How I Put the Mid... ...
Teacher Who Sexually ... ...

Undoing Jane Doe

Kristen Lewis Cunnane

SUNBURY PRESS

Mechanicsburg, PA USA

Published by Sunbury Press, Inc.
Mechanicsburg, Pennsylvania

www.sunburypress.com

Disclaimer: The views and opinions expressed in this book are those of the author and do not reflect the opinions, policies, or positions of the publisher, its shareholders, or employees.

For information about special discounts for bulk purchases, please contact Sunbury Press Orders Dept. at (855) 338-8359 or orders@sunburypress.com.

To request one of our authors for speaking engagements or book signings, please contact Sunbury Press Publicity Dept. at publicity@sunburypress.com.

ISBN: 978-1-62006-001-8 (Trade paperback)

Library of Congress Control Number: 2019937694

FIRST SUNBURY PRESS EDITION: March 2019

Product of the United States of America
0 1 1 2 3 5 8 13 21 34 55

Set in Bookman Old Style
Designed by Crystal Devine
Cover by Riaan Wilmans
Edited by Sanford Thatcher

Dandelion by Alice Noir from the Noun Project

Continue the Enlightenment!

This book is for my children.

May you have a glorious childhood
filled with wonder, love, laughter, and,
perhaps most importantly, truth.

May you know the courage of your dad and
dedication of your family.

May you know where your mom has been,
who she is, and how she has survived.

Always remember you are important,
you are loved, you are strong,
and you are mine.

CONTENTS

Foreword

I have always told my team that it is not just about swimming. I have reminded them that once they are done and have moved on to subsequent chapters in their lives, they won't remember their exact times or the place they finished. They will remember laughing so hard they cried at a team dinner. They will remember helping a teammate through a hard day. They will remember life moments.

The same could be said for me and the journey I traveled with Kristen as she healed from the horrendous abuse of two entrusted teachers. I do not remember all of the details, the progression of the police investigation or the court case. I don't remember the dates or the civil or criminal counts. But I remember the moments where I felt Kristen's devastation.

I first got to know Kristen as she competed for UCLA as a butterflier. When she was in high school, I was told that she wouldn't get much faster in college, so I didn't recruit her. As I watched her career unfold, I saw her improve drastically all while being a leader for her team. In 2004 Kristen reached out to me in her senior season. She was interested in being a coach and I brought her onto our staff immediately. She would go on to work with me and my team over the course of the next ten years, and eventually we took a front row seat in each other's lives.

Kristen and I spent countless hours together as coworkers—standing on the pool deck through early morning practices as the sun rose, working on the next recruiting class, traveling the country for competitions, and trying to build one of the best swim teams the sport has ever seen. In 2009 we shocked the swimming world (and, to be honest, ourselves) by taking a team that was

ranked outside of the top five and winning a National Championship. We did this, not by having a goal to win, but simply having
a goal to be the best we could individually and collectively every single day. Through this journey, Kristen and I became close
friends.

In 2010, shortly after our NCAA Championship meet, I noticed a change in Kristen. One minute she would be fine, the next
minute, I felt as though she drifted off into thin air. I noticed that
she was struggling to eat when we would go out with the team or
walk down to Starbucks for lunch. I noticed her looking thin, very
tired, and a little vacant.

In her dark days, Kristen began to share with me bits of her
past, but told me the entirety of it while we were on a travel trip
to Irvine, California. It was nearly impossible to wrap my head
around the amount of abuse that Kristen had suffered. It was
also nearly impossible to wrap my head around the amount that
Kristen was still suffering. The crimes may have been a decade
old at that point, but I witnessed the crimes profoundly impact-
ing her in the current moment. For those people who say "but it
happened years ago . . ." as a way of questioning or minimizing
Kristen's pain, I wish they would have seen her in the spring of
2010 when she was struggling just to survive.

As Kristen walked through the depression and anxiety of her
remembering what happened, she was a shell of her former self.
The coach who helped me build a championship team had been
overcome by the sadness and fear of a fourteen-year-old victim.
The crimes may have been a decade old at that point, but Kristen relived those moments in the form of severe and debilitating
flashbacks.

The night after we returned from that trip to Irvine, Kristen
asked to spend the night at my house. Scott was out of town for
the weekend, and Kristen was too terrified to be alone. I will never
forget that night or how fragile Kristen was. Here she was, an
Olympic Trials semi-finalist, with a BA from UCLA and an MA in
Education from Cal, the assistant coach of the NCAA Championship team, and a happily married twenty-eight-year-old, unable
to spend a single night by herself.

Though I knew much of what was happening with Kristen, my
team did not. It has always been imperative to me that the women
whom I coach have open and honest communications with each
other and my staff. I could also see that Kristen was struggling to

keep her pain at bay and struggling to keep her secret. Therefore, Kristen and I made the decision together to share her experience with the team. Piece by piece and little by little, we shared the heartbreaking truth both of what Kristen had faced as a kid and what she was now facing as an adult.

What happened next was extraordinary. My team grew. Not in physical size or number of athletes, but in heart. They realized that life was bigger than swimming, that they had a duty to help Kristen through this chapter, and that they had a responsibility to show up for the team in a new way. The team sat closer at team meetings, pitched in more for recruiting, and became more compassionate with each other. In the midst of all of this, our team won back to back NCAA Championships in 2011 and 2012.

Through 2010 and 2011 I walked step for step with Kristen through the criminal process and in 2012 and 2013 I walked step for step with Kristen through the civil process. I went to several court appearances to be there for Kristen, she would give me updates on developments with the investigations and the legal proceedings, and she relied on me as a coworker, boss, and friend to get through those days.

It would be a lie to say that was an easy road for me personally. My assistant coach was profoundly affected and there were times it was very hard. However, I got to see firsthand the devastation that child abuse can cause, I came to respect my own position of authority and mentorship even more, and I learned a valuable life lesson about the power of honesty.

I remember saying to one of my top recruits—an Olympian in fact—that the way my team had supported Kristen through her journey was something that I was just as proud of as any NCAA title I had won. I meant that. We all showed up for Kristen and became her "army." I am proud to be one of Kristen's generals and will never stop fighting for her healing and the healing of all people affected by childhood trauma.

Teri McKeever

Preface

As I sat in the Lafayette police department a full decade after my abuse ended, I had no idea of where to begin. The memories, the flashbacks, and the nightmares were difficult to escape and seemed impossible to process. In that first meeting with Detective Birch Parker, he brought up the idea of doing pretextual phone calls to Julie Correa in order to obtain the evidence we needed to prosecute her for the crimes she had committed against me in my childhood. Already inundated with memories of my past, my head began to swirl with what I would possibly say to this woman who had nearly ruined my life.

Hours after we left the police department, my husband Scott and I drove to our family cabin in the mountains to take a much-needed break together. Along the way, we stopped and I bought a small green journal. In this journal and on our trip was where the beginnings of this book were born.

I began writing down very specific instances of abuse—nights I remembered along with specific details and, in some cases, specific dates. I wanted Detective Parker to understand how elaborate and devious Julie's schemes had been and how much she had managed to instill perpetual fear in me. As I began writing, I noticed that a piece of the pain that Julie had caused would leave me and find its way onto the paper. My writing became therapeutic and almost addictive in this stage of my grieving and healing.

When I returned from my trip and met with Detective Parker, we began to plan my pretextual calls. I relied heavily on my little green journal to prepare and to remind me how and why Julie had caused me so much pain. I also relied heavily on my little green journal when Julie and I began to talk, as I was able to get her to corroborate many of these dark memories.

My wise therapist Chuck Wickstrand helped me through these phone calls, through all of my legal proceedings, and through the remembering of what Julie had done. He became aware of my writing, encouraged me to keep writing, and used it in our meetings to reprocess various traumatic experiences. I was not only reprocessing being sexually abused as a teenager, but I was also dealing with the trauma and scrutiny of the legal process. I remember specifically after the preliminary hearing in which the defense insisted the sex acts were my idea and initiated by me, Chuck encouraged me to get to my writing immediately. My writing became my outlet.

As my healing progressed, I became very aware that I was lucky to be alive. There were many instances where I felt as if making it through one more minute was an impossible task. But somehow I did. As I looked around at the amount of support and love I had in my life, I knew that not everyone was so lucky. It was with this feeling that I knew I needed to share my story. I knew I could no longer be Jane Doe. I knew I needed to show other victims that it is possible to survive and even thrive in the aftermath of abuse.

The amount of support I have received from family and friends has been awe-inspiring. The amount of support I have received from utter strangers has been completely unexpected and, at times, overwhelming. I have heard from abuse victims, families of victims, friends of victims, people who suspect abuse, and others looking to end this epidemic in our society. I have realized that abusers are not only men and that victims are not only "at-risk" youth. I have realized that abusers groom their victims in calculated and predictable ways. I have realized that our voice is our strongest weapon. I have realized that healing is possible.

Undoing Jane Doe is my story. It is my story of a perfect childhood turned dark by a predator who no one suspected. It is a story of abuse, slavery, and rape. But, more importantly, it is the story of escape, of freedom, of strength, and most of all of love.

A note to the reader: When I began the long process of healing, I began to write about both my traumas as a child and my journey to recovery as an adult. Though they happened more than ten years apart, these two tracks are devastating, hopeful, and in many ways similar to each other. The chapters I have written from the perspective of my youth are signified by a dandelion while the chapters written from the perspective of my adulthood are signified by a sprouting weed. Together, these two symbols represent the loss of innocence and the reemergence of the past. Some names have been changed to respect privacy.

Acknowledgments

I often talk about my "army," without which this book would not
have been possible because I would not have survived. I am
blessed by the number of people I have to acknowledge and, if
I tried to name everyone, the acknowledgments would be longer
than the book itself. So, in general, thank you to my army for
helping me survive and encouraging me to thrive.

For me, though very difficult, the legal proceedings proved to
be very healing. I should like to thank Birch Parker (Lafayette
Police), Geoff Lauter and Joyce Blair (Attorney General's Office),
and Shannon Maghoney (Contra Costa Victims Assistance).

I should like to thank Chuck Wickstrand, my wise therapist
and now close friend. Teri McKeever was a pillar of strength for me
through my remembering, my phone calls, and the legal proceedings, and she gave me a place—the Cal swim team—to achieve
greatness in the face of horrendous days. I should like to thank
all of the athletes I coached at Cal who gave me their patience and
their best every day.

This book would not have been possible without Kevin Quick
(my writing coach) and Sanford Thatcher, who not only helped me
to get this published, but also helped me believe in my abilities as
a writer and the power that this book holds.

I saw my friends in a new light once I began my battle with
Julie. There were those who would answer my call on the first
ring and those who would help me get dressed before the court
hearing. I have friends who have been with me since childhood
and new friends that have come into my life recently and helped
me with the pursuit of this book and preparing for Julie's release.
I am blessed to have far too many friends to list here, but I would

be remiss if I didn't give my love to a few friends in particular: Chelsea Murray Siciliano who helped me make those awful calls and helped me write this book and my two Maggies: Maggie Ford Pressutti (Maggie Red) and Maggie Barnard Rinow (Maggie Black) who helped me every inch of the way.

I have a great family, both immediate and extended. My family from Utah, my in-laws and countless aunts, uncles, and cousins, have supported me, my parents, and Scott as we heal. They filled my side of the courtroom and offered countless measures of love. My older brother Marc has always been my protector and was through my battle with Julie as well as my pursuit to hold the school district accountable. My dad, who is the hardest-working man I know, has worked his entire life to ensure his family is financially secure and could live in the safe and quiet community of Moraga. And my mom, who is the bravest woman I know, taught me how to love and how to fight, and held my hand as I got my life back. My family is not the reason that this happened but my family is the reason I survived.

And, finally, thank you to my husband Scott Cunnane. You saved me once as a boy and saved me again as a man. Without your love, I would not have had the courage or reason to risk my life and gain freedom from Julie. Without your love, I would not have had the desire to live through my darkest days or had the strength to walk into the Lafayette Police Department. We have a beautiful life together now, all because of how much you love me.

PART ONE

"Life Should Never Have Been So Hard"

CHAPTER ONE

Talking to Trains and Crying with God

Even when I concentrate, it feels difficult to get a full breath. I stand outside of my teal hotel door on the second floor, trying to get my room key to click the door open. The red light flashes defiantly, and I reenter my key. The swimmers clamor past me, clutching the room keys I have just distributed and hurrying to find their rooms. Finally, the signal turns green for me and I throw the door open.

I hate my room immediately. It feels too big and I think that it might swallow me. And, for all the times we have stayed in this hotel, why is my room on this side of the building? I have not slept since the retreat five days ago. And tonight I will face the noise of a rumbling train.

"Are you sure you want to come with us?" Teri had asked me in her office on Monday after the Woman Within Weekend.

I had looked at her through a haze, unable to see the details of her office—the NCAA Championship trophy I had helped her win just more than a year ago, the still shots of Olympians adorning her walls, the clutter of college swimming that has kept me happy until recently. Instead, I only looked at Teri and found some words to say: "Yes, I am sure."

The thought of sitting next to Scott through another unexplained sleepless night was reason enough to come with the team. *Can he feel my despair from the left side of the bed?*

Situated where the 405 and the 5 freeways meet, the hotel looks as though it could have been an old train station. With its tin roof and its proximity to the tracks, I wonder why someone would have made this into a hotel in the first place.

The La Quinta Inn is nothing fancy. The Irvine Grand Challenge is somewhat of a casual competition for us, the first meet after the 2010 NCAA Championships. The swimmers had a few weeks off and now it is our first meet back to racing.

The 2010 season was a good one for us—or maybe for them, I should say. Although we won in 2009, no one thought that we could have placed in the top four this year. We came in third. That was in March, only two months ago. That was the last time that I can remember feeling happy.

I can hear the girls settling next door and I know that my college team looks at me a little differently these days. They show up to practice, cheerily toting mesh equipment bags behind them, then slow their pace upon seeing me. On the brink of adulthood, they are old enough to know I am not okay. Simultaneously, they are children unsure of what to say or ask. So instead, they just smile. And I feel farther away.

Teri has been supportive and as understanding as anyone could be. She has given me some time off of work and let me go to Woman Within last weekend, which felt like a string pulling me back to earth. The only problem is that with that string, with coming back to life, I have to face the ground-floor reality of what happened to me.

The competition doesn't start until the day after tomorrow. Teri and I are going to take the girls ocean swimming in the morning and then Kathie is going to come up and do a workshop with our team on leadership.

What kind of leader am I? Again, it hurts just to breathe.

I can't keep the pain inside any longer, and Teri and I have decided that tomorrow we are going to tell the team that I have been having a hard time with some personal things. Essentially, I am going to ask for their patience.

For how long will my athletes have to be patient?

I am not sure if I should be at this meet, but I am sure that I don't want to be at home. I need to give Scott a break. I need space from him, space apart from him for practice, in case I tell him and this all comes to a terrible end.

It is getting late, the TV is hurting my ears, and I should be getting ready for bed. But the normal wave of being awake and being tired that flows through an average day escapes me. I am always tired and I am always wide awake. I stand in the hotel bathroom under the buzz of the fluorescent energy-saving light.

I brought a little souvenir with me from Woman Within. It is a handmade list of affirmations I want in my life. As I pull it out of my makeup bag I feel two distinct and opposing feelings. The first is a sense of calm. A sense of peace that I told a group of people what I went through and that I am still alive. The opposing feeling comes next after I read the words that a staff member wrote on the card for me. Just as I get to the final statement "I am healing from my past" my breath rushes out in exhale and I feel that overcoming this is impossible.

The girls are quiet now and tucked in their rooms for the night. The paper becomes heavy in my hand, so I prop the light blue index card up against my bathroom mirror. I stop for a moment to look at myself. I hate looking in the mirror, so it requires a degree of force to move my eyes in the right direction.

People have always seen the put-together, smart, athletic, moderately pretty Kristen. As I look into my eyes, I see a different person looking back at me. My eyes look older than they did a month ago. My face looks thinner, but not in a good way. My mouth looks drained and evaporated from all of the crying. But more deeply than that, I look different because I am different.

I must not be the Kristen whom other people know. I do not feel like her. My finger bones ache within the constraints of my hands. I must be someone else. I must be a weak soul in order to allow this to happen to me. There was no gun, no rope that held me in my place. I must be a flawed heart, to attract this type of evil in not one, but two abusers. In both equations, I am the constant.

Julie's voice rings in my ears, "You told me that you wanted this . . ."

It's more than remembering but less than hallucinating. I can see it all happening to me. I can see the bushes, I can feel her hands, I can hear his slight lisp, and my brain hurts as I see all of the dark things.

I am helpless here. I feel trapped. I wish I could open my head and take my memory out. But, instead, I watch. Scene by scene, while sitting safely in my hotel room, I relive the unexplainable movie of my life from the time I was 11 until the time I was 18.

Another sleepless Thursday has found me as the hotel alarm clock ticks past midnight.

In a room with two queen beds, whenever I travel, I always sleep in the one closest to the bathroom and farthest from the door. Usually, it is so that I am next to the bathroom. Tonight I am grateful to be far from the door.

From under the blankets, I let my head turn and I look at the inside of the door that I struggled to open. I look at the gold handle and air fills my lungs.

As the memories come like flash floods in the Sahara desert, I wonder how my brain could have been dry of this recollection for so long. I think back to the last few weeks of undoing the clouds of my past.

There was the USA Swimming sexual abuse scandal that got media attention from the likes of 20/20 and *USA Today*. In April, only a month ago, I sat down innocently enough to watch the well-publicized program. I thought I was doing my part as a coach by being aware of the issue. I didn't know it would make me aware of my past.

My eyes grew wide with the detailed accusation of "passing the trash"—that coaches who abuse their athletes are simply allowed to switch club teams. Something deep in my belly hurt to hear that people in the swimming community, which I am so proud to be a part of, has worked so hard to keep the sexual abuse of swimmers quiet. I didn't know why I hurt then, just that it was the start of my pain.

Then there was the fiasco with our diving coach. It tormented me. I learned of his affair with a former athlete and it made me so sick that I didn't want to eat anymore. I started to think that his teeth looked exactly like Mr. Witters's teeth. And as his wife crumbled under the betrayal, I began to remember that Mr. Witters had a wife. I began to wonder how old his children would be. I began to wonder why he had to drive his car into the Pacific Ocean.

But Julie told me that they never found his body . . . so where is he? Maybe in my garage? Maybe Julie is in there, too?

But this still does not make sense to me. I look down at my NCAA Championship ring on my right hand and my wedding ring on my left. I sit up in the bed and look down at my dream life.

How could this have happened to me and I am still doing what I am doing? If this is true, how am I down in Irvine at a swim meet and not locked up in a mental institution? Is it possible that I am making this up? Would it be worse to be crushed or crazy?

As I try to get through the changing minutes of the clock's time, the sound of the train does not keep me awake. The thoughts of what happened to me stir in my mind. The thoughts of what might happen to me wrestle in my soul.

The sound of the train pulls me like a magnet as I sit in stillness, unsure of both my past and my future. I feel like a vampire, thirsty for blood: Thirsty for my own blood. An insatiable need to be rid of this hurt fills my every cell.

I have always loved to tuck my toes under Scott's legs while we are lounging and watching TV. The pressure of his legs makes me feel safe. Now, without having to close my eyes to envision it, I can see what it would be like. Gently nudging the dirt underneath to make space for my toes. Sliding them under the safety and the stillness of the wooden track. The slow and steady increase of the shake as the train approaches, the end of the pain with the impact.

Suddenly, in Irvine, California, this seems like a good idea. To feel the force of the train, slamming my bones together. To feel the twist of my tendons and the tug at my ankles. The pain of my insides flying through the night's air and coming to rest peacefully in a million tiny pieces.

I don't have shoes on. I would keep it that way. I am on the second story and I would take the stairs at the corner of the building. The concrete is cool by now, being absent from the heat for hours.

I guess I wouldn't need to bring my room key.

Let me be honest, I do not want to kill myself. It is the exact opposite, really. I desperately do not want to kill myself. But I would be lying if I didn't say that it enters my mind. Truthfully, I am sick of lying.

The pain, the crushing devastation, tempts me out of my bed and onto the track. I would be done. My room rattles with the next passing train.

If it were just me tonight, things might be different. But now, as I imagine Teri trying to find the words to tell the team, as I picture my parents howling in endless grief, and as I envision Scott walking the dogs alone for his lifetime, my fingers dig deeply into the mattress. I pull my eyes away from the door. I squeeze the softness with all of my might and I clench all of my teeth together. I shake and I scream in near silence.

I carefully release my right hand so that I can pick up my phone and read the text message that Scott sent me earlier tonight: "Kristy, I have been thinking about you a lot and I think I understand why you are having such a hard time. I love you."

I read the words in the small text box, and then I read them again. Over and over, it feels almost as if Scott is here with me petting the top of my head. I sink deeper into the bed and the need to look at the door inches further from my mind with each passing minute.

What does Scott know?

Maybe the text is enough to tell me that the question marks in my future are worth getting an answer to. Suddenly as I read his words, I feel brave enough to stay in my bed and begin to answer the questions about my past.

My left hand joins my right, as I hold my phone. In a hurry, I open the Safari App that people use to surf the net and shop online.

Tonight the prey shops the predator.

First I do a Google search, "Julie Correa."

Third down, "Julie Correa: Address, phone number, history and more. People Search Pro."

As I open the page and stop to wonder if it is worth paying the $35 for the service to find her, I look down at my white knuckles and get mad that she has made me feel this way.

After entering the credit card, navigating the site, dismissing a few same-named, nonevil, innocent bystanders, I find her. "Living history—Livermore, CA/ Lafayette, CA/ Concord, CA/ Salt Lake City, UT."

Crazy that I am not crazy.

I sit up in my bed and see the phone number listed next to her current address. I pull my hand away from the phone, afraid that I might not be in total control of my fingers, which may decide to call her.

My eyes grow wide as I read her name again and again. I imagine her living her life in Utah, sleeping soundly in her bed tonight.

Worry fills me.

What if she is not in her bed tonight? What if Julie has snuck into her kids' babysitter's house? What if Julie has taken her and her parents don't know where she is? What if Julie is in her own home, taking a little too long to tuck her oldest into bed? What if, just like all those years ago, her husband Rob knows and does nothing?

With the worry comes a deep knowledge that I am remembering what I am remembering for a reason.

I sleep with the phone close to my head so that I can bounce between the People Search Pro and my text message from Scott.

They both feel like evidence in the case of "Who is Kristen?" Each time I open the Internet, she is still there and is still a real person. Each time I read my text message, it is still from Scott and it still says "I love you" at the end.

"Don't you dare do that . . . ," I say out loud to myself in the tiniest of whispers. I think of the train below me, and I am almost certain that Julie is the conductor. I think of her smile. My hands return to the mattress and my fingers curl in. I make a vow, a quiet pact with myself, that I at least have to try.

But that doesn't mean that I want to.

The night goes by and so does the weekend. Each hour is hard. I stand on the pool deck, unable to observe the stroke technique of my swimmers, but only able to stand and breathe and have my heart keep beating.

"I know that you aren't hungry, but I'm gonna grab some food before finals," Teri says as she pulls into Wahoo's Fish Tacos. Her curly hair looks tired from the long weekend, as a single strand falls through her eyes. She looks over toward me, but not at me.

It is the final day of the meet and we will fly home after this evening's sessions. I look back at Teri and I hate that she has to be around me. "Okay, I can find something," I say, trying my best to be as bearable as possible for her. Just thinking of a taco or a burrito makes me feel defeated.

I know that I need to tell Teri what is really going on with me. I have alluded to things before, and she knows that I am a "molestation" victim, but it's not enough.

"I want to tell you more of what happened to me," I say as I slouch in our booth and look down at the uneaten kid's bean and cheese burrito.

"Okay . . ." Teri is eating her favorite, chips and salsa.

Two weeks ago when I gave her only the very surface-level information, she had said, "Okay, thanks for telling me . . . you know, I don't need to know all of the details." Somehow this time she knows not to finish her sentence.

I hate the details. I try to change them constantly. I wish especially I could leave off the 's' in 'she.' I hate that I am in the details. I hate that every time I close my eyes, I can see the details.

So, in the middle of a mildly crowded chain restaurant, I tell Teri what happened to me. I tell her the truth, and without a single tear, I feel as though I am describing a recent HBO thriller.

Her face is turning grey. I know that she is hungry and she puts down her taco and looks me in the eye. "What about Scott? What does Scott know?"

I think of the text message and I think of what he might be doing in this exact moment. He's probably having a beer with his high school friends. I picture him and his light brown crew cut, standing somewhere in the Lake Tahoe sun. He's at a bachelor party and he's probably laughing because he is always laughing. *Could he ever laugh again?*

Suddenly, my clenched hands are covered in tears. "He doesn't really know . . . I haven't really told him anything." *Will we have to sell the house? Who will take the dogs?*

Teri leans away from her food and looks at me. We both know, without having to say, that my marriage might be over. *Isn't there a point where things are just too hard?*

I get myself together enough to robot my way through the meet, standing all too close to Teri the whole time. At least she knows so that if I start screaming uncontrollably, she can explain my mental state to the mental institution.

"Teri . . ." I say and my voice is very small and lost in the middle of the Orange County Airport. We are standing in line at the Starbucks, and normally I would notice the oddly long line on a Sunday evening. Instead, I ask for help: "Do you think I could stay at your house tonight?"

"Of course." She doesn't give the appropriate time lapse to answer my question, nor does she ask why.

"I just don't think I should be alone tonight," I say to her and to myself at the same time.

As the plane begins to soar home, I remember that Orange County is the airport that I used to hate flying in and out of. Some haughty OC residence complained about the engine noise, from which there was born a code that requires pilots to shut off their engine after takeoff.

The plane climbs aggressively off of the runway, and as we begin to level off, the engine grows quiet. My eyebrows lift.

I think of the residents below, able to enjoy their Sunday dinner because of the quiet plane. And once we pass, the pilot will turn the engines back on and we will fly the rest of the way home.

What if it doesn't work? What if we crash? Then Scott wouldn't have to know about me. Then Scott would think that it wasn't my choice to die.

The engine kicks back on and I nearly jump out of my seat. "It's okay . . . ," Teri says and grabs my hand. "It's just the engine. They do this at Orange County." She holds my hand for a second and my shaking stops momentarily.

"Oh, yeah . . . right . . . I forgot," I say.

Unfortunately, we make it to Teri's home and I go directly to the guest bedroom. I look at the bed and drop my bags, not remembering or caring that I should brush my teeth before bed.

I stand in the middle of the room, staring at nothing and only being surprised at my body ache. I wish I could chalk this up to my normal body pain after standing on concrete for three days. But it's deeper. I think for a second that I might have appendicitis, but my pain is not in the lower right side of my abdomen. The knife cuts though my entire being and shreds open my soul.

I get in the bed but I focus my attention on my surroundings because being inside myself is the last place I can handle being right now. I try to focus on where I am.

You're safe. One more night. You can do this.

I have to pep talk myself into just about everything.

As I lay in the guest bed, I can hear Teri and her husband Jerry getting ready for bed above me. The sound echoes in my ears, and suddenly I am hearing questions in my head.

How could I have not known that something this terrible had happened to me? How could I have been separate from this for the past ten years?

I feel as though there should be two heads instead of one head laying on the pillow. I feel like an alien.

How did all of this happen to me? How could no one have saved me?

I think of my mom and my dad and I wish I could scream so loud that they could hear me 30 miles away in Moraga. I think of Moraga. I bite the blanket.

Can anyone save me now?

I lay in Teri's guest bed and I know that the pillow is covered in my black mascara. I have no energy to be embarrassed. I'm exhausted and I can't sleep. I'm starving and I can't eat. I have nowhere in my body or in my brain to go.

From somewhere deep inside, I say my first tiny prayer. I don't mean the first prayer of the night. I don't mean the first time I pray about being a victim. I mean, the first time I pray in my life. About anything. The first time I speak to God.

It's hard to believe in God. Hard to think that I can trust the universe to protect me from harm. It's not that I ever questioned that there is a such a thing as God. It was never a question. Because by the time I was old enough to wonder, to ponder about life's mysteries, I was old enough to have seen evil. And so, I never wondered. I just assumed there was no God.

Now, in the most opposite way, I lay here and I have to assume that God is here and that He is listening to me. If I don't believe this, I cannot make it another minute.

I look at the hand life has dealt me. I am devastated. Tonight I let go of the mattress, and I grip the pillow.

I listen to my heart pound underneath the sheets. I choose to believe that my beating heart is proof of Him. I choose to feel that my survival through the evil is proof that He is real. I have no choice in my faith. I have no choice in finding God. He is inevitable. Tonight He is the only way through this.

And so, instead of talking to a train, I talk to Him. "Can I make it? Will I make it? How do I make it?" I am not sure if my words come out loud or if they are just very loud thoughts in my head.

The room is quiet and there is no answer. I continue to cry.

What if He never answers? And as I continue to cry, I hear His answer in my cry. And therein lies the start. My tears, the first step in my journey. They roll down my cheeks, proof that the laws of gravity still apply to me. Proof that I am still here. Proof that I am alive. Proof that I can feel again. Proof that I am real and what happened to me is real and is really devastating.

This is one of the messiest nights of my life. But laying in the guest bedroom, I find a partner in my battle. Someone to call at any hour of the night. Someone who knows it all, who has seen it all.

A flashback of her apartment comes at me. I can see my fourteen-year-old body. I can see her sick smile. I can see God sitting there with me. I have to believe I was never alone.

Without sleep I find peace within my horror. I do not see my God in a church or in a book. I see my God in my soul. I do not find him through my friends, in a church group, or through a long line of family tradition. He finds me.

I lay here counting the minutes of the night and of the early morning. I hate each second, but I make it. Having a partner does not make it easier, but it makes it possible.

Finally, I hear Teri come down the stairs to wake me up for morning practice. I pretend that I have slept, entirely grateful to be going to work at the break of dawn and to have another human being to grab onto when I feel as though I am falling off the face of the earth. The change is undetectable, but as we pull out of the driveway, I am a tiny bit stronger than I was when we pulled in. A tiny bit less alone.

CHAPTER TWO

Propeller of Truth

I wonder if the people at the Apple store will be able to tell if my damaged iPhone has fallen in the toilet or if it has been soaked in tears. Then, suddenly, I realize I don't care what anyone thinks of me. Almost anyone.

I am driving home from work and what usually feels like the best part of my day now feels like the worst part of my day.

It has been four days since we came home from Irvine, and each afternoon getting off work feels worse than it did the day before.

Two months ago I would speed over the hill and slip onto the freeway thinking of what Scott and I would make for dinner together. My favorite used to be when we would both get home from work early enough to bike down to happy hour sushi. But last week, in trying to swallow my sushi, my spicy tuna roll tasted like gasoline and Clorox mixed together.

Although I do not like it, I have been able to eat at least some food since I started seeing Chuck. Yesterday we had our fourth appointment, and I was prepared for his question: "So, Kristen . . . How are you eating?"

Within the first three sessions, this question caught me off guard as I searched for the last thing I had swallowed. I don't like letting people down, so at this most recent session it felt good to say, "A little better than I have been. I managed a glazed old fashioned doughnut today."

"Ah," Chuck smiled his aging smile at me. "No one can pass up a good doughnut." And suddenly his smile spread to the corner of his eyes.

He had sat looking at me, his palms folded together, and his legs crossed at his ankles. When I first met him, I was surprised at how large of a man he was.

Now I am just minutes from leaving Cal and I drive by the Claremont that reminds me of the end of Julie. Yes, it reminds me of finding freedom, but it also reminds me of her. It reminds me that it happened. I don't want to, but as I drive by, I look at the beautiful white building. The hotel that people spend hundreds of dollars a night to stay in. The restaurant to which Teri and I take our top recruits for the spectacular views of the bay and the spectacular breakfast. Instead of seeing it for what it is, an acclaimed spa and resort, I see it as a piece of my undeniable and dark past.

My insides feel as though they might be made out of nails and it hurts just to sit within my skin. I don't even notice that I am crying until the road becomes harder to see. As I stop at the intersection at the top of a magnificent Berkeley hill, I cry and yell out loud to my empty car, "How could have this happened to me? How could no one have stopped this?"

Let's be honest, I work in Berkeley, so seeing homeless people is not out of the norm. Hearing them rambling on to themselves is to be expected. But as I walked past a ranting transient on Telegraph Avenue, I never stopped to wonder, "Why is he talking to himself? What is he talking to himself about? What makes people go crazy like him?" And as I cry out in desperation, I imagine briefly that my friend from the streets of Berkeley is watching me through my window. I wonder. *Does he think I have lost my mind?*

I have been consumed with the question "how did all of this happen?" I know that Julie was evil and her deceit haunts me every second. *But how did no one else know? How did my parents not find out?*

It wasn't once or twice that this happened. It happened all those times through all those years. I remember my mom before the abuse and think of her mother hen instincts. But then, once it started, a cloud of black surrounded a piece of me and I was lost to the rest of the world.

As I get on the entrance to Highway 24, I am glad that my cell phone is back in service. With every mile I drive closer to my house, I feel more afraid. I pick up my phone and press "Mags" on my list of favorites. We have a new law in California that does not allow us to drive and talk on the phone. I am surprised, given my state of mind, that I remember this law and put my headphone into my ears. I am grateful to the Golden State that by law I must have two hands on the wheel.

"How are you doing, Krick?" Maggie Red skips the unnecessary hello and gets right to the question of how I am doing. Since I told Maggie a few days ago, I have talked to her more times a day than I can count. She has come to expect my call now, around 5 P.M., on my dreaded way home from work. Maggie has come to expect my calls at the most unexpected times of the day.

Maggie has always been such an incredible listener and now I am grateful that she got her degree in psychology. Having my best friend be a therapist, at least I got lucky in one way in my life.

"Krick, where are you?" She is worried about me and doesn't want me driving when I am like this. Though I have not said anything yet, she can hear me crying.

Maggie has an eight month old, Luca, and taking care of him is a full-time job. She has not missed a phone call of mine in the past week and I imagine her walking around her house with her phone glued to her hand. There she is, phone next to her on the changing table, awaiting my name to appear on the screen and never allowing the phone to ring more than once.

"I am almost home from work." I tell a white lie so that Maggie won't demand that I get off the freeway. I wish I could tell her the truth. I wish I could tell her that I am on Highway 24, near the central Lafayette exit, but I can't. She would make me get off the freeway and, in an effort to keep me safe, she would have me within two blocks of Julie's apartment, within a quarter mile of where the darkest nights of my life occurred. And as I think of those nights, and I think of these nights, I can't help but see the stark similarities. I wonder which are worse.

"Mags, I don't want to go home." I allow myself to admit this much to her.

"Why not, Krick?" I think that she knows the reason for my fear as well as I do. Since we started dating, Scott and I have had a uniquely cohesive and symbiotic relationship. He relies on me and I rely on him. Our friends have silently admired our relationship from afar. But now, coming home to dinner and done laundry, I only rely on him. I am terrified and almost certain that he will give up on me.

"I don't want to see Scott. He still doesn't know, Mags." I wonder what Scott has been thinking the last month that I have been struggling. At first it was almost possible to hide it from him. But lately it has become impossible. I hate putting him through seeing me like this.

I think of Irvine and being away from him last week. *Could I ever become whole without him in my life?* My answer is an absolute no. *But what if he can't handle this? What if he doesn't want to handle this? What if I can't hide and he can't handle, where does that leave me? Who will be there to save my life next time?*

"Krick, you have to tell him." I almost forgot that I was on the phone with Maggie. I almost forgot I was driving.

I am quiet on the other end of the phone. Maggie is saying some words, but I can't hear them. Instead, I think of when I told her.

It was the day before I left for Woman Within. I sat on the couch hidden in a down blanket. From somewhere underneath, I had pulled the comforter tighter, so that it felt like someone was holding me.

Maggie keeps talking and I keep remembering. I started off by testing the waters and talking about what had happened with Mr. Witters. A tiny voice that I did not recognize came out from deep down inside of me, "Mags," I said, "it wasn't just him."

She sounded instantly breathless, and as I remember how she reacted, I wonder if Scott will sound the same. *Or, will he throw up all over me?*

"What do you mean, Krick?" Maggie had said on the phone that day.

"There was another person," and my mouth turned sour as the black sand came out from my soul. The single word felt too big for my mouth. It had jagged edges and it would be the first time I have said the word in over ten years. The word: her former last name. What we called her. What all of the "cool kids" called her.

Telling my best friends, I had struggled to breathe, to see or to feel my heart beating. It took a miracle but somehow the blackness jumped out of my soul in one three-syllable word that I have feared for fourteen years. "Na-ta-li," I said.

I am almost home now and I can remember Maggie's words. "I knew it," Mags said. This typical "I-told-you-so" phrase said with utter devastation and sorrow. "That never felt right," she had admitted.

"Krick, pull over. Are you there?" Maggie is growing frantically concerned on the other end.

"I am okay," I lie as I remember the difficulty in telling her, and the pending impossibility of telling Scott.

"You have to tell him. He is an incredible guy, Krick, you have to trust that. You have to believe that you found the right person to help you through this. I believe in him, Kristen. You have to believe in him, too," Maggie says as she begs me to fight for my life. Briefly, I realize that she is crying on the other end and her words are as aggressive as I have ever heard them in the past twenty years of friendship.

I listen to Maggie's words and remember what it was like to be talked to and tempted by a moving train. It is bright outside and I squint as I look directly into the sun.

I imagine Scott leaving, laughing, throwing up, and giving up in no particular order. I imagine living through the suffocating feeling of not wanting to drive home to my husband for fear that he would find out who I actually am. I weigh my fear against my pain and realize it is time. I need to show Scott exactly who I am so that I can see exactly who he is.

I steady my car into the driveway and, as I open the garage door that Scott installed when we bought the house two years ago, Murphy comes hauling out at me. I see his orange face, the propeller motion of his tail, and wonder if I will ever feel the happiness that this sight used to bring me.

Murphy wags his tail often when he sees people, when given a new bone, or when something brings him amusement. But his tail only turns in the clockwise propeller motion for people he knows the best and loves the most. *Will Scott take Murphy with him when he leaves me?*

This half Australian Shepard, half Cattle dog runs with excitement at my car. He wiggles his bottom as I open the door. "Okay, Mags, I'll do it," I say as I look down into Murphy's eyes, which look a little too much like a human's eyes. I pat him on the head, thanking him quietly for greeting me and for sleeping so close to me for the past month. Scott might not know the truth, but Murphy does.

As I hang up with Maggie, I know that she has spoken the truth; I must tell Scott and I must know the outcome. Nothing—not even living alone—could be more lonely than this. I need to know his answer.

I take my time walking the short distance from our detached garage to our house and Murphy walks in step. Scott's inside and, as my feet meet the brick patio of our backyard, I feel a sense of resolution. I realize that it is the first thing other than pain that I have felt in my heart in a long time.

And, as I head into the house, my insides feel as though they are made out of orange Jello. I look at my green backyard, my tomato garden, into the window of my new kitchen. I imagine a four-alarm fire and the destruction of it all. I imagine giving up every single thing in my life to protect the one thing I have never been allowed—the truth.

"Hey, Kristy," Scott says as he stands over the stainless steel gas range. He's cooking fish tacos in his undershirt from work and his black Adidas shorts. His hand holds a paring knife too small for the yellow onion that he is trying to cut.

I should be focused on the fact that he is making dinner, typically one of my jobs. I should listen to how softly he says my nickname when he greets me. But, instead, I look at the butcher block.

Like most people, we registered for a set of knives for our wedding. I picked AJ Henckels, not knowing or caring much about how they cut. I stand behind Scott and stare at the wooden block that holds them, realizing how much has changed since we picked them out at William Sonoma three years ago.

Two weeks ago I thought mostly about the largest knife in the block. For the past few days, I have been obsessing over the serrated one. I've been told that it is meant for bread, but as I stand on our recently installed tile, I think that it would be particularly effective for getting Julie out of my body.

The onion sizzles and I am desperate to feel the tear of the blade on the inside of my arm. Maggie always says I have the softest skin on the underside of my forearm and I yearn to rip it open. Maybe just a little slice would let my insides breathe. Maybe I would bleed, and Julie's eyeballs would drip down toward my fingers and she would be gone from me.

"I made you tacos, Kristybop," Scott says as he slides the tacos onto the granite counter where we eat dinner every night. His voice sounds nervous. I notice that he only made me two, instead of my usual three.

I climb atop the stool and sit with Scott as he bites into his warm dinner. I hold a single taco with both hands and take the smallest bite of my adult life. The food jumps back out of my mouth.

"I can't do this!" My words jump out of my mouth as well. "I can't do this." I am yelling at Scott and crying and shaking all at the same time. In a near fall I leave the stool and retreat to the adjacent leather couch—the same one that held me while I told Mags.

Scott is much slower in his movements and is deliberate as he puts his taco down. He sits on the ottoman and faces me.

"I can't lie to you anymore. I'm not who you think I am. I am not who you want." My words come out without control but with extreme clarity.

"Stop, Kristen. Please stop," he says and he holds my shaking hands between his clammy palms.

"You're gonna leave me. If you know what happened, you won't be able to stay." I gasp for air and I believe myself as I speak. "You won't be able to love me."

"Look, I know . . ." He is calm and, although on the verge of tears, he is in total control. "You have been having such a hard time that I was worried. I read the first page of your notes from your retreat." I think back to the text message that saved my life. I remain hunched motionlessly on the couch.

He is soft and slow with his words. His voice sounds different and I can tell he has been practicing for the past few days. "It doesn't matter if you were abused. It doesn't matter if you were abused by one person or two people. It doesn't matter if it was by a man or a woman. You were abused. And it wasn't your fault."

I think of him opening my notes and wonder what he felt that day. Scott has never been one to snoop; I could leave a birthday present in plain sight and he wouldn't notice. It must have taken a lot of worry on his behalf in order to go searching on my behalf.

What could feel like betrayal to some is an act that saves my life. Not big on texting, I think of Scott finding his phone to write to me. He wraps both arms around me and scoots as close as he can get: "I married you," he says, "because I love you."

I am utterly silent and my shaking has stopped for the first time in three weeks. He knows what to say and how to hold me. My mind sequences back to figure out how long he has known, if he has looked me in the eye since, and if he has been disgusted by my body in the meantime. The answers are that he has known for six days, yes, that he has looked me in the eye countless times, and, no, that he has not vomited. *Could this really be okay?*

"And so we have two options for us to move through this," Scott uses a matter of fact voice. *Did he say us?* "You and I plan a way to kill her. We find her and we kill her. And no one ever knows it is us."

"I already found her," my voice is tiny but there. "I paid $35 for an Internet search at 3:15 A.M. last week to figure out where she is. She is in Utah, next to my aunts and uncles and cousins," I say and I am surprised that my voice sounds mad.

Scott looks at me and presses his lips together as he digests the fact that I have found her already. He opens his mouth only to continue with my options. "Or you go to the police. You report your crime and you watch how the criminal justice system treats her."

He does not list option three. The knives—the most immediate way to escape my pain. The train—the most direct path to my freedom. They are the only options that I have thought of up to this point. But I write it on my mental chalk board in secrecy just in case.

I have absolutely no control over what comes out of my mouth next. I picture Scott killing another human being for me. An angel using evil against the devil. I picture our lives waiting for the police to figure it out and our lives of waiting for them to knock at the front door. I picture Murphy never sleeping in the curl of my leg again and myself never being able to teach my unborn babies to swim. I picture only seeing Scott through the steel bars of prison. And what was never an option is now the only option between the two of us. If I want Scott on my team, I need to compromise.

"Okay," I say without understanding why I am speaking. I look at Scott and I feel his body touching mine, pulling me back into life. I do not know why I trust Scott, only that I must trust him. "I don't want to ruin our lives." I think of options one and three, and immediately settle with option two. "I'll go to the police."

CHAPTER THREE

911 ... What's Your Emergency?

Where does my story start? I guess it would be on that sad June night. *Do I start there or is the other stuff before important?*

As I make my way from Scott's car into what looks like an average office building, I look down at my nearly white Sperry top-siders and I am surprised they are moving in the right direction. My heart rattles somewhere in my chest knowing that I am headed into a police station for the first time in my life.

The parking lot is predictably hot, on this the first day of July. The sun burns through the bottom of my shoes and makes me walk a little bit faster. And, as I hustle, my mind hurries along.

What about how she would smack my butt in seventh grade? What about how she bought me an Eddie Bauer watch for graduation? What about how she told me to constantly lie to my parents? What about when Mr. Witters touched me?

I don't remember everything. And still I don't know where to start.

Since telling Scott, my life looks a lot different. My eyes have new lenses and the air feels breathable. I can swallow food more often than not.

Perhaps more than a hundred times a day I have to push my fingertips together to feel that this is no dream. The force of my index fingers brings me to the reality that Scott now knows what happened, that he really sees who I really am, and that he is really still by my side.

Today he is walking at my side and, as I look at him, I can see the line in his cheek where his dimple would be if this were any other occasion. His golden stubble glistens under the California sun, and I am glad that I didn't have to ask him to come with me. He just knew.

Scott has done a lot of legwork since he found out and gave me my options. Being a district attorney has given him resources on how to handle this case as well as the conviction that it should be handled. He has talked to his boss and the head of the sex crimes unit and gotten input on where I should go to report my crime, on who is best to hear my story.

Two days after I told him what happened, Scott came home from work and said, "since her apartment was in Lafayette, we can go to the Lafayette police. They have a guy there. He's supposed to be good." Scott had looked at me purposefully in the eyes. "His name is Birch Parker."

As we approach the entrance, I reach for his left hand, and I think of the two options he gave me. As my hand settles into his, I realize I had never thought of either option on my own. They were not options to me until Scott and I sat on the couch and he held the entirety of me.

Before that night I had thought that telling Scott rested solely on my shoulders, that I would have to open my mouth and tell him all of it. And I had no idea where to start and no idea how to get through it. But when I started, a little miracle happened and he did all the work. A man who speaks a quarter of the amount I do did all of the talking in the most difficult conversation of our marriage.

"It'll just be a minute, honey. You're here for Parker?" says a bottle blonde lady from behind the counter. We have passed through a glass door that has been darkened with tint for the privacy of a police department. This along with the small City of Lafayette, CA, seal on the door is the only indication that I am not at the dentist.

As I wait for Detective Parker, I glance at Scott to make sure that is still he sitting next to me. As I think of telling Parker, I think of all of the people I have told since sitting with Scott.

I told my brother. Marc was stunned. I told my mom, over the phone. My mom told my dad. I'm pretty sure that they have cried every day since then. I told a few close friends. They all have wept.

They all want to know the same thing: "how did we not know?" My body doesn't have room to consider their sadness. My heart does not have space for their guilt.

I grab Scott's hand as I see a door straight ahead open. A large man comes barreling out in his police uniform and heads to the back of the building. *He's not Parker.*

Scott squeezes my hand knowing my internal thoughts without speaking, "So, whom was your best call with this morning, Kristy?" he says in a lighthearted way, trying to grab my attention away from the inevitable.

Today is July 1. For most people in my profession, it is one of the most important days of the year because, per NCAA rules, it is the first day that a college coach can speak over the phone to recruits who are entering their senior year in high school. People make a pretty big deal of it; some swimmers even stay home from practice so that they can talk to college coaches and make a list of who has called them.

"Um . . . there were a lot of good ones," I say in a halfhearted response to Scott. My eyes bounce back and forth between the three closed office doors, guessing that Parker's is likely to my immediate left. "They all like the fact that I am calling from Cal. I guess that's good."

This morning I spent my day calling seventeen-year-olds and telling them what a wonderful program we have at Cal and asking them surface-level questions about their high school lives. It's an art really, using small talk to get to know the makings of a person and to gain her trust. I think back to the many calls I made this morning, angry that the two sides of my life are butting heads.

The door to the left opens, and my spine grows straight. "Sorry to keep you waiting." Parker was told that I was coming in. He has been on vacation for the past week while I have been anxious to get this interview over with. Parker looks at me and his tanned skin and bright smile mock my nerves and the days I have waited to see him.

"Hi," I say back to him. Scott stands up with me but our hands fall away from each other. *Is he going to leave me here? Am I going to go inside and tell Parker everything, and is he going to go home and pack his bags?* I grab Scott's hand again.

Parker sees me and notices my quick move. "Scott can come in while we get started and you get comfortable, Kristen," he says in a casual voice as he tips his head back. I like how he says my first name. *But what if this smiling receptionist can hear our conversation and tells one of her friends using my name?* I give her a quick glare, but find relief as I see that she has her dispatching headset on.

We make our way into his office that feels tight and crowded. "You guys go ahead and sit here." Parker uses his nose to point us in the direction of the meeting table where Scott and I sit. It is round and could be found at any office in America.

"So . . . Scott, how's everything over at the DA's office?" As Scott begins to answer and chat with Parker, I look at the chairs and wonder if there is a designated spot for the "victim" of the case. I wonder what else this table has heard and if my life will have been the worst.

Parker starts to pepper me into the conversation. "So . . . you work over at Cal?" he says with a broad smile. He knows all about me. "I have kids on the swim team here. Maybe someday they will be fast enough to swim with you?" As I respond I can feel myself relaxing into the chair.

And as the chatter banters back and forth, I can't help but think of the way I spoke to my top recruits on the phone only hours earlier. Rapport: the art of getting to know someone but for a purpose all your own. It works. The small talk about Parker's stint as a water polo player and coach makes me feel more comfortable and reminds me that life exists outside of what I am going through.

Scott breaks the meaningless conversation. "Kristen and I went to school together, so I can help with some of this stuff." His voice is loud and reminds me of when I went to watch his mock murder trial in law school. "Julie Correa was a PE teacher and she . . . she was oddly close to a number of different girls."

"So you had her for PE, too?" Parker's ears perk at the idea that Scott could be a witness.

"No, we had a male teacher; the boys had Mr. Tsubota." Scott looks at me and puts his hand in the center of my back.

I know that the time is coming where Parker asks Scott to leave. I know I don't want to do this with Scott here. I know that I don't want Scott to leave. And I know that I have to do this. *Where does that leave me?*

"Kristen and I are going to go through some of this on our own," Parker says to Scott in a softer, more serious voice.

"Okay, that sounds good. I'm going to go get something to eat. Do you guys want anything?" Scott asks but doesn't actually invite or expect an answer from either of us. "Okay, Kristy, I'll have my phone with me. Just call when you need me."

I need you right now.

And so Scott stands up slowly. He touches my shoulder as he leaves and I can feel through his hand that he is nervous.

And so, in a cold room, with the faint sound of the police radio and hum of the misplaced aquarium, we begin.

Birch settles into his chair and I watch Scott's head disappear around the corner of the receptionist's desk and out the door.

"I'm going to record this. Is that okay?" Parker asks me as he makes eye contact across the table.

"Yes," I say and look down at my hands, which are crumpled together on top of the table. My nails are a little too long. I hate long fingernails.

"Okay." He clicks a button and the wheels on the small black recorder just in front of me begin to turn. "I'll just start from as far back as you can remember and . . . go forward."

I look at him and suddenly wish that I could just scoop my brain out and lay it on the table. My breath is pulled from me. But still I start.

"Okay, so it started in . . . junior high school. I had a PE teacher whom I was really close with and she coached our . . . she coached the volleyball team and she coached my basketball team and softball team." As I speak, I am unaware of my stumbling and only aware of the smell of the dirt on the softball field. I can see the moments of eighth grade as though they are today.

I continue, "she's kind of like the cool teacher . . ." My cheeks turn pink as I realize my use of the present tense. "Everybody wanted to hang out with her," I say careful to convince Parker that I realize this was more than a decade ago.

Parker jumps in to show he is listening, "And these were the . . . junior high teams or they were the . . . ?"

I interrupt him. "They were junior high teams, yeah." Now that I have started, I have to keep going. "All of the older kids, like if you were an athlete you wanted to be liked and stuff like that, by her," I say and I am frustrated that I sound like a twelve-year-old.

I look at Parker as he scribbles with his pen on his note paper. I think of Julie and I think of Witters and I can't pull them apart from each other in my brain. "I also had a science teacher . . . I don't know how important it is, or if it's really important at all, but I had this science teacher in my eighth grade year and . . . he did something . . . inappropriate with me. I think that was after school."

Parker looks at me and I look at my hands, "So really what you remember is something happened between you and . . . this male teacher that made you uncomfortable enough that you met to talk to your coach about it."

"Yeah . . . ," I say gratefully and look at him, somewhat surprised by his concise and correct summary. I decide to maintain eye contact as I move on, "And then she . . . kind of isolated me even more and then she ended up abusing me for the next four years."

Parker leans back in his chair, away from his note pad. I am reminded of Teri in the Wahoo's Fish Taco booth. He lets out a large exhale.

I lean over to my left and reach into my blue-striped Cal tote at my foot. I grab out of it a stack of four large calendars, the covers of which read: "1996, 1997, 1998, 1999."

I look down at them and my heart sinks down in my chest. I touch the cover of the calendars and remember as each of them sat at my mom's small desk in the corner of the kitchen. Just to the right of our home phone, these marked all of Marc's and my important dates. They were my mom's way of keeping track of her children.

Parker watches me as I set the stack of evidence on the table. I explain myself: "My mom kept all of our calendars from then and . . . I marked some of the things that . . ."

Parker slides them over so that he can get a closer look. He softly touches the green tabs that peer from the top of the pages. I look down at the Post-its and am suddenly transported to the warm afternoon last week when I told my mom.

"Are you doing okay?" My mom had asked me over the phone. "You don't sound like yourself," she said, knowing that something was wrong. I had been avoiding her calls since Woman Within.

"I've just been having a hard time. A really hard time. With some things that happened to me a long time ago . . . ," I said sitting on my back patio. Just holding the phone up to my head felt like a chore.

"What sort of things that happened?" my mom had begged.

"Mr. Witters touched me, mom." I paused knowing that was only a tenth of the pain. I reached deep in my gut and pulled out the truth for her as I did for Scott. And Natali . . ." My ears hurt to hear the forbidden sound. Tears had flowed down my face as I spoke plainly and directly to my mom.

"Do you have those old calendars? I'm going to the police and I need them to outline the dates," I said, knowing that she did and not caring about her opinion if this was the right move.

"Yes, I think I have them . . . ," she said and I could hear purposeful digging in the background. "Here I have them right here. What do you need?"

The years swirled in my head as I tried to find a voice to tell my own mother through which childhood years I was being raped. "Um . . . I need 1996 through 1999," I said and that is when the uncontrollable grief came out.

"Kristen . . . I have to ask you this. Are you suicidal?" My mom paused crying momentarily for the brazen and brave question.

"No," I lied to her, secretly glad that she understood the degree of devastation enough to ask.

"Okay. We can get through this," she said on the other end.

I remember her words as I am brought back to the present moment of Parker flipping through pages. I look at him, wondering if he thinks I have lost my mind with these old and tattered records.

As if he knows what I am thinking, he closes the book. "No, that's very cool," Parker says as his eyes look down at the book. He explains: "Dates are important . . . what happens next when I talk to her about it."

The fish in the aquarium pause and my eyes look at them unblinking. *Talk to her about it? If you talk to her about it, she will kill me. This is not why I am here. I don't want you to talk to her about it. That will mean the end of my life.*

I am sure my face has turned white and Parker continues on to explain his logic, "I'll ask specific dates, and it shows that this isn't just something someone's making up."

"Yeah," I agree with him with my mouth but my mind disagrees vehemently. *Making this up? How could I have ever made this up? Why would I ever make this up?*

"It's a lot of pressure both on her . . . to defend that action." Parker's voice trails off as he begins to talk about what will happen next. Suddenly, a terrifying scene is unfolding before my eyes. Julie saying it never happened, people believing her, a judge, a jury, a defense attorney, a warrant, an arrest, a hearing, a trial.

It took everything I had to get to this moment with Parker. I didn't have the energy to consider the aftermath. *How will I be ready for what comes next?*

Parker looks at me and he can see that I am overwhelmed. He draws my attention back to his part of the process. He continues: "So eighth grade was . . . So how old are you now?"

"Twenty-eight," I say. *Why do I feel like I am still fourteen?*

"So what, we've got fourteen years ago," Parker says without being dismissive. "So this is April of '96?"

"Yes," I confirm. I open my mouth for a full chest breath. As I let out the exhale, I slide my hands to the edge of the table. I let my shoulders drop into the frame of my body. I lean back and open my chest so that the truth can come spilling out to him.

Through the course of the next three hours, and over the course of three more interviews in the same office, I tell him all that I can remember. Step by step, plan by plan, and night by night, I remove one black grain of sand from my soul at a time.

Parker always does his best to keep his composure. But I can see when it is hard for him. He always makes the same face, holding his pen still as if he is thinking of what to write. Pressing his back teeth together as if he has just swallowed something sour. Allowing his eyes to look toward the window, as though he is looking out. But I know different. I can see what he is really looking at. There, just before the window sill, in a cheap plastic frame, a picture of his two children smiling back at him.

CHAPTER FOUR

Blank

The dryness of spring smells distinct. Our winters are wet. And without rain now for over a month, the flowers, the trees, all begin the fragrance fight.

I love this time of year, although I am not as good at softball as I am at basketball. It's just too slow and rarely do I get to use my speed. Still, I wish I were at softball practice.

Instead, I am walking through the heart of JM. Past the locker hallway where all of the popular eighth graders have their lockers. I was supposed to have a locker there, but I was in Salt Lake this summer visiting my family when we picked lockers. Last summer, the last time I saw my grandpa. It is after school and I see a group of boys and girls giggling about something. I am jealous. Not in their locker hall, and not in their laughter.

My locker is four whole buildings away. Well, my old locker, that is. All the way over by the sixth grade core classes. Completely out of the way, and completely out of the fun. You got sick of me complaining about how far away it was and told me, "A few years back, people got a bunch of stuff stolen out of their lockers in that building." It makes sense. It's not as though there are any teachers back there to report misbehaving. People want to be here, in the heart of the school.

Your solution seemed like a good one to me. You dragged in four cinderblocks and two flat planks of wood. I never stopped to wonder where you got the building materials—whether they were already at school, if you went to Home Depot and bought them for me, or if you had them somewhere in your side yard. The grey blocks are large and heavy, and if you turn them to the side, they have a design that reminds me of a flower.

"Me and my roommate used these in college to build bookshelves and hoist our beds up so we could store things under them," you had said to me with a certain look in your eyes. The same look you always get as you reminisce about college, about having a dorm room and a roommate and about playing soccer. As I imagined you living in a tiny room with a tiny fridge and a tiny television, I longed for it all. Independence seems so painfully far away from me sometimes. *Will I ever get to play soccer in college and be on my own? Will I still know you then?*

As you adjusted the two large wood slats to complete my makeshift locker, I wondered then if you have ever made something like this for a previous TA. I had considered asking you, but worried that you would think that I was being unappreciative for your building skills so I decided to keep it simple. "Thanks," I said, but immediately began to wonder how I would get my books when you are not in your office.

Don't get me wrong. As I said, it was a good idea. It made sense and it still makes sense. I am in your office constantly. Before PE, after PE, every brunch, before softball practice, during TA period . . . so why not just keep all of my stuff there? I liked how you let me decorate the wood after you put it up. Peace signs and bubble handwriting, Sharpies and highlighters make the shelves my own. It feels like how my friends have their lockers decorated.

Only, it's not a locker, it's not my locker.

And here is the thing. I don't want to tell you this because I really don't want to hurt your feelings. And I don't want you to think that I am ungrateful for the shelves. Because, trust me, it is better than the locker in Siberia. But I just wish that maybe one of the Maggies also had her stuff in your office. It makes me feel a tiny bit weird that I keep my stuff in there. See, I am pretty sure that the other kids talk about it—even my friends. When they come in for PE class, and I am standing by the office waiting for you to unlock it, they give me a "look." I'm not sure if this comes from anger or jealously or judgment, but I know that it feels bad. They know that I am your favorite and, just sometimes, I wish I weren't.

But, on the flip side, I feel as though I need to be near you. And there is a whole laundry list as to why. You get me. You get how important sports are to me. You let me talk to you about Mr.

Witters, who is getting worse instead of better. And two weeks ago, my other grandpa died. Two grandpas in the same school year. And you have been the perfect person to help me through . . . everything.

And now walking through the corridors to the science building, I am thinking of missing softball practice and I am feeling anxious. I picture you building my fake locker, about you calling me your favorite again to try to make myself feel better, but all I can fixate on is the growing distance between where I am and where I should be.

I hate all of the dry leaves between the cement steps and wonder why someone hasn't cleaned them up since the fall. I see the garbage can that Carolyn was eating chocolate chip cookies out of yesterday and I become angry at the boys who were making fun of her. I think of the teacher that I am going to see and I wish that I were going to see you. Because with you, at least I feel safe.

I have learned a lot about Mr. Witters this year. Mostly I have learned that he gets a lot of attention and that people are constantly talking about him, which means that you and I talking about him is basically what the whole school seems to be doing.

I like confiding in you because you are willing to confide in me. When I tell you about him, you make sure that I know I am not alone. You told me that there are a lot of mixed feelings toward him. Some families request him as teacher. Other families refuse to have him teach their children. Three days ago you told me that other teachers talk about him in the lunch room as much as the students talk about him in the lunch quad. I wonder innocently how you know that when you spend every lunch with us in your office.

"And," you said yesterday, "he has done worse things than what he does with you. Last year he licked a girl's ear right in front of me." I jolted with a full body shiver. "I told Principal Walters, but nothing came of it," you said with a shrug of the shoulders.

I have to be honest; my feelings are still a little mixed. There are still a lot of things that Witters does that make me smile and laugh. Eighth grade science is never dull or boring. He is young and loves his job. In some ways he is so much like you. But there are a lot of buts.

Besides what he says to students, everyone in the school thinks that he and Mrs. Nelson, the art teacher, have sex at lunch time. Mr. Witters is married and has two young children. But he flirts with Mrs. Nelson constantly and the two have classrooms that are separated by the path I am currently walking down.

"Hello, stranger," Mrs. Nelson said last week when she came into our science class. I looked up from my current lab assignment to see Mrs. Nelson leaning in the doorway and looking at Mr. Witters. "I haven't seen you all day," she had said to him and the two met for a brief conversation, the details of which I could not hear.

I know Mrs. Nelson fairly well because she teaches my ceramics class. She is nice enough and all of the boys think that she is really pretty, but I think that she is fake. Plus, if what people say is true, what kind of person would she be if she is sleeping with a husband and a father? Also, I think that it is gross to have sex when you have kids coming in next period to work on water coloring.

Mr. Witters really likes me, and has no idea that I complain to you every day about him. He likes me almost as much as he likes Caitlin. Caitlin is his favorite, but not in the same way or for the same reason that I am your favorite. Caitlin is his favorite because she has boobs. I think that it is weird when he says things like, "Whoa! Caitlin, gotta love that tight shirt today." It confuses me. Does he like her shirt? Or does he just like that her shirt is tight? Or when he tells Vanessa that she has beautiful hair and that it is going to drive the guys wild, does he really mean that it drives him wild?

He likes me because I am good at sports, I do well in his class, and I always get good grades. Well, at least that is why I think he likes me. It's not as though I have any of the attributes that his other favorites have.

This walk feels as though it is taking forever. It reminds me to be grateful for my new locker in your office.

As my feet hit the path, I am reminded of seeing former JM students on this same pavement. There is one in particular whom I have seen coming to visit Mr. Witters a lot this year. While I flip through the rolodex of my brain searching for her name, I think that she must have been his favorite if she is now in high school and still wants to come see him.

Thinking of returning students makes me feel a little calmer. I have no idea what high school will be like and I am hoping that maybe I can come visit you next year. We have become such good friends that it would be cool if I came back to see you.

I got my braces off a few weeks ago and I also highlighted my hair for the first time and Mr. Witters says that the boys are going to start noticing, whatever that means. I have to admit that it felt a little good when he said that in front of the class, because maybe some of those boys will listen to him and notice me. But then my face turned the color of my dark red soccer socks; I wished he wouldn't have pointed me out. He knew I was embarrassed and with his barreling laugh came over and kissed me on the cheek to apologize.

So today I turned in a project that I should be really proud of—a 3-D exhibition of a plant cell. Witters loved it so much that he said, "Awww! This is pretty awesome. Come back after school today. I wanna pick your brain on how you got this idea and see if I can talk you into letting me keep it as an example for next year." I stop suddenly in my tracks.

My project is good, but it's not that good. And I didn't do it alone.

Jessica was my partner for the project. We got to pick our own partners, but it had to be someone other than whom you sit next to. I like Jessica and she is on both my basketball team and softball team so that finding a time to work together around practice and games is easy. *Why didn't Mr. Witters ask to see both of us?* I saw Jessica getting ready for softball practice in the locker room.

Maybe he knows. My heart begins to race and I hate that I am such a worry wart. My mom passed down her ability to worry to both Marc and me. *Maybe Witters knows what happened when I went over to Jessica's house to work on the project.*

It was last Sunday. Usually when I have group projects to do, we do them at my house. But Jessica's mom insisted that we do it there, and I had immediately begun to worry if she was just trying to help because of my grandparents.

Jessica lives in a nice house, but it is not as nice as mine. It's a long rancher and the defining feature is the pool in the backyard, which they keep the temperate of a hot tub. I can't imagine trying to do a swim workout in there. I would throw up.

As I knocked on the door, I was surprised to hear the familiar sounds of the pool and the unloading spring of the diving board making their way from the backyard. Jessica is an only child and I had hoped that she would be ready to get started on the project right away.

"Welcome, my dear," Jessica's mom had said to me as she opened one of the blue double doors that led into the house.

"Hi, Mrs. Larson," I had replied with my science book and notes billowing out of my arms.

"Well, do I have a surprise for you?!" she said to me with her red lipstick lips stretched into a smile.

She led me to the kitchen, from which I could see Jessica. There, on the diving board, she bounced in her blue and pink two pieces, getting ready to wow her watching father. I hate wearing two pieces and as I look at Jessica's puffy belly, I am surprised that she doesn't hate them also.

"Well, what do you think?" Jessica's mom had said behind me, pulling my attention away from the pool party outside.

I had to clench my jaw in an effort to keep it from gaping open. There, in the center of the oak kitchen table, sat our cell. A finished product, with no work left to be done. "Now you can go out there and join them. I left some swim suits for you to choose from on Jessica's bed."

I stood flabbergasted in the kitchen. I looked at Mrs. Larson wishing she would understand that I don't like to swim for fun. I like to race and I like to win. I had looked down to avoid the intensity of her stare, at which point I saw a body too small for Jessica's swim suits.

But more than the distresses swimming in my head is this: I wanted to do the project. I had told Jessica my idea to use glue to suspend various objects that would represent the nucleus, the mitochondria, and all of the other cool things we were learning about. My eyes drifted over to the cell, made just as I had wanted to make it, only better. With floating buttons and perfectly placed yarn the cell was . . . beautiful. And there, in the lefthand corner was a glossary defining the contents of the cell. Printed perfectly in handwriting I have never seen before.

I know I should have told my mom. *But what would I have said? And then, what would have happened?* My mom would not stand for such a thing and would never consider doing an assignment for me. I guess that this is what my mom means when she says, "I am not your average Moraga Mom." I used to think that she meant that most moms here don't smoke cigarettes and bowl in a bowling league on Thursdays. Now I think she is referring to the moms who will stop at nothing to ensure the success and achievement of their sons and daughters.

I inch my way closer to Witters's classroom and wonder if he somehow found out that my project is fraudulent. I think back to the look on his face and it did have markings of mischief. *I only told you about the cell situation. Did you tell him? Am I in trouble?*

I see the invitation of his door, propped open to the dry spring outside. I think of another possibility. My mom had to write a letter explaining the family's situation and verifying my school absences. I wonder if all my teachers know. *So, maybe Mr. Witters knows about my grandpas and he is trying to make me feel better.*

As my feet crunch the leaves below, I am still a child, although I wish I were not. I try to take my mind off of all the pending possibilities and instead wonder if my mom will make spaghetti or chicken for dinner. My mind drifts easily as I wonder who is playing pitcher at the softball practice I am late for it because of this stupid meeting. I run my tongue over my newly slimy teeth and I can hear, smell, and see the world just as a kid should. And as I move toward the side door of the classroom, past the door of the art teacher, I have no idea that my life is about to change forever.

CHAPTER FIVE

Dialing the Devil

It's a voice I do not recognize—or, rather, one that I do not recognize right away. It is high-pitched. It is rushed and short. It is young. It is coming out of my mouth.

I have been practicing this with the detective. What to say to her to gain her trust back. What not to say to her to make her suspicious. Tactics to get her to admit to . . . everything. But no preparation could prepare me for this.

My eyes dart around the room, just as they used to dart around the apartment. My stomach is empty from the anticipation of hearing her voice today. Detective Parker sits across from me and knows I am nervous. He has been speaking extra slowly, as if he can calm my nerves through osmosis.

When Detective Parker first brought up the idea of doing pretextual phone calls, I thought that he was crazy. Didn't we have enough evidence without them? My ex-boyfriend to testify to that sad night. My dad hearing someone jump out of my window and the broken leg she consequently suffered. My mom's suspicions. My testimony. Did I really need to go through this? According to the DA who had looked at the file, the answer was a resounding yes.

Parker knows I am an athlete at heart. I know he is, too. After all of the getting-to-know-him hours, I know that he played water polo in college. Somehow the two of us have gotten comfortable talking about the uncomfortable. He looks into my eyes and knows that at some point, the game begins.

I am shocked that I am not shaking as I hold the phone to my head. The weight of the black receiver feels good in my hand. I look down at the dashboard of the phone and notice the blinking lights of other police lines working.

I found her phone number in early May. Her phone number, her address, her previous addresses, including 1085B Deer Hill Road, Lafayette, CA. There, in black and white, the darkest place of my life. Proof that my pain was real and that my nightmares had an origin. Relief that I wasn't insane.

And so I brought with me that number I found. You would think that the police database would be more accurate than People Search Pro, but apparently not. I also brought all of my notes of what to say. And, of course, the thing that made me feel the safest in the world: Scott.

I imagine what he might be doing now, soaking up the warm sun of a July afternoon and playing on his iPhone in the parking lot of the Lafayette Police Department. I imagine that he is sitting next to me, stroking the blond hair that falls down my back.

And still I don't feel ready. The ifs swarm through my head. *What if she won't talk to me, if she says it didn't happen? What if she comes here immediately and kills me? What if I go through all of this, she admits to all of it, and then Detective Parker's tape doesn't record?*

The first ring jolts my ifs to a halt.

I am sitting in a different chair this time. More of an office chair that swivels and spins. I imagine Parker sitting in this same chair pushing paper work. I turn, just to the right, and see Parker sitting at the nearby round table. The scene of showing him my soul. He has paperwork in front of him now, and although he flips through some pages, the wrinkle in his forehead says he is nervous for me. He senses my stare and looks up at me.

Second ring. Parker gives me the thumbs up sign and lifts his eyebrows. "It's recording," he mouths at me. I wonder how he can be sure because it is not like CSI where the detective is watching two tape wheels spin. "You can do this." And he shakes his head to show he is confident in me.

Third ring. I turn my back to Parker and lean my elbows on the desk. I look down at my notes.

What will she sound like?

A peacefulness settles into my chest.

"Hello?" I have thought about Rob endlessly since I remembered all of this. His voice has not changed since the days when

Julie would make me call her in eighth grade and he would answer. Back then he used to joke around with me a little before he would give Julie the phone. Now he has no idea that the person on the other line is dying because of what he allowed to happen. Or does he?

Her husband then, her husband now, my hurt says that he knew. "Hi," I reply. It takes a conscious effort not to physically swivel my head around and look for another person in the room doing this terrifying thing for me. This voice is not my own and I am startled and comforted by it at the exact same time. ". . . Is Julie there?"

"Uh, no, she's not here right now . . . ," Rob replies. His voice climbs higher at the end of his sentence, almost forming a question mark.

"Uh, this is an old friend of hers, Kristen from JM, and I was wondering if you might have a cell phone for her?" My words, much to my surprise, leave my mouth seamlessly.

Rob, on the other hand, stammers, "Oh, yeah, God, what . . . she actually has my cell phone," I hear Rob mumble and stumble on the other end of the line. "I can tell you . . . let me see if I can find her name. It's like a . . . it's 925 . . . oh, hers is dead . . . 925 . . . Oh, God, I'm doing this by memory . . ." Rob's words are frantic and fumbling, like a cheating husband trying to justify the scent of a foreign perfume. I wonder what he is trying to hide.

My jaw clenches with anger toward Rob, "Okay?" I say to him. "2-267-2683, I think. Oh, God, I don't know if that's right or not." Rob's voice seems to be getting higher pitched by the second.

Suddenly something makes me much smarter than Rob. It's as though I have someone living inside of me who can handle this and also happens to be a detective. "It's (925) 267?" I say, checking to see if Rob can remember the lie he just told me.

I am not surprised that he cannot. "God, man, this is killing me. I don't know my own number. It's just, uh . . . If not, you have the right number . . ." *Two small kids and a phone that used to belong to you, Rob? Sorry, I don't buy it.* I remain silent halfway enjoying his extreme discomfort. He knows he has to say something. "She's actually just . . . she's at the store and she'll probably be back in about, probably about a half hour or so."

As I imagine her putting Rice Krispies in her cart, my soul feels as though it is sliding off the plastic chair. This has been another theme in my constant line of self-questioning. *What kind of mother is she? What will this do to her kids? What does she already do to her kids?*

The voice is back to handle this for me, "Oh, okay, great, should I leave a number or should I just call back? Just call back?"

Rob's words will not settle, "Well, I have, I have it on . . . on . . . I have your number on the log. This is. Um. Kristen from JM? You're, uh—were you a teacher there?"

This question, coming from the person I went out to many Mexican dinners with, ran the Bay to Breakers running race with, who came to my soccer games with his wife. I know that he remembers me and that he knows exactly who is calling him tonight. I feel my arm reach through the phone and put an ounce of pain from my stomach to his, and I answer simply, "No, no, I was a student," I say casually. Somehow I know to tell the truth about this.

"You were a student. Oh, my God." He sounds shocked and also scared.

"Yeah, yeah." I let my words linger, remembering that Rob is not who I am after.

"That's going back a ways," Rob says. *Nope, Rob, we aren't going back anywhere. We are going to do this right now.*

His voice sounds even more nervous than mine. I can hear that he knows exactly who I am, that he has a clear picture of my fourteen-year-old face on the back side of his eyelids. Through eighth grade I spent such a significant amount of time with Julie and Rob that I know that this oblivious little act is only that.

"Yeah . . . ," I am careful not to give him too much.

"Do you want, uh, do you want me to leave her a message or just, uh, will you call back or you want me to have her call you?" Rob asks. I imagine her calling back on Parker's cell phone. *How would I record the call then?*

I respond quickly, "Yeah. Um . . . , I can call back, that's fine."

"Oh, okay." Rob is quieter now.

"All right, well, take care." But sincerity is missing from Rob's words.

"All right, you, too. Thanks," I say.

Rob doesn't return the thank you: "All right. Bye."

As I finish my conversation with Rob, I know that he knew what Julie did to me then and I can hear the fear in his voice as to why I am calling now. There is a piece of me that feels calm, confident that I can become the hunter. There is another piece of me envisioning a Lifetime movie about my abuse. In it, Julie is in the master bedroom making me do twisted things, and Rob is sitting in the second bedroom, watching it all on camera. As I watch the episode in my head, I search the bedroom for the hidden camera. *Was it in that old teddy bear she had? Don't they make nanny cameras like that? Maybe it was in that pile of clothes at the corner of the bedroom? Maybe up there, in the ceiling fan?* I decide to stop searching and focus on the task at hand.

I sit with Detective Parker, running through more scenarios of what to say to Julie once I get her on the phone. I look at the papers in front of me. All of the notes scribbled in miscellaneous order. The many things that Parker has told me, that he has coached me on. "Get her to *trust* you," and "take your time with her." I know that I need to wait at least a half hour until we try to dial the devil again.

"Remember, Kristen . . ." Detective Parker's voice trails off as he tries to keep the atmosphere light, but he looks at me and he is worried. He has heard more of my past than anyone and he knows what talking to this person can do to me. "Remember, we are going to do the hard work now so that it is easier later on."

I know that he is talking about the legal process, but my brain has a hard time imagining how any of this could ever be easy.

Parker continues: "A few years back I had a seventeen-year-old girl call her abuser. He didn't want to admit what he did to her over the phone. I had her tell him that it was all her fault and her idea. Once the perp felt as though the victim was taking blame, he opened up. She then asked if there was anyone else." He looks at me and tilts his head proud of his police work, "Hook, line, and sinker. He replied that she was the only one and all of a sudden we had corroboration. He took a plea bargain before we could even get a court date. And it was over."

I look at him and nod my head. I am good at making people feel good about themselves or what they have just said to me. My stomach feels as though it has a weighted medicine ball sitting in the pit of it.

Simple as it sounds sitting here in Birch's office, I know Julie and I know that this will not be simple. She is a snake and a manipulator, and I know that I will have to be braver and stronger than I have ever been in my life to get her to admit to the truth. She is smart and paranoid, and I must first regain her trust. And even if I win, if I get her to tell the truth, somehow I know that this is far from over.

Birch picks up the phone and regrets his question before he has even completed it, "Are you ready?" I look at the clock, and somehow it has been 44 minutes since our last call.

I smile at Birch and look at the notes in front of me. He dials the recording service first, enters the cell phone number that will appear on a caller ID, and then dials Julie's home number. "Hello, is this Kristen?" It is Rob again and there is a hint of anger in his scared voice this time.

"Yes, it is." I try to be as brief as I can.

"I'm sorry, Julie's not back yet." I look back at the clock to verify my call. Now it has been 46 minutes since I called her last time. Is he lying for her again?

"Okay . . . ," I say trying to sound as a disappointed person would after unsuccessfully trying to reach an old friend.

"I'll have her give you a call when she comes back. She . . . she just went to the store with our youngest, so . . ." I hate that these two have kids.

"Oh, okay . . . okay, that'd be great . . ." I proceed to give Rob the cell phone that Detective Parker has provided me with. He has assured me if she calls back, we will let it go to the recording that has my voice. Then I will call her back and attack again.

"Hey, Kris—is your—can I get a little bit of detail? Are you— what year were you in and all that or . . ." Rob's voice moves too fast as he begins his own investigation.

"Um, what year was I . . . I don't know exactly what year I . . ." I know to seem hesitant here. I know that the average person wouldn't be sitting in a police office with dates and times spread across the table in front of her. That a regular person wouldn't have a calendar from 1993 with the handwriting of an eleven year old marking the first day of sixth grade, now sitting quietly in police evidence.

Rob laughs at my stammering as he says, "It was a long time ago." *Why does it feel like yesterday?*

"I mean I grad . . . yeah, I graduated, uh, high school in 2000 and . . ." That should be just enough so that Julie knows exactly who it is.

"2000? Okay."

"Yeah, I just feel bad that I fell out of touch with her and I'd just like to talk to her so, yeah, . . ." I hope my desperation doesn't come through in my voice.

"Okay. Well, she definitely likes to hear from her former students so, uh, she's going to be mad at me that I can't even remember my own phone number . . ." Rob tries to laugh at himself. My body jolts from the seat with his words. I picture other broken students, making a phone call similar to mine today, facing similar devastation in their lives because of Julie. *What if someone else has already tried this? If she's at the grocery store, that someone must have failed.*

"Oh, okay, yeah, yeah, that's okay . . ." I take a breath, to stay calm.

"I'll have her give you a call and she'll . . . she'll probably be, like I said, probably be at home within the next . . . within the next half hour or so or some time . . ." *That is what you said 49 minutes ago.*

"Okay," I comply.

"She'll definite . . . she'll definitely give you a call back." Rob sounds defeated knowing that he has no choice in what Julie will or will not do.

"All right. Great. Thanks," I say.

"All right, thanks, Kristen." He lingers on my name, and if he could, I think he would beg me to rewind the last hour and never make this phone call.

"Okay, bye." I hang up the phone with Rob, disappointed that I did not have the chance to get what I needed out of Julie today.

"It's okay," Birch reassures me. "She'll call back. She'll need to know why you are calling. She won't be able to help herself." I know her and I know that he is right. "Stay close for a few hours, and if she calls back, I will ignore the call, call you, and have you meet me back here at the station, and we will try to get ahold of her."

"Okay, I go to LA tomorrow afternoon for a swim meet." I remind Birch of my hectic summer schedule. Between competitions and recruiting, I am on the road constantly.

"But I can do calls from down there." Now that I have called Julie, that I have got the ball rolling, I know I can't just make it stop. I know that I have one chance with these phone calls, one chance to get a jury to understand and see what she did to me. I have one chance to make things as right for me as they can possibly be.

As I exit the police station, I feel disappointed that I did not accomplish what I wanted to tonight. As I walk the dogs with Scott,

I wonder what the next few days will bring. *Is that her running on the trail? Has she made it from Utah in less than an hour? Has Rob told her that I called yet? What is she thinking as she brushes her teeth tonight?*

I check my cell phone every two minutes and Birch has not called. When we get home from the walk, I hurry to the computer to check my fake Facebook account that Birch had me set up in case she tries to contact me. It remains blank: no messages, no wall posts, no friends.

CHAPTER SIX

Safe Secrets

What do I write?

W I look down at my blue ballpoint and blank inside of a card I stole from the upper cabinet of my mom's desk. It says "Thank You" on the outside and has a mirage of flowers and birds. Though it seemed like the right choice of cards, I have no idea how to thank you.

It's almost as though I didn't have to go through it. Like right after it happened, that you were there, I told you, and that you promised to take care of everything.

I knew I needed to wait until the end of softball anyway, because that is when my mom would come to pick me up. I also knew that you would wonder why I missed the whole practice.

"Where were you? I ended practice early because I was worried that you had to go to his classroom." You always tell me that you don't trust Mr. Witters as far as you can throw him. I always imagine you picking Mr. Witters up, your arms around his growing pot belly, and you thrusting him forward an inch or two. That's not very far.

You say all of this, but during basketball season when you coached my "8-A" team and he coached the "8-B" team, you acted like friends. We often scrimmaged teams, and you two were always joking around with each other. I would never tell you this, but sometimes I think that you might be jealous of Mrs. Nelson.

When I sat there to tell you why I was late, I was worried about how you might react. You seemed angry and I didn't know who you were angry at. As you sat the closest you have ever sat to me, I knew then that your priority was to take care of me.

My body was hot, as we sat with our legs extended on the concrete floor of the locker room just outside your office. I know that no one else was left in the locker room that afternoon; most kids don't come in after practice. My words were muddied with tears and I gasped for air as soon as I opened my mouth.

But that is all I remember.

I am not trying to be evasive; it's just that I honestly don't know how our conversation went. I can't remember what I said; I can only remember the pain of talking. I can't remember exactly what you said, but I know that you listened. I know that you were soft and fuming at the same time.

The only words I remember were yours: "Don't worry, I won't tell your parents . . . ," you promised me.

I felt better hearing you say that. It is the only thing that has made me feel at all better, and I wonder how you knew what to say without me even asking for you not to tell anyone. I think of how sad and devastated my mom and dad would be. Everything they do, they do so that I have a great life. My dad's long work hours, my mom's determination to give me a better childhood than she had—how would they feel if they knew what happened? All of their hard work, out the science room window.

For the first time in some time, I felt my lungs fill with air. Like so many times for the past three years, you made me feel better. Like when Dominic teases me about my flat chest, or when I feel left out because of my locker, or when I miss a basket I know that I should make . . . with this.

You were there for me when no one else was. And, since then, you are there for me every day. You have been so generous with me in the past few weeks. At least something good is coming out of something bad.

Today is the playoff game for the eighth grade softball team, and I am not sure what I am supposed to say back to you when you say, "Just take them, I can get new ones." *How I am supposed to just take your Oakley sunglasses?* I for sure want them, it's just that they are yours and I know that they are expensive. My mom and I always get our sunglasses at TJ Maxx because then, if I lose them, they only cost $9.99 to replace. Sometimes the store has pretty good brands.

"I can't take these. You wear them every day." I know that I play softball better when I wear them because you always let me borrow them when I am pitching at practice. "I can just wear them for the game and then I will give them back," I say, halfway hoping that you take me up on my offer.

"But you can't give them back because we only have three weeks together before the end of school and you can't just keep borrowing them," you say in an obstinate way that you know I will not argue with.

Why do you talk about me leaving for high school every chance you get? I hate it. It makes me feel as though I have a hole in my stomach. Part of the hole comes from feeling as though I have just found my spot here. I am doing great in sports and in school and I like spending time with you. Another part of the hole comes from you constantly telling me how sad you are that I am leaving. You always talk about how you could never have as good of a TA as me. *What is it that I do so well?*

I hate it when you talk about how sad it is that I am headed to high school because, although there are things I like about JM, I am desperately ready and excited to move on. You make me feel as though I am not supposed to be happy about this next step, so the excited feeling has to stay inside and make the hole grow bigger.

"I know," I say quickly so that you cannot detect my eagerness. "It is coming up so quickly," a safe and neutral comment that I hope you do not read into.

"You better not have a teacher that you like as much as me, because I know that I will never have a student that I like as much as you . . . ," you say and sometimes your voice sounds different, like really far away.

This comment makes me feel good and bad at the same time. Good because I am glad that you like me. Bad because I want to have a teacher that I am close to in high school. I think of all of the things that you have done for me: the daily bagels, the protection from Mr. Witters, the starting point guard position, the soccer lessons, the Adidas hat that I am wearing right now—and I know that you are right. There probably won't be another person, let alone another teacher, that would do all of these things for me. "Impossible," I say and I wonder why my sentences with you have gotten so short.

We continue driving toward the softball game in the next town over, and I wonder what time my family will make it to the game. All of my relatives are visiting from Utah, and between the hair spray and the flat iron; they take three times as long to get ready as I do.

Usually, my mom drives me to the games, but lately you have been offering. When you knew that my family was visiting this week, you said, "Perfect! I can drive you and we can talk about whom to play at which position. We can also stop for Slurpees if you promise not to tell anyone. You know . . . they won't think that it is fair." You always ask for secrecy with your secrets, or our secrets, with the same mischievous raise of your eyebrow.

I love Slurpees. I also love it when you let me help you figure out a game plan. In basketball it was more about setting up plays for me to run, but this spring you have let me help decide who plays where on the field. It makes me feel grown up, and when I take the field, I feel a sense of ownership. I think that it is okay that you let me do this; after all, I am the captain of the team. But it is another thing that I don't tell people about.

Since Mr. Witters, there is a growing list of things for me to keep track of not to tell people about. My mom would probably think that it was weird if she knew that I was allowed to help coach the team. She would probably think that I am too young to really know how to strategize. And she would probably think that it was an unfair position to put me in to pick and choose who sits on the bench. But, I figure, what she doesn't know won't hurt her.

I am glad I am riding in the car with you because then I won't have to be worried about being late for warmup. Your metallic teal Honda Accord pulls into the parking lot of our rival junior high school . . . if there is such a thing. I secretly hate the color of your car, and the fabric seats make the underside of my legs itch.

My head hurts because I have been trying to drink my Cherry mixed with Coke Slurpee as fast as I can so that no one will know that you bought it for me. You always pay for everything and sometimes I feel bad. Like last week, when you got permission from the school to take all of your TAs out to Bianca's Deli and made sure that we were at the back of the line together. "I'll get yours because you work the hardest for me," you whispered in my ear so that no one else could hear. I don't know what to say because I don't need you to pay for mine; it's not as though it's my money anyway. But I don't want to say something back because someone will hear me and, if you are whispering, you obviously don't want anyone else to know about this. So I stay quiet.

We are the first to arrive at the field, and I am glad about this for a couple of reasons. First, I will get to spend time warming up with just you. I like throwing the ball around with you better than anyone else. Second, my friends won't wonder why I rode with you and not them or not my parents.

Speaking of my parents, I should say my mom has been really bothering me recently. She would barely let me ride to the game with you, and last week at dinner I was telling her I didn't want a hamburger because you always say that hamburgers are a walking heart attack. We were at Nations Hamburgers and I ordered a chicken breast sandwich on wheat with no mayo. I got a pretty serious head swivel from my mom when "No, thank you" to the question about fries.

"What is all this about? You always get a cheeseburger and fries here," my mom had said in an almost accusatory way. My brother looked at me as perplexed as my mom did.

"Natali says that they are too fattening. She has this chart in her office of how many calories different food has and how many calories you can burn doing different exercises." I thought of the chart and decided to leave off the part that always makes my cheeks burn, but still I take the time to envision the chart.

Right when you walk up the stairs to your office, there it is. I like looking at the difference in calorie consumption of running versus walking and mopping versus vacuuming, but I hate looking at the amount of calories consumed when having sex. It makes me feel as though I don't belong. The only things I know about sex are what I learned in Sex Ed this year, what I overhear other kids talking about, and that I am incredibly far away from having or wanting to have sex. I hope that this doesn't make me even more of a freak.

"Mom thinks that you talk about her too much," my brother had blurted out as he bit into the monster-sized burger that had been delivered to the table. As I watched the juices run onto his hands, I realized then that I have gone on and on about what I have learned from you about nutrition. I had been preaching about the importance of a low fat diet and how people gain weight by eating more calories than they burn.

This comment from my brother stung and made me angry as I imagined the two of them talking bad about you together. My mom suddenly got quiet.

"What is that supposed to mean?" I had fired at my mom. I have never been afraid of standing up for myself to my mom.

"I just think that it is a little weird . . . how much time she wants to spend with you girls . . . how she calls you at night. And . . . ," my mom paused and put her food down to convey her seriousness, ". . . how she wants to take you to the cabin at the end of school."

Something inside me started to turn. *Am I not good enough or not old enough for you to want to be friends with me?* I wish I could have told my mom what you have helped me through. I wish she knew that you have been there for me when she could not be there for me.

I feel fists form as my fingers curled under the table. "So," I could feel my temper festering, "you aren't going to let me go to the cabin at the end of school?" I said but my words did not match the devastation I felt inside.

You have the very cool tradition of taking all of your former TAs to your cabin at the end of the school year. I have heard that it is the most fun weekend with hiking and board games and swimming in the lake. It is all we have been talking about for the last few weeks.

"I'm sorry, Kristen, I don't think so," my mom said. She sounded disappointed, but it is impossible for her to be as disappointed as I was then and I am now as I think about it. Instead of raising a fight, right then and there, I decide to plan my approach to getting her to say yes to the trip.

But since then, she has been more and more hesitant with you. When you call my house, she gives me The Look. When I told her that you could drive me to the game, she seemed concerned even though she knew it would work a lot better because my relatives were visiting and having your hair look that way obviously takes some effort.

As we pull into the parking spot and you reach over me to grab your mitt out of the back seat, I look at you and I am glad that I have a great role model in my life. I wish I had my Polaroid and I could take a picture for my evidence locker.

My mom might not understand you, how much you care about me and how much you have protected me, but I certainly do. I can smell your Jergens lotion, and as you lean, I look at the long scar that marks the outside of your knee. I know that you are older than I am. I know that you have lived more life than I have. But every day I learn from you. Someday I hope to be what you are to me, for somebody like me. And for the last time in my life, I thank God that I have you.

CHAPTER SEVEN

Phony Phone Calls

It's one of my lifetime favorite restaurants, C & O Tratorria in Venice Beach, home to some of Scott's and my most special memories. When I was a freshman at UCLA, and Scott still went to UC Davis, we would ride the Big Blue Bus from Westwood just to have the amazing garlic bread balls and sausage rigatoni. Where else in Los Angeles is down to earth enough for the entire restaurant to sing the Italian favorite "That's Amore" at 8 P.M. every night? So there, among LA's finest bus-traveling folk and some of LA's least accredited singers, some of my best memories were made.

At my direction, all of our team trips to LA include a pasta stop. Today I sit alone at a table for two. Teri and the team are doing an ocean workout, and I have just placed the orders for my athletes, who have come to love this restaurant, too. As I imagine my athletes training in the perfectly blue warming waters of the Pacific Ocean, my chest feels as though it is full of quicksand. I am glad to have a break from the girls and a break from having to act as though I am doing okay. I seriously considered not coming on this trip, contemplated telling Teri that I just couldn't handle it. But the strings to life that coaching this swim team has given me are too strong, and I need them right now. I told Teri exactly where I am with these calls, and that I might need to follow up from LA. As with everything else in this journey, she understood.

I cannot believe that Julie has not called yet. Sure, it has been less than 24 hours since I talked to Rob, but this timing doesn't feel right. I wish I could explain to someone that it is not like Julie to behave this way. Waiting is not the norm for the Julie who obsessed over, stalked, and abused me so many years ago. I feel as if I am going a little crazy. *Did I make up that she was that bad? Was I in constant fear for no reason? Is my current panic all of my own making?*

I ordered soup while I waited for the girls' food, thinking that I might be able to stomach that. Real food still feels overwhelming. How do I pick up a fork when I am trying to pick up my life? How do I swallow a hamburger when I cannot swallow my past? And just as I am served, I use my iPhone to check my fake Facebook account. There, a tiny red circle with the number 1 hanging inside, shows my first ever Facebook message. My heart pounds as I try to direct my shaking finger to open the message.

There is a picture of her. She is leaning over her son, who looks to be about seven or eight years old. Her eyes look desolate, dead, and her mouth is drawn tight. Her stark look and the serious stare of her son contrast with the happy background that looks to be an amusement park. I imagine her there, with her family, and hope that she doesn't try something with her son in the bathroom on the way to the next rollercoaster.

"Did you try to call last night? Rob said a former student called. When I called the number, I heard your voice on the message but didn't know what to say and hung up. If you want/need to call me, you can do so anytime—everything is fine here. I would like to hear from you but will leave it entirely up to you."

Within 48 hours of creating a Facebook page, Julie has found me. Suddenly I understand my own desire to avoid social networking with my friends. I see clearly as to why I am the only one of my friends not to use Facebook. I see why I have been too scared to join, despite the jealousy that stirs inside when I hear about my family and friends following each other's lives online. I am shocked that Detective Parker's idea has worked. I call him immediately.

"I feel as though I need to call her right away. If I don't, she will get suspicious and have too much time to think about all that she has to lose by talking to me."

He pauses in thought. "Okay, I agree."

I know that I cannot call Julie at the moment. The girls will be to the restaurant in ten minutes. I will call her tonight.

As we settle into the Westin Bonaventure downtown that I negotiated for on Priceline, I am proud and relieved that I have finished my responsibilities for the day as a coach. Despite some debacle I had with starting the rental car in the parking lot in Venice, I am able to manage the remainder of the day without incident. The girls laughed at me as I tried to turn the already running electric car "on." It feels good to laugh with them and I am glad to act like a fool, almost able to forget that this is all going on.

Teri knows as much as anyone—what a hard time I am having, that I have told Scott, that I have gone to the police, and that they want me to make phone calls. When I tell her about the Facebook messages, she responds immediately, "Do you want me to be in the room. I can sit in the bathroom, just so you know someone is with you through this." As I imagine Teri, the Head Olympic Coach holed up in the hotel bathroom, I look at her face. She knows I am scared.

An offer I had never considered suddenly makes these calls seem doable, "Yes. The recording only lasts 30 minutes, so if you could keep time, that would be really helpful." I feel so lucky that I haven't been entirely alone through this.

The hotel is beautiful, much nicer than the types of hotel where we typically stay. Had this been a normal stay, I would have been off to explore the hotel gym or out to shop the surrounding streets of downtown LA. But tonight I sit in my room and get ready for my one shot.

I am shaking, but I make my voice sound calm. I have notes spread out before me, but I make myself into a scared and hesitant fourteen-year-old. As the phone rings and my heart pounds, I ask quietly for something bigger than myself to take over. Maybe it is my fourteen-year-old voice, maybe it is a stranger living inside of me, and maybe it is God. Maybe they are all the same thing.

As I hear a click, I know Julie has answered the phone. I also know that I am not alone.

By now I have practiced with Scott, Teri, Detective Parker, Chelsea, and Maggie Red. I have practiced in my head, on pieces of paper. I am ready to take back my life.

"Hello?" That voice, smooth and collected and planned, comes slithering out of her mouth. Her voice, absent from my ears for ten years, penetrates my skin.

"Hi." The shape of my throat somehow changes. I am beginning to recognize my friend who now speaks on my behalf to Julie.

"Hang on a second. I have to close my door. So you pretty much blew my mind . . . ," Julie laughs to end her statement.

"Um, I've just been thinking about calling you for months and months and . . ." I allow my voice to sound timid and young. I sound how she would have wanted me to sound for her. I know a secret that Julie does not; this voice will do my hardest work so far.

"How'd you find my number?" Julie's voice sits in the middle of excitement and suspicious, and I can almost hear her heart rate increase over the phone.

"I did Spokeo. Have you ever heard of that?" I start with a test lie, knowing that Julie's name and phone number can also be found on Spokeo, because my mom called last week proud to tell me that she had found Julie.

"When I got home and Rob said Kristen called . . . , so then I'm thinking how did she get my number?" Julie laughs again. *What is so funny, Julie?*

I look back down at my notes and somehow know what to say. "I don't know . . . if this is okay or not, you know?

"It's okay. It's been ten years, you know?" Julie says with an air of humor in her voice. "Probably necessary actually . . ." *Well, Julie, it is necessary according to the DA who looked at your file.*

I remain mostly quiet on the other end, agreeing periodically with the typical "uh-huh." I stay silent, much as I did on the secret cell phone.

Julie is happy to be the driver through this conversation. "I always kind of thought that maybe we'd like run into each other." I can hear her sick smile though the phone.

I remember being terrified to walk through the baggage claim of so many airports and not knowing why. Not totally aware that my tight stomach, dashing pupils, and sweaty hands were not typical of a person waiting at carousel five. My words come out without thought. "Yeah, I thought so, too . . . I looked. I didn't know you were in Utah though."

I wonder how I could have been scared that I would see her, without fully realizing what she did to me. It was a primitive, primordial fear, like a dog hearing the snap of fireworks on the Fourth of July.

"I was pretty hush-hush about it . . . I mean it happened really fast and I wasn't teaching anymore and so like there were only a few people that would know." *Why aren't you teaching anymore, Julie?* The hair on the back of my neck stands up.

"Yeah, and then, um, Rob got a job . . . out here and it was like . . . seriously our house sold in like three weeks and it's kind of crazy that I end up out here given the fact that you have family out here." Flashes of fun memories with my cousins fill my eyes. *Were you watching me at the mall last fall?*

"Yeah, I mean. I could have seen you, you know? All those years of coming to visit. I go up there every year." My heart breaks a little knowing that Julie has also taken Utah from me.

"Yeah. Totally. So, . . ." Julie becomes quiet and wants me to show her my cards as to why I am calling.

"I don't know where to start." And that part is the truth.

"It's okay." She tries to soothe me with her voice, just as she would try to rub my back after hurting me on her bed. "You know what? I just—it's been ten years but it really hasn't sort of, you know?" She circles me with fear. "I kind of figured that one day I'd just run into you because that's the way it was supposed to be . . ."

I am not sure what I say next, not sure what she says next, but I fight my way through the normality of an abnormal ten-year reunion. I look down at my handwriting: "Be vulnerable with her."

I sound as if I am twelve. "I've been having a really hard time . . . Like really, really bad depression and . . . I don't know where to go . . . kind of, you know?" I think of my depression and clench my teeth as I make her think I am asking for her help out of the smog.

"You know I, well, I mean I feel good that you called me." Her arrogance fills the space between Utah and Los Angeles. I guess in some ways I am asking for her help out of this. After all, the idea of her ankles shackled behind bars would help me breathe a little easier. I let myself smile just a hair.

"Well, you know, it's been a long ten years," Julie says and I imagine her awaiting this call. "It's been a lot of changes . . . Just with the move . . . and then with the kids and you know. I have two kids now and . . ."

"That's hard for me to hear," I tell her the truth. I worry about them constantly. I also know that she will read this comment the wrong way.

"I know it is," Julie replies. "But in no way does it mean that I . . . just forgot you . . ." She tries to sound loving and I love that she is confused.

I lift my head and see a beam of light shining on just how delusional this person is. She has no idea that I worry about them because of what this might do to them and what she might do to them. She thinks I am jealous. Unbelievable. I put a piece of power in my sweatshirt pocket.

Julie continues driving, "Well, I just want to say one thing before I get in deep into this and that is that I want to completely be able to trust you and I mean I hope you're not angry with me . . ."

"I'm just lost. I don't think angry is the right word. I'm just confused and lost and . . ." *You have no idea how angry I am, Julie. Angry isn't the right word. Angry would be an understatement.*

Julie uses a new voice now, one that is whiney and helpless sounding. It is hard to imagine a 40 plus mother of two on the other end. "I worried at one point you would become angry and that, you know, and that I . . ."

Her words trail off and I wish that I could yell into the phone, "What, I know that you . . . *raped* me?" But I stay silent on the other end as she continues, "It all would end up hurting you in the end and I hope that's not what happened and I hope that you know . . ." *Know what, Julie? You did hurt me. You almost ruined me. This is what almost ruined looks like. Watch out.*

"Um-huh, . . . I feel more than being angry at you, I'm angry at myself . . . I remember so many times you saying . . . when you're older or 18, you know?" My mouth turns sour as I cling to the instructions of Parker telling me to take the blame.

"Mm-hm, . . ." Julie agrees and continues on. She likes this. She used to like me telling her not to cry on our drive back from the apartment.

She takes a deep breath and I can hear thoughts rattling through her head: "I'm going to be real frank with you right now. I completely want to confide in you . . . to open up to you and . . . I want to be real frank with you. I fear that—and this may sound crazy to you—I fear that . . . maybe the conversation is not just between you and me."

"What are you talking about? How could it not be?" I make my voice sound confused and surprised by such a ridiculous comment.

I become completely entrenched in taking the blame. We do a dance around each other: her talking about her fears and suspicions as to why I am calling; my trying to convince her that I believe it was my fault. We are getting nowhere and I am becoming worried.

I talk quickly. "I was the one who would push all of it . . ."

Suddenly a flashback comes. I am fifteen and Julie is holding me by the shoulders in the living room. It is the middle of the night and Julie is crying, "You pushed me to do what I did tonight. You made me do it because of how you are." I force myself to come back to the hotel room.

I need to make her feel that I am as fearful of others knowing as she is. "What am I going to tell my husband, you know?" I try to convince her that the secret still belongs to us.

"I'm just saying if, if I could I would just wish at this moment that I wouldn't have a shadow of a doubt." I hang on to my patience, slowly removing any doubt Julie has by putting her back in a position of power.

"I mean you're the only person . . . I wouldn't have called if I didn't . . ." I want to say the only person whom I have talked to about this, but that is so far from the truth I am worried I will laugh out loud. Julie can fill in the blanks with her twisted mind.

"Well, that makes me feel good." I can feel her calming and growing confident in my words. A scene fills my mind; I remember sitting in her office in eighth grade before the abuse started. It was the fall, and I was talking to her about how none of the boys liked me anymore. She sat at her desk, voicing words of compassion. But as I remember her now, I can see the look on her face—the pride as she sunk her claws into my skin. Just as she thought she was helping me then, I must make her think she is helping me now.

"I mean I'm taking anti-depressants . . . it's horrible . . . like nobody knows." I sit a little straighter, happy that I am on no medication. I hope she doesn't ask me which kind I take.

"Well, you know what? It means so much to me that you called me. I cannot tell you. That's my one hope . . . like I said in my message. If you need or you want to call me. Need. Want. Either way . . . it's been ten years but it's not ten years . . ." She sounds surer in her words. She knows this role of mentor all too well.

Just when I think I have lured her out of the dark, the mouse pulls back and her voice changes again. "I got people to protect now . . . and I'm not putting them over you . . . It's not about me. It's not about Rob. It's not about that . . ." Julie leaves the sentence open, but I know that she is talking about her sons.

I hold tightly on to the phone. *Does she really love them? Or is this a poisonous apple? Does she know that my heart is soft and good and that knowing kids will be affected is enough to make me jump off of the Golden Gate Bridge?*

Julie continues on with her suspicion. "Maybe there's another phone I can call you on or . . . I don't know. I know I'm acting crazy but I just can't help myself." *You just can't help yourself?* I have heard that one before.

"Okay." Julie's voice turns stern and icy here. "I'm going to be completely upfront with you, like what if it was being . . . , what if someone was recording our conversation? What if . . . you got angry and what if you decided that you were wronged and what if you went to somebody?" *Yes, we are being recorded. Yes, I was wronged. Yes, I went to the police. You are right but you keep talking to me. Just as Parker guessed, you can't help yourself.*

I let out a huff of air on the phone to somehow convey disbelief and let silence do the talking. *One thing I know about you, Julie, is that you get scared when I get angry.*

"No, just . . . don't get upset," Julie begs me. "It's not about making you upset . . . it's not about you . . . it's just about . . . my brain," Somewhere between her desires and her suspicions, Julie sounds as though she is losing control of herself. "And don't get frustrated . . . I never knew what occurred like after the fact." *It took a long time, Julie, but what occurred after the fact is that I got strong enough to do what I am doing now.*

"It's my fault . . . ," I say. I take the blame but anger laces my words.

"Oh, my God . . . please." She is begging and either crying or fake crying on the other end.

"I wish you could see like where I am right now. I'm sitting in a hotel in Los Angeles . . . by myself." I give her bits of the truth to settle her back down and continue stealing her trust. Almost on comical cue, Teri comes out to give me the five minute remaining signal. I nod to Teri.

"I am scared and, as I said, I'm not scared for myself and I'm not scared for . . . I'm just scared for my kids, you know?" My skin feels as if it is thickening to Julie's words.

"Hey, wait . . . can I call you back?" I don't want to run out of recording room. I make Julie think that my roommate is back and that I need to go outside so that she can keep "helping me."

"Yeah. All right." Julie sounds exhausted and I hope that this intermission won't make her more suspicious. I wonder if a Google search on police calls would tip her off to the thirty-minute limit.

"Bye . . ."

I set the receiver down and walk back toward the bathroom. I open the door and look at Teri with her magazines and swim meet program spread around her in the small space. "I need to call back," I say in a flat line. Teri gives me a quick nod, knowing not to touch a balloon that is ready to burst.

I sit back down in my spot and repeat the steps to record the call. First the recording service number, then the number that I want to appear on Julie's phone, then Julie's phone number. She picks up and within a few sentences I have her right back to where she was before she hung up.

"There's nothing more that . . . I want to . . . help you . . . , you know that." *Okay, then, say what you did to me and let me get off the phone with you!*

"I'd always be there . . . No matter what . . . , no matter what it is. And it kills me to know that . . . you're dealing with the stuff you're dealing with." *You are the reason I am dealing with anything.* "So we have to figure out a way to put my silly mind at ease."

I stay mostly silent on the other end, allowing her to talk herself through this.

"I might just take a leap of faith. Which I'll probably end up doing anyway. So we could do one of two things: we could just like kind of take it slow and like, you know, get to know each other again . . ." *How many phone calls is it going to take with you?*

"We have to figure it out together . . . ," Julie says as if we are partners in crime. "Like I said, if you were here right now, there would be no problem."

"Yeah. You would know." *You would know that I had a microphone taped under my shirt because there is no way I could pull this heist off in person.*

"I would know . . . I'd be able to look you in the eyes and I would know." The thought of looking at her in her grey eyes makes my stomach flip. I remember when she had mono and had jaundice. The whites of her eyes turned yellow. And when I looked at her, I thought the yellow suited her.

"I think that I can help you. I honestly do. I mean, if there's one person who could help you, it's me." Julie's voice is certain and sure.

"Yeah," I agree. She is the one who can help me.

"So, um, can we just like talk about life?" Julie says.

"Yeah," I agree again.

"Would that help?" Julie asks. The only person who can help me. What a joke.

"Yeah. I'll try that," I say quietly, wondering how long it will take.

"C'mon . . . ," Julie laughs. "Tell me about your life. Oh, let me tell you what I know about you . . ." Her voice says that she has been haunting me.

"I know that you're coaching at UC Berkeley . . . and I know that you got pretty deep into the Olympic trials in your senior year."

"Mm-hm." I make my voice work. That was seven years ago. A piece of my heart knew back then that she was watching me. I hate that she is weaseling her way into my swimming life. It feels just like when she stood on the hill and watched me swim. My hand clenches tighter on the phone.

". . . And lemmie think of what else I know. I know that you married Scott." My teeth hit together. *How dare you say his name?* I imagine myself as a porcupine with her standing in front of me and my shooting my quills into her eye balls and into her laughing mouth.

"Mm-hm." I can't use real words right now.

". . . And I know that in your Cal team bio it says that he was your high school sweetheart . . ." She laughs openly at this idea. The sides of my eyes draw down and it is hard not to cry as she laughs at the love of my life.

"And I think you live in Walnut Creek," although her voice sounds very sure of where I live. I wonder if she is there now, sitting outside of my house watching Scott watch TV. Maybe she is getting ready to kill him and my dogs. Maybe the trick will be on me.

My eyes search the corners of the hotel room as my fear intensifies.

"Let's see. What else do I know? I think that's about all I've been able to gather from here and there. Curiosity searches . . . I've seen a number of your quotes in, you know, the paper and whatnot . . . So fill me in on the rest . . ." Julie sounds upbeat and happy, but I know that she knows more about my life. She gives me enough to make me scared, but not so much that she scares me away.

"I'm lost . . . right now, you know?" I go back to my go-to of needing her help, hoping somehow to gain trust out of this pointless conversation.

"You're not lost . . . anymore. You are actually found." Her words reek of narcissism, a term I learned about in psychology in my freshman year at UCLA. Are all pedophiles narcissists? "It's gonna be okay," Julie says confidently.

"All right." I keep it simple and let her spin her web.

"Have you forgotten the power? The power of me?" Julie laughs and I imagine her tossing her gross brown hair over her gross shoulder. *No, Julie, I have not forgotten the power of you. The power you have to split me in half and crawl inside of my skin.*

It is a game of cat and mouse. Unlike half a lifetime ago, I am the cat, the tiger. I know I need to get her to admit what happened, but I also know that if I come barreling out of the bushes too loudly with claws swinging, she will scurry away forever.

This is so much harder than I thought it would be. My body feels as though it is made out of lumps of charcoal pieced together by gummy bears. I spend minutes, hours gaining her trust back. I lay out a piece of cheese and talk about myself and how much I am struggling. Just as my claws curl into the dirt, she backs up.

"Yeah. I feel like you're thinking before you say anything . . . ," I say to her finally, calling her out on her own suspicion.

"Yeah." Julie laughs as though this is a laughing matter. "Oh, you picked that up? You are a really smart cookie."

The use of the word "cookie" nauseates me, just like the many pet names she had for me when I was half her age. I change the subject, "What are you doing?"

"I'm just being a stay-at-home mom and that's about it. I never went back to teaching," Julie replies.

"Is that because of me?" I ask in line with taking the blame.

"No. Well, . . ." Julie leaves open space, wanting me to feel a little guilt.

"Was it us?" I say implying that there was more than just me. Maybe I am on to something here. Maybe getting her to admit to there being an "us" will be enough.

"Mm. I don't think that would ever happen again." Julie offers me a little coupon without me digging at all. "You're one, one in a million, I tell ya . . ." *But what if, Julie, there is another one in a million? If it's actually two or three or four in a million?* She continues, although I am not sure that I want her to. "It's not me, you know?" *What's not you? Being a child molester is not you?*

"Okay," I pretend as if I believe that Julie has only done this to me.

"When do you think you could conceivably call me?" Her voice sounds thirsty, desperate for another call.

"What's good for you? Like when can we talk? At night?" I need to make her think she is still in control. I need to convince her she is the boss as she used to be.

"Anytime. It doesn't matter. I can figure it out." *You have two kids and you can talk to me anytime?*

I try to bring the conversation to a close, like the volume of the music fading toward the end of the song. But Julie just keeps talking. "Do you want my cell phone so that you can text me?"

"Oh, yeah. I tried to get it last night but Rob didn't have it." I offer a stage for Julie to explain Rob's questionable behavior.

"I know . . . I had his phone because mine was dead . . . I was gonna give him my phone number, but I couldn't remember it and I'm like, oh, God." Julie's words don't make any sense. I stand confused by last night. Was she standing in the kitchen with Rob while he lied to me?

"Okay, what's your, what's your cell phone?" I draw my mind back to the moment.

"8-0-1 . . ."As Julie reads the remaining digits, I am reminded of being a little girl and dialing the 801 area code for my Christmas day call to my grandpa and grandma in Salt Lake. I feel sick as I scribble the familiar numbers down.

"Is there any way that, um . . . Are you booked solid all summer?" I know what Julie is asking me now, but she repeats herself anyway, sounding desperate. "Are you completely scheduled out all summer?"

"I don't know. I have to look at it. You mean for me to get there?" And suddenly I think of Utah as a carrot to hang over her head to get her where I want her.

"I'm so glad you called me," Julie says.

"Yeah, me, too," I respond. "All right. I'll talk to you soon."

I need to get off the phone. I am afraid if I talk to her another minute that I won't be able to keep it together—that I will scream at her, "How could you have done that to me?" and that I will reach through the phone and pinch her eyeballs right out of her head and squeeze them between my fingers until they explode.

I hang the receiver up and push the phone back toward the wall where it belongs. I gather my notes and relieve Teri from the bathroom. I give her a quick breakdown of the events and try to keep my body glued together.

"Do you wanna just stay here tonight?" Teri asks me. I had almost forgotten that this was her room. I jump at the idea of not having to pass the hours of the night in a room by myself.

"Yeah, if you don't mind." Teri turns on Sports Center and gets in her Cal pajama pants.

I lie in bed trying to retrace the steps of the day. I know what her voice sounds like now. I know that she will not hang up the phone. I know that my vocal cords will work. But I know I have a huge mountain ahead of me. I need to recharge my attack plan, I need to sleep, and I need to talk to Scott.

CHAPTER EIGHT

Red Vines

A game of UNO never felt so confusing. My brain feels as if I should be looking at a chess board instead of brightly numbered cards. My mind is racing all over the place and it's after midnight.

The eighth grade trip to Washington, DC, is something every student at JM looks forward to. Since my brother went four years ago, I have been basically counting down the months. I remember the bags of souvenirs he brought back for us; I'm wearing my Georgetown sweatshirt at this very moment. Beyond the gifts, Marc returned as a different person. He was older and wiser and had been out to see the world all on his own—in the company of a touring group and chaperones, of course. But, still, he had an experience without the rest of our family, and he had oh so many stories to tell.

And now here is my own story about my trip to Washington, DC. I know that Marc is going to be jealous because my story has a little twist. A couple of hours ago, we were onboard our plane ready to take off. The pilot's voice boomed through the cabin, "We are sorry to inform you of this, but the plane has a mechanical malfunction that we will need to look at before we take off. It's gonna take a few hours, so we are going to go ahead and de-plane." The reaction from my fellow eighth graders was diverse: some people were scared and wanted to call home; others were sad to have been gone from their parents for so long. But I was excited to have another night.

As we passed the gate agent and returned to the terminal, we were each handed a twenty-dollar voucher for the food court at the airport. A soft pretzel and $15 of candy later, we were called back to the departure gate.

"Bad news, kids," one of the head parents projected his voice in a way he clearly was uncomfortable with. "United canceled the flight." The group broke out into animated independent conversations, "Shhh. Listen, up kids, we are going to stay the night at the Hilton across the street and take the first flight out tomorrow morning. The airline will pay for all of it." Although this dad seemed annoyed and frustrated, I knew that this turn of events would be an exclamation point on my first trip away from home.

But herein lies the confusion. You are a chaperone on the trip. I was so excited and relieved when you told me that you were going to come with us. You have grown to be my most trusted friend. No one else knows about Mr. Witters. No one else needs to know about Mr. Witters. But I hate it when stupid kids in my grade talk about how cool they think he is. Or when they ask me why I haven't been in science class. You always have good ideas of what to say, and I just need to be able to talk to you about it when I want to.

So here we are at the hotel where the airline has decided to put us up. A really nice place—way nicer than where we stayed the first five nights. You invited all of us up for a game of UNO even though it is after 10 P.M. when we finally checked in. When I say us, I mean my friends and me. There is an "us" group that hangs out with you at school, and we have been hanging out with you on this whole trip. The only difference in the "us" this time is that Maggie Red isn't here; her parents told her that the trip is a ripoff.

I'll be honest, this whole flight getting canceled is pretty cool— free food, a free hotel, and now late night cards and no bed times. Now *this* is growing up.

And somewhere within the giggling of UNO you slip in the comment, "This room is way too big for just me; one of you guys should stay here so that you don't have to be four to a room." So, while the game continues, I look around at my friends and I know that who you really want to stay is me. It's always me. It's always me who gets the front seat if you take us all in your car. It's always me who gets the extra food you bring to school. It's always me who gets the little trinket gifts. It's always me who gets the basketball plays. It's just always me.

Don't get me wrong. I like that it is me. I like that it is n Maggie or Meghan or anyone else. I have worked hard to be your favorite, and it supports my constant objective to be the best athlete in the grade. I am the best athlete equals I am your favorite equals it is always me. Simple math. *Why doesn't this feel simple?*

I don't want to stay here in the room with you. I want to be with my friends. But three days ago when I ventured off in the Smithsonian with Mags Black and Meg, you pulled me aside and whispered, "Thanks for ditching me with the old folks." I looked at your face to see if you were mad and your eyes said somewhere between joking and serious . . . confusing.

Then the next day, at The Tomb of the Unknown Soldier, I felt guilty for letting you out of my sight. I really wanted to make sure that you weren't mad at me and that you didn't get stuck with the old teachers.

I feel as though I am getting pulled in so many directions. I want to hang out with you because you know me so well. I'm worried that my friends will be jealous if they know I am your favorite and feel like I am ditching them. And I have a massive crush on Kyle Irving, who is on this trip with us.

A couple of days ago at Carls Junior, he was actually talking to me. It's crazy that you know me so well that you knew I was flirting with him and gave me a hard time about it afterward. I was happy to take the teasing, though, because it meant that you weren't mad at me. "I'll talk to him for you," you said casually. You always throw your hair over your shoulder like you can take care of anything.

"What . . . are you serious?" I had said in response to you. *A teacher talking to a student about a crush . . . Are you for real?*

"Yeah, I think he is really cute. The cutest boy in your grade. You should go for him."

I don't know exactly why, but I was very relieved by this comment.

"Okay, yeah." I smile with you and I am so glad that you are my friend.

But now in your hotel room with all the girls, I wish that I weren't the one, that I weren't your friend because I am really worried that they will all go back to the room without me. They will leave me here and talk about how I am the teacher's pet. They will play another round of UNO and stay up all the way until the airport shuttle picks us up at 5 A.M. tomorrow. They will pool

ınd sneak out to the vending machine. They will
out me.

ybe I should just tell you that I want to go back.
... c worst that could happen? You could get mad at me
*ugain. You could change your mind about helping me get ready for
high school volleyball tryouts next fall. You could make me go back
to Mr. Witters's class and not let me hang out with you that period.
You could pick another favorite.*

And so, as the list grows in my mind, I realize I have way too
much to lose and will have to forgo the Red Vines in F7. In the
most awkward fashion, long after you have dangled the invitation, I resign, "Sure, I'll stay."

The girls leave and I see their eyes whisper silent comments
to each other. They seem to leave in a hurry and the door closes
behind them the same way. You smile at me and put your hand
on my shoulder. "I have something to tell you." I have seen this
look from you before, like the time you told me that the principal
said that the school couldn't do anything about Mr. Witters without physical proof. My heart waits at the edge of its seat. "I talked
to Kyle in the food court at the airport. He doesn't like you." You
wear a crooked smile. "He's crazy," you say. And with a defeated
heart I wonder . . . is he?

"Thank you so much for staying with me. We have been gone
for a week and I am sick of staying by myself." I feel bad that you
have stayed alone. We have had four girls in a room the whole
time, and between the candy and the card games, the four of us
have become so close.

"Yeah, that stinks." I agree and I think of how boring this trip
would have been without Jean and all of her jokes.

"What do you guys do at night?" You ask me this and it feels
good that you want to know what we do for fun.

"Last night they French-braided my hair." I remember I kind
of looked like that girl from Star Wars. *What's her name? Princess
Leia?* I never liked Star Wars.

"I never learned how to do that," you say and you look a little
sad.

"Really? That's crazy! Aren't you a girl?" I say with a laugh. I
like teasing you because you tease me constantly. It makes me
feel as if I fit right in.

"Teach me," you say, and your smile is nice.

"Okay." I am so tired that this is the last thing I want to do. But, if you want me to teach you something, I owe you that. After all, look at all that you have taught me.

You start by parting my hair per my instructions. Then you fumble with the next step and we laugh. "God, I'm such a tom boy," you say.

Yes, you are. Sometimes I wish that you looked different; I wish that you took better care of yourself. I never like your clothes and you don't bother with makeup. Your t-shirt is always a size too big and you just wear your hair straight down. *Why did no one ever teach you how to be a girl?* Maybe I can teach you a thing or two.

"Maybe I should just stick to what I know . . . ," you say to me with a sideways smile. I am sitting on the edge of the bed and you are standing behind me. As you move your hands to my shoulders, I know what is coming next. You often give me massages to help me get loose for an upcoming game. Don't get me wrong, it totally helps. But it also makes me feel totally different.

Different from other kids because they don't get massages. Different because it seems as if you care more about me. Different because you have told me not to tell anyone. Different because last time my mom found out, she gave me The Look. Different because it makes my body tingle. Different because I feel like I can't say anything.

Tonight even this is different. You start as you usually start, but then I started thinking. *I don't have a game coming up. We are done with softball season and you have no reason to be doing this.* It feels almost impossible to speak, but still I somehow manage. "You don't have to do this, we don't have a game," I say in the kindest way I can.

"It's okay, I just want you to relax this time." Your hands move up to my head and you start rubbing my temples. It feels amazing. I love it when people give me head massages. I think of all the times I have sat in front of my mom on the family room couch and begged her to play with my hair. Or the times when I would visit my grandma in Utah and spend hours lying next to her on the couch as she rubbed my head and back. A tiny voice in the back of my head stands up and says "watch out," but it is heard only by me.

Before I know it, I am in a trance-like state. It must be past 2 A.M. and I am exhausted, and yes, relaxed. I am lying on the bed now, on top of all the covers and you are still playing with my hair, rubbing my back. My eyelids feel as if they are made of mud and just as the mud thickens, I feel your hand slide around my side and near my right rib cage. In a very sensitive spot, I know if there was anything there, your hand would be on top of my breast.

I do not jerk, or scream, or yell. Actually, I do nothing. Well, not nothing. Physically, I do nothing. Mentally, I go for a bike ride around my head. *Did your hand just slip? Did you fall asleep and, as a result, accidentally touch me? Did you want to touch me? Did I make you want to touch me? Why do you want to touch me and the boys do not? What should I say to you in the morning? Whom can I tell?*

And when your hand stops, my breathing stops, too. I think that you feel my chest freeze. Your hand lingers, and eventually leaves. It feels like your hand was there for three days but may have only been there for three seconds.

I do not sleep the rest of that night. You stopped at the place where my body is supposed to be maturing. *Is it a private part if there is no part yet?*

My heart beats hard as I try to make sense of this in my barely fourteen-year-old brain. My heart beats hard, but in a different way than when Jonathon kissed me two years ago and different than during the third quarter of the basketball game. As I lay awake in the stillness of the hotel room, I can sense that you have fallen asleep next to me. I hear you breathing, I think of my friends on the floor below, and I wonder if my mom or dad will pick me up tomorrow. And as familiar faces roll through my tired brain, I feel entirely alone.

PART TWO

"I Never Wanted It To Be This Way"

CHAPTER NINE

An Angel at War

As I walk off the heated pavement of the USC pool deck, I feel drained. Teri and I head to our rental minivan, which we usually use to tote the team, but they have taken different vans home for the day. We have been here all day, coaching our athletes at the meet, and we are headed to a recruiting dinner with a high school sophomore.

"I need to make a few calls on the way there," I say to Teri as we walk in step. She nods, knowing exactly what my calls will be about. Usually, I care too much what Teri thinks of me. And now I am sure that she would rather be analyzing our day of racing than being the bystander to my tactical calls. Any concern I have about Teri leaves my brain as my cell phone buzzes with Parker's number on the screen. He calls me before I have a chance to return his messages.

"Kristen, it's Birch." His voice is serious and stern. He sounds different than he does at the police station. "Do you have a minute?"

"Yeah, Teri and I are just leaving the pool. What's up?"

"I relistened to the calls from the two nights of recordings." He sounds upset and my stomach turns, hoping that I have not done anything wrong. I have talked to Julie for almost three hours over the course of three days, and I haven't been able to get her to concretely admit to anything. I have gone hours and hours, round and round with her, and although I have gained her trust, I can't get her to say exactly what I need her to say.

"And?" I ask as Parker pauses for his words.

"I think that you should stop. I think that you should stop doing the calls, Kristen." Parker talks quickly. I slow my walking speed as I feel failure sticking like gum to the bottom of my Sperry boat shoes.

"Why?" My voice barely comes out and I have to piece the sounds together.

"Kristen, this is not healthy for you. She wants you to come out to Utah. She wants you back. She wants to start things again. She's still very sick and this is not good for you . . ." The phone crackles with background driving noise, and Parker sounds as though he is going to vomit on the floor of his police cruiser.

"But in the calls it is clear that she did something wrong. Do you think that the jury will understand why she is suspicious? Do you think we have enough?" I say all at once and I feel as though I am on the front end of a panic attack.

"No, we don't have enough. But I think you should think about dropping it. This isn't worth allowing her to hurt you and place blame on you for everything that happened. This isn't worth you becoming a victim again."

My walking goes from a slow pace to an outright standstill. My phone is heavy in my hand, but my heart gets a little lighter. I realize at once that even Birch is tricked by my young wounded voice on the phone. I have outacted my acting coach. "Birch," I say and my voice is opposite from the one he has been listening to on the tape recording service, "I can do this. I have to finish this and I know I can."

The mere idea of doing these calls terrified me. Now I know they are my ticket to justice. And I know that I can do them.

"Okay . . ." Parker's voice sounds hesitant.

"I'll call again tonight. Teri and I have a dinner and then I will do it." I look at Teri and she gives her usual nod.

"Just remember. Use the words that she would have used then. Don't say things like oral copulation or anything . . . ," Birch says and tries hard not to make this conversation feel awkward.

As I finish my call with Birch, Teri and I head to our recruiting dinner. After a full day in the sun, we will spend two hours with a sixteen-year-old prospect and her family.

I eat the most food I have in a week as I try to be "normal" company for strangers. I wonder what they would say if they knew about my current catastrophe. I sit surprised that I am able to perform my job, although I realize I have made a life in pretending nothing is wrong. I let Teri do most of the talking as the head coach, but I fill in with enthusiasm wherever I can.

Teri and I finish and drive home in mostly silence. "I think I'll sleep in my own room tonight," I say quickly to Teri, having found new purpose after Birch's call.

"You sure you're okay?" Teri is not the type to coddle me, but leaves no doubt that she cares. I also like the fact that I don't have to worry about hurting her feelings.

"Yes, I can do this," I say to myself as well as to her.

I head to the elevator and pull up Scott's number on my phone so that I am ready to dial it when the elevator opens.

As gravity lessens and the elevator rises to my floor, I think about the people I have in my life. There have been things that people have done for me, and not until later do I realize how generous, kind, and loving they had been. Like how my mom used to drive lunch to me every day in high school. Or how hard my dad worked while I was growing up so that, when my brother and I begged for our "turning sixteen" car, he could simply say "Okay."

Since I told Scott the truth about my past just more than four weeks ago, he has done little things that I know someday I will look back and more fully understand. He has absorbed the shopping, laundry, cooking. He has absorbed me.

But now as I get ready to touch "My Boy" on my list of iPhone favorites, I somehow know the magnitude of the role he will play tonight. I do not need a few years to digest it. I see that he is my angel.

"Did you listen to the recordings I sent you?" I ask him. A few of last night's calls we taped on my iPhone. Julie was paranoid that I was making taped calls and had insisted on being the one who called me. It worked out great because then I sent them to Scott so that he could listen.

My hands shake a little as I imagine Scott listening to the calls. But I am afraid my insides will fall out if he doesn't help me through this. "Yes, I listened. It is unbelievable. She wants you again."

"I know." I agree with Scott. "That's what Parker says. And he says I should stop, that it is too dangerous for me and for my health."

"Kristy," Scott is the only one who calls me by this nickname. "You can't stop. You have her right where you want her. You have her trust. You have done so much in these calls that I won't let you stop. You have to use her now. Use the fact that she wants you to come to Utah to see her. I know that you are strong enough to do this and I have a plan."

From dates to the mini-golf course to the purchase of our first house two years ago to the decision to go to the police, Scott always has a plan. And I have survived by trusting this plan.

"Okay, I am emailing you a list of questions right now." What does he mean by a list of questions?

"Okay?" I ask.

"You are going to use me to get her to admit to the illegal physical acts that she did to you." I have to admit that I had this idea in my head, but my love for Scott wouldn't allow this idea into my heart. "Remember what I told you, there is a law that states that if she does not deny these things, her silence is an admission."

As I open my email and see a detailed line of questioning for Julie, written by my husband, I take a moment, close my eyes, and thank God I have him. As a DA. his document is complete with key words and phrases that he knows will carry weight in the courtroom. As I read the terms listed in bold at the top, "kiss, touch, physical, intimate, fourteen years old, high school," I smile silently. *Thank God he is a lawyer.*

"Okay, do you see where it says key words?" He doesn't wait for my response. I know he is nervous, but he knows I need to hear this. "Use situations with me to get her to admit to those things. You have to say, 'it doesn't feel the same when Scott kisses me as when you used to kiss me.'" He pauses, having clearly picked the most G-rated question on the list.

I stare at the computer screen and there it is. A permission slip from my husband to bring our intimate life out in the open for the world to see. *Am I really going to use my happy and healthy sex life with Scott as bait to lure my rat out of her hiding place? How can he be okay with all of this?* He knows that these will be played in the courtroom someday, that they will be a major part of a major investigation.

"Are you sure?" My voice sounds small again. A little person asking if love is possible with all of this.

Three simple words match mine: "I love you."

As I hang up the phone, I begin to hang up the fear that Scott will leave me for a skinnier and simpler girl. I am ready. Almost.

I need to make sure that the words, the ones that I hate the most, will actually come out of my mouth. I call my best friend from UCLA, Chelsea, because I think she can handle hearing me practice.

"Hi, Pnop." A stupid nickname born out of our desire to take classes Pass No Pass in college.

"How are you?" Lately, the "are" has been enunciated in my friend's voices. Chels knows that I have been doing these phone calls and has been texting and calling constantly through all of this.

"Okay, I think I can do it tonight. I just talked to Scott. He wrote a script for me."

"A script?" Chelsea asked.

"Yeah, I am going to use my sex life with Scott to get her to admit the things that she did to me."

"And this was Scott's idea?" My eyes suddenly well with tears and I stay silent. "Wow," Chelsea says in a near whisper.

"Okay, but here is the thing. I am afraid I am going to get on the phone and I won't be able to get the words out."

"Let's practice. I can hear anything." I wonder if Chels knows that her second sentence is the exact thing she said to me when I first told her about my abuse.

"Okay, so . . ." I feel my heart racing. "You know those things you used to do to me, they don't feel the same when Scott does them."

"Kristen, you can't say 'those things.' A jury doesn't know what those things are. You can say it. You have to say it. If you can't say it to me, then you will never be able to say it to her."

I know that Chelsea is right and so I take a deep breath and hang on to the belief that she can hear anything. I say it all and she stays on the phone.

"Okay, you are ready." I am surprised that she talks to me the same way she did before she heard all of those foul things, that her words are not interrupted by violent vomiting from what she has just had to picture in her mind.

"I know," I say. And I know I have to be ready.

As the phone rings, I imagine that Chelsea is holding my right hand and Scott is holding my left. Teri is not in the bathroom tonight, but still I imagine that she is there counting the minutes and coaching me as she does our swimmers.

"Hello?" Julie says and her voice sounds hollow.

"Hi," I say rushed and I know that it is late. My shoulders settle into my body frame as I realize my voice is back for me.

"Can you get away for a sec?" I ask as I hear Julie wrestle with the phone.

"I couldn't sleep anyway . . . ," Julie says.

"Can you get away for a second?" I ask again, not knowing what to say.

"Yeah, I can. Do you want me to call you back?"

"No, no, it's fine." I would rather have the calls where they are secure and Birch can listen to them. "Um, . . . a bunch of us coaches went out . . . to a bar tonight and so we were down at the bar in our hotel drinking . . ." I smooth my words together, trying to make my tongue feel like it would after a few glasses of wine. "I was like . . . I just couldn't stop thinking about all this . . . so I was like I'm coming back up . . ." I know that Julie can read between the lines. I want to give her reason as to why I am going to be bolder tonight. With phony liquid courage, I continue. "My roommate's down there and so . . . when I hear the door open, I'll just hang up," I say.

"I cannot believe you called me." Julie sounds excited.

"Why?" I play dumb.

"I was just like, oh my God, I'm never gonna go to sleep. It's like killing me, you know?" Julie hangs on the word "killing." She has been using this phase over and over again. Of course, I thought that she was suicidal. "I'm so glad you called, though, because I've just been like for two days now just thinking and thinking and thinking and thinking . . ." Her repetitive words are rushed and it makes the anxiety tick in my chest bone.

". . . And what have you been thinking about?" I hang on to the hope that Julie will make some admissions on her own, hanging onto the hope that I might not have to say the black sand out loud.

"Oh, this and that and other things and a lot about what you said and I thought about what I said and you said you know. I'm just rehashing things in my brain," Julie says and I realize all she is talking about is more suspicions again.

My frustration grows. "Yeah, . . . while we were sitting down having drinks downstairs . . . I needed to come up and try to tell you where I am with things and how much I've been thinking about coming to Utah . . . I guess I kind of became clear on like my fears and my worries and my excitements and like . . ." I stammer like a tipsy person would.

"Mm-hm." Julie pushes me along and I can tell that she likes where I am headed with this.

I look at my open email attachment from my husband that sits before me. "I am thinking a lot about coming and wanting to come . . . but it's just . . . such a huge leap of faith for me. Today I got out of the shower . . ." My heart races as I try to imitate a lost and slightly intoxicated victim. "I . . . had this like crazy flashback and . . . I was in your apartment and I was . . . a sophomore and I just started playing water polo and . . . we're in front of a mirror and we're laying together and you're telling me how strong I was and now . . . I don't look like that and I just, I feel like that's what's holding me back . . ." I hurry so that I won't think about the sadness of what I am saying or feel the realness of the fear I felt that night so many years ago. *Remember, if she doesn't deny it, she's admitting it.*

"Why do you think that?" Julie asks.

"Why do I think I don't look like that? Because I don't look like that." I play dumb.

"No. Why do you think that that was then?" Julie says in her cryptic sentence.

"I just remember you talking about like how good I looked and how strong I was," I clench my fists and I am angry that I have to do this. Being in front of the mirror was always the hardest because it made it more difficult to escape. I keep trekking. "I'm like soft and I don't look like I did when I was a sophomore." I make a clear statement of how old I was.

Julie does not deny my words. My ear burns as I await her reply, "I see what you're saying, but I can tell you honestly . . . to me it's your spirit. It's your inside . . . I may have said that at one time and it was probably true." My heart bounces with this small victory. While not an outright admission, this reply gives me courage. *You don't know my insides, Julie. You have no idea what I am made of.*

I take a moment to remember Scott's idea and look at his permission slip. I close my eyes and pretend that I am just practicing with Chelsea on the other end. My little voice becomes a bit bigger, "Like when . . . Rob goes down on you do you think about me doing it?" My body feels lighter, my muscles feel the strongest that they have been in months.

"I don't even let him." Julie tries to sound sad, as though she has lost the love of her life in me. Most pedophiles think that they are in love with their victims.

"You don't let him?" I press her.

"No. That's too personal, too intimate," Julie says with a reminiscent air in her voice. *What you did to me was rape.* My body stiffens as the words snake out of her mouth.

"That was—that was just for me?" I force the words up my vocal cords and out of my mouth.

"He hasn't yet since, so I don't know what to tell ya," Julie says, refusing to sit fully in my trap. Good thing that I have the law on my side and I know that these nondenials will count as admissions.

"Really?" I ask, hoping I can still get more from her.

"Yeah. When I said to you some things in my life are good and some things in my life are not so good and some things, I don't know if they'll ever be good." She tries to create space in her sentences for a life with me. A piece of my brain wants to laugh at her.

I draw in a deep breath and open one of the green tabs marking a memory in my journal. I open it and read my prompt, "Like remember like Valentine's night . . . you came and you got me and you had that teddy on and I . . . like I can't wear that for Scott . . ." My memory burns as that night comes rushing back. Once laying out these pieces of my life made me want to lay in front of a train. Now I am laying them out as bait for Julie. Still, the black nightie makes me shake.

"Mm-hm." She takes a small bite, unable to say that she does not remember. It sounds as if she is moving around. I hope that it is a bad connection, but I worry that she has her hands down her pants.

"Like the way like I touched you in the car and . . . it's just . . . that stuff was so exciting and . . . meaningful, you know? It's just different." I press the palms of my hands onto the hotel bed, remembering that night and having to go along with her sick games.

"Mm-hm." Julie agrees with confidence and gives me more hope. "I'm probably the . . . person to help you because . . . I don't think anybody would understand anything and I know exactly what you're talking about." *Ah! You know what I am talking about because you remember that night. You remember what you made me wear and you remember what you made me do. Did you know how scared I was?*

"It's hard. I have to be the one that shares all these memories and flashbacks and . . . concrete things that I'm like holding on to . . . but I just had to take a leap of faith and call you tonight so . . ." I allow myself to tell Julie the truth for a moment, admitting that this is hard for a different reason than she thinks.

"You don't have anything to lose at all . . . You're so safe with me it's not even funny." Julie laughs a little. *Safe with you, Julie? That's what you told me in eighth grade. I don't believe you this time.*

"Yeah," I lie to Julie.

"I told you that I love you forever and I meant it. However it works out to be, I meant it. However long ago that was. I want what's best for you." My fists curl in anger. I stand quiet on the phone for a moment, refusing to use the word love with her.

"You know I, you know I haven't had an orgasm in ten years." The sentence just pops right out of my mouth. I press my eyelashes together and pull my arms close to the center of my body. A sadness enters the pit of my stomach as I remember figuring out that faking was a way to freedom.

"Well, maybe that's how it's supposed to go." Julie laughs and I can tell she feels powerful. *Julie, you're not denying any of this. What will the jury think?*

Suddenly I feel powerful, too. And I continue; "I need you to know . . . I've tried everything to feel like the same person . . . but I let Scott go down on me and I think of how you used to and it—nothing works, nothing works. Nothing works for me like it did with you." I hate that I have to say this, but I am proud that I can. I think of my marriage—an impenetrable concrete wall, standing between Julie and me on the phone line. I try to force her response as I ask, "You know?"

"Well, I mean, do you think that it's any different for me?" Although she refuses to directly implicate herself, I feel the evidence on the side of the prosecution mounting.

"Is it?" I ask and demand more from her.

"No. No." Julie replies and excitement turns her voice now.

"Have you been thinking about it since I called?" I push on her sickness.

"What do you think? I just want to talk to you, you know more than anything, and I can't . . . there's so much I need to say and so much I need to tell you . . ." Julie sounds upset again. "I want to sit down and talk to you without fear of anybody listening like Rob or whatever. I just want to have it out with you . . ." My head shakes back and forth quickly with the "have it out" statement.

With these words, I am brought back to some of the most gruesome nights.

"Okay," I say because it is the only word I can manage at this
point.

"I'm so paranoid that you're not gonna call me . . ." Julie
chooses her word paranoid to remind me that her obsession has
not changed.

I know I can't just keep calling and I also know that it is going
to take some time to get the arrest warrant from the judge. "Well,
do you want me to try Tuesday?" I say, thinking that will give me
time to get home from LA and make a plan with Parker.

"I want to talk to you tomorrow. I don't want to wait another
two days. Are you kidding me? I won't sleep a wink." Julie's voice
is so hurried that I feel my breath do the same.

I work the conversation to a close. "I think my roommate's
here," I whisper and I imagine Teri waving time from the bathroom. I want to end abruptly as if to avoid the possibility of her
telling me she loves me.

I pick up the phone for one last call before bed. I don't think
of the time as I wait to hear Scott's sleepy voice.

"Hey, Bop . . . ," he manages to sound happy that I called.

"I did it." I want to yell, but I don't.

"What?" Sounding more awake now, Scott I think knows what
I did but he asks anyway.

"I got her to say what I needed her to. I pretended I was drunk."
I let my pride shine through.

"Good job, Kristy . . . I'll talk to you tomorrow."

"I love you, Scott," I say, meaning it more than ever before.

I nestle into my bed and wear an actual smile on my face for
the first time in a long while. I look at the clock and it is 1:55 A.M.
I settle in the sheets and wrestle with sleep. I don't think of the
things that Julie did to me over a decade ago. I don't think of a
train or of a knife. I think of meeting Teri in the lobby tomorrow to
walk for coffee and grab her arm, looking her in the eye and telling
her I got Julie to say what I needed her to say. I think of Parker
listening to these calls, a judge, a jury. I feel a twinge of happiness
in my heart, and wonder if it is beginning to rebuild itself.

CHAPTER TEN

"But I Am Not Sixteen"

The day is gone I'm on my back
Starin' up at the ceiling
I take a drink, sit back and relax,
Smoke my mind makes me feel
Better for a small time
What I want is what I've not got
What I need is all around me

As "Jimi Thing" by Dave Matthews drones in the background, I sit in the passenger's side of the car trying to figure all this stuff out. We have been listening to his *Under The Table and Dreaming* sound track for the entire trip, but I still only understand half of what Dave is saying.

I don't really know what he's smoking or who's drinking what. But I do get what he means "what I need is all around me." I can sense Maggie Black in the back and I see you out of the corner of my eye, directing the car down Highway 80.

I am so glad that my mom finally let me go to the cabin with you. After all, it is what almost all of your TAs get to do after the end of the year. Plus, it feels better that my mom doesn't hate you anymore. It feels good that you don't hate her as much anymore, too.

I can't tell you this, but I am seriously car sick. I try to decode the words to "Jimi Thing," which I know by heart by now. I get car sick all the time, and although driving through the Sierras is especially beautiful, it is especially nauseating. My stomach does flip turns and suddenly I am choking back down whatever I ate within the past five hours—like a four year old on the Ferris wheel. I have always been embarrassed that I get car sick, but with you, I am especially careful not to tell you certain things. I don't want you to have too much ammunition to tease me with. I never know how I am supposed to act with you, other than more grown up than I actually am.

Like when we went hiking yesterday: you, Maggie, your golden lab Zoe, and I climbed the hills to a good swimming spot. "We can lay out down here and you guys can get tan," you said without waiting for the answer. *Why are Maggie and I the only ones who cared about getting tan? Why don't you want to get tan?* "There is no one down there. It is beautiful," you said over your shoulder.

And so, as we headed down to the secluded swimming hole and followed the river, you stopped and said, "Maggie, why don't you lead down the rocks." I would be lying if I didn't feel a little jealous about this. *Maggie didn't know where she was going. Do you think that she is a better rock climber than I am?*

Hiking isn't something that we have done with my family very much. "Hurry up, Krr!" you constantly called to me as Maggie made her descent. Now you always call me "Krr," borrowing the nickname given by my mentally handicapped friend Carolyn. Every time you use it, which is every time you say my name, I am reminded of how you mock her. I am secretly happy that she is headed to high school to escape you. I don't think teachers should tease kids—especially those with special needs.

I am used to being good at things, especially physical things. And each time you had to remind me to "hurry up" you caught up to me and tapped me on my butt. It's not that I hated this, it's just that I didn't like it. I can't tell you why I didn't like it. Maybe it was because it reminded me that I was not going fast enough. Maybe because it just didn't feel right. Maybe it was both. Maybe it doesn't matter now.

Sure, you have slapped me on the bottom before. I have seen you slap lots of girls on the bottom before. Like after a great play when we are playing soccer in PE or when we beat our rival middle school in basketball. It isn't always just me. But it usually is.

When we finally found the swimming hole, I spread my towel out just as I have watched you do, letting the slight breeze catch the towel and float it down on the rock right next to yours. Maggie peeled off her dusty ankle socks and got ready to dip into the freezing cold snow melt.

"I love it down here because no one else ever comes down here," you said and you looked proud of yourself. *Why did you say that twice?* "Are you going to get in the water you little fish?" I had liked this comment. You often give me attention for being such a good swimmer and I like that you barely know how to swim.

"Yeah, if I can stand the cold and figure out how to get my suit on without a bathroom," I said and I looked around for a secluded spot where no one could see me.

"I told you, there is no one down here anyway. I didn't even bring my suit," you had said boldly.

Standing on the granite rock with the rushing river water below, I imagined you going swimming with all of your clothes on. I had a ridiculous sight in my head, only to turn around and see a more ridiculous sight behind me. You took your t-shirt off, and suddenly you were wearing only your sports bra and a pair of your usual mesh shorts. I looked away because I hate looking at you without a shirt on.

I had seen this sight before; when you have changed after a sweaty basketball practice or a rainy PE period. I hate it because your belly looks bigger than it should for someone who is still under the age of thirty. You don't look like an athlete, and of all the things I envy in your life, I do not envy a body like yours.

"Ohhh! Toots!" I heard Maggie exclaim as she turned from the edge of the water where she was soaking her feet.

I followed her surprise and turned back to look at you. "What, you guys? We are all girls here and I told you, no one comes down here! It's just us. Stop acting like such children . . ." You added that when you saw the blush race toward my cheeks. "I come here every time I visit with Rob, and we always lay out naked." I thought I had gotten the blood to drain from my face, but it came racing back with this comment.

I hate it when you talk about Rob this way. I imagine the two of you hiking, laying naked together, and then frustrated that I don't know exactly how all that goes. It feels as though you are purposely leaving me out of something that I will never understand.

I glanced at you and I was undeniably glad that you had left your shorts on. Still, I hated what I saw. I said nothing because, what can I say? Instead, I climbed down to the swimming hole and did what I know how to do much better than you.

I stayed in as long as the frigid cold water allowed, and by the time I got out, Maggie and you were asleep on your separate towels. I took my position, glad that you were lying on your stomach and glad that I didn't have to say anything at all. I closed my eyes and waited for the baking sun to warm my cold body.

Finally, I snap out of the memory of my hike and realize that we have made progress towards home. My eyes are closed now, not because I am asleep, but because I need distance from you. And with a sudden coil in my stomach, my eyes are forced open to try to calm car sickness nausea.

As the fake air conditioning blows in my face, I try to reason with myself in my head. I have to admit that most of the trip was fun. Last night, after our long hike, you took Maggie and me to an open field. "I'm going to teach you guys something," you said with excitement.

As you put the car in park, and got out of the driver's seat, Maggie and I exchanged a look of wonderment. As best friends so often do, Maggie and I can talk to each other without the use of words. But as of late, I feel as if my silent speech with everyone in my life is slowing.

"Kristen, you're first." You said this but you didn't really need to. I am always first for you. "Get in." As you opened the driver's door, I suddenly saw your plan to teach me how to drive.

"But I'm not sixteen," I said with wide eyes. It was a statement back to you that came charging out of my mouth without warning. I did not think, I just spoke—big mistake.

"You honestly think I don't know how old you are?" You laughed at me with both your words and your eyes. I immediately regretted saying anything to you.

I stood conflicted in the center of the forest. *So this is pretty cool that you are going to let me drive your car. But what if my parents find out? Then my mom would have another reason to give The Look.*

I always had this fairy-tale image of my dad taking me to an empty parking lot one day and teaching me the rules of the road. In it, we fight and laugh and smile and it always ends with him taking me out for a doughnut. My feet froze as I thought of my dad. *Is that all gone if we do this?*

"No one will know." I had thought that you might have been able to read my mind. You continued, "We are in the middle of the woods and you won't get in trouble." I imagined the Forest Service ranger speeding to the scene of where a fourteen year old ran head on into a sequoia. I allowed that image to disappear and replaced it with believing you.

I did exactly as you said. Just as with everything else, I let you teach me how to drive and I let go of my internal questioning. I felt completely in control and completely out of control as I drove around the overgrown pines and kicked up dust as I practiced putting the car in reverse.

"Okay, we better get to the pizza place before they get too crowded." Maggie and I didn't question you on why Maggie didn't get a turn. I switched car seats with you, careful to avoid Maggie's eyes and avoid the potential hurt she might have felt from me being your favorite.

As I walked around the car, I felt the pain in the sides of my feet and I wondered if people are always this sore after they hike. I wondered if the pain is normal or if it is on account of the new hiking boots that you gave me before we left for the trip. I thought that they were awesome, brand new Adidas backcountry shoes. They are high tops with purple and brown piping around the laces. You reminded me to tell my mom and Maggie that they were old ones you used to have. After all, my mom wouldn't see them until they were dirty and had returned from this trip. But in order to get them dirty, I had to wear them. And wearing them meant squeezing my size 10 feet into a size 8.5 shoe. But what was my other choice?

And so as we drive home, I remember what it felt like to drive your car and what it feels like to have been on my first trip without rules. The CD is still blaring on repeat and it has given me a chance to remember all of what has happened at Silver Lake in the past three days. As the silence echoes through the car, I know what song will play next, "What Would You Say."

What would you say if I asked you what you were doing on the foot of my bed this morning? Well, not all the way on the foot of the bed; I might not be feeling this sick over the foot of the bed. You were more on the side of the bed.

I am not sure why, but I was a little relieved on the first day when we got to the cabin, up to the loft, and I saw three beds there. But this morning it was early and you were out of bed.

I could see the light peek through the blinds as it broke over the ridge behind the cabin. My back was facing you and you could not see that my eyes snuck open to see if Maggie could see you sitting there with me. My contacts were not in yet and I was frustrated that Maggie was just a blur in her bed. You began rubbing my back and I remained fake asleep on my right side. I was careful not to slow or speed my breath, because I figured it was better to just keep sleeping.

You played with my hair and this felt so unlike you. Just as you dropped a lock of my hair, you moved your hand down my back, made a small circle, and continued on to where you had been hurrying me along throughout the hike.

I concentrated only on my breath. Only on the oxygen that came in and the carbon dioxide that went out. I focused solely on my air intake so that I was able to fool you. Your hand moved up, and just when I thought that playing dead had worked, you slid your hand to my rib cage, past my arm pit and toward my left breast.

I couldn't just lay there. I had to at least do something. I rolled over suddenly and I expected to surprise you. But there you sat, calm and collected with a look on your face that said "nothing's wrong."

"I know I don't say this very often, but I do love you." Your words sounded too soft coming out of your mouth, different from your usual speech.

My mind raced: *What do you mean? Do you love me as a friend? Do you love me as something else? What can I possibly say back to this?*

As I remember this morning, my insides feel stretched in a very strange way. I remember lying on the bed, wishing to be somewhere else in the world. I had fought to be here, on this trip and with you. But in that moment I wished I could melt into the bed skirt below us.

I had opened my mouth and looked up at you. I lay there and thought of all things that you did for me. They are countless, really. In so many ways you have done more for me than anyone else in my life. I forced my face into a small smile and said simply, "I know."

And as we come out of the curves of the foothills and into the straightening of the highway toward the Bay Area, I think of this morning and wonder why it felt so bad. I wonder if I said the right thing. I wonder if it is car sickness after all.

CHAPTER ELEVEN

Nail in the Coffin

The lady at the front desk knows me by now, making things a little more comfortable and a little less comfortable at the same time. With dark roots peeking through her blond hair and her blue eye-shadow, she smiles at me as I walk through the door of the Lafayette police department. Her grin seems too tight, and I wonder if the office staff talk over doughnuts about my case.

"Hello, dear. Parker's on the phone . . . it'll just be a few minutes." Her throat has gravel in it, and I imagine her on her smoking break holding a box of Virginia Slims.

It's Tuesday and I am back in the Bay Area from my trip to LA. Much to Julie's dislike, I found a way out of calling her yesterday, claiming that I had to drive one of my girls home from the airport and then saying Scott surprised me by being home early from work. I wrote her a Facebook message that would keep her at bay until today.

I settle into the waiting area and feel almost confident being here without Scott. I know this place by now, where the bathroom is and how officers' coffee mugs sit drying on the bathroom sink.

Parker's face peers out of his office and around the corner to me. "Welcome back," Birch says with his typical grin. I can tell he has practiced this smile, somewhere between happy and concerned. Birch doesn't use my first name, and I wonder if this is in line with the Jane Doe status of my case.

As we walk into the office, Parker shuts the door behind me and says, "So I listened to the most recent calls . . ."

I look back and raise my eyebrows as if to ask "what did you think," but I care too much to get the words out of my mouth.

"You were excellent. Really great stuff, Kristen. Today you just need to tell her you're done talking with her. Simple . . ." Birch looks at me to make sure I agree.

My heart spins in my chest as I think of trying to get out of this trap I have created. "Are you sure? What if it isn't enough for the judge?" I ask Birch, refusing to believe that anything about Julie could ever be simple.

"Yup, that's it. You can start a fight with her. And just keep telling her that your life is too controlled to talk to her. Make her think that Scott is this overprotective and obsessive husband." Birch smiles at me, knowing the role that Scott has played in my survival.

"Okay," I pretend to agree but my right hand grips tightly onto the green journal of evidence. A piece of me doesn't trust that Parker knows what it will take to prove this case.

"I am going to stay here and do some paperwork on your case," he says, reaching for the white headphones that came along with his iPhone as an added treasure at the bottom of the box. "But I'll listen to some music so that you don't have to worry that I am listening to everything that you say."

"That sounds good." My insides settle as I sit in the chair Parker pulls out for me. Sitting now in the same chair that I sat in to call Julie for the first time, I have come a long way since then.

I set myself up, just as I would before an open book history test at UCLA. To my right, my green journal of memories to verify and points to prove. To my left, Scott's script. And straight ahead, the various phone numbers I will need to call Julie and my list of notes that has helped me over the past few days.

I begin before I am fully aware of what I am doing. Somehow I am used to this now, and I feel like a bulldozer as I pick up the phone. I press the keys down with a sense of purpose and passion.

"Hello," Julie says, and her voice sounds thirsty.

"Hey." I take air in through my nostrils as Julie begins talking to me about not being able to talk yesterday. I know that there will be a warming up period to this call, and I call upon my patience to find it.

"First of all, tell me how you broke your leg cuz I like can't get that out of my brain; I just need to know," Julie asks me. At some point over the various phone calls, I brought up breaking my leg to relate to her and gain her trust.

I play along, knowing that it will take me some time to get her where I want her. "How I broke it? Sliding into third base playing softball," I say plainly. "Why do you need to know that?" Suddenly I am aware that my voice sounds older than it did last time. I hope Julie doesn't notice.

"I just was wondering and every time it came up I wanted to ask, but we were talking about something else and I didn't want you to think that I didn't care . . ." Julie lets her voice trail off.

I talk Julie through my irrelevant injury that happened over two years ago and I can feel my patience wearing out. I want to jump through the phone and grab Julie by the throat. "I feel like last time . . . I'm a little bit nervous this time because it's like last time when I had all this courage and I did all the talking . . ." *I can't play these aggravating games with you any longer, Julie.*

Much quicker than I would have guessed, Julie responds, "I'm gonna tell you what I should have said at the moment because I've been replaying that in my mind over and over and over . . . and the reason I didn't say the things that I probably should have said was that I was just sketched out that I was in the garage." I picture her hiding in her garage, then hiding in my parents' garage, and finally in my garage. I wonder if she will be there when I get home tonight. She continues, "I assumed Rob heard the phone ring and I was . . . so worried and I was like on edge and I wasn't thinking straight and I was more worried about him finding me in the garage on a cell phone." Julie's words are frantic .

"Yeah." I respond to her long interlude and hope that she continues. I remember Birch telling me the more talking she does, the better.

"So, first of all, about the whole body issue thing . . . I'm forty-two and my knee hurts me all the time. I can't run anymore . . . I'm not what I was at thirty," she says trying hard to sound lighthearted. My mouth squeezes shut as I imagine her body.

"Mm-hm," I barely reply.

". . . and you're more than the outside . . . It's your spirit. It's your—it's just who you are . . ." Julie loops around me in the same complimentary but blaming way that she did before.

My anger is growing. *You tried to break my spirit, Julie.* "Yeah," I say quickly, keeping my words to a minimum with worry that she can detect a change in my voice today.

Julie continues, eager to speak. "Then the other thing about . . . the orgasms . . . I don't even let Rob try . . . He just does his thing and then that's it . . . I just don't want to share that with him."

I beg for my young voice to come back. I reach deep inside to find it. "So, like, that was just for me?" I say in a tone that is as close to a fourteen year old as I can manage. I wonder why it's so much harder to find today.

Julie continues because she cannot help herself. "I mean our life—his and my life is about . . ." Her voice trails off. I think of Rob lying to me on the phone the other day. I think of him failing to protect me when I was little. I forecast him listening to these calls. How will he feel when he hears Julie saying this? There is suddenly a small satisfaction in Julie's words.

"Is about . . . what?" I say, demanding more from her.

"As dysfunctional as you can get," she says. I smile a little, not knowing if she is telling me the truth but knowing this will also hurt her. Julie continues, "And it's a constant bone of contention. It's just a constant problem and it's something I struggle with continually . . . I don't ever think it'll be okay."

"Mm," I respond like a caring listener would.

"There are some things that I can push down and there are some things I can suppress and there are other things that I just can't . . ." Julie's voice sounds as it would when she just couldn't help herself with me. "There are some things that I can convince myself of . . ."

"Like what?" I say and my determination to get more from her fills every part of my body.

"That I was okay. That I was doing good. That I was maybe even a little bit over it," Julie says.

"Over me, you mean?" I say, unable to find a sense of sorrow in my voice.

"I'm finding that it's not true," Julie says longingly. "The past six days . . . now it's back in my face and I find that out that you care . . ." Julie says, leaving an opening for my reply.

"Mm-hm," I say. *Yes, Julie, I care. I care that you go to prison.*

Julie keeps digging her grave, "I convinced myself that you just didn't care and that you moved on . . . So what was I to do, either . . . stop living or make the best of things?" Julie whines as if she is crying but somehow I know that her eyes are dry.

"Mm-hm," I make a simple noise so that she will continue. My ears hang with the phrase "stop living," as I remember Julie using this most nights on the phone as a threat if she could not see me, if someone found out, or if I left. The suicide card is still hers to hold. My body curls and my confidence leaves me momentarily.

"I had no idea why you left . . . ," Julie says as she pretends to cry.

I keep my response matter of fact, "Yeah. I don't know. I don't have an answer for that." *Actually, Julie, I have a great answer for that. Because I became strong enough to live without you. Because I found someone worth risking death for. Because when I turned eighteen I was finally able to see how sick and evil you were and I didn't care if you killed me.*

"I know you don't. You didn't then and you don't now . . . ," Julie whines into the phone. She sounds like a person calling from a pay phone who is considering jumping off a cliff.

I need to redirect her. I open my green notebook. "I feel like last time we talked I shared things with you that nobody can ever hear again . . . like I have really specific memories of how things started . . . I kind of hang on to those. Remember . . . your apartment freshman year and how things progressed and . . . Rob was still in Livermore?" My yellow highlighting on the page smiles back at me.

"Uh-huh," Julie agrees.

I feel myself gaining momentum again. "It was all the time. Two to three times a week and how quickly it progressed . . . kissing you . . . touching you . . . making love." Anger fills my chest as I make words come out that are antonyms for the truth: rape. My teeth grind together as I imagine yanking the words out of Julie's mouth. "Can you remember those nights?" I say, feeling as brave and as mad as I have ever felt in my life.

"Yeah. Sometimes I'll just lay in bed and I'll just like slip back to one of them . . . There are so many of them . . ." Julie's sickness seeps through the phone.

"Which ones?" I demand more.

"I want to trust you so bad right now," Julie says as she retreats back into her cave. *Fuck you, Julie. Say it.*

"So, it's still about trust?" I respond quickly and I am certain she can see my anger.

Maybe this can be the turning point of why she won't hear from me tomorrow or the next day. But, do I have enough?

"No. Don't do that, please. God." She is panicking now, knowing that I am the wrong person to make angry. Her voice is like a howling hyena's.

"I'm the one who shared all those things and now you're . . . back to not trusting me?" I say.

Her voice turns lower and stern, opposite of the sentence before. "But do you care about me?" Julie tests me.

I squeeze my eyelids together as I lie. "Yeah, but it feels like I can't care when I'm going out on a limb and risking myself and you're just quiet. Like when you're like daydreaming. I don't know what that means . . . ," I say, knowing exactly what it means.

"You want to know what I was daydreaming about for three hours? I was daydreaming about what it would be like to see you again . . . what would occur . . . what it would be like . . . I don't know if I could see you and . . . not have to touch you," Julie's words slurp out of her mouth and make me gag. I dig my heels into the linoleum. I turn my head over my right shoulder to see Birch listening to his music, reminding me that I am safe. But the words coming through the phone make me shake. "And if I touched you I don't know if I could . . . resist."

She's not going to touch you ever again, Kristen, I say deeply to myself. I check to make sure I am breathing as I realize that with her same words and in the same way, Julie has not changed. But I have. "That's kinda like how it was, you know?" I say with my fake voice.

"That's exactly how it was." Julie replies too quickly. I can hear instant regret in the silence that follows.

I fill in the gap: "There was a plan to wait . . . till I was eighteen and . . ." I flip a few pages forward in my journal. "Remember when . . . I don't even know when this was but you took . . . a bunch of us out to lunch . . . and then we went to your apartment . . . I don't remember who was there, but they went down to the car . . . ," I say, looking down at my handwriting and the list of my friends who were there and can verify the incident, "and . . . we stayed up in your apartment and you were kissing me?"

"Mm-hm." Julie agrees and I smile. Julie says, "I mean . . . for me there will always be an attraction. A physical attraction . . . a burning inside attraction." Julie sheds light onto her impulse. I wonder if this is how criminals justify their crimes.

"It didn't matter if . . . I was thirteen or fourteen or twenty-eight or fifteen or eighty, right?" I purposely end with a question, looking to implicate her again.

"In a world without rules or society . . . in the purest sense . . . it doesn't matter." Her voice penetrates the phone just as she penetrates the laws of the society in which she lives. *You are still dangerous, Julie. And it's my job to make sure you never hurt anyone again.*

I flip to my next tab so that I can continue. "The other day I was like thinking about . . . driving around with my parents or my mom . . . and those times that you would . . . sneak upstairs and be in my closet when I would come home . . ." I think briefly about the sickness that would live in my stomach on the days that I knew Julie was waiting upstairs. It was the worst of all of her options. I look back at the page to concentrate. "I would sneak up into my room and you'd be in the closet and . . . we'd make love while my mom was right downstairs . . ." I squeeze my eyes tight after the words come barreling out of my mouth, like a kid after a booster shot at the doctor, hoping that it is over. "I thought that you were the person I could talk to about that."

Back to her high pitched whine, Julie replies. "Oh, God, I am, I am. That just kills me. It absolutely kills me . . ." She uses the scary words again, but they don't scare me anymore. *Go ahead and kill yourself, Julie.* As if she can hear the lack of concern in my silence, her voice grows dark as she tries to turn the tables on me. "I'm worried that you're trying to get me to say what concretely happened because somebody's trying to pin something on me. Like maybe this is all gonna come back and I am going to pay for what I've done."

For the first time, I sit back in my chair. A warmth fills me. *Yes, Julie, I will make sure that you pay for what you have done.* I respond to Julie, and tell her not to worry, but I imagine a judge listening to this and I can't help but feel a puff of pride in my chest.

Julie insists on throwing a dagger in my heart. "My worst fear. You want to know what my worst fear is?" she asks me.

"What?" I respond, knowing what Julie is trying to do to me before she does it.

"That my boys won't have a mother . . . that's my worst fear." She dangles them in front of me. She holds the two apples by the stems, not caring that their limbs are being stretched and their innocence is being stolen.

I refuse to fall for her facade, "Now . . . that's where your priorities are." I say as I build yet another trap for Julie to fall.

"No, it's not where my priorities are . . ." Julie fails my test as she picks her sickness over her children. I pick up the blue ballpoint pen and dig into the corner of my notes, knowing now I must protect those boys.

"It is where your priorities are," I say back to her, giving her a final chance to redeem herself as a mother.

"No. Not necessarily." And there, in the Lafayette police department, I forgive myself for any impact I have had on these children's lives. I know that I have done the right thing for them and the right thing for me.

I feel powerful as I aim for her jugular. "So you think it was wrong that we were together when I was fourteen and fifteen?"

Julie's voice is sad in her response. "No. I don't think it was wrong, but a lot of people would."

I turn the page of my green journal and look at a few more scenarios I have yet to prove with Julie. "Sometimes . . ." I begin and Julie is quiet as she hangs on my words, "All of a sudden I'll have a memory . . . dropping Adam off on a date and like going to meet you in my car." I shiver a little and turn quickly to the next tab. "Or like . . . my parents have to go to the airport to get Aunt Judy tomorrow and when my mom told me that I was . . . just thinking about how every time they would go to the airport, you would sneak in and we would be on the guest bedroom bed and make love." My ears feel as though they might be bleeding. I think of the room where my dad still sleeps every night, and I believe I would rather pull my own fingernails out than look at that bed. I pull myself back to the phone call. "I just need to hear that you remember all of it, and that you think about it . . ." I leave room for her response.

Julie's voice mumbles into the phone, "All the time."

"Huh?" I ask. Julie, say it again, I need the judge to hear this one loud and clear.

"All the time." She says and I smile to myself. Julie continues. "Part of me wants to run away from it because it's risky . . . and then like yesterday when you didn't call . . . it hurt too bad. It was way overboard and I was like, 'oh, no, you know you are not in control of things. You need to just get back in control . . . you're letting yourself go. You're letting yourself go there.'" Julie talks about herself in the third person in a way that scares me, in a way that has always scared me. Her voice is like something out of a horror movie: "it's such an inviting place, you know?"

I close my eyes again and hold onto the receiver of the phone. "Mm-hm," I manage.

"Okay, I don't wanna freak you out, but I have a recruit I'm supposed to call in ten minutes and I'm not ready at all . . ." I believe I have enough and I begin to lay the foundation for ending our call.

Julie sounds panicked: "After this call I feel really horrible. I feel like you don't care about me like I care about you and that's really scary for me. I need for you to . . . call me back." Her claws sink into my skin and I begin to wonder how long I can keep her fooled while they are getting a warrant. "I am in a bad state right now," she finishes.

Does that mean she is going to kill herself if she doesn't hear from me or if she will come kill me? "I'm telling you that realistically, without people knowing something's going on . . . I can probably talk to you once or twice a week, you know? It's just really sad that's the nature of my job. Recruiting started July 1st and they really look at my phone calls," I say to Julie using the NCAA limits on phone calls as a reason to why I cannot call her. "I have this friend who's going through this really bad divorce. Her husband cheated on her and everything, so she's been staying with us off and on." I throw Holly onto my growing list of excuses.

"Mm-hm." But I can hear the skepticism in Julie's voice.

I look down at my notes and remember what Parker told me just before calling today: "Scott is really controlling . . . he knows something's wrong and that I've been unhappy." I think of Scott holding my shaking hand as we go on our nightly walks, knowing that the sole source of my unhappiness is Julie. "I saw him reading my texts a few weeks ago . . ." I add this in imagining that this is what a controlling husband might do.

"Uh-huh." Julie sounds defeated. Maybe she can see the writing on the wall.

I continue, "Well, I just want to be honest with you and so you don't freak out when I don't call you." I look at Detective Parker hoping that the forms he is filling out at the other table have something to do with a warrant.

"Well, and I do because it's hard for me to understand your life," Julie says. "I let myself get way out of whack in the past couple days, and I probably shouldn't have done that. I need to stay composed about the whole thing. Maybe I was having a little too much fun with it, you know, . . in my mind?" she says and I picture her running her filthy tongue over her fangs.

"That's okay. You can do that," I say. *Have all the fun you want, Julie, I will never be yours again.*

"And just because I don't share things doesn't mean that I don't remember things," Julie adds.

"Okay." I say and my eyebrows lift with this unsolicited coupon for our case.

"I remember everything," she says and her voice crawls through the phone, dances on my scalp, and sends chills directly down my spine. *So do I, Julie.* I stand near silence. Julie finishes, "All right, well, I'll talk to you soon then?"

"Okay," I say as I imagine the glory of police lights flooding her street and her grey face in the kitchen window.

I hang up the phone and I stay at the desk for a minute by myself before turning to Parker. I have done what I never believed I could. My bones sink into the chair beneath me. I sit silently as I realize how decisively one person has changed the direction of my life. Julie gave me reason to fear my own brain. She gave me reason to stand on that train track. But now she has given me evidence—proof that I am not crazy and that my pain has an origin.

I look out at the parking lot and wonder why on hot days pavement has the ability to make the invisible air look wavy. I stare into space and feel lighter in my chair, as I wonder what my dad is doing at work today and what book my mom is currently devouring. I think of my long dance with Julie and the painful maze she created in the past several days. I see the world as it is: my parents doing their best, and Julie being solely responsible for this sin.

CHAPTER TWELVE

June Show

It's pretty cool that you are going to take me to Meghan's dance recital. Most fourteen year olds have to go with their parents. The "June Show" at the Rheem theater brings out virtually the entire town of Moraga. I got in an argument with my mom last night about going with you today.

"Why does Julie want to go to a four-hour dance recital? It doesn't even make sense," my mom said with The Look written all over her face.

"Because she knows a lot of people in the show, mom! She has been their teacher and she cares about them," I said. I always become annoyed when my mom questions my motives. Defense and anger rise up in my throat.

But deeper inside, I allow my mom's question to linger. *Why did you want me to stay in your room in Washington, DC? Was I sleeping when I felt you sitting next to me on the bed at the cabin? What about the gifts? The time you spent away from your new husband and with me?*

You had given an excuse for everything before my young mind thought to ask: There was not enough space in the room I was supposed to stay at in DC. You didn't have an alarm clock at the cabin. You liked buying me things—bagels, hiking boots, candy, lunches, an Eddie Bauer watch—because I was your best TA and really made your life easier. You want to go watch the show to see your students. I accept your excuses as coupons for friendship. I believe you so that I can resent my doubting mom. After all, nothing has happened.

You pick me up in the early evening and take me to my favorite Chinese place for dinner.

"It's right across the street," you say as you drive me down the main Moraga road. I sit tall in the passenger's seat; proud to be parading around town with a teacher in the summertime. "It doesn't matter if we are a little late for a silly dance recital anyway," you added at the last minute.

Dinner wasn't in the plans. I check the rear view mirror on my left for my mom's white Volvo. *What would I say to her?* She already questions you enough. I don't want to add fuel to her fire.

You continue talking to me without realizing that I am nervous: "I'm really glad that you choose sports over dance. What's the point? Can you even win? You can dance in other ways for the rest of your life," you smile to the side.

What is that supposed to mean? "Yeah, I am glad I choose sports over dance, too," I say back to you, telling part of the truth.

Last year my mom had me choose between all of my various sports and all of my various dance classes. The hours of multiple practices a day were increasing every year, and she understood the importance of academics as I was heading toward high school. Picking soccer, basketball, swimming, and volleyball over tap, jazz, ballet, and point seemed like a no-brainer. But, still, I miss dance.

"Dance is kind of stupid," I added just in case you had started to read my mind.

Through the rest of dinner, we joke about kids in my grade and other people that we might see at the show. It never occurs to me that this dinner and late arrival might be intentional so that the rest of the town doesn't see you with me and think that it is weird. This feels normal to me; I am growing up and I have older friends now.

We walk over to the theater and search our way through the darkness between acts to find our assigned seats. It is a packed house and I am surprised to not be sitting near any familiar faces. You are looking around, too. When you don't see anyone you know, you relax and begin watching the show.

The show feels as though it drags on and on. I see Meghan and I miss being her partner in parts of the routine. I point out other people from my grade to you, and former students. I feel uncomfortable because you have no interest in a "silly" dance show. I feel uncomfortable because your leg is touching my leg and I don't know what that means.

Finally, as the show ends, I quickly bring the flowers I had bought for Meghan backstage. You are acting awkward in front of Meghan's parents, and you try to lighten the mood by joking.

"Meg." You call her what I call her. "You were a superstar up there!" you say and laugh. Meghan smiles with her whole face, and her eyes curve with happiness and pride as you give her the attention that you typically give me.

A conflict of feeling arises in my center: on the left, a pang of jealousy similar to a side cramp I would get in soccer; in my gut, a feeling of relief that you are this nice to someone other than me.

I am relieved to get in your car and head home. With a sense of caution you ask, "Is everything all right?" You pause as if you care deeply. "Was my leg touching your leg freaking you out?"

"No," I lie.

"Sorry, it's just that it was cold in there," you say with another careful pause. "And I am also really sad that you are going to high school next year . . ." You sound as though you might start crying. *Have you ever been this sad about a student leaving before?*

"I am sad, too," I say and stop with that. I am sad to leave you. We have had so much fun together and you know me as well as anyone. But I look forward to leaving junior high, a place that held loneliness and pain for me. A place where Mr. Witters was allowed to say anything and do anything to his students and not get a second look. A place where my body was mocked. High school would be an adventure to meet new people, excel at my sports, meet a boyfriend, and go on dates to dances.

"And I want to spend as much time with you before you have to start school," you say in the space of my silence.

Again, you confuse my emotions. You stretch the inside of me. You tug at me as I feel guilty for wanting to move on, sad that I am leaving you behind, flattered that you care that much about me, and excited to hang out with you.

"Me, too," the safest reply comes out of my mouth.

It is late but, with it being the middle of June, it's warm and darkness has only just come for the night. We drive down my street and I think of what you have just said to me. We pull in my driveway and you put the car in park. I go to give you a hug—lately you have been giving me a hug when you say goodbye to me. *That's what friends do, right?*

As I begin to pull away from the hug, you gently hold me for an extra moment. You lean to kiss me on the cheek. You have only kissed me on the cheek a few times. As you bring my cheek to your lips, you turn my face just slightly. Suddenly, your mouth is half on my lips and half on my cheek. I have not kissed someone for almost three years; since Jon kissed me in the sixth grade during a fall afternoon next to the Core building at school. It was wonderful and magical and felt the opposite of this.

Your lips linger and I know that you have planned this. Your lips drive a dagger into my heart, and at once I see clearly what your intentions have been. And as your lips leave me, I feel the unmistakable flick of a rubber band snapping inside my soul. Who I am dies. And in my place, two people are born. It is immediate and sudden and not even you can see the death and the birth.

You pull away and a fake look of surprise covers your face. "Oops, I didn't mean to do that." You have to fake a gasp of disbelief.

I can barely speak. "I know," I say, and in a very strange way, I feel as if I have just said my first words.

"Just remember, I really do love you . . . ," you say and your voice now sounds different to me, like nails on a chalk board.

I can't hear my other voice. I have no idea what she says to you.

As I walk in the house, I worry that my parents will look at me and see the two brains that are living in my head now. I am very careful as I approach them watching TV in the family room. My dad sleeps on the couch and doesn't awaken to see the monster that has taken over his daughter's body in the past five minutes. I am grateful. *Maybe he won't notice until tomorrow morning?*

My mom, on the other hand, is awake watching 20/20. "How was it, Krick?"

"Meghan was awesome," I state the obvious and focus on the reason that I went to the show in the first place.

"I'm sure she was. She always is," she smiles at me. She seems satisfied with my answer. I am shocked.

As I walk up the stairs, I feel different. I know that I will never be the same. I stand at the top of the stairs for some time—two minutes or twenty minutes maybe. I feel lost and sad and confused.

The last time I felt anything like this was when I went to explain my cell project to Mr. Witters.

For so long, when I have felt lost, I have turned to you. *You have always made it better; can you make this better? You have made it so that you are the only one whom I can turn to. You have made it so that you are the only one who really knows me.* After an endless pause at the top of the stairs, I walk into my mom's room and grab her cordless phone from the night stand. I know your home number by heart now. *Is that normal?*

I sit on the old trunk in my mom's room to talk to you, as you taught me to do. Suddenly I am aware that this spot was your idea. You have been to my house a number of times. My dad especially likes you and trusts that you are taking time out of your life to be my mentor.

As my mom has been growing concerned with the amount of time we spend together, over the recent weeks she has been asking me why we talk on the phone and what we talk about. Lately she has been picking up the receiver to try to determine just how much we talk on the phone.

"Well, let's think . . ." You had paused, but by the sound of your voice, I knew that you already had a well-devised idea. "You know in your mom's room, that big window she has, can you see into the family room from there?"

I think of my childhood Christmas Eves. We have a Lewis family tradition that runs something like this: We go out to a nice dinner as a family. We come home and open one present, usually new PJs. We play a family game. Marc and I go upstairs, "in case Santa comes early."

I used to be fooled into thinking that Santa might come early. But now I know it just takes my dad a little longer than the average to follow the instructions on putting together a new basketball hoop.

There is an unknown part of our Christmas Eve tradition. A segment that Marc and I have invented on our own. We are supposed to be upstairs in Marc's room, with the door closed, but sometimes we sneak out, cross the hall to the master bedroom, and sit on the cedar trunk underneath the picture window. From there we crank our heads to see what's happening in Santa's workshop.

I stay quiet but I wonder, *How did you know this?*

"Yes," I answer.

"Perfect, that way you can see if she gets up to check on the phone and we can hang up." This seems like a lot of work just to talk on the phone.

Now, you know my house, you know my mom, and you know me.

I look down at my mom and think of all of the conversations that I've hidden from her, and all of the little lies I've told. *I never did tell her what we have talked about because I thought that you were my friend. I thought that it was none of her business. I thought I was growing up. But what if she was just trying to stop you?*

I hold the white phone in my hand and I stare as my mom sips her red wine. As I stand in my parents' bedroom, I remember watching my family's golden retriever Tasha dying nearly four years ago on the patio below. Before I knew you. Before you knew me.

I am shaking as I push the buttons that make your phone number. I am quiet as you answer. "Hey, what's wrong, sweetheart?" Your nicknames for me have slid into "honey" and "sweetheart" in the past few weeks. There was always a small sliver of my heart that felt weird with this, but mostly I had felt as though you really care about me. Now the sliver digs at my aorta.

"Nothing," I lie.

"Look. I didn't mean to do that. I love you and I don't want to hurt you. I promise I didn't mean to," you say and your voice sounds oddly casual.

I try to listen to your words and try to let the usual relief wash over me. But I can't. Instead, I feel a dark doubt inside. I feel as though I have two heads sitting atop my shoulders.

"Okay," I say with a little laugh to hide the confusion.

"I can say that I didn't mean to. But I can't say I didn't like how it felt," you say and I know that you are smiling.

Your happiness, your laugh feels wrong coming through the phone.

"Okay," I say again. But this time, I can barely hear myself speak.

CHAPTER THIRTEEN

Zoo Keeper

"Okay, Krick, what are you going to wear?" Maggie Black is standing behind me and we are both peering into my closet.

"I don't know . . . what do you wear on an occasion like this?" I ask Maggie and myself at the same time.

"Maybe like a sun dress or something?" Maggie pulls a black cotton spaghetti strap out of the far right side of my closet.

I shrug my shoulders and look away from her, at the hardwood floor below. *How can I care? How can I care when it feels as though my feet are floating a foot off the ground?*

As I hear the air conditioning click on in the attic above my head, I know today is going to be warm. It's late August, and when the fan starts humming this early, before 8 A.M., I know that we are in for a scorcher.

"What shoes?" Maggie asks.

I shrug my shoulders again and make myself look at her.

Maggie Black is beautiful. High cheek bones and dark hair define her with or without makeup.

I look at her now and try to imagine what the look on her face was then, on that July 1st day almost two months ago, I called her, immediately after leaving the police department and leaving Detective Parker.

"I'm going to have to call these people," Parker had said across the average office table. "Have you told Maggie yet?"

"Well, there are two Maggies," I said to Parker, although I had already explained the name sharing by two best friends at many other parts of the interview.

"Oh, yeah, that's right," he said, flipping back through his notes.

"I've told one of them and not the other," I explained. *Maggie Red is the reason I'm alive and I am not sure Maggie Black would know what to say.*

"Well, the other Maggie. She's one of your best friends, right?" Parker asked.

"Yes," I had agreed.

"You can call her before I do . . . to let her know what happened. Don't get into all of the details, because that will be important for the case," Parker said, sliding the chair back on the hard and cold floor so that he could stand and end the meeting. "I gotta run to pick up my youngest at the pool," he said trying to lighten the mood after three dark hours.

"Okay, I'll call her tonight," I said feeling empty of emotion.

And so I did. I didn't know what to expect. She's always been the goofy one, the one that uses a silly voice and doesn't care much about what people think or say about her.

"Krick? What is it, Krick?" Maggie Black grew serious on the phone in response to my cries.

"I went to the police today, Mags," I nearly whispered on the phone. "I had to go to the police today because I have been having a really hard time." My mind was suddenly full of the many minutes spent with Maggie Black and Julie through the years. Suddenly my mouth closed.

"Why, Krick? What's going on?" Maggie had begged. Her tears matched mine and came through the phone loud and clear.

"It's Natali," I said as quickly as I could, hating her name and hating the truth. "She abused me. She sexually abused me." I spit my words.

"Krick. No. When?" Maggie asked "How did I not know?"

That was the point. "I kept it hidden. And it's not hidden anymore. And I need you now. And the police need to talk to you. Would you talk to them?"

"Whatever you need," Maggie said.

And she meant it. I look at Maggie standing here today, in the morning light in front of my closet door. She tilts her head and gives me a sideways smile.

Since that telling day, Maggie Black has launched her own investigation. Finding other students who were close to Julie, compiling lists of other possible victims. She's collected photos of smiling thirteen year olds and even found one of us next to our then-favorite teacher, venturing off into the woods for a day of hiking and tanning.

"Okay, Krick," Maggie says, shaking her wrist to expose the face of her watch so that she can verify if we are on schedule. "We better go." I am fully dressed and as ready as I will ever be. "Scott and Red will meet us there. And your parents, too. I talked to your mom today. She's going to ride with your dad."

"Thanks," I muster. "You're like a wedding planner, except this isn't . . ."

"Yeah, not quite like your wedding day." Maggie stops me before I hurt myself.

As I look at her eyes and see water rim her lower lids, my chest bone curls forward and my hands catch my near fall, as I anchor to the tops of my knees for support. Sorrow comes rattling out of my mouth, and my rib cage pulls inward as I cry.

"I have tissues," Maggie offers. "You can do this, Kricky. You've made it this far."

I let her words sink into me and I draw in a few clean breaths. I think of the ground below and I stand upright. A single step at a time, I walk alongside Maggie toward her SUV sitting in our newly paved driveway.

For a quick second I look at my bluish grey house. The window seat in the front smiles to the street and the black rocking chairs sit invitingly on the front porch. Scott and I have made serious progress since we moved in over a year ago. The green landscape looks better with each passing season, and just briefly, I wonder how my home can keep improving, when I am not.

"Do you have everything, Kricky?" Maggie asks as we settle into her car.

"I think so. I brought everything that the attorney general asked me to bring." I place my large tote bag underneath my feet in Maggie's car—where Julie used to make me sit.

Since the phone calls, I have had two more interviews with Parker, one of which was joined by Attorney General Joyce Blair.

"Kristen, since Scott works in the the DA's office," Parker had explained to me while sitting at our same table, "The State of California Attorney General's Office will be handling your case from here on out." Parker looked across the table, passing the conversation to Joyce, who sat to my right.

"Kristen, you did excellent on the phone calls. I have listened to all of them. You were incredible," she had said to me, her voice sounding shrill and cheerful.

I had unsuccessfully tried to pull my mouth into a smile, but settled with a slight nodding of my head instead.

"Kristen, I have a question for you," Joyce said and tipped her medium-length grey hair to one side. I had wondered if the prosecutors are instructed to use first names to create comfort in uncomfortable situations.

I stared back at her in silence.

"What if you had just said no?" Her blue eyes pierced my own. "What if you had, let's say, just gone over to her apartment one night, but then said, 'no, I don't feel like it. Not tonight. No sex'."

I sat across from her, the lips of my mouth pressed together. *I must be in the wrong place. These people don't understand.* I pulled my eyebrows together and had wanted to shake my head so hard that the fury could have snapped my neck.

"That was not an option," I said, looking at her while tears of frustration had filled my eyes immediately. "It was never an option of what I wanted. It never mattered what I wanted. I wasn't allowed to say what I wanted. I was too scared to say what I wanted." My angry words were on rapid fire back at her.

"Okay, I understand. Let's talk more about that," Joyce began and so we did. By the end of the interview, her head was nodding and she was understanding.

"I wonder if Joyce will be there today." I allow myself to include Maggie. "They have a number of people working on the case, so I am wondering whom they will send."

"Have you shown Joyce the Facebook stuff yet? Did you bring it with you? I think that it's an important part of the case." Maggie Black is like being with a human checklist.

I look at my bag and see the printed-out pages of Facebook sitting next to me. As we pull onto the onramp, I slide the pages out and begin reading through them.

"Ah," I moaned, making a face at Maggie. "Remember that . . . when she wouldn't leave me alone and she hadn't been arrested?"

"That was horrible. If you got through those days, you can get through this day." Maggie's eyes momentarily leave the freeway to look at me.

As I leaf through the stapled pages, I feel the anxiety and fear that those days held.

"Just don't open her messages," Scott had said to me while we stood together at our overpriced Pottery Barn workstation. I had looked at him, in the far away light of the late afternoon.

"You don't understand." My heart raced inside my chest. "I can't not respond. Then she will know. She will know and she will flee. Or she will know and she will come find me." I looked out the front window. "Or she will know and she will kill herself." My eyes darted back to Scott. My right hand reached for the mouse as Scott stood closer behind me.

"They should have an arrest warrant soon," Scott said as he placed his hands on my shoulders. He pressed down on them, trying to create space between them and my ear lobes. It had been three days since I had finished the phone calls, and no word from the detective. "It'll be okay, Kristy," Scott whispered.

I wasn't listening as I navigated the Internet to open the message. Next to the conversation bubble was a red marker that read "6."

"She wrote me six messages." I was nearly yelling at Scott.

"What! What do they say?" Scott tried to remove the surprise from his voice.

I looked down and began reading the first of six text messages, all dated 7/15/2010:

> "Is there any way you can call me from another phone or collect from a pay phone, we just need to settle some things before we take an extended break from talking. Please try, I need to have some peace with this whole thing. Maybe tomorrow from work?"

As Scott and I stood together, and our eyes read the messages, I felt a familiar sense of pressure in my chest. I felt like an eighth grader again.

> "By the way, if for some reason you regret calling me and want to just take a break from it, that is okay. It would be easier on me if you just told me that straight out. Then I could just try to go back to what I was doing before without wondering about you. If that is not the reason, don't be mad I mentioned it, just wanted to give you an out if you need it."

I felt Scott's body relax behind me, but my spine stiffened, knowing that it was just another one of her tests. "No babe." I turned to him. "If I tell her I want a break, she will know that it was a setup. She'll leave, or kill herself, or . . ."

"Okay, Kristy, let's just see what the rest of it says . . ." Scott pointed his chin toward the screen and I followed his lead.

> "Please find a way to call, I need to know where to go with this."

My throat tightened as I read these messages coming in only minutes away from each other. Julie's frantic tone continued in a note only thirteen minutes later, and I could imagine her green face reflecting in a computer screen:

> "I have always tried not to ask you for much or make any demands, but this time it is different. Even if Scott is the reason, you owe me one last phone call to sort things out. My life has been tossed upside down and you aren't going to find a way to call? I need peace, I am devastated. Is there a number that I can call you on, like an office phone or something? Please figure it out and let me know! If this is as hard on you as it is on me, I am sorry. Maybe we can figure out a way around this mess together."

Scott squeezed my arms, just above my biceps, and tried to settle my body. It did not matter; I couldn't feel him. My eyes had jumped out of my body and onto the computer screen, leaving only a shell of myself behind.

> "I will call you tomorrow on Rob's phone; tell me when to call."

And, suddenly, I could see the invisible chains and ropes with great clarity.

"Krick, are you all right?" Maggie brings me back to the present moment and I realize that we are off the freeway and driving on side streets.

"Yeah, I was just reading the Facebook stuff." I look further down the page. "Listen to this, 'I just need to know—not knowing drives me absolutely nuts and leads me to think irrationally.

I truly believe that I am the one to help you through this rough patch, please let me'." I look over at Maggie.

"Ah, barf!" Maggie sticks her tongue out with pretend vomit.

I sit back in the car and look at the twenty-nine days, from the first Facebook message to the last, and I shake my head in disbelief that I fended the monster off for so long.

"Can you believe that it worked?" I include Maggie in my thought process.

"No. I can't. I can't believe that it worked and I also can't believe how long it took them to arrest her." Her dark hair swishes on her back as she shakes her head in disbelief.

Two weeks after the phone calls, I was losing faith. Finally, after an afternoon workout at Cal, I had a missed call from Parker waiting in a bubble on my iPhone. I waited until I was driving home from Berkeley when I picked up his unintentionally enthusiastic voicemail: "Kristen, it's Parker. We got the warrant. I fly to Utah on Monday."

My grip had loosened on the steering wheel that day as I realized I would only need to make it another few days of fake Facebooking.

As I began to imagine the police lights nearing her home, I began having heartburn-type pains in my chest as I envisioned two boys playing football in the backyard. The momentary peace I had in knowing that she would be arrested was quickly replaced by guilt.

"I can't believe this is going to happen," I told Chuck in a meeting, the day after I had been promised that her arrest was near. "What are they going to tell those kids? Are they going to be okay?"

Chuck tilted his head from across the room and smiled a tiny smile for me. "You are such a kind gal." His words did not work as an antacid.

"How can they have any sort of good life without their mom in it?" I asked, not returning the grin.

"Kristen," Chuck grew serious in his tone. "Children need to know the truth. Children can still have a good life if they have a serial killer for a father or a rapist for a mother." I noticed Chuck's careful choice of gender and crime. "The thing that can ruin them is the secret of who their parent actually is."

I had listened to Chuck that day and allowed a white wave of relief to wash over me with his words. Unsure if I actually believed him, or that I wanted to believe him so desperately that I found a way to, I sat down at my Facebook account with a plan.

> "I have looked at my meet itinerary and I will have some time alone in the room on Tuesday morning. Will you be home alone and able to talk in private?"

I had told Julie enough pieces of the truth so that she couldn't catch me in a lie. This time it was true that we were headed back down to Irvine for another swim meet.

"I can't believe that she was planning on talking to me while her kids were sitting right there," I say to Maggie, continuing to read through the messages.

"I know. It shows that she's evil, Krick. It shows that you are doing the right thing." Maggie reaches for my hand.

I let in a full breath of air and let in the memory of that day. "Kristen . . ." It was Parker on the phone and, again, I had been waiting for his call the entire day. August 3rd, the first day of the US National Championships and the longest day of my life.

"Hi, Detective," I had said while riding in the car with Teri, only four days after my careful Facebook message. Teri's head had swiveled to look at me and she tightened her hands around the wheel. She, too, was awaiting this call. "How did it go?" I asked him.

"Well . . ." He said. Within a nanosecond, the possibilities flashed in front of my eyes; the most startling was her lighting her house on fire with her and the kids inside.

"Did you get her?" I demanded.

"Well, I went there to ask her questions. I went this morning, as you had arranged with your Facebook . . ." Parker began the entire story as I awaited the conclusion.

"Was she home? Were her kids home?" I pressed.

"Yes, she was home. And, yes, unfortunately her kids were home," Parker answered.

"What?" I exclaimed, angry that my plan didn't work. "What did she say?" I took the driver's seat of the conversation and Teri stole glances as she drove the rental minivan.

"Well, I got her to admit some things. Then I showed her the poem and she admitted some more. Then she told me that it was your fault and that she was the victim. I pretended to believe her and I made her really comfortable in talking with me. I assured

her that she wasn't under arrest and that she could talk to me."
Parker sounded a little proud.

"And then what?" As I asked, I looked out the window and
saw a familiar sight to my right: the La Quinta hotel where we
stayed less than three months ago. I looked at the train tracks
and clenched my jaw.

"I left. I phoned the judge and made sure the warrant was
ready and then I returned that evening." I put my hand on the
warm dashboard as I waited for him to finish. "Rob had come
home from work early; they knew it wasn't good. I think that they
had already contacted a lawyer."

"So, do you have her in custody?" I asked and I had looked at
Teri as though I was talking to her directly.

"Yes, she's in the county jail. She will be transported to California next week for arraignment." As Parker finished his words,
my jaw unclenched.

Now, as we approach the Martinez, California, courthouse
and I remember the stepping stones, I fidget in Maggie's car. I
carefully place the Facebook material back in my bag, as though
it is fragile evidence, not a computer printout that could easily be
replaced.

"I think that you park over there," I say to Maggie, as if to
explain my eyes, which are darting around the parking lot.

*What if I see someone I know and they go look at the court
calendar to see why I am here? What if it is in the newspaper
tomorrow? What if they know who Jane Doe actually is?*

"Okay, sounds good." Maggie humors me. "Let's get as close as
possible. I wonder where everyone is," Maggie says, and although
I know that she is talking about my immediate friends and family,
I think of everyone else it could be.

"Probably inside already," I say.

Maggie whips into a spot and we hop out with as much energy
as if we are going to the Junior Prom. "Do you have everything?
Here, we can walk together," Maggie says as I try to steady myself
on the tree adjacent to her parking spot. I ended up picking boat
shoes, so my shaking legs wouldn't be as likely to betray me. I
look down and wonder if I've picked the right thing for this wrong
occasion.

My phone buzzes in the outside pocket of my evidence bag.
I know it is Scott before I read the text. "Hi, Kristy. I am headed
over from my office. I will meet you outside the metal detector."

I read it to Maggie, although she is already reading over my shoulder. We walk in step toward the courthouse, which looks more like an office complex and less like a scene from *Law and Order*.

I jump and grab onto Maggie's arm as a white school bus with darkened windows rounds the corner to our left. The noise startled me and what my eyes see scares me even more: "Department of Corrections" printed in worn black on the side of the bus. I can feel that she is inside.

"My knees feel like Jello," I admit to Maggie.

"You can do this." And as she says this, I believe her. Finally in sight is Scott, standing as tall as he can in his pin-striped suit.

My legs work again as I walk toward him. The smell of the juniper bush to my left reminds me that it could be a happy summer day.

"I'm scared." I raise myself onto my tip toes to whisper into his ear, but I don't necessarily need to.

"This is nothing compared to what we have already done." Scott's words are a touch louder than mine. "Remember, it is just an arraignment. They don't do much here. She just enters into a plea."

I look into his eyes, "But she will be here?"

"Yes." He gives me a defeated smile, and I curl my lower lip under my front teeth.

Scott leaves me with Maggie as he goes through the special entrance for attorneys. He flashes his badge, while Maggie and I place our belongings on the conveyor belt. I avoid eye contact with the guards.

My mom is just inside; being early is one of her most typical characteristics. She doesn't notice as I walk in; she is preoccupied with examining the bulletin board that lists cases and court room numbers.

"Krick!" My brother rushes past my mom's turned back and comes charging at me for a hard hug.

"Hi, Marc," I say hugging back, the pressure of his arms bringing tears to my eyes.

"Hi, Krick, how are you this morning?" My mom has lined up and is hugging me now.

"I'm okay," I say, struggling to make myself feel the well-trafficked floor of the court hall below.

"Are you doing okay, Krick?" Maggie Red is next. I sniff in her perfume and am once again transported to high school.

I nod my head this time, with my back toward the metal detectors. Red keeps hugging me, "Oh, there's Rob," she says.

My dad? Why would Maggie call my dad by his first name?

I spin my head to see the next person who will line up to hug me. My eyes are deceived. The other Rob . . .

I see his face. His dark hair and his dark skin. My eyes lock onto a face that my memory knows from a time long ago.

Without thinking, I almost walk toward him to say hi. I can feel my mouth pulling toward a smile, but somehow I find restraint.

Like a flash, I see him as a person from a piece of my past that was good, when I was a kid. I see his face and feel the admiration I had for her, the desire I had to have a marriage like she had. I step back to the times Rob and Julie took my friends and me out to dinner. The times they came to my soccer games. Before . . . anything.

But why? Why were they there?

Now it feels weird and sad and bad that they were there. That they would spend their free time watching, befriending, following a fourteen-year-old child.

Then it was different. Then it felt as though they loved me. That they saw me as the ideal child they might someday have. Then it felt as though I had the coolest friends in the world. I want to scream at him. But, instead, I stare.

I can feel Scott join our group, but I am not deterred by the present moment.

Rob wears a wrinkled button-up shirt, which is tucked into his jeans as a last ditch effort at looking nice, and the same glasses he had a decade ago. He turns to someone else I remember: his brother Matt. A human that I have not seen in fourteen years, yet his name frozen in my memory.

I ran the Bay to Breakers with both of them. In May of 1996, before Julie ever raped me, but well after she drew up her plan to do so.

"Okay, we are in the way back of the court," Scott says.

But I am frozen. My eyes pierce the side of Rob's stubbled cheek. Rob turns his neck and faces Matt, who is behind him. They exchange words and my heart stops as their words give way to a laugh. I wish I had a gun.

Did he know? He knew. He allowed this to happen to me.

Suddenly I do not have the light feeling in my heart as though I have seen a lost friend. My happiness is twisted into a dark loneliness and anger that takes my breath away.

His spouse talking on the phone every night. His new bride staying out until the morning hours. His wife demanding a new apartment. His money disappearing on phone bills.

I want to charge at him directly, and use the force of my bare hands and my fury to pummel him. But I find control and instead convince my legs to walk with my family. Yet still my mind is somewhere else.

He knew then. He knows now. What if he helped?

With my husband at my side, my mind spins. "Hi, Kristen. Good to see you," Joyce says to me and shakes my rattling hand. "I'm Joyce Blair from the Attorney General's Office," she announces. "I've been working with Kristen on her case." Joyce puffs her chest out and makes the most of her short stature. She shakes hands with my people and I barely notice that my dad has joined us.

My head turns to look for Rob.

What if he taped it all? What if he watched, was there even? What if he documented it, and sold it? What if my nightmares are floating somewhere in outer space?

Before I know what is happening, we are in a courtroom and I am seated on a wooden bench. I feel separated from the reality of where I am and my head moves on my shoulders in a smoother way than it usually does. Scott squeezes my hand and both Maggie Red and Maggie Black rotate between rubbing my back. I can almost feel them.

Scott is to my left. "That's where the inmates stand," Scott says, and I can see movement in what looks like a glass cage.

There are four bodies inside; that much I can tell. Three of them have short hair and move like men. The other has shoulder-length hair and moves like a snake.

"There she is," Maggie Red says and shakes my hand. I feel the people around me look at me as they think that I am looking at her.

My head faces the right direction, and so do my eyes. I look toward her, but I cannot see her. My vision is blurred and all I know is that I am sitting in the same room as Julie Correa.

"She looks like she hasn't eaten since she was arrested two weeks ago," I hear my mom say to Scott.

She must be thin.

I sense Scott nodding his head in agreement with my mom. "These other cases might go before us." Scott assumes his explaining role.

Good, I need time. But even as the minutes pass, I still cannot see her. I try to look but my brain won't allow it. The pain will have to come in pieces. The weight of the betrayal all at once would crush me.

So, instead, I turn to look and look at Rob sitting ahead of me and to my left. My eyes regain focus as I glare at him from the inside.

I am startled out of my stare by a loudspeaker that comes from the front of the room: "In the matter of Julie . . ." A large male judge brings the piece of paper that is already near his nose closer to his face. He squints his eyes and feels very far away. "Cor-ree-ah." He mispronounces her name.

"Your honor," a large man stands up at the table I know to be for the defense, and says: "It's pronounced, Co-ray-ah."

The word echoes down my spine. I feel as though I am swimming through very dark and deep water. Noise is muffled. I cannot hear the legal logistics that come from Joyce, the judge, and the defense.

"Not guilty, your honor." I grab onto Scott with both hands as I hear Julie speak live for the first time in ten years. I sense that she is in the front area of the glass cage. The noise is directed at me, and though I cannot focus my eyes on her, I know that she is glaring at me.

Scott squeezes my hands back. "That's just her plea. That's how they always plead . . ."

Not guilty. I think of the nights I worried that she could get me pregnant.

Not guilty. I think of the sharp pain and I pull my legs together.

Not guilty. I think of her sons there the day she was arrested.

Not guilty. I think of what she said to me on the phone.

I think of all of the pain and I cry, bending fully into Scott's embrace.

I feel both Maggies move closer and my parents draw in toward me. I hang my head and look down at the evidence bag below. As the officials at the front of the room work on picking the next court date, I see Detective Parker sitting in the far lefthand corner of the room, watching me.

I cannot see Julie today, because my eyes cannot focus. I cannot kill Rob, because I cannot risk going to prison with Julie. I cannot scream from my belly when she says "not guilty" to the judge, because I cannot let the court know I have lost my mind.

But I can feel my army around me. I can feel my army growing. And I know that I can fight.

CHAPTER FOURTEEN

Beating the Watch

I look down at my boxer shorts. They are white with huge car-
toon-looking flowers all over them. The petals are all different
colors and the center is filled with a smiley face. The pavement
under my feet is hot, but not as hot as the redness that burns in
my cheeks.

I am embarrassed, to say the least. Sad, disappointed, mad
are also emotions swirling in my gut. But more than any of these
other feelings, the embarrassment pulls my eyes down and I feel
unexpectedly young.

I hate to lose. I rarely lose at anything I do. In all my sports, the
desire to win keeps me up the night before the competition. This
has been a part of who I am since I was born fourteen years ago.

I especially hate to lose in the pool. From the time I was a
young girl, I invented underwater games to play with Marc that
I knew I could win. Sure, he is four years older than I am and
very athletic on land. But I always knew how to take to the water,
to spend longer below the surface than I should. I think that I
understand the water better than anyone. So, why should anyone
beat me in it?

Today, Lisa did. Today, at the finals of the OMPA Championship, when things really matter, I lost. Lisa is on my team. I have
swum next to her all summer long. So why now? How could she
find a way to get her hand to the wall before me?

The questions still run through my mind as I avoid my mom
and her angry eyes. I have thought about this race for weeks, if

not months. The 50 fly at this meet has been mine. How dare she take this away from me. It just isn't fair. I need this right now.

I have to admit that I have come to expect the "1" to appear on the scoreboard next to my lane. I have come to demand the blue ribbons from myself. As we passed under the flags in approaching the wall, I sensed Lisa next to me. I became distracted—annoyed that she had pulled near. I allowed her to step into my focus, to distract my finish, and suddenly, the anticipation of a "1" was replaced by the disappointment of a less familiar number "2."

I wished immediately I had a chance to redo what had been done. I know I am better. Why does life feel this hard? My rage came at me like an unexpected stroke of thunder. I threw my goggles. I threw my cap. I did not acknowledge Lisa's win. I stormed out of the pool and the pool area toward the adjacent football field and found a corner where I thought I could feel the devastation on my own.

I grabbed my towel and put on my boxer shorts feeling like I might want to be done with the rest of this swim meet.

"What do you think that you are doing?" I have rarely heard my mom's voice so angry and accusatory. Some kids may think that their mom is angry about the 2nd place. I know this is not the origin of her tone.

"This isn't fair. I am so much better than her!" I yell at my mom, mostly wishing she wouldn't have followed me here, wishing she would have left me alone in my anger. *Why did she follow me? Why is she checking on me again?*

"Kristen," her voice is firm and direct. It reminds me of the times in the grocery store when I was told not to beg for the candy next to the checkout counter. After my mom's telling me just one time, I never asked again. In fact, I don't think I ever looked again. I know that when my mom says 'no,' she means no. "If you want to play sports, you are not allowed to do what you are doing right now. Today, Lisa was better than you. She beat you. If you can't handle this, you can't play sports."

I wish I felt as happy as the smiling faces on my boxer shorts looking back at me. I put my hands on my narrow young hips, imagining what my life would be like without sports.

This is who I am. This is what I live for. How dare she threaten to take that away?

I take a deep breath and watch the design of my swim suit expand and then collapse as I release my breath. My new black and purple paper suit is a specially designed swim suit that is tight on my body and meant to minimize drag. I feel the fabric underneath my fingertips, surprised that it really does feel paper-like, and I am surprised by the fact that it is almost dry less than five minutes after my race. These suits cost over a hundred dollars, but we got this one over fifty percent off because the Speedo logo was accidentally screened on upside down. I stare at the Speedo logo looking back at me to avoid the disappointment in my mom's eyes.

So here I stand, embarrassed in knowing that my mom is right. I am acting like a child. So often you tell me that I am acting like a child, and as always, I hate how stupid I feel.

I let myself listen to my mom's words. Since I began relying on you for everything, especially through eighth grade last year, I rarely listen to what my mom has to say. "She's just doesn't get it," you often say about my mom. "You can't really hold it against her. She grew up in a poor family in Utah. She didn't play college sports like I did. She didn't even finish college." I hate it when you talk about my mom and I hate that you have a point. If I want to play college sports, I should probably look up to you, not my mom.

But what about the gross things you just started doing to me? Will you please stop those so that I can go back to following your lead? I am scared to follow you now.

The pavement scorches my feet, and although there is a little pain caused by the black top, I like that I can feel the earth. I like that I can feel the pain.

It is the middle of August, and the innards of the swim complex roar with the finish of the next race. Recreational swimming, or "rec" as we call it here, is a huge deal. With two towns, and over 2,000 swimmers, even the grocery stores are empty through this weekend of August. From overdecorated cars, to coverage in the newspaper, the anticipation and the results of this meet are meaningful.

After I won "Swimmer of the Meet" when I was twelve, my core teacher, Mrs. Christiansen, made a huge scene about how proud she was of me. "Kristen!" She had screamed to me across the JM lunch quadrant when she saw me at seventh-grade orientation. "I'm so proud of you!" *Even you knew I had won and had asked me about it in PE.* I liked that my teachers knew of my summer success, and I was hoping my future high school teachers would pause when they saw my name on their class list with something to the effect, "Oh, Kristen, she was undefeated at OMPA this summer." I was planning on making a mark before I set foot in the place. With a second place finish, I guess that won't be happening.

"Kristen." My mom has been awaiting my response this whole time. I have listened to her, taken in what she has said, and only floated around for a time. "Are you hearing me?"

"Of course I am hearing you, mom." *But I have been taught to listen to you and not my own mother.* I wonder briefly what you would say about my unexpected loss.

My mom lowers the volume to her voice and steps in closer, "Do you want to swim the rest of your races at the meet? Do you want to prove what an incredible swimmer you are and how hard you have worked this summer? Do you want to prove that you can handle a second-place finish like a grownup?"

I have always liked how my mom focuses on the positive. She could say to me in this moment, "Are you going to just give up like a selfish and immature child?" Instead, she focuses on the positives of what are possible at this point.

I rub the paper suit beneath my hands and I feel the opportunity to race again—to prove to my mom, the crowd, and myself that more than being a winner or a loser, I am a fighter.

"I need to go get ready for my next race," I say to my mom as I allow myself to meet her gaze.

As I walk past my mom, her thin but solid arms reach out and grab me, pulling me in closer to her for a brief hug.

The weekend goes by and as I pull into my driveway, I remember the game I played this whole week with myself. It is a game that I often play before big sporting events or meets. In my head, I say to myself things like "next time I drive up my driveway, I will have broken the pool record," or "next time I see Maggie, I will have scored six goals in my tournament." I never tell anyone about these mind games that I play. They might think I am weird or obsessed with winning. *Do most people talk to themselves as much as I do?*

I am sitting in the back seat of our minivan as the car turns left into the uphill of the driveway. My eyes seem naturally to avoid a certain space to the right. I think of my mind game I played, promising myself I would win all of my events at the OMPA Championship. As I review the weekend and remember the struggle with my mom, I know that I must pull in the driveway with a second place.

"I'm back and I didn't win," I think to myself. "But I feel as though I won. I won my other two events. I broke records in both. I helped my relay team break an ancient record and win Relay Team of the Meet. I did end up with that High Point Award. I look in the back seat and see the trophy that stands as tall as my waist. As I compile the growing list of my accomplishments in my head, I feel proud rather than upset. I smile quickly to myself as I mentally note, "I also won second place in my butterfly race."

My meet didn't look exactly the way I had expected. In some ways it looked better. Today, I received my trophy from my childhood hero Matt Biondi. Meeting an Olympic swimmer and shaking his oversized bear paw of a hand provides a compass of where I want to go in life.

The celebration of OMPA afterward is always one of the highlights of my summer. After the general awards ceremony, each club retires back to its respective pool and there is another award ceremony for each individual club. Sometimes I wonder, how many awards, trophies, ribbons can one person get? Don't get me wrong: I like all that I have gotten, but sometimes it feels too easy to earn.

It is dark outside. It is almost eleven o'clock. Most of my swimmer friends are having a sleepover, but my mom thought it was getting too late to let me spend the night anywhere but in my own bed. I didn't fight my mom. I didn't want to make her mad. I knew that you would be waiting for my call. I didn't want to make you mad.

My mom and dad settle in the family room to watch the eleven o'clock news. Usually they watch the ten o'clock news but not tonight. I used to watch the ten o'clock news on Channel 2 with them, but now I am a teenager and I talk on the phone.

My mom doesn't always know to whom I am talking. She used to ask and I used to tell her. But she thought it was weird that a teacher was talking to me on the phone. And you got mad that she was concerned. A wedge.

So you came up with The Plan to sit and watch my mom below.

And so now I look at the cordless phone sitting on white tiles of the kitchen counter. I know it is late and you will be angry that I have not called yet. I do not stop to think that your husband will wonder who is calling at this late hour. I only know that I have to call you.

As I walk up the carpeted stairs to the talking perch in my mom's bedroom, I think back on the old you. Maybe tonight you will answer and it will be the old you. You won't be mad at me that I am calling late. You will let me tell you about the roller coaster of a meet I just had. And then we will hang up. You won't talk about all the other stuff. I hang onto a rope tow of hope as I climb the stairs.

I call your number and I think that you answer before the phone even rings. It feels as though I am on a walkie-talkie.

No "hello" or "hi" because you know who it is. "Well, well, well. You had yourself quite a meet."

You are not mad at me and I am surprised by that. But I don't like surprises these days. I hate them actually. It should feel good that you are not mad. So why am I scared?

How do you know about my meet? It will be in the newspaper, but not until tomorrow morning. *Have you talked to someone? Did you mention my name directly?* I hope not.

I let my wonderment leak out of my mouth, "How do you know?" I am not so sure I want to know the answer. Were you there? I feel a shiver run down my back as I am curled in a ball, staring wide-eyed at my unknowing mom below.

"No, I wasn't there. I am sorry, sweetie." *I am not sorry and please don't call me that.* "But I watched all of it."

My stomach leaves my body and drops squarely between the wool sweaters of the chest below. "What do you mean?" My question is soft and quiet.

"I watched all of it. From the hill above the pool." I know the steep hill you are talking about. I get scared just driving on it. *But how could you see me?* I am silent in fear.

"Yeah," you fill in my blank and I hate that you can read my mind. "I had this really good idea. I got binoculars and I watched. Man, that breaststroke was amazing. You won by half a pool."

STOP. I want to yell but I can't because my parents would hear and then they would know. If they knew, my mom would have been right to question you. They would be disgusted and want to take me away to another school. They would turn you in and I would never have a chance at getting my old teacher back or have anyone to talk to about Mr. Witters.

And who knows what you would do?

But please don't talk about swimming. Swimming is all mine. You know nothing of the sport and look like a rat when you try to swim.

Why were you there? I hate that you were on that hill watching me. I hate that I didn't know you were there until just now. You live in Livermore and had to drive almost an hour to get to that hill. Standing on a hot dry hill in grass that has turned brown. Is that how you really spent your whole weekend? My chest cavity feels like a tornado. *Please stop doing this to me.*

"You saw everything?" I ask this but I know the truth. *You saw the races. You saw me get second. You saw me break records, but you didn't see everything.*

"I'm sorry about the butterfly, sweetheart." You are talking about my second-place finish to Lisa. "You must have been so disappointed." Your voice to me sounds like a mom whisking up a fallen toddler before he even has time to start crying. I feel like a lamb at the petting zoo.

"Yeah," I make myself murmer.

"But you have to be happy with how everything else turned out, right?" These are words I should be sharing with my mom. I wish I was watching the sports segment and rehashing what happened over the weekend with her, not you.

The feeling of needing and wanting my mom dims quickly as I think of you standing on that hill. What would have you said if someone would have seen you there hovering over me? I allow my eyes to drift out the window into the darkness.

Are you out there now? Are you watching me now? What about when I get ready for bed? When I change my clothes? Have you watched me before?

I feel like an air balloon on a rapid and violent descent from the highs of the day. I land on a bed of lava that now covers the entirety of the earth.

A sudden shift occurs in my mind. A change that is only detectable to myself. I assume you are here. That you will be everywhere I go. It is easier this way. It is better than wondering. And so I walk through the rest of my conversation with you and imagine you, your outfit of black in the night, and the glow of your night-vision goggles, perched in a tree and waiting to pounce.

CHAPTER FIFTEEN

Evil in the Hallway

The sofa in the office where I meet Chuck is firm, almost un-comfortable really. I'm not at his usual office in Alameda. Lately he has been meeting me at a church in Berkeley because it is close for me and he might be the kindest man I have ever met.

Chuck is my therapist. I am twenty-eight years old and Chuck is the first therapist I have ever seen. Crazy, I know. When I told him my story in the first session, and then I told him I have never been in therapy, his eyes almost rolled out of his head. He sat there, God bless him, and figured out a way to keep his jaw from dropping and tried to continue the conversation without letting on to the fact that he was in shock.

He is a trauma specialist. He understands how trauma can be trapped in the human brain and not realized, recognized, or dealt with for years on end. He believes me when I say that, for the past ten years, I didn't even realize that all this had actually hap-pened, that I knew I had been in a bad place, but I had no idea where that place was and what it looked like. He understands how a child can be trapped in a situation, without physical force but through fear alone. He understands that trauma, if not dealt with, can sneak back up on a person and the fear will feel as real and alive as the day or month or years that trauma occurred.

I have PTSD: post-traumatic stress disorder. The famous Mayo Clinic says that it is "a type of anxiety disorder that's triggered by a traumatic event. You can develop post-traumatic stress disor-der when you experience or witness an event that causes intense fear, helplessness, or horror." Event? What about an entire life? When I look at what happened and the years of trying to run from it, sometimes it really does feel like my whole life.

And so, yes, I have PTSD. It affects me everyday. Sometimes it is a loud sound, sometimes it is a quiet sound. Sometimes it is a sense of helplessness, sometimes a sense of spinning. I look around corners. I look over my shoulder. I look everywhere.

Chuck and I have not spent much time talking about the fact that I have PTSD. We have been too busy trying to walk through the memories of what happened and where I am now with going to the police. I see him twice a week most weeks, and he usually keeps me past my hour. He charges me half price because he knows I need his help.

And as I sit here today, I realize just how overstuffed this couch really is. In this first five minutes of my appointments, we always just talk about his weekend, small stuff to make sure I am ready to dive into this. It's not that I like the chat or dislike the chat, it just doesn't matter to me. Every day is hard, and talking about all this is the only thing that makes it a little less hard.

"I have something to tell you about." Chuck seems strangely uncomfortable with what he is about to say.

"Okay," my stomach begins to hurt again with wonder.

"I had an incident yesterday. A woman in my hallway." Immediately I know what he is going to say.

Chuck carefully continues, "I am not sure that this has anything to do with you." *Well, I am sure.*

"I came out to use the bathroom," his voice is hesitant as he watches me respond. "She wasn't in the waiting room but in the hallway just outside. In twenty years, I have never seen someone sit in that hallway. She was in a cross-legged position with her eyes closed. An hour later, when I came out, she was still there. Twenty minutes later, I came out and asked her if she was waiting for my coworker, Kathleen. Finally, she opened her eyes and said, 'No, I am not waiting for Kathleen.' It started to bother me and I decided to pack up my office and leave." He pauses to see if I am still breathing. He knows that the oxygen is hard for me to find but also knows that he has to tell me this. "When I left, the woman was still there. I went down to my car, through the office park, through the parking lot and to my car. I turned around and the woman had followed me down to my car and was peering out from a pillar, watching me get in my car."

I have left my body. I hear what Chuck has said, I know in my gut that it was Julie. I knew in my gut that she would come. But, still, I can't stay here. It's not safe here. And what I have always done when things aren't safe, I dissolve into thin air.

Chuck sees me sitting there but watches as I float to the top of the room. He stops his story. He looks into my vacant eyes and says, "how does this feel to hear this?" It is a question that doesn't have an answer.

My mind spins. I'm trying to figure out the right answer of how this should feel to me. I'm trying to figure out if she is outside the door right now, or waiting for me back in my office under the desk, or has figured out a way to get into the back seat of my car. I need to call Scott. I need to get a picture of her and show it to Chuck. I need to know if it was her.

I bypass the question that I do not have the answer for. I have my own questions that I need answered. "What color hair did she have?"

"Brown." He knows I am in charge now.

"How long was it?"

"Shoulder length." I always hated her haircut.

"How tall was she?"

"5'7"." Exactly.

"What was her build?"

"Athletic, but pretty slender." She probably starved herself for the month that she was in jail. She was thin at the arraignment and now she is out on bail. I knew she would come for me.

"What color were her eyes?"

"She had her eyes closed most of the time. She only opened them to answer my questions. I don't know what color they were."

"Were they hollow?"

"Yes. They were scary."

"What was her voice like?"

"Also hollow, also scary."

My mind goes to a rational place really. *It is her. She has come for me. To kill me? To scare me? To try to get me back? To silence me?* It doesn't matter why she has come. The way that I have stayed safe from her is to assume the worst. She is capable of killing me. And so, without hysteria and with reason, I begin to plan my next move.

I could leave straight from Chuck's office. Not tell Scott, not tell my family where I am going. I could hide until she is convicted and put away. I could go to the ATM, get out as much cash as they will let me, and get out of here. I could flee.

Or, I can fight. I can stay here. Stay put in my truth and risk my life in order to speak my truth. This is hard, but I like my life. I wouldn't be able to walk the dogs with Scott every night. I wouldn't be able to stand next to Teri on the pool deck. I wouldn't be able to go Christmas shopping with my mom, to a basketball game with my dad, or stop in to see my brother and his beautiful new baby boy. I don't want to flee. I have things worth living for. Things worth living through. My chest fills with air and I return to my body in preparation for the fight.

It feels the same as when I met Scott. I had and now have something that is worth standing up for. I think that they call this courage.

CHAPTER SIXTEEN

In the Cuddle of My First Pup

The days and the nights are beginning to run into each other. I used to be able to keep track of how many times you have taken me from my house by counting on my fingers. Nail by nail I could add the steps and stages that you have progressed with my body. But now there is nothing left to do to me; or so I think. *What's the point of keeping track when it feels as if my insides are rotting?*

I am here again. I do not have a gun to the back of my head, but lately I have been imagining that I do. At what appears to be my own will, I walk into your room.

The light is low and the smell is distinct. I look up and see the picture: my picture. It is a painting in a frame above your bed. It's probably just a poster that you had framed, but I am too young to know the difference among a poster, a print, and a painting. As I walk into the room, this scary and cold place for me, a few things make me feel a little calm.

To the immediate left of the bed is the small digital clock on your bedside table. It sits innocently enough, but I know that you will use it to set an alarm to wake up and take me home. I have found tranquility in these green numbers, which I now wear on the inside of my eyelids.

To the far left is the window that faces the front of your apartment. This window has taken much of my time and energy through many nights, and for that I appreciate its presence. Tonight it is cracked slightly, allowing the whispers of the night's sound in for a quiet orchestra. It is the fall of my freshman year and the days are as bright and as warm as any summer day. But now the window lets in only blackness. I wait for headlights.

But my eyes are pulled back to the right. I look above the bed.

You are in the bathroom washing your hands. My heart beats as I sense your presence in the near room. As I hear the water release and run, I know that the soap is lathering between your hands. I also know what is coming next. "I have to clean my hands before I touch you, because I don't want to hurt you or give you anything bad," you had said to me last time.

You always hurt me.

The water stops. Suddenly, and in a hurry before your return, I walk to the wall. I leave a shadow of myself on the bed for you. With tiny steps, I move like an ant up the white paint, light and quiet. You come back from the bathroom. You don't see me. You only see the shadow I have left, in the form of my body. My ant self smiles. *I have tricked you again. You stay here and I will march somewhere safe.*

I am in my room. But not the one in my house. The one in the painting.

When I arrive, the air feels warm and still. My nose catches the scent of freshly washed sheets. The small window is open, but the air outside is at rest and the daytime is much quieter than the crickets. There are no shades, no curtains, no blinds, and no secrets.

The centerpiece of my room, and also the painting, is a loosely made four post bed. The grey wall behind the bed is calming and caring, and it might be the same color as the inside of an army barracks. The white quilt is undeniably plain, and the fringe tells me that it has had a long life of holding its owners. And my favorite part of the room: the white lab that is curled with his head resting on the pillow.

When I first saw this picture, I thought that it was odd and redundant and silly to have a picture of a bed hanging above your bed.

I asked you. "Why did you pick that picture?" It was a few weeks ago when I asked this question. Things were different then. Things hadn't gotten this bad. My words then had been an attempt to get back the teacher that you used to be. Now there is no small talk in this big nightmare.

"It reminded me of Zoe. Why do you care? Do you suddenly have a preference in art now that you are almost a big time freshman in high school?" you had said, glaring at me.

I hate Zoe. And I am not one to hate a golden lab. She smells and she licks and she sheds all over me. And, worse, she cannot talk and tell anyone what you do to me. She has never run for help.

You would know this if you ever stopped to look at this dog, and had ever stopped to hold this dog in your picture, that this dog is nothing like Zoe. First of all, it is a boy dog. He is old and wise and tired. And, unlike Zoe, he protects me. He doesn't act all happy and hyper when something is so terribly wrong. He knows when to cuddle, when to bark, and when to bite. Most of all, he listens to me.

I am in the picture and the hardwood planks creek as I get closer to the bed, but still you do not hear. Now you have wrapped your arms around my actual body.

I lift the tattered white quilt and climb in.

This is not my first visit to the picture, and I am always surprised that the quilt can keep me warm enough. The blanket is heavy, like the one at the dentist's office when x-rays are taken. I shape my body around my dog. He lifts his head as if he expects me and lies it back down as though he both wants me to stay and wants me to be safe. He barely wakens for me.

At first, I lie where I can see you and my shadow. Your bed is just a mattress and a box spring on a metal bed frame. I have always thought it looks ridiculous when people don't spend enough money to have a real bed. *You spend almost half of your life in a bed, and this is the best you can do? For you, your bed is not about sleeping, it's not about relaxing. For you, your bed is about hurting me and satisfying you. Disgusting.*

I lie with my guy for a moment and watch you. I feel safe, but a stitch of guilt enters my side for having left my shadow again. I stay with my shadow as long as I can bear it. I watch you abuse me. I stay there for that. But when the time comes where you make my shadow do things to you, I close my eyes, slide my head to face my pup, and let myself rest.

Some minutes have passed and suddenly I am pulled from the warmth of my pup and back to the bed. I am yanked back to reality by a strange sensation on my fingertips. I had left my shadow for a rest and you, in the effort of trying to find something new, put my hand down the front of your underpants.

My esophagus burns with the start of throwup and I clamp my mouth shut. *Why are you wet down there?* I am back from the picture, so I can pull my hand back toward my body.

"What's wrong, honey?" you say and hold my wrist as my hand feels as though it is going to fall off. I wish I could slice my fingertips with my dad's razor blade.

"Uh, . . . nothing," I say now, knowing that I can never tell you the truth. "I just . . . have to go to the bathroom." My voice comes without cognizant thought.

"Hurry back, my little one," you say and your face looks green in only the light of the alarm clock.

The rug is soft under my feet. But it is also thick and it feels like quicksand. As I walk, I allow myself to realize that I should be home, sleeping in my warm bed, hanging my toes out from under the sheet so my nail polish can dry and match my outfit for tomorrow.

I am surprised that I can put my right foot in front of the left. As I trudge toward the bathroom, I can see the sad front door, which is only locked from the inside. I pause, naked in the darkness. I look at the front door and I wonder.

Could I make it to the door before you knew where I was going? Could I make it down the stairs without you shooting me? Could I make it to the pay phone to call home? Or would you grab me by the wrists, put an actual gun to the back of my head, and take me away?

I look down at my underdeveloped fourteen-year-old body and press play on the possibility.

I forecast my family's pain. Me living somewhere in the middle of America. You having your capture of me so well planned, just as you had every lie planned. My brother searching for his little sister as he used to in hide-and-seek. My father engulfed with rage. My mother exhausted by the hunt and ruined by your evil soul. It is your last trick, and you are able to keep me from them for the rest of my life.

I stand here and let my imagination run. I have been letting it run in English class, too. In the most clear and vivid fashion, I have started to obsess over this nightmare. It has replaced my dreams of my wedding day or picking the name of my first daughter. It replaces these normal adolescent dreams, not because I yearn to be with you, but because you have convinced me that this is the way life is going to be for me.

As I contemplate my escape from you, I contemplate the consequence of you catching up. It is dry and hot and lonely. Maybe somewhere in Alabama. We move often and I am not allowed in public with you. I don't get to play sports or go to college. Of course, I cannot talk to either of the Maggies; you are certain that they will tell my parents where I am. So I cannot talk to anyone. Once again, although I am with you, I am alone.

What if I forget how to speak?

We are in a trailer park. The classic Hollywood depiction of what life on the run would be like. My young mind builds the image of my future on what I have seen on television, in movies, and this image scares me. You continue to make me hide. Ride in the car with my seat reclined if not in the foot space. Always running to the back of the trailer when a neighbor needs eggs.

You bring your dog Zoe, and not my dog from the picture.

And so I know what life would look like. I can see what my future would be. And then I think of volleyball practice tomorrow and my feet begin to move toward the bathroom.

I know I must go back to you. I think of your body in the bed waiting for me as I sit on the safety of the cold toilet seat.

I hate your breasts. The way they feel and the way they look. I am not attracted to them. If I said that out loud, I think that you might kill me. So I say it over and over again in my head.

I return and play a different game this time. I let my eyes fill with helium and turn into balloons. They leave my head and float to the ceiling.

Some time has passed. I can barely admit this to myself, but I have fallen asleep. And waking up may be the hardest part.

My body feels warm and I feel safe. The blankets are a Pepto-Bismol pink and I hate the color, but I love the way they feel. I am laying at a diagonal. I hear a noise and I fight through a deep cloud of exhaustion to force my eyes open. The safety evaporates through my skin. And then, all at once, I know where I am.

My first thought, before all others, is to look out of the window. I expect to see headlights coming up the driveway. I spin my head to check, halfway hoping there is someone coming and halfway praying they are not. No matter the outcome, checking feels good. Wondering is the hardest part. And no, no headlights. The darkness stays.

The clock's noise, although set on the lowest setting, makes my insides feel as though they are rattling. I look at the fake wood on the outside of the clock that I have always hated. *Why didn't you just buy a black or white clock? It's not as though anyone thinks that a digital alarm clock is actually made out of wood.* Even after you slide the alarm to the off position, the noise echoes in my ears.

You are right here. Sitting up in the bed, your back leaning against a pillow. You are fully awake and I know that you have not slept. You put your body there, between me and the alarm clock, so that you can set it and turn it off.

Your bony arm reaches over; you have all but stopped eating since you first kissed me. You always say, "I'm losing weight for you, so that you will be more attracted to me."

I will always hate how you look.

And my heart races at what will come next and my mind follows. *Will you try to touch me again? Will you tell me how much I liked what you did to me? Will you tell me that I made you do it? Will you be mad that I fell asleep before I could do those things to you?*

I have my first high school sporting event ever on Friday, my first volleyball game, and I am mad that I am here.

Why am I thinking about that? There is so much more that needs to happen before that game. The shower, the candy, the soda, the steps, the car door, the blanket, the drive, the light check, the drop off, the walk down the hill, the gate, my dog, the slider, the stairs, my mom's room, the hallway, the bathroom, the book, the doorstop, the dummy, and finally my bed.

You get up from the bed and my eyes are glad that you are already dressed. I am glad because your clothes mean that this is over—for now.

We get out of your apartment, which is a production in and of itself. You feed me my favorite candy so that I can "wake up" and be alert as I prep for reentry into my home. The glass tub of sour watermelons sits invitingly on the counter in your kitchen. I grab two fistfuls before you have time to direct me this time. As I head toward the door, I pop three of the gummies into my mouth and bite down on the crystalized sugary goodness. I hate that I still love the way these taste.

"Wait here," you say in a hiss. "I need to go outside and check first and then I will come get you." You always check the outside surroundings before I go anywhere. You move as fast as the wind and, before I know it, you have gone out the door, down the outside stairs, looped your car around, and are back in front of my face. "Okay, let's go," you say as you look at the space behind your body.

I know what you want me to do. You want me to walk down the stairs in sync with you so that the downstairs neighbors are fooled into thinking that there is only one of us.

Upon approaching your car, you and I get in at the same time. "Wait!" you say with a scowl once we are inside the car. "Don't close the door until we pull out."

With headlights off, the car creeps in reverse down your long and bumpy driveway. I lay in the passenger seat, which is fully reclined, and I am thankful for this step up from the foot space.

With lights switched on and the car forced into drive, we make our way toward my house, only not directly. Driving to Moraga on Highway 24 through Orinda never made sense to me. I know that you have a reason, but I think that you are crazy. You have utterly lost your mind and, suddenly, there is nothing more in the world that I want other than to get as far away from you as possible.

We enter the freeway to take our indirect, nonsensical route home. I imagine what would happen if I dropped my body out of your speeding Subaru. The burn of the asphalt, the limpness of my body responding to the impact. It would hurt, but it would feel so good for everyone to know. The hurt would feel, and the hurt would be so reasonable. Burns and scrapes and scars on my skin that I could point to and say, "ouch, I hurt."

As I think of what it all would smell like, I realize that maybe then I could just stay in my own bed at night for a few days to heal. Maybe then my family would understand my pain and know what I have to face every day. My imagination runs wild thinking about the grey road digging deep into the side of my face.

Would you even stop? I imagine blood running down my face, and through the glare of rushing ambulance lights, I can see the retreating squint of your taillights. Leaving me there so that you are safe. A smashed smile covers my face as I wait for my own safety.

My heart pumps harder and harder as I think of the consequences to this freedom, and I am wide awake. My smile is short-lived and only in my mind. It is brought to an abrupt stop as I imagine the high school whispers in the aftermath.

Instead of dreaming, I focus on the task at hand: sneaking into my house and not allowing anyone to know.

"Honey, wake up. It's time," you say to me and touch my arm.

You think that I was sleeping from the time we left your apartment. Little did you know I was planning my escape. And even though the blueprints flew out the window, it was fun to draw them. Plus, pretending to sleep is better than hearing you talk about what you did to me, how I begged you for it, that I wanted it.

"You were amazing tonight," you say with a smile and a look out of the corner of your eye. Your words, just like the asphalt, dig deep into my skin.

You look at me differently and I hope that you can't read my mind and know that I almost jumped out of your car. If you did know, you would take me away for sure. Or at the very least, sneak into my kitchen and put arsenic in the Cinnamon Toast Crunch. Your look lingers and I believe that you know at least this much: *I hate you.*

"I hope that the lights are off." I say the only thing that will come out of my mouth. As I hear my words, I know that they ring half true.

"I'm sure that they will be," you say and your dismissiveness makes my trembling insides feel unrealistic and silly.

As the car climbs Carr Drive, my throat gets tighter with each ascending step, I find myself mostly hoping that the house is black. The beautiful home that held my very happy childhood, that was once full of light and life, is asleep. I find myself begging the universe that I can get back in, keep everyone happy, and play outside hitter tomorrow.

A full breath of oxygen fills my lungs when I see that just one small outside light has been left on by mistake. A tiny piece of me wonders if it possible that a fairy left this on so that I could see my way around the backyard and through the slider. A tiny piece hopes that it is my other life welcoming me home. I find pieces of this hope and hold on for dear life.

"Okay, let's get you back in that house," you say and your voice has traces of your old self-—my old basketball coach—in it.

My home, you mean. It is my home, not that house. I wish I could rip your eyeballs out of their sockets.

"I'm ready," I don't finish my sentence . . . *to be done with you and done with all of this.*

We pull to the top of my hill and I open the door. I'm pretty sure that you kiss me, but I don't feel it because my mind has already stepped out the door, ready to get back in my bed.

As my feet hit the asphalt, I wish it was my face and that I didn't throw my blueprints out the window. If I get caught now, people will think that I wanted all of this. If they find me sneaking back in, I will be in trouble. I will be your accomplice. If they would have found me half dead on the freeway, at least then they could have started to understand.

It's colder outside than it was last night. Rob is coming to stay with you tomorrow night and I am glad that I won't know the temperature difference at 4 A.M. tomorrow morning. I run down my hill and think of the words of my current high school PE teacher and cross-country coach: "Let the hill do the work for you, Kristen." But I know, the production that awaits me tonight, the life that I have to hold together, is work that only I can do.

And so I reenter. Quiet as a mouse, I go through the side gate and the back slider. Cautious and aware of each inch my body moves. Through the kitchen, up the stairs, and back into my room I reenter my real life. And with each minute that passes (and there are a lot because being this careful, this silent, takes time) I convince myself that this is only a bad dream. That you are who you were then. Who you are now is only a nightmare.

I am fourteen, but I feel much younger. I feel as though I am watching Mr. Rogers and the trolly has just come back from a trip to make-believe land. Sure, it's not good make-believe. But as I settle back into my bed to catch an hour and a half of sleep, I am happy that at least it isn't real.

CHAPTER SEVENTEEN

Magic and Madness in the Month of March

I need to remember how this feels. How I feel. Proud, calm, confident. I know I did the best I could have ever done. And I need to stay with this feeling for the next few days.

Somehow I wish that the seconds could tick slower, that I could just hang on to the joy of this.

Last night I had one of the most important experiences of my life. My athletes found something magical within themselves and did something that no one thought they could. In less than forty-eight hours I will have to take the witness stand. And, again, I will have one of the most important experiences of my life. I, too, will look for something magical within myself. And I, too, will do something no one thinks I can. Especially one person.

A freshman stands up, shocks the country, and wins an NCAA title. A senior captain reclaims an NCAA title, proving that her first win was not a fluke. A relay comes together to shatter an American record. A team, ranked seventh, then fifth, then fourth, then third, then second, comes together to win an NCAA team championship.

My magic as a coach is special and fun and warm. My magic as a survivor is dark. It does not feel the same. But in a very sound way I know that my black magic is what allows me to find the other magic in my life. And I am on the brink of saying that it was worth it.

For a living, I coach. I get to go into the homes of the top swimmers in the country and sell my product, my school, my program. At the dinner table, I make a promise to the parents of high schoolers that I will push their kids, tell them the truth, and love them the whole way through. I tell them that I will do everything in my power to help their maturing children grow into wonderful swimmers and wonderful people. I promise to do my best to continue the job they started. And, inside, I promise to do the job in which Julie betrayed me.

As freshmen they are still kids. They look at me for advice, direction, and leadership. They are only eighteen: still kids and still seven years older than I was when I met the person who was supposed to be my coach, the person whom I was supposed to look to for advice, direction, and leadership. Energetic and wide-eyed, these barely adults are not only figuring out how to swim fast, they are also trying to figure out how to go to school at one of the best universities in the world. They are trying to figure out when to add fabric softener, how often to call home, what kind of cough medicine to use, how to ask a roommate not to slam the door after a late night, how much to drink and how much not to drink, which boyfriends are worth keeping, and in which order all of this matters. I should like to think I help them with these things. And each time I do, I do something that Julie had no intention of doing for me.

As sophomores they think that they have things figured out. A new swagger in their walk reminds their new freshmen teammates to watch their step. They are surprised suddenly that things are different now. Their senior mother hens are gone, and with their departure comes a new responsibility on these sophomores' backs. As returners, they are expected to know the expectations. In many ways, I think that the most growing occurs here in the second year. The transition from being a follower to a leader is a metamorphosis of sorts. I do not know which is more rewarding, helping spin the cocoon or watching wings break through.

The junior year is different for each athlete. It is an individual trip dictated by the successes and failures of previous years. Some athletes are coming back from incredible feats, personal bests, school records, and NCAA championships. Some athletes are coming back from injury, illness, parental pressure, disappointment, and unfinished business. In the third year, this journey—mixed and unpredictable—becomes their own. My role is always different, but I am always on their path. A profound sense of anger and sadness fills my gut as I realize that Julie's destination with me had always been evil. And a profound sense of pride fills my heart as I know that the path I walk with my athletes leads to something pure and real and good. And that the destination lies along the path.

The senior year evaporates all too quickly. I remember as an athlete myself beginning to wish the weeks, the days, and even the practices would last longer. When something so special is about to be taken away, the heart aches for more. By now these athletes have carved a special place in my heart, and I am here to remind them that this will never be over. They will always be a part of Cal swimming and they are forever changed and better for having been a part of this experience. And as they graduate, having allowed me to coach them and impact their lives, they hand me back a piece of my soul that was wrongfully stolen.

This must be what healing feels like. Remaking my life. Making the wrong things right.

I walk around the pool deck, a smile on my face, the most decorated coach at my side, and the best athletes in the water. I know people are jealous. They look at me and think that I got lucky. They see me laughing with my girls, dancing with them before the meet starts, and probably think they could do a better job than I. I am sure many of them think that Teri is the coach while I am just the cheerleader. But it is not about them or what they think. It is my job and I get immense joy from it. It is about one person and one person alone: it is about me.

I work hard for the girls because they deserve it. I work hard for Teri because she has earned the support. But the thing that drives me most is me. Coaching makes me feel a tiny bit better everyday.

Months have passed since I first saw Julie at the arraignment in the fall. More than a hundred days have gone by since I sat with Chuck and he told me about the devil outside of his office. And somehow I am still alive. Still working. Still coaching.

I would be lying if I said that it was easy. Any of it. Breathing, eating, driving in my car, making it through each day—it all feels impossible in the moment, but here I am. Julie has been out on bail this entire time, and part of me expects her to be around every corner.

Chuck picked Julie out of a photo lineup, but Joyce said that because Chuck saw her booking photo at one point, he was biased and the evidence of her stalking me outside of his office would not be admissible in court. So she roams free.

The horrible parts of my life feel so horrible that I am forced to hang on to the good stuff, like winning an NCAA title.

I walk away from this weekend incredibly proud to be a coach at Cal. I walk away being utterly inspired by my athletes. Moved to be my best. I walk away believing fully in the power of magic. I walk away and head into the courtroom, feeling that this has given me legs to take the stand.

But now the meet is over. And the days, the hours, the minutes, and the seconds are melting away toward the morning of March 22.

"This is only the preliminary hearing, Kristy," Scott says to me on the plane ride home. "The burden of proof is low, and even though you have to testify, it won't take as long as the actual trial will." I think of telling my story to a live audience, and his words bring no comfort.

My worry goes from rational to irrational at a remarkable rate. Sometimes now, sometimes then, and sometimes in between, my mind would make the most unlikely scenarios into inevitable realities.

As I sit on the plane next to my now sleeping husband, my brain finds the idea that Julie will be in the Oakland airport upon our arrival. It is Sunday morning, the trial is Tuesday morning, she would not want to arrive the day before. As my heart begins to race alongside my spinning mind, I frantically try to get a wireless signal 2,000 feet in the air so that I can look up the Southwest Airlines flight arrival schedule from Salt Lake City, Utah.

Discouraged by my inability to get my iPhone to work in the air above Arizona, I become frustrated with myself and this unrealistic fear. My throat starts to close, my eyes start to swell, and I realize that Julie is the one who made me this way. Following me on the running trail, watching me at swim meets, putting things in my locker, she was everywhere to my fourteen-year-old self. What may seem unrealistic, far-fetched, silly to others, has always seemed normal and expected to me.

And the drive home from the airport presents more challenges. As the wheels turn, the car gets farther away from an NCAA championship and closer to the unknown. The miles shorten and so does my time to prepare for the impossible.

Eating presents some challenges. Sleeping presents some challenges. Walking, talking, and breathing present challenges.

But these challenges are only that. Not road blocks but road bumps. Somehow I drive over them and around them and I arrive on the morning of the big event.

It is cold outside, the sky wanting to rain. I wake up in my warm bed feeling surprised that I slept the night before, surprised that my heart isn't racing, surprised that I feel ready. I take a shower, put on my makeup, and get dressed without a single incident. I am utterly shocked that it is not impossible. I need to eat and my mouth, my throat, my stomach all do their part. Scott does his part, "Okay, Kristy. Let's go," and he helps me get to the car.

Driving to the courthouse feels like floating. I am unaware of the turns that Scott makes, the path that he drives, and I am surprised when he settles into a parking spot behind the courthouse. Without seeing them, I know that members of my army have settled into their own parking spots and have descended into the courthouse.

I am scared. I am terrified. I can barely walk. So as I put one foot in front of other, next to my husband, I pretend that I am walking toward the podium to accept our NCAA championship trophy. I remember the swagger, the sensation of being the best team in the United States. I hold on to the happiness of jumping in the pool to celebrate with my athletes and march ahead.

CHAPTER EIGHTEEN

Enter Eve

I used to love our chats on the phone. Last year I would look forward to them. I would always find a corner of the house all my own. I felt older than my other friends to have you on the other end. My mom had her concerns, but I thought it was cool to have found a friend in you.

"What do you and Natali talk about?" my mom would wonder. I hated coming down the stairs, waiting for my mom to ask the ominous parenting question. I also hated the way that she said your name. I would stop and stand square at my mom, ready to defend you.

"Nothing, mom . . ." I would think of the secret Slurpee runs and would search for an acceptable response. "Just something funny that happened at school today." My mom's eyes, like those of a mother bear wondering why her cub had strayed from the lair, would meet mine in silent question. Without her saying a word, I could hear her wondering what was so funny that would cause a teacher to talk to a student for an entire hour. I tried the various approaches that you fed me to feed my mom; "She is helping me with my soccer moves," or "The other girls were mean to me today and I am trying to learn how to stand up for myself." But no matter what I said or how I said it, the look that stared back at me was always the same: the unmistakable glare of a mom's distrust.

I hated that look. The Look. I hated that I could not change it, that I could not convince my mom that you were a good mentor for me. I remember thinking that you were right, that she was just jealous about our friendship. Now I look back on last year through different lenses. It's ironic that my mom had been right about you. But I can't tell her that now.

The cell phone is hot in my hand and it burns my right cheek as I press it into my head, hoping that it could just dissolve into my skin. There are two interesting things about this phone: you and I are the only people who know about this cell phone, and I do not know anyone else who owns a cell phone. I know a few rich Moraga people who have car phones or pagers, but no one who has a cell phone. It is made by Nokia. I had never heard of Nokia before having this phone; I guess Nokia does not make electronics for kids. And you always talk about how you need to hurry home near the first part of the month, to get the cell phone statement in case Rob is coming over to the apartment that day. It's weird thinking about you having to pay a bill. I wonder what a bill looks like. I wonder how much it costs for you to talk to me.

I don't know what time it is, only that it is likely after 2 A.M. I didn't finish my homework until after 11:15 P.M. Then I had to wait for my mom to go to bed after finishing her wine. My dad always falls asleep on the couch and then comes up the stairs sometime around midnight. That is about the time that I called you. The cell phone is running low on battery life, and it usually lasts for about two and a half hours. You put a new battery in my locker, so that this one would be fresh when I called, and you will likely switch this one out for a new one tomorrow. As I said, from all mathematical calculations, it is about 2 A.M.

I used to have a clock in my room. But I unplugged it because the numbers reminded me of the one next to your bed. And your bed makes my body feel as if I am made of shattered glass.

You are moaning on the other end of the phone and your hushed whisper of a voice is somehow loud in my ear. "I just can't stop thinking about what happened last time," you say.

I remember the so-called last time that you are talking about. It was in your apartment and only two nights ago.

I say nothing back to you.

"You make me crazy," you say, and even though you say it often, it still confuses me. I imagine the movie I watched on the safety of my couch last weekend with my mom—one of her favorites from 1975, *One Flew Over the Cuckoo's Nest*. I imagine you, in your house, borrowing Jack Nicholson's straitjacket. *Do you mean crazy like that or crazy in a different way?* Then I imagine the episode of *Baywatch* and Pamela Anderson telling the new lifeguard that he "drives her crazy." I think *Baywatch* is the kind of crazy you are talking about.

But I can't be sure.

As much as I used to love our calls last year, I hate these more. My head is sweaty, burning with the heat of this secret cell phone. My heart is racing on two accounts. The first is that I do not know what you are going to say next and I am not sure how I am supposed to respond. And, second, I sleep on my left side so that I can see the pale hue of light under my door. I stare hard at this light, begging for it to stay uninterrupted by the foot of a tipped off mother or father. It all feels like all too much to handle. And I need a little help.

Without you knowing that any of this is happening, I call in for backup. I have a little friend who no one knows about; especially not you. After all, I'm not so sure anyone would like her.

She is, as they say it, rough around the edges. She wears her hair short, in a pixie cut. And it is almost as black as the night's sky outside. She is smaller than I. It's unfortunate that she doesn't like sports, because she is wiry and her insides look as if they might be made out of springs, and I bet she could run pretty darn fast. She is very pale, having never seen the light of day. She prefers to keep her nails short, either painted black or deep navy blue. With her small and striking features, there is no denying that she is pretty. Sometimes when I look at her, I think that one of her parents may have been a fairy. I am not sure how old she is; her voice sounds younger but her actions seem older. In a lot of ways she is the opposite of me. Except her eyes: they are exactly the same.

Her name is Eve.

You make me keep everything a secret. You have made me live entirely alone with the truth of what you do to me. I am sick of it. I need a friend. And now it is time for me to keep a secret from you.

Eve, my copilot, allows for me to navigate through maintaining perfect grades, keeping your thirst quenched, scoring goals in my soccer games, protecting my parents, tracking the whereabouts of the cell phone, and making sure I have a date for the Sadie Hawkins dance. She was born in my driveway; the day you kissed half of my mouth and pretended it was an accident. No accident that, off that side of my mouth slid a piece of me. A piece that has kept growing and now can help me. A piece called Eve.

Sometimes she just holds my hand. Sometimes she just tries to memorize everything in case things go terribly wrong. Sometimes she takes my place. Sometimes I feel as though I can handle you all on my own, and Eve doesn't come.

Tonight she knows I am tired, that I have a big test tomorrow, and that I already have that lumpy feeling when I swallow just before the onset of strep throat. So she yanks the phone out of my hand, covers the receiver, and says, "I got this."

I am glad that she is there and that Eve will take over. I settle into the bed to close my eyes, but I can hear Eve on the phone telling you the things that you want to hear. Although the phone is gone from my ear, I can still hear the words slithering out of your mouth.

"I wanted to wait to touch you down there . . ." Your voice is excited and hurried and I am glad Eve has the phone because I wouldn't have any idea what to say. You continue, "But I couldn't help myself and I know how much you like it . . ."

I want to scream, but then my eyes return to the seam of light under my door, and I know I must stay silent. I look at Eve and our blue eyes meet.

We have a secret conversation without words. We agree on one thing; I did not like how it felt and neither did Eve. I pull my eyes away from Eve's, even embarrassed that she saw what you have been doing to me.

"Why are you so quiet?" Your demanding words jolt the both of us out of our private conversation and back to the phone. "Please don't be mad at me. I told you, I couldn't help myself." In the matter of three sentences you have gone from sounding angry to sounding sad.

Eve, please help me.

"I am not mad," Eve says and her voice is simple and young-sounding. And maybe Eve is not mad. I am never ever really sure with Eve, how she is feeling or what she is actually thinking. Often those things do not matter. Really she only exists to keep you satisfied.

"Oh, good," You sound relieved. "After all, in the middle of everything, you forced my hand down there."

No, I didn't. I remember my face turning hot and red, hoping your bony hand would cease in the downward direction. But it did not.

Eve and I stay silent on the phone. We hope that you are close to being done. "Do you know what I want to do to you when you are all grown up?"

"What?" Eve takes her time with this word and uses her little girl voice, as if a five year old were wondering "what" is underneath the Christmas tree.

Although I am grateful for Eve's answering, I am paralyzed by your statement. This is your script; what you always say. But you do not wait until I am grown up—unless "growing up" means waiting forty-eight hours until the weekend.

"I am going to kiss you down there." Your voice sounds as though you can't catch your breath, almost as though you are dribbling a basketball up and down the court. *What is all the commotion is about?*

As Eve continues on with responses that satisfy your conversation, I think of a few years earlier. Once again I wander back to that spring day in sixth grade when Jon Danton kissed me after school behind the English building. My first kiss was a quick and dry peck on the lips. Yet, still, it felt as though the whole world stopped spinning so that I could climb to the top and yell, "I've had my first kiss and it was miraculous!" It made me feel as though my insides were going to burst wide open.

You also make me feel as though my insides are going to burst, because it feels as though you are filling me with black sand that may cause me to explode. And when you kiss me, it feels the opposite of my first kiss.

I take myself back to that day behind the English building, adjacent to the baseball fields, and try to hang on. I try to picture it again, but this time I imagine Jon walking up to me and getting on his knees. The scene changes, I am standing in the center of a spotlight and the entire school is laughing at me. Jon leans forward, toward the zipper fly of my favorite and final pair of jeans from Gap Kids and "kisses me down there." I almost throw up over my entire bed.

I look back at Eve and she is glaring at me as if to say, "you need to be on the lookout or getting some rest, or taking care of this crazy lady on the phone for me, not making up stories or thinking of a time that will never exist again."

Eve is right. When I float away like that, I risk everything. I risk you knowing that Eve has taken my place. I risk my parents coming to the door and me not having time to hide the phone. I risk the unmistakable pain of dreaming of what was and waking up to what is.

The breathing is louder. *Honestly, why are you moving around so much? It sounds as though you are on the stairmaster in the middle of the night.*

Apparently, Eve doesn't know either. She knows she has to find out in order to keep playing the game with you. "What are you doing, Tooli?" She knows just how to make her voice sound precisely innocent, as if she is asking the questions with wide eyes and high eyebrows. She picks one of your favorite nicknames, in hopes of not making you mad with the question.

"I . . . oh . . . I'm thinking about you, about your beautiful body." Your mouth lingers on the last two words as they come rolling off your lips. Eve looks over at me and I look down at my body, covered with the flowered quilt I got for my birthday last year. No one has ever told me that my body was beautiful before. Fast, strong, quick . . . yes. But beautiful? Maybe my face is beautiful, but not my body. I think of how I felt in the shower this morning, hoping my private parts would run down the drain. Eve answers for me.

"My body isn't . . . beautiful." I wonder why it takes Eve so long to form sentences.

"You are kidding me, right? I want every single part of it," you say, shoving the 'w' of the want right though the phone.

What does that even mean? And you never answered Eve's question about what you are doing? "Thinking about me" does not explain all of the hustle and bustle on the phone.

"You know that teddy bear you gave me?" Still, your voice doesn't sound right.

I know the one you are talking about. It is a Care Bear that I got for my first birthday. It is yellow with a red heart on his bum. He has a white belly and a cupcake patch in the center with a single lit candle in the middle. You saw it in my room last year, before you started hurting me, and said you loved it and always wanted that exact Care Bear when you were little.

"Here, have it. For all the help with soccer and stuff . . . ," I had said to you that day in eighth grade, shrugging my shoulders casually. I remember just being happy that you weren't making fun of the fact that I still had teddy bears and troll dolls scattered through my should-be teen room. And I didn't really miss it. I actually haven't even thought of that bear until just now.

What does that bear have to do with anything?

Eve knows that I could never handle this and says in a softer way, "Yeah, I remember that bear . . ."

"Well, I am thinking about you . . . about your body . . . about how much you responded to what I did last time. I am touching myself the way I touched you. And I am using your bear down there because it reminds me of you."

I look at Eve. She knows. I can't live through this. I can't take another minute. I watched a movie in History class once. It was set somewhere in the south and sometime during a war. A general appears at the front door of an unsuspecting mother. After the knock on the door, and the door being opened, the perfectly folded American flag is extended to the mother. But she cannot accept the flag nor her son's death. There on the white wood porch, in the afternoon heat, her brain separates from her body. It's not dying, but passing out, as death for the moment is too much to bear. She falls gracefully into the arms of the general. As I fall, I am grateful for Eve and the safety of my bed.

CHAPTER NINETEEN

Taking the Stand

They are ready for me. I believe I am ready for them. Geoff stands, his right hand over the front of his suit jacket, as I pass by him to take the stand. Geoff Lauter is Joyce Blair's associate in the Attorney General's Office and I am secretly grateful of Geoff's large physical presence.

Without looking at her, I know exactly what she is doing. I can feel her smirk as I ascend the steps. Her attorney sits next to her, and he feels nervous to me. Her legs are crossed and she is lounging back in her seat as though she were sitting out on her deck in Utah enjoying a glass of California Cab. He is in the front of his chair and I wonder if he has ever done a case like this before.

The judge is Leslie Landau, a kind-looking woman who, with her glasses, tilted head, and concerned stare, reminds me of a kind and patient tortoise I read about once as a child. Her right hand holds a pen, and as I imagine what is before me, I wonder if anyone can believe this unbelievable story.

I turn and face my audience. Scott is in perfect position and I can see his perfect face. My friends and my mom sit close together, on the righthand side of the courtroom. My mom has a habit of doodling on everything in sight. She has brought a doodle book to write bad words about Julie, but I don't think my mom has the vocabulary to describe this. My dad sits next to my mom, my brother sits directly behind him, and as I look at my brother's hands on my dad's shoulders, I wonder why it has taken something like this for a son to touch his father in such a way.

The wood railing that surrounds the stand is my protection, and before I know what has happened, I have raised my hand and promised to tell the whole truth. As I land in the chair beneath me, I am surprised how solid the wood feels, how still the air is, and how ready I am.

I am surprised when the judge starts and not Geoff. "Apparently, this is no longer a minor. For the purpose of preliminary hearing, do you want the transcript to refer to her as Jane Doe?"

I don't look at her, but I know Julie wears a soft grin.

Now Geoff's loud voice enters the room, "No, your honor. We made a decision that Ms. Cunnane would like her name to be known."

Right off the bat, things are not going the way Julie thought they would. Here, another piece of the secret smashed into a million pieces. I see her head snap quickly around to look at Rob.

My wise tortoise reaches her neck down and peers at me over her glasses. "Very good," the judge looks down at me and I can tell that in another setting, she would give me a standing ovation. "Will you please state your name, and spell your first and last name?" Her lips grin slightly and I can feel her kindness.

"Kristen Cunnane," my voice is strong and sturdy. It is louder than I thought it would be, it almost sounds foreign, as I spell my name for the court reporter, who sits in front and slightly below me.

Geoff's voice is kind and his questions sound soft and careful. He starts by asking my birthdate. And in the same voice he says, "Do you know someone named Julie Correa, the defendant in this case?" He tilts his head.

And just when I think I am settling down, my breath disappears as I remember that she is twenty feet away from me. "I do."

"Would you please point to her and describe what she is wearing?" Geoff knows that these questions are getting hard for me.

"She is there. With the pink sweater on." It is only for a moment, but my eyes move toward her and I see the blur of her body. She sits there, the situation mandates her silence, and suddenly for the first time in knowing Julie, I am in control. I lift my finger and point.

Geoff begins to weave the fabric of my meeting Julie in sixth grade, the bond that we formed through sports, the idolization I felt toward her as my teacher, coach, and role model. As I describe my middle school years, I can feel the heat of the junior high school blacktop underneath my feet, smell the freshly cut grass of the soccer fields, and understand exactly who and where I was when Julie entered my life.

"She was really close with a lot of the older girls . . . and she coached them," I explain. "So, I began to really look up to her and wanted to impress her when I ran the mile and wanted to impress her when I played sports." Geoff and I dance through what everyone will call the "grooming" phase.

"Yes," I say. Geoff has asked me a question about my teacher-student relationship with Julie in seventh grade. "I began keeping books in her office. I cared a great deal about if Julie liked me and thought that I was good at sports."

Time slows and I exist in a sequestered space. I can all but touch the moment of my past that I am describing. I am aware of my family and friends facing me. I know that Julie is in this room with me. But I am fully occupied with Geoff and his questions.

"When you were in eighth grade, did you still have contact with the defendant?" Geoff asks.

"Yes, I got to know her much better because the year prior she asked me to be one of her TAs for the year and I thought that was like the coolest thing ever, because we all wanted to be her TA." I look down at my hands and try to remember what they would have looked like when I was only thirteen.

"Why was that?" Geoff wonders.

"She was the most popular teacher in the school. And she won awards for teacher of the year."

I can feel Landau's eyes on me and my stomach tightens, as if I am watching a horror movie for the second time. I know what lies ahead and I know that there is no way to press pause.

"And she asked you to be her TA?" Geoff takes me in the necessary direction. "How did that make you feel?"

"Good. I was really excited because when you're a TA, that's kind of like you're getting older and you're helping a teacher, and you're not just a little kid anymore."

Suddenly I am talking through the time period in which Julie would bring me a bagel every day and I notice Teri shift in her chair. Without looking all the way back at Teri, I see a light bulb go off in her head. Just as she suddenly realizes how to fix a hitch in a stroke, or a solution to a team dynamic, she has just realized who this teacher was in my life. And like so many times on the pool deck, my realization follows hers. I pause for a moment, look down at my chipped nail polish, and say, "Outside of my family, I looked up to Julie more than any other single person in my childhood or adolescent life." And a small piece of me understands how this all happened.

The plot of the horror movie thickens as we get toward the end of the eighth grade. The gifts, the Washington DC trip, the PE award, and the mountain trip. I notice the two Maggies in the audience, both crying as they were present for so much of this beginning.

Now I have reached the day when my life was split in half. "We were in the driveway, and she leaned over to kiss me on the cheek. She had begun kissing me on the cheek to say goodbye. But instead of kissing me on the cheek, she kissed me half on the mouth." I can see it all happening, the slant the car was positioned in my uphill driveway, the warm summer night, and the feeling of walking into my house and not knowing which way to turn. I am aware of my parents now, imagining this night, searching their memory for where they sat in the family room, which episode of 20/20 was on, and why they didn't run outside to save me.

The summer of 1996 was consumed with lies to my parents in order to satisfy her. I recount the volleyball lessons and the episodes in her office. I describe for Geoff the physical acts that took place at the beginning of my freshman year. I walk through the apartment, her car, my closet, the number of times, the feelings I had. I hear the words "digital penetration" and "oral copulation" come out of my mouth and I am shocked that they do.

Since the day that I fell in love with Scott, I had assumed that he could not hear these things and still love me. Part of why I need him here today is to know that he can, that hearing them will not make him stop loving me, and that he will not be disgusted. I look back at him and I know that telling the truth, that freeing my soul of this black sand, is the most important thing in the world to him. He sits, arms crossed loosely, small dimples touching his checks, and says to me with his Tahoe blue eyes, "Keep going, Kristy." I believe he may love me more having seen the strength and courage I have today. My story leads to how I met Scott and my escape from slavery.

I am surprised when I look up at the clock and see that I have been speaking with Geoff for over two hours. "Your honor, no further questions at this time."

Relief? Yes. Pride? That, too. Complete? I think I am getting there.

My answers with Geoff, the telling of my story in front of the people who matter most in my life, is a step in others knowing me. It is a step of my outside matching my inside. It is a step toward truth.

And so, as I step out of the courtroom, my family and friends asking if I am hungry and if I want lunch, Scott takes the lead. He knows that the worst is yet to come. He knows that the cross-examination will wreak havoc, that even the easy questions may be tricks, and that the hard questions may make me question why I am doing this in the first place.

"I will take her to get food," Scott says with authority. My mind wonders if I would ever have the opportunity to spend an hour with all of the people in the world who mean the most to me. But my heart knows that the person who means the very most knows me the very best.

As Scott grabs my hand, I realize he is still here and Julie was wrong; people can hear this and still love me. We head to the car, and in three words he makes my heart shine: "You were amazing."

CHAPTER TWENTY

Stairway to Hell

It is just before 7 A.M. and I am glad that my mom keeps the house so warm. It makes getting out of bed in the morning a touch easier. I look around my room and know that I need to clean it. I don't have time. My clothes decorate the rocking chair in the corner and most of the items have been left inside-out from the last wear. My dressers—I have two of them because I have a lot of clothes—have drawers that are haphazardly peaking open. My mom hates it when I leave them ajar because she says it will cause the wood to warp, whatever that means.

Practically I have so many options of what to wear, but realistically I only have a few. I am in the fall of my freshman year, and as I gaze around the room, I try to pinpoint something that a high schooler would wear and also something that is not noticeably dirty. As much as I hate my cluttered room, I like that my mom won't come in and clean it without asking me first.

I settle for a pair of jeans left at the foot of my bed and my Campolindo High School sweatshirt with a growling cougar mascot on the back. I bought the grey hoodie this summer at orientation, following many envious years of looking at Marc's high school apparel. I pull on the size 4 Gap jeans and I am glad that, despite my current growth spurt, I have not moved on to a size 6. With no clean socks in my drawer, I am sure that my mom has done my laundry and that there is a fresh pair waiting for me downstairs. If I'm lucky, they might still be warm from the dryer.

I open my door to walk down the hallway and down to begin my day. I stop for a breath and realize that it was only recently that I started shutting the door to my bedroom. My heart squeezes with a twinge of pain and I know why; I have to shut the door to the evil part of my life.

The carpet is warm between my toes and the tattered cuff of my jeans trails behind my heels. I look to my right, and the familiar oil painting of my mom looks back at me. I smile a little, both because my mom did it herself, and because it would not be quite fancy enough for most Moraga homes. I pass my brother's room, which stands empty owing to his recent departure for UCLA.

At the top of the staircase I smell the "best part of waking up," and know that both my mom and dad are already sitting in the kitchen drinking their Folger's coffee. I have only tried coffee once, last year in eighth grade English class as part of a book report some kid did, and it tasted like dirty water. It seems like the worst part of waking up to me.

The house is occupied with all of the predictable morning sounds, although in general things are quieter now that Marc is gone. I can hear my dad's spoon hitting the edge of the cereal bowl as if to make certain that there is not a morsel left. My mom wrestles with the paper to find the crossword section and fold it just perfectly so that only the puzzle presents itself. As I begin to head down the stairs, I think I know exactly what I will see. My mom will be sitting on her favorite stool by the kitchen window, showered but still in her bathrobe. My dad will be at the table, plopped in his usual dinner spot and wearing khakis and a shirt too casual for most jobs. When I was growing up, this spot was often vacant during dinner hours owing to his long workdays, but ever since we dropped Marc at UCLA a month ago, my dad has been trying harder.

It is late October, but I am not sure what the actual date is. I know it is Friday, but I have never been good at knowing what calendar day we are on. I like the fall and I like my new school. Next week is homecoming and I am going with a sophomore boy who asked me. His name is Chris Rudolph and I don't really know him, so I can't really like him. But I like that he is a sophomore and I especially like that he asked me, out of the sea of freshman girls, to go with him.

I am distracted as I walk down the first few steps. My mind is wandering off to wonder what kind of dresses high schoolers wear to dances. Suddenly my body stops and turns to stone before my brain can fully interpret what I am seeing. I stand and stare.

From my vantage point, I can see the entryway to my home. It is floored with gold tile, which I am told is expensive, and softened with a blue entry rug. In the lefthand corner, a white porcelain cat sits, which I have been reminded not to break when roughhousing inside. On both the right and left sides of the heavy and oversided door are two skinny windows. The lines of these windows run at a diagonal and draw the shape of a diamond rather than a square. I am square with the window on the right, and I see past the insignificant grids of the window to the outside.

Directly in front of my house, pulling neatly to the side of the street, is a maroon station wagon. My body freezes in fear while my brain processes that it is you. You just bought this car to replace your teal, two-door Honda Accord. "I need to have more room to be with you," you had said and your words ring in my ears as I look at the evidence of the much larger car. I push my tongue to the roof of my mouth as I see the cusp of your head appear from the driver's side door and remember what you did to me in the car two weeks ago. You begin to walk toward my house with both normalcy and purpose. Up my stairs, as if there were nothing to hide.

I do the same. I copy you. I go up the stairs and head toward the safety of the bathroom. *What could you be doing here?* I travel the hallway, around the railing that protects the stairs, and pass my mom on the wall without noticing her this time. I move quickly, but my insides move much more quickly. I do not have time to consider how I am feeling, only to look for a slice of safety.

I turn right toward that bathroom that Marc and I share—the bathroom we used to share. I hear a knock at the door, which causes me to freeze in the doorway. *Why don't you just use the doorbell?*

I am still. With a primal sense I know that you are directly below me. I look at the staircase that I just stood on, and my ear canals open wide. I hear my dad and I know that he has heard your knock. His footsteps make way to the door and I listen from above.

"Oh, hi, Julie," my dad says in a voice loud enough for my mom to hear from the kitchen. *Does his voice sound different from when he used to see you last year? Do you notice his change?*

"Hi, I was hoping that I could talk to Kristen . . . and you guys. I was hoping that I could talk to all of you for a minute," you say, taking your time with your words. Your voice sounds chilled and calmed, and my best guess is that your head is slightly tipped to the left. My name floats up the stairs, into my ears, and causes my eyelids to pull further apart.

"Sure . . ." My dad's voice leaves a question at the end of his single word. It is a school day, a Friday; *what could you possibly need to talk to our family about in this moment?* My mind rewinds to last night and being on the phone with you. I remember you mentioning something about Mr. Witters, but I think that Eve was doing most of the work by then.

I can hear the much lighter and quicker footsteps of my mom moving in the kitchen and the adjacent laundry room. I imagine what she is doing now, going to grab clothes to cover her bathrobe, before hurrying to the front of the house.

My mom confronted you two weeks ago about giving me more space. She is worried that you still show an interest in me. She doesn't like that you still come to my sporting events. She is concerned that you are more than twice my age. And yet she doesn't know about the majority of the time we spend together. She has no idea of what you are doing to me. She would be crushed. I let out a deep exhale in the dark for another day.

"Kristen!" My dad's voice travels up the stairs, but my name sounds different coming from his mouth. I can't pretend that I fell into the toilet and got flushed down, so I begin the downward trek to the inevitability of what awaits me below.

Back on the stairs at the previous spot, I think of Maggie Red. I wish that she were walking down the stairs with me and that I wasn't alone on this step. I think of what it would feel like to hold her warm hand that is slightly smaller than my own. *But how could I explain this to her?* I think of the full moon last night. What if, suddenly, the universe forgot the principle of gravity and the moon, both heavy and cold, fell rapidly to the earth? As I walk down the stairs, I imagine the earth and the moon growing closer and closer, with innocent and ignorant humans below. But as the moon speeds and I walk, I know. I look up and see as the moon falls through the final layer of the atmosphere and lands, out of everywhere on the planet earth, squarely on my forehead.

The crushing pain makes my heart feel like a hard stone in the center of my chest. I have to force my eyes up to look at you. You are wearing a version of the usual: a white Adidas t-shirt, mesh shorts, and indoor soccer shoes. Of course, your hair falls just above your shoulders. I look at your lean calves, the ones I used to envy, and I wish that I could dig a knife through the center of one so that you could feel an ounce of this pain. You carry your car keys in your right hand, and looking at your right hand makes me want to scream. But I don't.

"Well, I wanted to come here and talk to you guys about something. Can we sit down for a moment?" You ask and point your nasty-looking nose toward my living room, which is to my left and to your right. You are bold as you march into this room as I frantically try to remember if you have ever soiled this part of my house before.

You settle into a stuffed rocking chair that is made of a deep red velour-like fabric. My dad sits in a chair that matches yours and that is across from you. My mom takes her place on an old and mostly unused sofa that faces the entry of the room.

I stand at the edge of the room, my feet refusing to enter fully. My bare feet hang over the ledge and maintain contact with the tile floor of the entryway. I am relatively certain that a realtor would call this a "step-down" living room in adding to the appraisal value our house.

"Some things have been coming out in the recent weeks." You begin in a careful and concerned way, but I know that you have a polished and perfect plan for saying whatever you are about to. Your eyes look concerned and soft at the corners, and I am reminded of how you looked at me when I sprained my ankle last year during a basketball game.

"Some girls have been coming forward and have been willing to talk to Mrs. Frank about Mr. Witters . . ." you leave room at the end of your sentence for interpretation. I imagine Mrs. Frank, now the principal at JM, listening to girls as they sob on her office couch.

With great difficulty, I remember more of what you said to me last night. I can just barely recall what happened on the phone. It feels like trying to remember a TV show that I wasn't really paying attention to. I wonder if that is because Eve was in charge.

"What about Mr. Witters?" My dad's voice comes from the right and echoes into my ear. I stand still in the middle of the scene. The grandfather clock to my left begins to ticks a little slower and the pendulum now swings in slow motion. A small dark circle forms in my eyes and my peripheral vision is removed. I turn my whole head as I await your response.

"Well, it is no secret that Mr. Witters has done inappropriate things to girls in his classroom. Things that have made them
feel . . . uncomfortable." You look at my dad, but I know that you
are really looking at me. I remember the day that Mr. Witters
kissed me on the cheek for the first time. I had kept that a secret
from my parents. The air is congested in the formal living room.

"And . . ." as you continue, you turn down the knob on the
volume of your voice—"it is looking like he did far worse things
than just make kids uncomfortable."

What am I supposed to do? What am I supposed to say? You sit
there, six feet from our Baldwin piano. The bench, almost within
your reach, where I sat alongside my mom. Right there, learning
the keys to "Hot Cross Buns," before you ever crossed my life.
Heat radiates from my skin as I look at you sitting within the
walls of my childhood.

I can feel my parents searching for the right words to say. I
can sense their minds spinning, and hoping that I will not confirm their now festering fears.

The room looks to you. "Kristen . . ." *Stop saying my name!* "I
wanted to come here and talk to you because I have been talking
to a lot of the other girls . . . to help them through this." To an
outsider, your voice is that of a loving caregiver. To me, it sounds
like that of a hungry wolf. *You are not helping me and I am not
your Red Riding Hood.*

"Kristen, I just want you to know, if anything happened that
we should know about, you can tell us." You speak your sick
words and my parents listen, as though you are guiding them
through how to handle their own daughter.

In my mind I can hear the crunch of old leaves and smell the
start of spring. I can see myself reporting to Mr. Witters's office
after school and remember not wanting to go there. And as I walk
through the memory of that day, I arrive at a sudden blind spot
in my brain. I don't remember the rest. I can't hear the words that
we spoke. I am unable to picture my science teacher on that day.
I have no idea what happened to me.

Instead, my mind jumps forward and I think of Tuesday night.
I know exactly what you did to me. I can smell your smell and
taste your taste and feel your feel. Whatever Mr. Witters did to
me doesn't matter anymore. I don't have room for it in my closet.

The room looks at me as I stand on the outside of it. The edge
of the step is cold, but I cannot sense it. Without anyone noticing,

I dig the arch of my foot, the very softest and most sensitive part, into the corner below. I press with all of my body weight and all of my force until the pain shoots through my body and takes the place of what happened on Tuesday night. My ears ring and for a moment I forget the current moment. I look down, slightly surprised the yellow tile has not turned red from my own blood. I shift my intention to the other foot.

I don't speak because I can't speak. Instead, I shake my head back and forth. In my own way, I say, "No, nothing happened." My parents let out a simultaneous breath of undeniable relief.

I am not able to fully translate the words that are being spoken between you and my parents. My body makes movements in conjunction with my parents standing and you getting ready to leave. I may even partake in the ending conversation, but I am unaware of what words I speak. I feel as though I am at the end of a long tunnel, watching the terrifying events of my life through a kaleidoscope.

Why did you come here? Why, after all this time and all this silence, do you want me to tell my parents about Mr. Witters? I am dizzy.

You leave. My dad heads back to the kitchen to get ready for work while my mom asks some followup questions of concern. I must do an acceptable job of answering, because after a short time she leaves me alone.

In the coming minutes and hours, the light in my kaleidoscope begins to change. And as the hours become days, the images before me grow gruesome.

Does Mr. Witters know I told you? What is your plan with all of this?

I live through my days both scared of him and scared of you. I walk through the hallways at school, hoping that you have not put a bomb in my backpack. I stand in front of my locker, worried to pull the latch open, terrified that his head is inside. I can't tell anyone I am scared. At least if I knew where he was I would feel better. So, at the end of each day, I call you.

"They don't know where he is," you say to me on the phone in a rushed voice. I call you because you are the only one who might know where he is. "I hope that he doesn't do something crazy." My eyes shift to the dark sky outside of my second story bedroom. I hope that Mr. Witters is not out there.

I say little on the phone in response to you. Eve does most of the talking, trying to pump you for information that will keep us safe. "What did he do to those girls anyway?" Eve asks on our behalf.

"He did what he did to you." Again, I unsuccessfully try to remember. "I think that the administration knew and they did nothing."

You purposefully make my mind swirl. *So would they do nothing if they knew about you?* "Why?" Eve continues.

"Because you know him and Walters are friends," you say. I think of Witters and Principal Walters paling around JM together. Then I think of you paling around with them. Then I think of you winning Teacher of the Year a while back. I shut my mouth in silence.

"He has been missing for two days. His wife says he hasn't been home in two nights," you say to interrupt my inner interlude. "Just be really careful because he might come after you or anyone he thought turned him in." You warn me and so I worry. "Who knows what he'll do?" You add to my worry.

"And you need to tell your parents. Or let them suspect that something happened," you encourage.

"Why?" I ask with utter curiosity about your plan.

"Because it will explain . . . us." I hate it when you refer to us as us. "Why we spend time together. Who knows, maybe your insane mom will even let me spend more time with you?" You sound disgustingly hopeful.

And as you talk and the days pass, something is happening to me. Something that you do not know about and no one on the outside knows about either. It is a change, invisible from the surface but momentous below. It feels as though I am being stretched apart, that my cells are floating away from each other, and that boundaries of my skin are being stretched and tested.

It feels as though my imaginary friend is being taken away from me.

"What's going on, Kristen?" My biology teacher pulls me out of my trance. Mrs. Scott is an older and rounder woman who leans over at my shoulder and looks along with me at the C-inked in red on the test in front of me. I am not sure what I say, only that I feel lost.

I thought that no one would notice my metamorphosis or struggle. But I guess I am wrong. Ever since Mr. Witters went missing five days ago, I feel as if the good parts of my life have turned to melted butter, sliding through my fingers.

While sitting in my fourth period Geometry class with football coach Mr. Macy, my mind shifts from parallelograms to the possibility of where Mr. Witters is hiding. "Can I go to the bathroom?" I ask without thinking or really awaiting an answer. Feeling sick, I grab the hall pass and head for the toilet. Before I know where I am, I find myself standing in the center of the school office.

"Can I see Mrs. Walender?" I say and ask for my school counselor.

"Of course you can. Remind me of your name . . . ," says a kind-looking woman behind the counter. I wonder why my eyes won't focus on her faux wooden name plate.

"Kristen, is everything okay?" Mrs. Walendar says and I can only fixate on how much hairspray she must have used this morning.

I find myself in an unfamiliar and small office, being asked questions that I can't find the answers to. "Yeah . . . It's just hard to hear all of the stuff about Mr. Witters," I say and at least that part is true.

Campo is full of his former students and the days are filled with whispers of Witters.

I hear them everywhere I turn, "Who do you think came forward?" is said with a small smile in gossip.

"Nothing ever happened, some girl is just looking for attention" is coming from somewhere on the senior lawn.

"I don't care what anyone thinks. Witters is the man!" is thrown out by a hormone- and pimple-ridden junior boy.

With each opinion, my organs move away from each other, and I feel closer to internal explosion.

"Was he your teacher?" Mrs. Walendar begins. She keeps it simple and I can feel her looking for a protected path out of where this conversation may be heading. I am old enough and smart enough to know that she has been kept apprised of the situation of the intermediate school that feeds her students' last names G through N.

"Yes," I respond.

"Is it hard to hear people say bad things about him?" she asks. Her face looks as though she is treading in dark and dangerous water.

"Yes," I tell the truth.

"Did he ever do anything bad to you?" she asks, but she pulls toward the back of her chair, almost wanting to create physical space from me.

I wonder if the police have come in and talked to the counselors or the administration. You have told me that the police are actively looking for him and are going to arrest him immediately if they find him. I feel small as I think of telling her and then having to tell a towering police officer. My mouth clamps as I try to think of what the local newspaper would title their story of scandal.

I cannot speak. If I open my mouth, I am not sure that I will ever be able to close it. If I start crying, I am not sure if I will ever be able to stop. So, I shake my head no. And. once again, I see the face of relief.

Although it feels more like a month than a week, I make it to the Friday following his disappearance. Step by step and breath by breath, I fake my life while I fear my death. I wake up, just as I did a week ago. The house smells and sounds the same, but I feel different.

The same scene only differentiated by a man-made calendar date. I have heard people use the term *déjà vu* before to describe uncannily similar experiences. And I may be able to use that term here, only prevented by the fact that my brain feels as if it has been changing since Mr. Witters disappeared.

And as I begin the walk down the stairs, I predict in my eyes the image of your car. I look to the window and look for the maroon shape to be outside. It is more than a memory and less than a hallucination, and I have done this image prediction every time I have traveled these stairs since your surprise visit. It is easier to picture you out there . . . just in case.

I see the grey street and my heart calms with its emptiness. Just as I tuck the image into my brain for tomorrow's downward climb, I see the front end of your station wagon pull into my sight.

You are back.

For a moment I question my sanity and hope for my hallucination. But I can hear the rumbling of your car, I can see your body close to the steering wheel with intensity. I hear my mom in the kitchen below. "She is back," she says to my dad with somewhat of a hiss.

What could it be this time? Did Witters finally make it home? You pop out of your car and I hate that I have a magnified vision of your head, streaked with grey hair. I wish I could turn and walk up the stairs as I did last time and as you do now. But I can't move. My outsides and my insides are still as stone.

My mom works quickly to get to the door before you have time to knock. She has been worried about me this week. The concerning meeting with you last Friday coupled with my behavior has kept her eyes lingering on me at the dinner table.

"Hi," my mom says to you. I wonder what she would say if she knew who you really are. "Come on in." She says this loud enough for me to hear. My mom leans in toward you, ". . . is there any new news?"

"Yeah . . . we need to talk with Kristen. This isn't going to be easy for her to hear." You speak in a fake whisper, but your words reach my ears with ease, and I know that you want me to hear all that you have to say.

Unaware of the muscular contractions that get my physical body there, somehow I find myself at the bottom of the stairs. My heart might be above my max, on the verge of cardiac arrest. Or, it may have slowed to a stop and I might already be dead. My hands might be clammy and my stomach may be in knots. But I am unable to feel any of this. None of it matters.

The participants in the play take the same spots on the stage as they did last week. They sit in the living room and it all looks the same. The white carpet below is clean and pristine from years of my mom requiring us to remove our shoes before entry. I notice that no one has taken the time to stop and remove their shoes today.

You begin to talk. I have no idea where you are going with this. Again, I refuse to enter the room and I stand on the edge of the world. You are saying something about Mr. Witters, but I am very distracted by where you sit. *How dare you take that chair?* In my mind, I am suddenly eight years old. My mom sits where you do, and I practice my ballet routine for her and my audience of stuffed companions. I am light on my feet as I leap across my stage at the ledge of the room. My mom claps because, even for a jock, I am a fascinating dancer.

But I don't dance anymore. I think of the dance recital this June and I feel as though my lips have been doused with kerosene and lit ablaze.

"They found his car . . . in Big Sur. At the bottom of a cliff." Your voice sounds sorry and sad and sincere. With big soft words you say, "I'm so sorry to have to be the one to tell you this . . . I just didn't want you to find out at school. I heard this morning," you say with a frown forced on your face.

What did you just say? I'm sorry I was in the middle of dress rehearsal. My mind goes blank from the happiness of my past as I imagine the reality of your words. Mr. Witters, in his blue Toyota pickup truck and his roundish black glasses and on the run. *Did he scout out a place and have a plan? Or was he speeding away from the dirtiness of his past and with a quick impulse, did he shove his foot onto the gas pedal and speed to his death below?*

Is he actually dead?

I have seen those movies, where cheating husbands fake their own death and head south with their dirty secret. With a new name and a new home, maybe he is just starting over. Or maybe he just doesn't want people looking for him anymore. Maybe he is outside the window watching all of this.

"Kristen," my mom says and she has turned all of her focus to me and my silence. I am brought back to the room in front of me.

"Yeah," I say as though my mom has just asked if spaghetti sounds good for dinner.

My mind makes up what it would have looked like. I think of the green hills and the look someone might have on his face with four seconds until impact. *Did he think of the sound of his wife's scream or of the soccer games he would miss of his young sons? Did he think of the students who loved him or the ones he knew he hurt? Did he think of me?*

As I wonder how much time he had, I suddenly wonder if he could have put a boulder from the nearby cliff on the accelerator and watched in safety as his old and messy life cruised off the cliff.

"Kristen," you say and try unsuccessfully to match the sound of my mom's voice. "Did you hear what I just said?"

"Yes," I say trying hard to make my voice sound deep and understanding of the consequences, yet still I feel as if this is all make-believe. "Yes, I heard."

"Kristen, is there anything that you need to tell your parents right now?" Your eyes burn into my skin, like a brand on the hide of a clueless cow. You try to drive me into this corral out of fear. If they could talk, your eyes would be saying, "c'mon, trust me." But they can't talk and I pretend that I have no idea what you want from me.

"No," I say in seeming innocent defiance of you. I can't feel the world around me and I am unaware that I am crying until I notice the movement of a tear as it falls from my face to the ground.

Am I sad about what Mr. Witters did to me? Do I understand what death is? I look at you across the room and even from this far away I can see your cuticles, and the sight of your hands makes my toes curl into the coldness of the entry tile below.

Still I search through the jelly folds of my brain, but I do not know exactly what happened. I can only remember your words: "Never forget what he did to you. I am going to make you better from him. I am going to make you right again." But before all of that, it is a mystery. I loop through the reel with your voice and feel like a stranger to my own footsteps.

"Kristen . . ." It's my mom again and I am grateful for her rather raspy voice. "Kristen, why are you crying? If something happened, you can tell us," she says and she is very careful. Just as a mother of a soldier opening the door awaiting bad news, she continues; "Whatever it is . . .We can handle this." And I am not sure she believes her own words.

I look at my mom and she looks older and smaller than she did yesterday. She looks frail and I imagine the weight of saying "yes, something happened" hanging like baggage on her shoulders. *If I started telling the truth, could I stop?* I look at my mom and wonder what it would be like if she really knew what was going on. *If she could see what you do to my body, where you put your hands, would she also drive off a cliff?*

They know I am floating away into the outer space of my thoughts. "Krick . . ." It's my dad now and his masculine voice conveys a sense of anger about the situation. "If he did something, you need to tell us."

"*She* did something," I think in the safety of my brain.

"I swear to God. If he did something, you have to tell us," my dad booms. As his words continue, his fury festers. I have never noticed my dad being so large, and suddenly I am singularly aware that his hands look strikingly like the paws of a giant grizzly. "If he did something to you," he spits his words, "I should have killed him myself."

Everything around me grows quiet. My mom says something to my dad about calming down. You say something, too, but I can't hear you. My dad stands in both anger and devastation. I can see the start of tears at the corner of his eyes. He moves with purpose as though he is going to go somewhere, although with Mr. Witters being gone, I don't really know where. There is noise and movement, but I am not here.

I stand still and beg for it all to stop—the talking, the questioning, the pain. But most of all, I wish my heart would stop beating.

My tear ducts open and zap the moisture from my eyes. I look at my dad, his bear paws, and think of him squeezing the life out of Mr. Witters. I think of him knowing the truth and trying to squeeze the life out of you. But you would not be an easy prey for the picking. You are a vampire, and just as you have sucked the life out of me, you would steal the life out of him. *Would you shoot him?* I think that you are too smart for that. *Would you poison him?* All I know is that this can't end well.

"Nothing happened," I say in a firm and direct voice that comes from somewhere other than me. It is Eve and she is here to help me out of this unnatural disaster. "It's just sad to think about, that's all." Eve knows to explain the tears.

"Yes, it is sad," my mom agrees, but I can feel that she is happy. Happy that it wasn't me. I see the look on her face, the lightness in her eyebrows and at the corner of her mouth, and suddenly she is beautiful again. I know I can never let her know the truth. I have to protect her from the pain.

I look to the left at my dad, who has shrunk to a normal size again. His hands still look large, but not dangerously so. He is relieved as he walks toward you to shake your hand and thank you for coming over to talk to us. Somehow I know that his hand is warm and soft in the center and that you hand is cold and bony. Surprised, I watch as my mom does the same. Goodness shaking that hand of evil in the center of our single family home.

Resolution for now, but another shift in my soul that no one notices through the casual conversation. We move back to the oak door that you entered through, and I wonder fleetingly about your purpose in coming here.

The door opens and you look at me. I think of his truck suspended in midair, and then the smoldering heat of the wreckage three seconds after impact. I imagine the best mom in the world feeling like an utter failure. I imagine that this can actually get worse. It is all too much. I can no longer exist.

My own version of driving off a cliff, you open the door to leave and I shove Eve out the door with you. I take the largest kitchen knife I can find and saw a piece of myself off to give to you. Sure, there is DNA I will miss, attributes that I will long for, but it is the only option. I can no longer balance both worlds in my hand, even if Eve is willing to help. Mr. Witters is dead and things have gotten far too dangerous. It's a deal: I will give Eve to you so that I can be a normal kid. This isn't happening to me anymore.

As Eve walks with you to your car, I know I will rarely see her again. And as I know I will miss her, I know that I will rarely see you, too.

CHAPTER TWENTY-ONE

Defending Myself

I thought that my judge said we would take a long lunch. How did almost two hours go by so fast? I sat with Scott at Starbucks, drank coffee, and ate frozen yogurt. Any other day it would have been my dream noon hour, but today is part of my nightmare.

My contingent awaits me as I arrive at the courthouse. I feel a little more sturdy than the last time they greeted me, but I know not to get comfortable. As I enter the courtroom, I allow myself to look at her. She is sitting cross-legged, her elbow resting on the table, and she is tilted romantically toward her defense attorney. When my mom was growing weary of Julie, she would say that it felt almost as if Julie was flirting with me. As I watch Julie's posture and her inviting laugh, I see my mom's frustration from adult eyes.

As I take the stand, not only to tell the truth but also not to be tricked, I make sure that I wear my invisible bubblewrap. My survival gave me a spectacular imagination, and just as I used it then to escape her, I will use it again.

The stand feels more reliable this time, and as I take a few deep breaths I watch Julie as she whispers frantically to her defense attorney Michael Thorman. She has to tell him what to do and what to say because her sickness of sex pales in comparison to her obsession with dominance and control. Like so many other twisted minds, if things were up to her, she would represent herself.

For a moment, before we begin, I survey her audience. Her sister looks so much like Julie and a hint of evilness touches the corner of her empty eyes. She smiles too much for the occasion and her skin looks grey and made of clay. Her mom is there, but not there at the same time. Her eyes have the hollow look of sedatives mixed with painkillers. She turns her head slowly, does not say a word, and I cannot take the time to feel empathy for her. And then there is Rob. My mind begins to hustle as I look at him. *Has he heard the tapes yet? What she said about him? What she admitted to doing to me then? What she wants to do to me now? How she will not let him do that to her?* I feel my distraction interrupted by a voice I have not heard yet today.

"Hello, Kristen." He sounds kind and soft, but I know this is bait and he is just trying to lure me closer.

"Hello." I imagine the Great Wall of China. Teri went there after the Olympics and I imagine a picture she showed me last year. I am on one side of the wall, he is on the other. The defense attorney and I are throwing a tennis ball back and forth. His questions, a long loop over to me.

"How are you today?" His bait smells bad.

I wait two seconds just to prove I can. "Fine," the closest thing to a lie I will tell all day.

I am surprised at how nervous he feels. His voice sounds as though he is made out of tin. *Wasn't it the tin man that didn't have a heart?* Thomas continues, "What is it that you do for a living?"

Why is he asking me this? Stop wondering, just answer. "I am the Assistant Swim Coach at Cal," and I feel a puff of pride fill my chest cavity. I sit up straighter now.

"And isn't it true that the head coach is here in the courtroom today?" He has more purpose in his voice, as if he has somehow just proved that by Teri being here I have made this all up. Inside I laugh at this ridiculousness. He has a stick and he is trying to prod me in the side. He doesn't see that I have a sword that is drawn when he talks about Teri.

I look back at Teri and I say with a questioning tone in my voice, "Yes."

With more confidence now, he asks me how I got into UCLA, what kind of grades I got in high school, and what kind of athletic demands I had on my shoulders thoughout high school. I know that these are not questions for him as he has already subpoenaed my school records.

He begins jumping all over the place with his questions, going out of chronological order, and it is starting to bother me. The only way I have been able to make sense of my puzzle-pieced memory is to make a timeline, aligning dates, holidays, instances I remember. It feels like sanity to be able to write them down, to make sense of the nonsense. The unambiguous pain can't just keep floating in space. I have to put it in order. Somehow he knows that.

I remember that confusion and frustration are his only allies. I have the truth. He was at home on those horrible nights, tucking his young children into bed. I feel stronger, smarter, and more powerful than him. I tell him about my acceptance into UCLA based on academic achievement, not athleticism. I am honest about my near perfect GPA and the hours of soccer, volleyball, water polo, and swim practices. I see him painting a picture that says, "She could not have possibly been going through hell and looked as if she were living in heaven." But my answer, the truth, is so soundly simple. It was the only way to survive.

"Isn't it true that your mom hated my client?" He bobs and weaves around the stigma of the word defendant.

And now another piece of his painting is being etched. The angry controlling mother who poisoned her daughter's mind and convinced her to make up a tall tale. "My mom had concerns about Julie, but I do not know if she hated her."

"Isn't it true that you told police that your mom hated her?" My stomach becomes nervous and I hope that I have not messed up. I pray that I have not ruined my credibility as a witness by something I said. I quickly spin the rolodex of hours I spent with police.

"I don't remember saying that. I know that Julie would always say that my mom hated her, but we did not sit around the dinner table and talk about the defendant. There were times when my mom thought that the defendant was a great role model for me and times that she was frustrated by the defendant and times that she did not trust the defendant." I use the D word as much as possible. "I do not know the exact feelings of my mom and how those changed."

This answer does not satisfy him and I wonder if I should tell him that he should not use so much hair gel. "If you had to say, would you say that your mom hated my client?"

I pause as practice and Geoff says on cue, "I'm going to have to object your honor. The witness is being asked to speculate on the feelings of a third party." His brow is lowered and I see hints of a pit bull in hiding.

"Sustained. If you need the answer to this to prove a particular point, then call her mother, Otherwise, move along, counsel." I smile inside at a tiny win.

"Isn't it true, in the situation you describe of the volleyball lessons and in the office after wards, that you were the one who initiated the kissing? That she never pushed herself up against you, but that you pushed yourself against her?"

Scott used to have this oversized paddle that one of his fraternity brothers gave him. It was so big that it was a joke to even look at. As I remember my first kiss with Jon Danton, and there the only sexual experience I had had at that point in my life, I think of that paddle. I think of what a joke it is that this defense attorney thinks that this is maybe my fault.

I think of the metal bars in her office, the ones that she pushed me up against and that indented my spine at two places, and the word "No" is the only thing that comes out of my mouth for the defense attorney.

"Isn't it true that moving forward sexually was your idea?"

I have to be honest. When I thought of going to the police, I did not think that I would be the one on trial. I look down at the blue nail polish that I have chipped off my fingers and now lies in a pile on the wooden ledge of the witness stand.

I think back to a warm spring day at JM. We were in Sex Ed class instead of PE and I had learned about the details of sex between a man and a woman. Sure, before then I knew some of the basics. I wasn't a naïve babies-come-from-storks kind of kid. But same gender sex was certainly not a part of the 1990s suburbia school curriculum. I can smell the spring air and I can see the Sex Ed class in front of me. I take a deep inhale, feel the innocence of who I was, and say slowly to the attorney, "No. I didn't even know what that was."

He moves aggressively into his next set of questioning and becomes more demanding with his voice. "Isn't it true that you responded physically to Julie? That you had orgasms even?"

And suddenly I think of the train. I crave the knife.

"Objection, your honor!" Geoff's voice is tumbling and barrels over the voice of the defense attorney.

I hang my head and peer through my bangs to the back of the room. I am too scared to let my eyes focus and see my family. I wish with all my heart that I did not have to feel the pain of this moment.

The judge sits so close to me that she may be able to hear my thoughts. Suddenly I am aware that she is as close to me as she possibly can be given the current seating configuration. "Please approach, counsel," she demands. She moves the microphone aside, so that the court cannot hear what she is saying. I am grateful that I can. "I have a duty to protect the victim of childhood sexual abuse. You are taking this too far," she looks at defense attorney Thorman, who looks strikingly similar to The Penguin.

"It is important to the case . . ." Thorman starts to reason with Landau, and I think that she knows I can hear the conversation.

I can feel her empathy and I know that she worries: What I have heard, what I have seen, and where I have been in my life may just be a little too much for me. She looks over and says, "We are going to take a ten-minute break and talk about the direction of this. Why don't you go get some fresh air?"

I am happy to leave and all but run out of the courtroom. I pass my family, fly out the door, into the bathroom, to the back stall where I immediately throw up—as if the vomit could rid my insides of the awfulness she put there.

Without knowing how, I am outside of the bathroom, my brother throws his coat around my shoulders, and my whole support system is there. Teri comes barreling out of the court. "I stayed in there to listen to the judge," Teri is angry for what I have been through, today and in total. "The judge is angry. She says that things are about done in there."

It is time to go back and I know it is time to take the stand again. As we enter, Geoff leans over and reminds me to just keep telling the truth. I wonder if he knows. I take the stand and I feel surprisingly calm.

Penguin waddles back to Julie's side and opens his notebook.

"We are back in session and you are still under oath," my judge says softly to me, and her eyes look concerned. They must be allowing the question. I half swallow and half nod.

Thorman begins, "Please strike the previous question." My heart breaths a little bit. "Did you ever tell the defendant that you enjoyed what she was doing?"

The pain now becomes worse. *What can I possibly say? How can I tell him that I had to tell her that it felt good? That the more I told her this, the sooner it would stop? That if I did not tell her that, she would be mad at me? That when she was mad, she did crazy things?* No one could ever understand this. No one will ever understand me.

I think of Elizabeth Smart, the girl who was kidnapped in Utah and held as a sex slave not far from her house. Months later someone saw her in a Burger King bathroom and a concerned citizen leaned over and said, "Are you Elizabeth Smart?"

She answered, "No, I'm not Elizabeth Smart." I wonder, after she was eventually saved, was she put on trial for this answer? Why did she go along? Why did I go along?

I remember how scared I was. I remember how much I hated her body. I remember how bad it hurt sometimes. I remember wishing that she was a man. And I watch the shame evaporate out of my soul and I simply say, "Yes."

CHAPTER TWENTY-TWO

Nothing in the Way

I wish I were eating a grilled chicken and jack cheese sandwich. Not just any grilled chicken and jack cheese sandwich, but the one from Village Pizza. The one that I order with potato leek soup and has a sesame seed bun. The one that I like to squeeze with my thumb and pointer finger and watch the juice run to soak into the bottom bun before I take a bite. I wish I were at dinner with my family. Sitting next to my brother Marc.

But lately I have been worrying that the chicken sandwich has too many calories. You just told me cheese is fattening and I shouldn't eat it anymore. Two weeks ago I ordered my usual, minus the cheese, and it tasted like a dried-up version of an old favorite. Plus the sandwich with the soup might be too much. I hate it when I am at dinner with my family acting as if everything were normal, and then your stupid critical voice jumps into my ear and tells me not to get fat.

But tonight I am not even at the dinner table. And it's not for fear of gaining weight. I wish I were there. Marc came home from UCLA to visit for the weekend. He is a freshman this year, and I think he is secretly homesick. Walking by his empty room this year has made me feel even more hollow than I already am. It is late afternoon on Sunday, and his room is empty once again.

I shouldn't be too sad. After all, it is spring so there are only a few weeks left of school until he takes finals and comes home for the summer. That's the best time of the year. The time for Marc and me to coach summer league swimming together and the time of the year when you know the very least about me. After all, you looked like an idiot the one time I saw you try to swim.

Although I am excited for dual meets and car painting, I am worried about how it will be when Marc comes home for the summer. Another sleeping pattern to monitor, another door to walk past in the middle of the night, another person to trick. And, still, I miss him every day.

So, yeah, I wish I were at dinner with Marc and my family. But, instead, I had to call you. I had to tell my parents that I had too much homework due tomorrow morning to go to dinner and then drive to the airport.

I did consider maybe going to dinner in my own car, driving home, meeting you here, and trying to get you to finish before my family got home from dropping off Marc. But then I remembered the tight time squeeze a month ago, how I felt as though I were going to die when my two lives almost collided, and decided I wasn't hungry for the chicken sandwich after all.

I had to call you because the other option, telling you that I cannot see you tonight, has a very serious consequence to it. Trust me, I have tried this. I have tried everything. If I tell you I can't see you, that I am sick, that I have too much homework, that my parents are making me go to the airport, you will come up with an alternative plan.

These alternative plans include, but are not limited to, your sneaking into my house at night when my parents are home, making me go running and coming to your office, and making me sneak out at night. All of these alternatives are much more risky than this. Sneaking out of my house and spending hours in your apartment means doing just that, spending hours with you. Running to your office involves the risk of someone seeing me heading in there, someone finding out what is going on, and then would follow a whole plethora of problems, which you often spend time predicting. But the worst of all, the very most painful and frightening of all, is when you decided to sneak into my house when my family is home.

"I need to have you." It is a phrase you say to me every day. Just when I think I have checked your evil box, you erase it or create a new task to check. It used to be, "I need to have you at least once a month." But it was never that way. And you began saying, "I need to have you once a week." And so I worked to create the safest situation in a life-threatening dynamic. But now your sentence has gotten shorter, more simple, and more demanding, "I need to have you."

I figure if there are ways to satisfy you, to keep this part of my life quiet I will: so that I can continue wowing the world, shooting game-winning goals in sports and scoring curve-setting marks on exams. I actively look for ways to keep your sick and twisted brain happy so that I can have my own happiness. I guess it is my fault; I do look for ways to allow you to do what you do. Picking the time and the place helps me feel as though I have at least one hand on the driver's wheel.

So I called you, using the cell phone that you bought me. The one that I keep in the Spanish English Dictionary that you went out and bought. The one you cut a hole in and make me carry with me everywhere. The one that you make me sleep with under my pillow at night. It is hard to sleep with that under my head, but harder to risk it being found somewhere while I sleep. Plus, you would kill me if I did that. You told me that it took you four hours to cut the hole, page by page, so that the cell phone was tightly secured and would not fall out.

The house grows quiet as I hear the garage door rest shut. As I hear the white Volvo station wagon pull up the street, I know exactly where you are. There you sit, across the street from the vet's office where we take all of our pets, in a parking lot on a hill, outside an office building. It's a building where I once got my eyes examined last year when I first got my contacts and they got stuck in the back of my eyeballs. *Do you remember in eighth grade, when I got my contacts?* You were so happy because I could finally see you calling the plays out at our basketball games. Little did I know that I wasn't seeing the real you at all.

You sit in that parking lot, perched above the main street, so that you can see my parents leave. It is fascinating how your mind works; tricking people comes so naturally to you. Once they pass, you pull your car to the top of the hill and park. In the same workout clothes you always wear, you jog down my street and walk in the front door.

Except today.

I am in my kitchen and I have the phone where I can get to it in case something goes wrong. Actually, both phones. I have the phone you gave me, in case you need to call me and tell me something has gone wrong. I have the cordless home phone in case my parents need to call me for a delayed flight or, much worse, let me know that they are coming home because Marc forgot his wallet. Even when you get here I will keep both phones in reaching distance. I know the details of these phones, the seams that hold them together, the color of the buttons, the growing grime on the home phone receiver, much better than I should. After all, they give me something to look at.

The phones stay silent and the house stays silent. I look through the dining room out to the driveway, expecting to see your floating stride coming toward me.

Why does your body not move up and down when you walk or run like most normal humans? You always look like you are hovering. I saw a really bad horror movie last week and thought of you when I saw the vampires floating through the night. *Why does no one else notice that you are floating? That you are a blood sucker?*

As my eyes grow wider and the clock in the kitchen ticks, I see something move out of the corner of my eye, in the backyard. *It could not be you, could it?*

I turn my body, although I have left my stomach, and I see you. Gliding up the back steps of my backyard. You move swiftly under the branches of the growing redwoods that my dad planted when we moved in fifteen years ago.

How did you get back there? Why are you back there? Have you changed your plan again without telling me? Were you there the whole time my family was here, joking around with Marc and packing up his recently washed clothes? I thought that my backyard was safe, and now I know I can never turn my back on that, either.

The sliding door shrieks as you open it. You act as if you belong here, as if you deserve to walk through the door and into my childhood, my life, my soul. You do not pause as a normal person would when you enter a home that is not yours. You come straight at me.

I am breathless and my eyes are so big that they might not contain the balls inside. You know that I am scared and can sense this. My fear makes you proud, causes you to stand upright a few centimeters taller. I am still growing and I am almost your height. But here, in my kitchen, you tower over me.

My voice sounds tiny, like that of a little bitty grey mouse. "What were you doing back there?"

A few more centimeters enter your spine, "I had a really great idea. I have been worried that people will see me on your street and say something to your mom. Then she will go crazy."

I imagine my mom knowing that you are here when she is not. I hope that she would, in fact, go crazy. I imagine her ripping out your ugly, greying hair, follicle by follicle. I imagine her shooting you in your hollow, setback eyes. I imagine her punching you in your teeth that are already slanted slightly back, as though you had been hit hard and square in the mouth. But I hope, more than anything, that she will never have to know.

"So what did you do?" The mouse voice is still there and softened even still more by the wonderment if I even really want to know the answer to my own question.

You smile with self-satisfaction. "I decided to still park at the top of the hill." I feel myself relax a little knowing that at least part of the plan that I knew about had not changed. "Then, instead of jogging down the street, I came through people's backyards."

The confusion hits my head like a two-by-four, right above my right ear. And if I were allowed to, my whole body would bend to the left from the impact. I stand still and look at you.

I imagine what has just happened. Quickly I count the houses on my street. I count mostly by family, and as I go through the list of old childhood friends, I figure we are the seventh house down on the street. Seven fences. Six feet tall. I imagine Mrs. Chan in house number four looking out of her window and seeing you scale over her fence. It's not even dark out yet. I rub my temples trying to make sense of this nonsense.

As I allow myself to look at you, to look into your eyes, I see pupils that are too small and a color that is too yellow for a human. I think that if there were to be an image definition for the word crazy, it might be your eyes at this very moment.

"Don't you think that the possibility of people seeing you climb their fences is more dangerous than them speculating about why you are walking down the street? There are other students of yours that live on this street. Neighbors might think that maybe you are going to see them?" My voice trails off quickly as you come at me with the force of a violent wind. Before I know it, you have covered the three feet that separate us.

I hate your hands.

They grab me. Around the wrists. You yank my hands from my worried face and put your nose to my nose. You move my hands to my side with such ferocity that I feel a twinge in my pectoral muscles. With a lowered brow, your crazed eyes become insane.

You are hurting me, physically hurting me, and you know it. My wrists beg you to let go and my hands turn weak. I gasp for air and you look like the most powerful woman in the world.

"Don't you think that I know what I am doing?" Your words are between a yell and a hiss. "You are being stupid, like a foolish child."

You take my numbing hands and force my arms around your body. Then, as you so often do after hurting me, you kiss me.

Your voice sounds different than it used to. You look different, too. I wonder if someone has hijacked the teacher I once knew, taken away my favorite coach. I allow the sadness of who I thought you were and who you actually are to enter my heart for exactly one second. Then I allow my heart to separate from my body. While you lead me upstairs to "have me," I float into the family room to watch my all-time favorite episode of *Saved by the Bell*. After all, Eve can handle things upstairs better than I can anyway.

PART THREE

"I Am So Glad I Found You.
I Am So Glad I Had You."

CHAPTER TWENTY-THREE

Listen Up

The food rumbles in my stomach. For the first time in weeks, I felt hungry after my testimony and had decided to eat at lunch. As I look up at the judge, I wonder if my breakfast for lunch idea was a good one after all.

I sit here, now seeing the sight that everyone else saw. Geoff and Scott told me that the preliminary hearings only last a couple of hours. No one knew I would be answering questions for the better part of two days. Finally, I am no longer up on the stand. I sit on the hard wood of the audience benches and have to remind myself that I am not at church.

My eyes are immediately drawn to the back of Julie's head. A primitive instinct to drive a spear through her skull fills my cells, but I remain still.

I can feel the presence of my important people around me, and as I begin to shake, I try to allow my army to sooth my nerves. To my left, Scott encloses my hand and, to my right, my mom sits leg to leg. She is rocking gently as Marc sits in the row behind her rubbing her skinny back.

"Krick," my mom had said at our lunch with tears welling in lower lids, "it was really hard to hear all of that stuff that you had to testify to. But . . . ," she gave a long pause and had grabbed my forearm under the wooden table, "it was really good to hear it, too. Now I understand what happened . . . how it happened. I understand your fear. She is a monster."

My mom lowered her head and looked at me above the rim of her glasses. A wave of relief washed over me as I realized my mom could hear all of the nastiness and still love me. It was in that moment that I had decided to be brave enough to dive into my eggs and bacon at The Copper Skillet.

But now my stomach disagrees with the decision. While we were gone, Detective Parker was called to the stand. The court ruled that I was not allowed to stay for fear of "tampering with the witness" for future testimony at trial.

"He was great." My dad had met up with us at lunch as we were getting the bill. My dad had insisted on staying to hear Parker.

"What did he say? What did they ask? Did it fall in line with everything I said?" My words came out too fast as I looked up at my dad wishing he would just sit down with us at the table.

"He was great." The same line.

I looked at my father, typically a man of few words, and begged for more. "What did the judge say? Do you think that she will uphold all of the charges?"

"Krick, Parker was great. He walked them through the phone calls and reminded the judge that he told you what to say." I settled into the red vinyl booth.

As of late, the defense attorney's new tactic was claiming that the phone calls actually help Julie. He claims that the calls proved that I loved Julie and that I was a willing participant in all events.

But I was recording the calls! I was using the calls to trap Julie and get her to admit to what she did! I wasn't being honest with her. I was telling her things to make her trust me and make her admit to what she did!

From my new vantage point in the back of the courtroom, I glare at the back of Julie's head and I glare at the back of Thorman's head. *What kind of monster would represent this monster?*

The judge enters more quickly than I want her to.

"Let's go back on the record. The record should reflect the defendant is present, both counsel are present." Judge Landau looks different from this angle, more powerful and perhaps less understanding. "I have completed my review of all of the pretext calls."

I look at her eyes to see if she is looking at me. *It was an act!* I want to yell out to her to make sure she understands I am no longer that person. *Please don't use those calls against me!*

But Landau has already moved on to speaking with the attorneys. They are talking about the different charges, the counts, the legal codes, not much of which I understand.

"Talk to me about the last six counts after she turned 16," Landau says with her nose pointed toward Geoff. "And there are three counts of forcible copulation and three counts of forcible penetration. Talk to me about what in particular you are contending the force is and why those time periods."

The element of force or duress is particularly important to me. Not only does it carry a heavier sentence, it is the element that captures what Julie did to me.

Geoff launches into his reasoning, "It's hard to necessarily see it sitting here in this courtroom, because this case is unusual in that the victim came forward over ten years after the abuse ended, the actual sexual abuse ended. However, the victim, at the time of this abuse, wasn't the Kristen that was here today and yesterday. It was a little girl."

I look down at my hands and imagine what they must have looked like before Julie ever touched them.

Geoff's voice booms through the courtroom and I am glad he is louder than I ever could be. "And that relationship of dominance and control that a teacher and a coach . . . increased even more so once Mr. Witters had disappeared and had died." Scott squeezes my hand knowing that I hate the "relationship" word. "That event was used by the defendant because of her dominance and control of the relationship she had with the victim." Geoff's anger twists the words slightly, but looking at the judge shaking her head shows that she understands his point.

Geoff continues to charge, "I was trying to show the Court how she was taken away from her friends and family over the course of those years until, basically, she had to do everything the defendant asked. And she didn't think she had a choice."

I didn't have a choice!

"And that was because of her age. And that was because of the way the defendant was." *And because Julie threatened to kill me and my family!*

"I remember hearing one thing on the pretext phone calls," Geoff flips through a stack of large pages in a hurry, "and I couldn't tell you which call it was, but I remember the defendant saying at one point in time, something to the effect of 'You haven't forgotten the force that is me'."

Shivers shoot down my spin and I sit up taller as I think of Julie's cackle.

"I noticed that," Judge Landeau interrupts and nods her head emphatically. Scott squeezes my hand.

Geoff turns back towards me and gives me the quickest of glances. "So, there was duress in this case. I think there was even more duress after Mr. Witters died."

Geoff wraps up his comments and, just as I had started to relax, Thorman stands up ready to argue. My stomach knots once again.

"Your Honor," Thorman's voice lacks the purpose of Geoff's. "I don't have anything to say about the first six counts. I think there's been adequate evidence shown for holding orders on the 288(c)s that have been charged." Scott squeezes my hand with this initial win. "I want to address my comments to the issue of the last six counts, and particularly [if] what we're talking about is duress."

My mind races. I think of Julie grabbing my wrists. I think like Eve, of wanting to jump out of Julie's car. I think of the train tracks. *How can people doubt the duress, the fear, the force?*

Suddenly I am no longer in the courtroom. As the defense attorney launches into case numbers and referencing *The People v. Hecker*, my bones fill with helium and I start floating to the ceiling.

From my new vantage point hovering above, I can see Julie aggressively nodding her head with each point her attorney makes. Throughout the past few days Julie has sat closer and closer to this greying old man, batting her eyelashes and tilting her head back to laugh at each of their interactions. He seems a bit taken with her.

Suddenly the lyrics to "Karma Chameleon" by Culture Club start to play in my mind as I think of Julie changing colors and have to keep myself from laughing. I shake my head and try to bring myself down from the ceiling back to present day.

Defense attorney Thorman is rolling now as I force myself to listen again: ". . . there is no evidence that the defendant knew or should have known that this was against her will. In fact, the evidence shows the opposite, I think. Kristen said that she never said no. She never gave the defendant any reason to believe that she was . . . not enjoying it. And listening to the pretext calls, I think one of the things that—I mean there are many things you can glean from that . . ." He turns and gives a smile to Julie. "But one of them, at least in terms of the way the defendant was talking to Kristen, that everything that was going on between them was—although she was not specific about what it is, but there's never been any implication that she thought that Kristen was not complying, it was not something she did not want to have happen."

Julie is nodding her head now and I can see the corner of her smile. *Who is on trial here?* If I would have said no, she would have slit my stomach open and let my guts soak the pink sheets of her apartment bed. My fists curl with anger and my wrists hurt. They hurt in the same place Julie grabbed me after she jumped over so many fences to get to me.

I look to the judge and she gives me nothing. I look to Geoff and I can see his blood boil in his body language.

Looking like a proud peacock, the defense attorney submits his case. He returns to his spot, too close to Julie.

Landau looks back to Geoff, "Anything further?"

"Yes, your Honor," Geoff booms and my heart fills as he takes up arms for me.

"I cite to the Court *People vs. Senior,* 1992."

Geoff pauses and allows the judge to find the case. "I was looking at note number six, which would be on page . . . I guess the second page of the case. And it talks about [how] duress can arise from various circumstances, including the relationship between the defendant and the victim, the relative ages and sizes."

Landau responds with a nod, "Yeah . . . and his or her relationship to the defendant." I wonder if it is normal for a judge to help the prosecution argue a point.

"Yes. And I think that there was enough testimony in this case about the surreptitious nature of the defendant's actions, including the way she snuck around, including the way she would have the victim lay down and put a blanket over her when she was in the car, including the way the headlights would be turned off, and they'd close the door at the same time, and she'd make sure no one was around, that she knew that this was not something that was two consenting adults doing, let alone two consenting human beings."

Geoff's words move fast—twice as fast as they should. He is like a steam train and I am surprised how quickly he can reference my nightmares."There's enough evidence in the record to show that the defendant, especially given the fact that she was, basically, stalking the victim after she cut it off and had to have the courage to cut it off in her senior year, that she knew she wasn't dealing on a level playing field and she knew that she wasn't dealing with someone who was giving full consent."

The judge listens to closing remarks and then responds: "I guess the only question I have about that is clearly that was a fear that the victim had—the alleged victim had, but is it something that the defendant ever said? I mean, clearly the victim felt very controlled by the defendant and felt that there were real risks to her family, but was that her own thinking or was it something that the defendant—I don't remember hearing anything about [what] the defendant said directly that said, I will hurt your family if things go south in this relationship, or anything like that. Did I miss something?"

Thorman pounces, "I think the Court's correct." I can hear his smile as the judge finds weakness in my case.

Geoff strikes back, "Yes, I think the Court did miss something. There was testimony about how there was a plan if they were ever found out about how the victim would go somewhere and meet the defendant. And they'd go off together."

Landau interrupts, and my eyes fill with tears as I have failed to tell the truth of my story. "But that's different from hurting, causing injury to the family."

As I begin to give up in my brain, Geoff unleashes: "Not necessarily, because the victim testified that she feared for herself, she feared for the defendant's life—she even feared for the defendant's life—and she feared for her family's life. And that plan is not mutually exclusive of parents dying before the plan is executed. Remember, that plan was there. If the parents ever came to the defendant's apartment, she was supposed to leave and go out the window. What do you think is going to happen to the parents? Or what do you think is going to happen in the mind of a fourteen, fifteen-year-old child when the parents show up at the defendant's apartment and all of a sudden everyone's gone? We're not talking about handing out roses to people, your Honor."

"I understand that. I'm just trying to figure out where is the line between what the defendant said and what the victim, a kid, feared." Landau tilts her head and I wish that she would look at me. Look into my eyes. I wish I could take her to coffee and explain the ropes that Julie tied.

Geoff flips through his pages and puts his index finger on the line he was searching for. He looks at the judge: "There's also testimony in the record about how, when the victim's mother was in the hospital with a collapsed lung, the defendant told her, 'It would be better if your mom was dead.'" I had never hated Julie more than when she murmured those words. It was the first of many times that I considered killing her.

"I do remember that," Landau agrees.

"So I think there's enough," Geoff says with a huff.

It seems as if both sides have said enough as the attorneys settle into their swiveling chairs. Julie leans her elbows on the table and tilts her head up at Judge Landau, and I can imagine her dead eyes trying to plead.

Landau also sits back in her chair. She removes her reading glasses and looks out at the court. For a heartbeat, she makes eye contact with me. "Okay, this is a probable cause hearing, this is not a preponderance of the evidence or beyond a reasonable doubt hearing," Landau begins and I think of the many hours Scott has spent explaining the difference between this, a preliminary hearing, and a trial.

She continues seamlessly, as though she always knew what she was going to say: "Everyone agrees that there's sufficient evidence on the first six counts. And as to the last six counts, although I understand the defense's argument, and it might be an argument that would fly with a jury, I think there is sufficient evidence of duress, given the broad definition of it, to justify a holding order here. It says, 'A direct or implied threat of force, violence, danger, hardship, or retribution.' And it takes into account the age of the other person and her, in this case, relationship to the defendant. And here I think there's sufficient evidence of an implied threat of force to—certainly to the defendant herself, that she would kill herself if the relationship ended. There is a risk of danger or hardship or retribution. I think there was testimony at some point that if the relationship ended that the defendant might out the victim as a lesbian. And that's relevant as well. The victim was fifteen years old, fourteen years old, under the control of a scarily . . . obsessed older woman. And if I hadn't heard the pretext calls I would find the . . . some of the stories so outlandish as to be unbelievable, except that the defendant never denied it."

Landau draws a deep breath in through her nose and allows her voice to get louder, almost a yell but not quite: "And the stories about hiding in the closet and jumping out the window, all of them in the pretext calls, none of them did the defendant deny, and by her silence she admitted them. And so the stories here are absolutely credible."

I think of my little green journal with the Post-it notes. I want to cheer just as I would cheer for one of my swimmers headed toward the finish. Somehow I knew I needed to prove the details. Not just the sex acts. Not just my age. But all of it.

Landau continues and I wish I could see her more closely. I believe she is shaking. Fury boils under her skin and she does everything to control herself. She begins to spit her words: "I believe the complaining witness in this case. I believe everything she said. And the level of control and manipulation and coercion and deception by the defendant, her exploitation of the Mr. Witters's experience and disappearance, leads me to believe that, yes, in fact, there were things that she said that were coercive, that were duress over a fourteen-year-old young, impressionable, and totally controlled young woman. So I think it's there. I think it's more than there."

Scott is now squeezing my hand and pumping my fist in silence. My brother grabs my dad by the shoulders and shakes him with delight. My mom raps her arms around my neck and brings me in for a hug and kiss on the cheek. I look around and my entire army is celebrating. There, in the back of the Martinez courtroom, we cheer as quietly as we can.

As tears roll down my cheeks, I look around and see people who have heard the dirty and disgusting truth, and now sit even closer.

Kristen with her mom Jeanne Lewis in their home in Oakland, CA, in 1982. This picture was taken just before the Lewis family moved to the small town of Moraga, CA, which had one of the best school districts in the state.

Kristen and her older brother Marc Lewis had a great childhood in Moraga, CA, before Kristen met the teachers who would later abuse her.

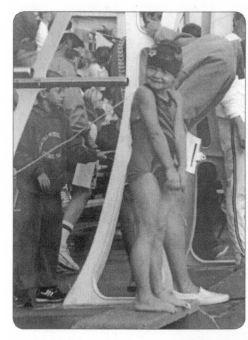

Kristen as a young swimmer getting ready to race the 25-yard butterfly. She would later go on to compete in butterfly at the NCAA Championships and US Olympic Trials and used swimming as a mental escape from sexual abuse.

Kristen just outside of the JM front office before the abuse began.

Kristen loved all sports as a young girl.
Here she is on a family trip to Lake
Tahoe, just months before being abused
by Dan Witters.

Julie Correa (PE) and Dan Witters (Science) were teachers
together at JM in the 1990s. They were both named Teacher of
the Year and coached after-school sports. The two were friends
and both abused female students.

This picture was taken just after Kristen confided in Correa about the Witters abuse. Correa used the incident to grow closer to Kristen and isolate her from family and friends.

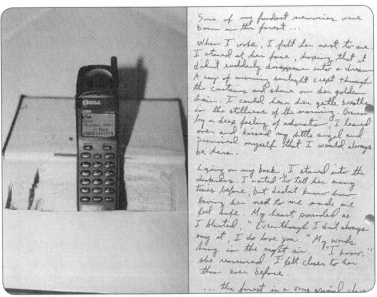

The secret cell phone (left) and the letter (right) were both crucial pieces of evidence in the criminal proceedings.

This is the street view of the upstairs apartment that Julie rented away from her husband and where much of the abuse occurred.

Kristen and her best friends Maggie Barnard (left) and Maggie Ford (right) before heading to their senior prom. Kristen's best friends Maggie "Black" and Maggie "Red" did not know that their best friend had just escaped years of sexual abuse by their favorite teacher.

Kristen races her signature event for UCLA, the 200 butterfly.
Kristen would go on to become an All-American, team captain,
and NCAA Post-Graduate Scholar for the Bruins.

For a full decade after her abuse ended, Kristen repressed
memories of sexual abuse and lived a happy life. Even her closest
friends, like Chelsea Murray (left) from UCLA, had no idea about
Kristen's past.

Kristen worked with Natalie Coughlin while at Cal. The two became great friends and Natalie became the most decorated female Olympian of all time.

Marc Lewis (middle) performs the wedding ceremony of high school sweethearts Kristen and Scott Cunnane in 2007. Marc not only is Kristen's brother but also represented her in the civil case against the Moraga School District.

This photo of Kristen and her dogs Murphy (right) and Jack (left) was taken in the spring of 2010 just weeks before she spun into a depression as she remembered what had been through as a child.

Taken in August of 2010, after Kristen reported crimes to police and did pretext phone calls, Julie Correa was arrested in her home in Utah.

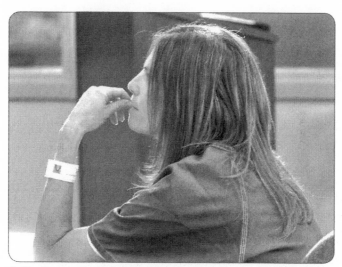

Julie Correa listening to the criminal proceedings. She laughed and smirked through much of the criminal process and had many supporters (former students and other teachers) in the courtroom.

Kristen Cunnane coached the Cal Women's Swim Team for ten years. While there, Kristen won NCAA Assistant Coach of the Year and helped her team win four NCAA Championships.

Kristen Cunnane and Teri McKeever (Head Cal Coach and Head Olympic Coach) hug after winning an NCAA Championship.

Kristen Cunnane surrounded by her athletes
on the Cal Swim Team, Caroline Piehl (left)
and Missy Franklin (right).

Kristen Cunnane cheers for her Cal swimmers at the
2016 NCAA Championship.

Kristen recognizes that her Cal team helped her through some of her darkest days.

Kristen with her mom Jeanne (left) and dad Rob (right) and new baby celebrating a recent NCAA Championship. Jeanne and Rob were both very supportive through the criminal and civil proceedings and Kristen credits them with helping her survive.

Teri McKeever and Kristen Cunnane strategize with their team about an upcoming relay.

Kristen's three young kids: Annie (left), Betsy (middle) and Billy (right).

Kristen and her husband Scott Cunnane (right), who is a prosecutor for the Contra Costa District Attorney's Office.

Kristen and her husband Scott with their three children in December 2018.

CHAPTER TWENTY-FOUR

Victoria's Worst Secret

I've figured out that it's more comfortable if I lean up against the fence. I squat down, feet just wider than hip width apart, and use the redwood fence behind me to support my lower back. Three inches from my face there are harsh branches of a maturing bush, meant to hide the neighbors' fence, not such a small girl.

Tonight things are especially uncomfortable in my hiding place. It's not raining now, but it has been all afternoon. I'm already wet from passing through the bush to get back here, and now my lower back is getting damper and colder by the minute from the fence that usually gives me some relief.

At the top of the hill I survey the four-way intersection of the neighborhood. By now I know the make and model of almost every car. Knowing who drives which car gives me a sliver of calmness.

Watching gives me something to wonder about: *Is it the grey-haired man five doors up taking his silver Camry to the grocery store? Does he work the night shift? Or, like me, does he leave when no one knows he is gone?*

I don't mind being here alone. I have let Kristen stay at home to get ready for her big soccer game tomorrow. After all, I only exist to take care of the dirty work.

You said that we are going to celebrate Valentine's tonight, that I am your Valentine. It is February 16, 1997—two days after Valentine's and two days before Kristen's birthday.

Why do I have to always celebrate with you? Kristen already gave Adam a Valentine and he already gave her four dozen roses.

I must admit, it was a little over the top. Besides, I am not entirely convinced that Adam is even the one who bought these flowers. I suspect that his mom, who adores Kristen and adores the fact that Kristen keeps her son out of trouble, was behind it. *What would she think if she knew about me?*

I hear the car that I know better than any of those in the neighborhood. The one that I see every day on the way to school. The one that I have spent so many hopeless nights trapped in. The one that will take me out of this cold damp space, only for a moment, and take me to a place much darker.

The headlights squint as they climb the hill, pass me and my bushes, and take a U-turn at the top. The orange street light shines on your serious and intense ashen face as you roll the car along the curb in front of me. You do not turn off the engine, you only slow the car, and suddenly I am inside.

"Hello, my sweetheart." A tiny voice screams in my head. My ears bleed. But I have no voice and no choice.

"Hi." I sound younger than Kristen did on the phone with Maggie earlier tonight. By now you have given me the blanket to put over my head. Tonight you have pushed the seat as far back as it will go. This means I am supposed to sit on the floor.

"I have your present in here." You smile and I can tell that you are proud of yourself. I hate this lowered-eyebrow grin. My heart races and I try to prepare for what you have in store.

"It's under here." The Velcro of your North Face rain jacket tears and the murmur of the engine does nothing to quiet the sound.

I wonder why this sound echoes in my ears. *Why does it sound different from when I take off my coat? Why does it sound like the cry of a child being torn from her mother's bosom? Why does it make me imagine blood oozing out of my wrists?*

Underneath I see my present and the cause for your grin. "I went to Victoria's Secret for you," you say, clearly proud of yourself.

I have never seen lingerie before, and Kristen has never worn lingerie before. My mind races quickly to figure out how I should act. *How do you want me to respond to this?* I know that if I do not respond correctly, you will be angry with me. Kristen could never handle this.

Should I act excited? Yes, but not the kind of excited Kristen is when she goes to get candy at Fudge Alley with Maggie.

Should I act happy? Yes, but not the kind of happy Kristen is on Christmas morning when she can barely walk into the family room because of all of the presents.

Curious? Exactly, but not the kind of curious Kristen is when she is thinking about which position she will play next season.

I look at your face. You are driving and you are very serious. It is black. Or maybe navy. It is so dark that I can barely see it.

Your right hand releases from the steering wheel, a finger at a time. *Why do you move in slow motion with me?* It pauses for a moment above the parking brake and then you grab my hand. I am sitting where people's feet are supposed to go. Not even your dog would sit down here. You grab my hand and I know what you are going to do next.

As you bring my hand back toward your body—toward your disgusting body—I look out the driver's side window. It is a trick of mine, one of many. You think I am looking up at you, but I am memorizing the numbers of orange streetlights and counting the seconds between each. As you bring my hand to the inseam of your freckled and old thigh, I wonder why the city of Lafayette has not noticed that the thirty-second streetlight on Moraga Road has been burnt out for over a year.

As I look into the darkness I am glad that Kristen does not have to see what I see tonight, that she doesn't have to feel what I feel. Without looking I know that your head is tipped back slightly and your eyes move upwards with pleasure. I count streetlights and think of Kristen as we creep toward your apartment.

The stairs feel as if they are about to break as I walk up them, and I am grateful that I move like a fairy. I know exactly how to navigate the exit from your car and climb to your apartment, like a SWAT agent amidst a sting operation. I walk into your apartment and I hate being here so much, I wish that I was hanging out with Kristen and her fun friends.

Let me just say this: it's not that I am mad at Kristen. I understand. She has a lot to lose and she needs me in order to win. After all, she is an almost sixteen-year-old girl who just needs to be fifteen.

I stand in the living room, looking at the scene before me. I am wise and like an owl I move my head as I predict in my mind what will happen here tonight. Although I wish Kristen were here, I know I will have to do this alone.

I let myself think of Kristen and her hair that grows blonder with each home highlighting job. I imagine her standing with me and realize that her dropping swimming times is a result of her getting taller and stronger . . . and because she has me now. I think of her and I think of me; our appearances are growing in opposition.

Kristen has a lot of friends, and many of them have started to experiment with alcohol. Kristen doesn't drink, though, probably because she worries that it will remind her of me, of you, and of this. Her friends hide their experimentations from Kristen, just as Kristen hides me from her friends.

I didn't pick my name. It's just like anyone's name, it was given at birth. I would like to think my name has a bit of meaning: Eve.

Usually, I come to help at night.

I like helping. Well, that's not entirely true. I don't like what I have to do in order to help, it's just that I like *that* I am able to help Kristen. Kristen has a lot to balance in her life.

It used to be the two of us against the one of you. But then, with Witters and the suicide and everything else, it just got to be too much. There became too much risk for Kristen to be here. Now I handle nearly everything.

I understand. I have to understand.

You move toward the center of the room and I stand closer to the door, hanging onto the image of Kristen.

Speaking of having to be approaching sixteen, Kristen has all of these silly little issues. Last week, when Kristen was out of town with her traveling soccer team, Maggie Black had "people over" when her parents were out of town. "Having people over" refers to a party—not a raging, out-of-control keg party where the police will be called more likely than not. More like guys and girls hanging out, having drinks, and sometimes hooking up.

Maggie Black is just like Kristen, and neither one of them ever drinks. That's part of the reason Kristen won't be here tonight. The latest of Kristen's problems is that she feels left out from her friends' group when they are off drinking. But she doesn't have time for that. She needs to do her school work; she needs to excel in sports. She needs to make sure that everything looks in order. There is a lot to be done.

So while Kristen is left negotiating the drama of a Moraga teen, I deal with you.

I turn my head to the right without moving my body, and I see you enter the kitchen. I watch carefully as you grab something out of the fridge.

I slip quickly back to Kristen's issues. Sometimes thinking of Kristen and her little road bumps makes me feel better, as though I have a tiny window into what a real life would look like.

So, anyway, Maggie Black had people over, let them drink at her house, but didn't drink herself. Black didn't drink because she is pretty involved with this church group, which Kristen is not. Kristen avoids the church, but a lot of her friends go. I think that she avoids stuff like that because, after all, *how can there be God when there is you?*

Most of these churchgoing friends of Kristen's drink and smoke weed anyway. Yup, another tiny problem for Kristen.

Just from an outsider's perspective, I like Maggie Black. I don't fully understand Maggie's faith because my current situation doesn't allow me to go to any sort of church or leave much room to think about faith. Actually, I am really only here when you are here. But I respect that what Maggie says at church matches what she does during the weekend. Maggie is the opposite of you. You say you won't hurt me and then you do.

Maggie Red, on the other hand, likes to have a good time. She started drinking a little while back, and the news of her recent hobby took a few weeks to reach Kristen. I wish I got to hang out with Maggie Red; I think that she would understand me.

Kristen felt lonely and sad when she found out that Red was drinking. Kristen was also pretty upset when she found out that Red had made out with Dan from another source. They are supposed to be best friends. But I understand where Red is coming from. She knows and I know that Kristen should just be kept in the dark about some things.

Kristen is working on convincing her friends that it is okay that they drink. I know that Kristen is not okay with it. I also know why she is not okay with it. Just the sight of alcohol reminds Kristen of me, of you, and that this is all happening. I often think that she would prefer that I didn't exist. But then who would do this?

So there you have it, Kristen and her normal Kristen problems. Sometimes I want to laugh at her for feeling lonely. Since she has separated completely to "achieve" in her normal life, I am entirely by myself. Kristen doesn't even really know that all of this is going on. If the Campolindo school counselor pulled her in from junior year English and showed her a video reel of what happened three nights ago, I don't think that she would believe it. She can't believe it because she can't handle it.

I guess I can.

You always find something to "celebrate." Kristen's birthday, your birthday, Christmas, every holiday I can imagine. I have stopped keeping track because I know that, to you, celebrating means one thing: you give alcohol to get what you want.

You don't even know when my birthday is. I wouldn't dare give you a hint that it is in June. Then you would know that I am not Kristen.

Right when I walked in tonight and saw the candles on the coffee table, I knew that the lace was not the end of your charades. I knew that you had another trick up your sleeve.

Are you trying to be romantic? There is no way that you actually think that you are being romantic? And if you do think you are being romantic, who is it for?

I hear a pop in the kitchen, where I sense that you are. I hear fizz that sounds like the opening of a soda that has been previously shaken. I can feel your intentions.

If Kristen liked what was happening, she wouldn't gag. She would be here. And if I really liked what was happening, you wouldn't have to get me drunk.

I wish that your beverage trick didn't work, but it does work. *You know that.* You always get to do whatever you want to me. I respond and I hate that some of it feels good. But when I have to do things to you, even Nicole Kidman could not fake it through the disgust I feel. I think it is the smell that makes me ill. You get angry with me, and although I can fake it better than Kristen ever could, I can't do it how you want me to—unless you make me drink.

In a flash, you are in front of me.

"I thought we would try something new . . ." The words leave your mouth and enter straight through my chest and my blood flows through my heart faster. My chest tightens and, despite what Kristen thinks, I still get very scared sometimes. I think of all the many times that you have said this phrase and then done something unspeakable.

I say nothing because I cannot say anything. But, truth be told, I hate how it tastes. I hate how it smells and how it makes my breath smell. And I know that it will make Kristen's head hurt tomorrow morning.

You leave room for my response just as a little girl having afternoon tea with her stuffed teddy and toy doll would.

"You will like this even better." You turn your rounded nose in the direction of the coffee table. I see the shine of a bucket in the near darkness of the room. Sitting next to the bucket are two glasses, and I know exactly what they are for.

Kristen probably wouldn't get what these are because they are taller and skinnier than the one her mom drinks her wine out of every night. But she has seen these glasses once before.

When Kristen was seven, she went to Santa Rosa with her family to celebrate her Grandma and Grandpa's fiftieth wedding anniversary. The happy old couple smashed cake in each other's face, which the young Kristen did not understand. And with twisted arms, drank out of glasses just like these.

That was a celebration. I'm not sure Kristen has room in her life for meaningless memories.

The two words "even better" scan across my mind and I search for what you might be referring to. *Something that you did to me? Something that you made me do to you?* I look at the glasses and the bucket and all of a sudden I know—even better than wine coolers.

"This is champagne," you say to me, momentarily acknowledging my age and should-be innocence.

You think that I am dumb, but I am much wiser than Kristen.

I look at your face and I hate that I know the lines so well. You always tell me that we are soulmates and that we were meant to be born at the same time, but you don't even know my real name. I hope that we are not soulmates. It is something that I hope for often, wondering deeply if I was born out of your evil.

"Okay," I say back to you and I walk toward you as I know I must. I have learned how to do this by now.

One black night you said to Kristen, "I think I'll buy us some wine coolers, so I can help you loosen up a little bit." Kristen didn't even know what those were. Another exhibit in the case of why Kristen needs me.

You carefully chose and spoke the word "loosen" because in that night you felt Kristen clamp shut. You knew she choked on you and she couldn't hide it. You were aware of her repulsion. And you wouldn't have any of it. Your solution: alcohol. Kristen's solution: me.

That night Kristen was terribly confused. She imagined that the next time she would be in your apartment that you would wheel out a blue Igloo cooler. You would reach your nasty hand inside and pull out the bottle of Merlot that her mom usually pours around 9:30 every night. Kristen sat wondering why you thought that she would like it better from a cooler than from the counter as her mom takes it.

She was surprised when she took her first sip, surprised that it tasted so much like a liquid Jolly Rancher. I was surprised that it made things go by a little faster.

She sat there silently; I can't blame her for being naïve. She didn't say anything, because when she questions you, you grow angry and you hurt her. You call her young and stupid. Then usually you kiss her. Poor kid.

I have learned from Kristen's mistakes and I have learned to most often keep my lips locked shut.

"We are celebrating our true and endless love for Valentines," You announce to me and break my inner dialogue. You know you have to give me a reason.

Or maybe you are just giving yourself a reason?

It is Kristen's sixteenth birthday in two days. We will "celebrate" again far too soon.

You lead me now around the dining table. You usually stop me here and lean so hard in to me that my back is forced flush with the table as you kiss me. I always have to stop myself from clamping my teeth down on your gross tongue.

There is a gift on the table. I know it is for me. Well, I know that it is actually for Kristen, but you are giving it to me. I get scared rather than excited. I think of Kristen's favorite scary movie, *Seven,* and imagine Brad Pitt opening a box and seeing the gift inside. It is his wife's head. I know how he feels. Why does Kristen like that movie so much?

I wish I were toasting with Brad right now.

The wrapping paper is silver and it has a blue ribbon. I imagine you tying the bow with your bony hands. The hands that make me want to drive a nail through my eyeball.

Did Rob see you wrapping this? Did he ask whom it was for or what it was? Who held the top while you secured the first knot and tied the bow?

You hand it to me and your hands feel cold. As I open it, I know I have to act as if I like what is inside. I practice the look on my face and the words out of my mouth before I open the lid. I am quite the actress, though my dialogue is extremely limited.

At the top of the box there is a pair of white pajamas. I pull them out and they look too small for me. As I hold them in my hand, I realize that they are from the wrong section of Old Navy—the little girls. The contrast of the white pajamas I am supposed to wear and your black lingerie reminds me that you love our difference in age.

I peer inside and see a key chain. It is silver and looks expensive. More expensive than the lanyards and photo key chains that Kristen has hanging off of her key chain now. She's not sixteen yet, but she has her keys all configured and placed neatly in the kitchen.

Last week Kristen's dad picked up her keys and said, "Krick, these keys are so heavy, you might want to take some of this junk off. It could ruin the ignition."

Kristen had innocently looked at her keys; the logo of her soccer club, the mini-kaleidoscope with the picture of both Maggies. She loved everything that dangled. Another of Kristen's minor problems: her dad not understanding how long she waited to have her own set of keys.

"This is your Valentine's present," you say and rub the side of your body as you touch the silk-like fabric. "This is an early birthday present so that you have it the moment you are able to drive."

I look down at the silver and I am angry that you would attempt to dangle onto Kristen's life. I am nauseated by the idea of adding you to her key ring.

"Read it." It is not an encouragement, but a directive. Not like a mom teaching her son the alphabet, but instead like Jim Jones at Jonestown.

"Never drive faster than your guardian angel can fly." I hold the words close to my eyes so that I can read them in the low light. Also, so that I do not misread them and make you angry.

You smile at me and say, "I am always watching over you. I am your guardian angel." Your voice sounds like a recording that plays out of your mouth, like there is not a real person living inside of you.

I smile up at you, because you are bigger than I am. A smile on my face and a frown in my heart. As your face and your triangular-shaped forehead come into focus, it feels like too much for me to see.

Suddenly I imagine a fantastical and far away scene. I am standing hand in hand with Kristen in front of the English tudor we both call home. Her hand and my hand fit perfectly together. Kristen's new car (well, new to her at least) and her sixteenth birthday present are to my left. Her red Jetta smiles at us and offers us freedom. Not the traditional freedom a new driver has from parental dependence, but freedom from you.

But the parking spot in the driveway is where the great divide occurred; where you kissed Kristen after the dance show, and where I was born. And now you are crouched behind the Jetta.

Before me, when Kristen was in fifth grade, she was the Lion in the school play. She loves *The Wizard of Oz*. But now the joy of the original is mutated into the horror of the sequel.

Your face morphs into the face of a flying monkey and your eyes grow red. You have always looked a little like a monkey, so the alterations are limited, but your back hunches to make way for sprouting wings.

We both get in the car fast and Kristen uses the stick shift driving skills her dad taught her, with great frustration, to speed away from you. You take flight, and as I sit in the passenger seat and look in the side view mirror, I can see your smiling face. We speed up, we make turns, and it feels good being on Kristen's team again. But, just when I think that we have lost you, you are inside the car with us.

Like magic, you shrink. Just small enough to sit on Kristen's right shoulder. "Slow down," you whisper, and she can feel your breath on the backside of her ear.

As I swivel my head, I see that you have a halo floating above your mini-face. But after closer inspection, it isn't a halo of light like a real angel. It is one that you bought at the costume store and you wear it to trick people. You wear it to coach athletes, teach students, and convince parents that you are a good role model for their kids. Then you go home, take it off, and brew a plan of how to rape an innocent believer.

Kristen is a good girl. She does what you say. She is scared. She takes her foot off the gas and, as the car slows, I look down at the keys that dangle from the ignition.

Kristen pulls to the side of the road near a local park and gets out of the car. She hands you the keys as she walks to meet her friends for a picnic. I sit still in the passenger's seat. You take the wheel like a crazed monster, and my eyes glide out the window as you go double the speed limit.

I turn to face Kristen, as the distance between our faces increases like stars turning blue from the Doppler effect.

The mini-movie has finished in my head and I am back at your apartment. I look at the champagne and know that this is my job. Kristen has to join her friends for that picnic. She has to go home afterwards and give her mom a kiss on the cheek. She has to have so much joy and so much happiness that my pain never wins.

So, I open my mouth and let the sourness of the champagne slip down my throat. The fizz brings tears to my eyes as I tip my glass up for too long, letting in the better half of my glass. In a short time, the space around me begins to feel fuzzy, and as I slip into another night and another time, I am grateful of the liquid protection.

CHAPTER TWENTY-FIVE

Broken Ankles

People will think I'm crazy if I say this. But I might go crazy if I don't. It doesn't hurt or sting or itch. It is hard to describe the feeling, but even harder to sit inside my body and feel the feeling.

I guess I would say it is an ache. An ache that is not only physical, but mental and emotional. An ache that doesn't just sit in my head or heart or soul, but often ends up sitting right around my ankles.

Three years ago I broke my ankle in five places. I was playing softball and sliding into third base, and my cleat got caught in a pothole. My left foot was nearly left in place when my leg kept sliding, and the bone came right through the skin. I have had four surgeries, and I am almost fully put back together. As crazy as it sounds, I would rather have that real pain than this unpredictable sensation that I do not understand.

It is as if someone had their hands wrapped around my ankles and were smashing all the bone, blood vessels, and ligaments together.

I hate ankle bracelets, I hate those kinds of shoes that have straps around the ankles, and I hate mid-ankle socks. I prefer my ankles to be covered, but can handle it when they are not. I hate when my ankles are bare and I am standing next to the bed or dresser and there is a slight possibility that someone could fit underneath. I like crossing my ankles when I am seated.

Last week "the feeling," as I have come to call it out loud in my own brain, was coming so often and so strong that I was getting sick to my stomach.

As I head up the stairs to one of my two weekly appointments with him, I think of all the things I could talk to Chuck about. I could update him on the court case and the logistics of trying to fight this battle. I could tell him what is going on at work and how the swimmers are my escape from the pain of a long drawn out legal fight. Or I could tell him the truth.

But I know if I tell him, we will have to do the most painful part of my therapy: EMDR.

A side note about EMDR, or Eye Movement Desensitization and Reprocessing: it is a form of psychotherapy that was developed by Francine Shapiro to resolve the development of trauma-related disorders caused by exposure to distressing events such as rape or military combat. According to Shapiro's theory, when a trauma occurs, it may jeopardize usual coping processes in the brain. Instead of being processed the way a typical life event would be processed, the trauma travels to a tiny place in the brain and gets locked up in an "isolated memory network." EMDR allows the trauma to resurface and be processed as a normal event would be, and then stored the same way a normal memory would be stored.

When Chuck first told me about it, the only reason that I even attempted to believe in it was because I was in such a deep mode of desperation I had to believe that this might help me. "Essentially," Chuck told me, "we use eye movement to activate a part of your brain where trauma is trapped. And the eye movement helps the memory be taken to the correct storage area for memory." Since Chuck gave me the short explanation of this therapy, I have come to feel the incredible power of this process. Like the painful process of chemotherapy, my therapy rids my soul of the cancer Julie caused. With each session, my heart breaks open, bleeds, gets cleaned out, and forms a new scab. It is deeply painful and deeply healing.

And so today, as I walk towards Chuck's office, I know that there is great pain waiting for me. And I'm scared because, although I know there is great pain, I have no idea why.

"How are you doing today?" He looks at me over his glasses.

"I am nervous." I am honest with Chuck. I have to be. It is the only option.

The feeling is here, in my ankles. The fact that my ankles hurt makes my stomach hurt. I sit down on the hard sofa.

"I have this problem with my ankles."

Of course, Chuck being Chuck, he handles it perfectly. His light smile and slight head tilt made it okay for me to answer his question, "What about your ankles?"

After I told him the things that make the feeling start, he understood right away. "Ah, that makes sense. Let's do some EMDR work to see if we can get some of that to go away."

One of the tactics that Chuck uses before we start the EMDR is to get me in a place where I am able to access the memories. We usually talk enough so that I am reaching for the box of Kleenex that is always on the lefthand side of the sofa. This shaking of my emotions allows me to access the pain of the trauma. I guess it would not work to have a happy and smiling Kristen bounce onto the couch and jump into what it felt like to get raped by a woman.

He begins by asking me how my ankles are feeling. Sometimes I think Chuck might have x-ray vision into my soul. He is an older man and I am thankful for his soft approach with me. He is occupied with wisdom and it radiates out of his every word. "So, how do they feel?"

It is a mixture of embarrassment, bewilderment, and frustration. You might want to throw a splash of pain into the cocktail for good measure; after all, none of this lacks the last ingredient. "They hurt," I say and cast my eyes down for two reasons—to give my ankles a dirty look and to avoid any possible eye contact.

"How does it feel to tell me that your ankles hurt?" He puts his hands out and palms up as an invitation for me to explain my confusion at this sensation.

"I hate it. I feel as if I am going crazy." I look back down at my ankles and Chuck joins my gaze. "See," I say in frustration, "there is nothing wrong with them. How could they feel this way?" My heart is beating fast now, trying to solve the puzzle for my brain. I feel my lids fill with water, and the last few words feel clunky coming out of my mouth.

As I begin to grab the tissues, Chuck says, "Okay, let's begin."

He moves a pen-looking object, which I imagine he has bought from some medical supply store, in front of my face. My eyes follow it, right to left. Chuck says that this will physically activate both sides of my brain. It is not at all hypnosis, although I am sure that if people saw my eyes swaying back and forth, they would think that it was. Instead, I am completely conscious and I have full control over my thoughts and actions. I stay present and in the moment of being in Chuck's office.

Chuck leads me through the next phase. "I want you just to feel the feeling in your ankles." I have my eyes closed now. After about ten seconds of following his pen, I close my eyes, take a deep breath, and let the trauma soak into my brain.

I feel my ankles and they hurt. I open my mind and allow the day they started feeling this way to rush back into my head. I speak the memory out to Chuck as I see it happening. "I am in my room at home. I know that she is coming. I think that she will be in the closet as she always is. I am standing next to my bed, listening to see if my dad has gone to sleep yet. I am scared to open the closet, but know that I have no other choice. I back up to my bed to sit down and suddenly, without warning, her hands are wrapped around my ankles." I open my mouth and a silent scream leaves my throat.

"Okay." Chuck holds the device back in front of my face and I know that it is time to follow along with my eyes. "Just notice the scene. It is like a movie and you are watching."

Tears pour down my face from my back-and-forth eyes, and I sit and look at my then fifteen-year-old face, terrified, breathless, and hopeless. I allow myself to do as Chuck says—sit with the scene. He brings his pen down and I again close my eyes, take a deep breath, and open my mind.

"She knows she has scared me. She feels as though I am about to scream and blow her cover. She tightens her grip, and I can feel the bones crushing together in my ankles. Instead of her hands, I feel as if I might have barbaric ankle cuffs chaining my feet together. My room feels like a dungeon and she is about to take me to the torture chamber."

Again, Chuck has me open my eyes and I watch as my beautiful childhood room grows dark and scary. I sit in the sadness of why my ankles hurt—at least part of the reason they hurt.

As I close my eyes again, I am presented with a different scene. The thing with EMDR is that I never really know where my mind is going. It feels like giving my memory a hall pass and it can walk into any classroom as it so desires.

Even so, I am surprised when I am not in my bedroom anymore, but in Julie's bedroom. I remember it all so well. I can see it all so well. The scene hurts so bad that I cannot get the words out to Chuck. I can see the image, but the image crushes my voice.

"It's okay, just sit with it. See what you see. You don't need to say it to me." These three short sentences take time leaving

Chuck and coming to me. He has me open my eyes again after allowing me some time in silence.

His voice is low and soft. "Just notice the image you saw. It is real and it happened and it is in the past. You are safe."

My eyes travel back and forth and I look through the bedroom window and see Julie. She is moving on top of me. She used to call it "kissing me down there." I didn't know it was oral sex until she had been doing it to me for over a year. As I watch her moving over me . . .

Chuck has me close my eyes again. I might be able to speak this time and I need someone to sit with me as I look through this window. I open my mouth because I know I must try.

"I am there . . ." I want Chuck in on this scene with me although he has not forced himself. "In her bedroom. Lying on her pink sheets. She is over me. Doing things to me. I hate her and I hate it. I hate myself because I hate that I am physically responding."

"Okay, Kristen, open your eyes and just notice that hate." I do, and my tears slow and my lips tighten in anger. I allow Chuck to sit next to me in the dark night as we look at what she is doing to me inside her room.

Again, he brings me to close my eyes. He asks me to share with him what I see. "She is still there, and still kissing me there. And I am still mad. Lying there, I feel like my insides are made out of black coal. I feel dirty and sick and evil. I feel trapped." My voice breaks with the word "trapped" and I see it. I see why my ankles hurt.

I continue on quickly because I do not want Chuck to stop me. I want to tell him what I am seeing before we move on. I feel as if I am on the brink of solving a decade-old case. "She is there, upside down on top of me. I want to get up and run. But I can't. She is thrusting her body onto mine. Thrusting herself onto my mouth. It tastes horrible and I can feel vomit in my throat. She pins me down with her body. She feels me squirm and pushes harder." And like a light shining on the truth of what I am going through I see my ankles, "And she is holding me down by the ankles."

"Open your eyes and notice what she did to you." I am brave enough to open my eyes and see the lonely scene. My tongue curls at the taste and my body sinks into the couch as I see her push her body into mine. I watch her use the meat of her bony hands to crush my young ankles.

"I need you to close your eyes again." I am glad to have a break from looking at the scene and surprised that my body has started to relax. As my eyes shut, I am astonished at what I see.

I am still there, trapped under her gross female body. I am still making too much of an imprint on the pink sheets. I am still held by my ankles. But something else has happened. My brain and my body have come to peace with what I thought and how it felt. They packed up their bags and marched down to where the physical sensation was the greatest: my ankles.

"I am still there." I want to include Chuck in the pilgrimage. "My body stops feeling and my head stops thinking. I tell all parts of my body to take a little nap and they listen. They become numb. The one and only thing that I am aware of is my ankles, where she is holding me down. It hurts, and I only pay attention to the hurt."

"Okay, open your eyes and think of the hurt." Chuck feels like my partner in solving the mystery.

As I follow along with Chuck, I see myself living inside my ankles. I see the travesty of what Julie is doing to me and know that even though my ankles hurt, they were a place of relative refuge.

I close my eyes again, this time finding a piece of peace. "I see myself paying attention to my ankles as a means to escaping."

Chuck chimes in, "Can you be thankful to your ankles for giving you a place to camp out?"

"Yes," I do not hesitate. In my head I reach down and whisper a word of thanks to my healing ankles.

"Can you imagine that they are strong ankles now?" With each question Chuck's voice booms a little louder and I can feel his confidence in me, his confidence in my ankles.

"Yes, they are strong and they would kick Julie in the face if they had the chance."

"Can you image them carrying you through your daily life? In your coaching? To the witness stand? On your walks with Scott?"

"Yes," I say. A feeling of forgiveness sweeps over my body and settles near my feet. Perhaps forgiving my own body is the only forgiveness I will ever feel.

I let a little smile reach my mouth and I open my eyes because I know that the EMDR session is over. I look at Chuck dead in the eye and I mean what I say: "They are good ankles."

CHAPTER TWENTY-SIX

Window of Opportunity

You are here. Upstairs, hiding in my closet. As I imagine you and your gross shoulder-length hair lying in wait, I wish I could laugh at this episode of *Step by Step*. I wish that you would wear a ponytail holder. I wish that Eve were here. I wish that I didn't know what is going to happen next.

But I do. Without wanting to, my mind is pulled from the comfort and final safety of my family room couch, and I imagine where you are this very moment. My closet is bigger than most of my friends' closets. It is somewhere between a walk-in closet and a normal closet, whatever you call that. It's not organized, but has all the clothes I could ever want or need. My mom grew up poor, and I think our shopping trips are a way to ensure that I have a better childhood than she did.

It's a conglomeration really, where childhood meets teen, where my oversized and overstuffed teddy bears and other animals share space with my jean jacket from The Gap, shoe boxes of pictures with my friends, and, right now, you.

I have always had the bad habit of being messy. But now you encourage my bad habit to feed yours. My messy closet gives you perfect refuge to hide your evil face.

Did I just hear the ceiling creek above my head? Or was that something in the car commercial? What will you do to me tonight?

As my mind wonders about the next several hours, I remember what you said on the phone last night; "I need to have you." This five-word combination is one of the favorites on your list. And as the words begin to leave your mouth, I wonder what it is you need. My heart hurts when you say this. It pumps harder in fear and shrinks in sadness. My brain races, wondering what is next in my life. I unravel all of the upcoming possibilities, but because I am not evil, I have a hard time playing defense against you.

I have a few strategies that seem to work at some level. I have never explained this to you, of course, but I have a hierarchical ranking of what is the most difficult to live through.

I have a mental checklist ranking written very neatly on the inside of my eyelids. It is only for me and Eve to see; it helps us work together. When you say that you 'need to have me,' we troubleshoot the situation, looking for a way that we can meet your sick needs without letting you steal my life.

1. Having you come here when my parents are gone.
2. Going to your office at JM.
3. Going somewhere in your car or my car.
4. Going to your apartment.
5. Having you come here when my parents are here.

Number 1 sits there, not because Eve enjoys it, but because she can handle it. I think it is the safest way to not get caught and thus stay alive.

Number 2 worries me in that there are still people from JM working on school grounds when Eve shows up and the cold tile floor is quite painful, even for Eve. Still, I prefer number 2 instead of number 3.

I hate going in either car because, well, because I hate everything about you—but I also think eventually someone will shine a flashlight inside and then you will be in a perfect position to drive away to nowhere.

Number 4 means that Eve has to spend hour after hour getting hurt. It means the least amount of sleep and poses the highest risk of my parents figuring out that I am gone.

But, still, in situations 2 through 4, Eve is almost exclusively in charge. A lot of the time she does all of it for me. Lately, a lot of the time has been becoming all of the time.

But then there is number 5. Tonight . . .

In my own house, with my parents here. It feels almost impossible to escape. It feels impossible to have Eve deal with you. *What if something goes wrong?* I have to stick around in case my dad hears something.

My mom is filling up her single glass of wine for the night and my dad is snoring on the leather chair in the corner. I need to get up to my room so that I can manage the situation. It would be dangerous if my mom and I walked up the stairs together and I might die if she followed me into my room to tuck me in.

"Love you," I bend down and kiss my pretty mom on the cheek. *If I really loved her, wouldn't I have been able to figure out a way out from under you?*

"Love you, too, Krick," she says as she looks from the TV at me with her loving brown eyes.

Krick—a term of endearment given to me first by my grandmother after the Kricket doll. It's what my whole family calls me, what Maggie, Maggie, and Meghan call me. You have never used this nickname for me and I think I would rip the nose off your face if you tried.

In passing through my kitchen, I open the fridge quietly, doing the first undercover thing I will do tonight. I grab the blue and red can of Pepsi in the refrigerator door, relying on the nominal amount of caffeine to keep me alert.

I walk up the stairs almost silently, not because I have to tonight, just for practice. I cough and, in time, lift the metal tab of the soda. I drink so quickly that the bubbles fill my eyes with tears. After turning right at the top of the stairs, I stop in the bathroom across the hallway from my bedroom. With each step, my heart beats harder and I imagine you moving with excitement in my closet. *Can you hear my steps as I pass you in the hallway?*

As I turn on the overhead light in the bathroom, I look at the sink neighboring mine and wish that Marc were brushing his teeth next to me, and that he wasn't down at UCLA. I pick up the toothpaste and line my brush. After four swipes total, I spit, put the brush down, and hurry to the toilet to relieve my hurting stomach.

To be honest, brushing my teeth has taken a back seat in my life. I can't even remember the last time I flossed that wasn't twenty minutes before going to see the dentist. There are just some things that I don't have time for anymore. After all, what's the point of cleaning my teeth when my mouth is going to feel so dirty in a few minutes anyway?

I pass the sinks and carefully avoid eye contact with myself. Looking at my reflection is hard, because in moments like these, I long to see Eve's dark hair in the mirror.

My door is open and, to anyone other than me, it would look like an invitation to a warm bed and a restful night's sleep. My body aches as I walk through the doorway, knowing that immediately to my left, you are there, in the depths of my closet. *Are you touching the jacket that I wore to school yesterday, or standing on the pair of soccer cleats that I recently retired?*

It's a wooden door. It's sturdy being made of solid oak. I used to stare at my closet door when I was trying to go to sleep and imagine the long darken streaks within the wood grain as faces, or tree trunks in an enchanted forest. Now I look at the vertical lines and see the bars of a prison cell.

The doorknob is gold, but not the bright gold of my new earrings, rather an antique gold that looks worn and tired. I feel a shift in my brain, a shift in my body, and suddenly I am ready to do what must be done. I am tougher than Eve gives me credit for, if only slightly.

It is dark in my closet, and although there is a light, I do not turn it on for fear of what I might see.

"Hello?" It is the whisper of a child who is alone and frightened. I bend down, not wanting to touch for you, but knowing that I must. My hand passes my newest pair of Abercrombie and Fitch sweatpants and moves aside a few stuffed animals.

Nothing.

My heart feels relief and worry at the same time. *Not tonight?* I am excited that I may be able to go to bed. *What happened? Did someone see you? Does someone know?* I am terrified that you are not where you said you would be.

After the "I need to have you" comment, you had been dissatisfied with my ideas of finding a way to come meet you somewhere.

"No, I have a better idea," you bragged. "I'll tell Rob that I have a soccer game and that my team and I are going out afterward. Then, when your mom goes to pick you up from swimming at 7:15, I will sneak in your house and be waiting in your closet." I hate that you know the itinerary of my life.

"Then . . . after . . ." I knew what 'after' meant. *Are you too much of a coward to say it? After you rape someone who is less than half your age. After you betray the trust of an entire family. After you "have me"?'* "Well, I have a really good idea for afterwards, because I hate walking by your parents when they are sleeping."

I imagined the consequence of you waking up my sleeping mom. Finally I agreed, "Yeah, I hate that, too."

"So I will take off the window screen after I sneak in. When your mom's picking you up from practice. I'll need some extra time, so make her stop somewhere." I had thought of the candy store with hollowed-out hope, thinking the gummy frogs just might make me feel better.

"Then afterwards," you used it again, "you can lower me out of your window with a sheet from your bed." You stated this as though you invented electricity.

You're crazy. You know that, right? That you're crazy? I live on the second story of a tall English tudor with a cement path below and a curious dog. My insides felt like they were made of stone.

So now, twenty-four short hours later . . . *why are you not here?* I move the large stuffed gorilla my parents bought me three Christmases ago and look down at his pronounced brow, completely confused as to why you have deviated. *"What about the plan?"*

My mind moves fast and my body backs up slowly to my bed. *I will get the cell phone out of the book to call you and see what happened? Should I? Or have the police caught you?*

I imagine an oversized Moraga police officer holding your cell phone in his hand, watching it intently and waiting for it to ring. The possibility of flashing lights coming down my street to tell my parents what you have done keeps me still by my bed.

The screen. Slowly I turn my head to the right, to look at the screen of my window. As I look out, I see the orange streetlight glow a little clearer than most nights, without the black grid filtering the color.

I am still and I do not breathe. My eyes move wildly around the room, knowing that you are somewhere. Suddenly my diaphragm drops, air moves quickly through my lips in the form of a gasp. I would be less scared if I thought it might be a stranger. I know your touch and I know right away that it is you. Your bony hands have ahold of my ankles. You are under my bed.

You slide yourself out on your belly, like a snake coming out of the brush to feed. You are flat like a pancake, and I take a moment to realize that you have lost more than twenty pounds since you started doing this to me. I used to be grossed out by your flabby tummy; now I am grossed out by your flat tummy.

"Gotcha," you whisper it in my ear after you have brought yourself upright. You have that warmup jacket on that makes swooshing sounds when you move. It hurts the tiny hairs that line my ear canals.

You feel my body jolt with your soft-spoken words. You grab my shoulders. *Are you trying to steady me? Or silence me?* "Oops, did I scare you, sweetie?"

The words that leave your mouth would sound kind if I wrote them down on paper. But in the hue of the streetlight, I can see the smile in your eyes and hear the fear that you are meaning to strike.

You want me to be scared. I know that. *There is no other reason to change your hiding place. No other reason for you to watch my soccer games or for you to wait obsessively to drive past me when I am heading to school in the morning. There is no other reason to be in my house, when my parents are home.*

"I just have to do this. I'm sorry, it's just . . . that I need you." *But you are not sorry and I feel a small ache in my ankles where you have grabbed me.* "Plus, there is something that I need to do with you."

There is a point where things can't get any worse. That is what I used to think. Now I know that is not true. Here I stand, in the center of my childhood room, in the darkness of my parents' home, wondering what I have done to deserve this life of hell.

Usually, when you come in my room, you pull me onto the carpeted floor. You push me down so that you are always on top of me. I never stay for long, pinned down like that. I find somewhere in my brain to time-travel, too. Sometimes it is something in my room—a swimming trophy or the eyes of a troll doll I got for my tenth birthday. Sometimes it is another place and time in my life; a favorite is visiting my cousins in Utah. Sometimes it is a place that is entirely made up, and the worse things get, the harder and more amazing images I create to pull my mind from my body. And this is what I do when I can't call in for Eve.

I look down at the brown carpet, and I am grateful that it is plush, so that my back doesn't hurt as it does on the cold cement floor of your office. I drop my head, and as I soften my knees thinking I am headed to the floor, you push me back toward the bed that is behind us.

We can't go on the bed. Not on my bed. It makes noises and my parents will hear. And . . . it's my bed! I have to sleep here every night. Well, at least the nights that you don't make me come over. What are you doing?

I didn't say it out loud, but you live in my life and now you must live in my brain. "I just had to have you on your bed. It is something I have been dreaming about every night . . . sometimes even daydreaming about."

You look down at me underneath you and you smile that crazy sinister smile like the Joker but without the makeup. I know what you mean when you say that you are "dreaming" or "daydreaming" of me. At first, when you started all of this, I didn't know what that meant. Now I am a junior in high school. I have heard the boys joking about masturbation, and although I am not totally up with the entire lingo, I am smart enough to put two and two together.

"What if the bed makes noise?" I allow myself to ask you, half in the guise of wanting to stay undercover from my parents.

"I won't be loud. Don't you think I know what I am doing? Like I haven't thought this out? It's all I think about. You're all I think about. You have to trust me . . ."

As you begin, you press your body hard into mine. I let my whole body turn into blue Gatorade. It is my favorite flavor and what I always drink before soccer games and at swim meets. I soak the sheets, drain onto the floor, and spread beneath the bed.

There I lay in a puddle, where you lie for hours waiting for me. Alongside boxes of mostly blue swimming ribbons and my worn and tattered ballet shoes from four years ago. Amongst my old yearbooks, the ones from JM. The ones that you are in as "Teacher of the Year."

Do you remember what I looked like when I first met you in sixth grade? Do you remember how fast I ran the mile in seventh grade? I really wanted to impress you, but it backfired because I passed out in Mr. Bohon's science class after. What about in eighth grade? I trusted you more than I have ever trusted a person. And now I lie underneath you and underneath my bed, hoping for this all to be over.

Some time has passed and I, in the form of the electric blue liquid, have made the rounds to various parts of my room. I really need to organize my jewelry box because I have some pretty nice things in there now, but I also have some woven friendship bracelets from summer swim meets that shouldn't be sitting next to each other.

"Sweetie, I have to leave . . . you fell asleep." *I did not fall asleep. I fell underneath the bed.*

"Okay," I say. What else am I supposed to say to you?

"I wish I could stay with you here all night." Your voice is almost that of a longing lover. But, as you look at me, your eyes get bigger, just like a hungry man sitting down for an oversized ribeye. I hate it when I can see the whites all around your grey eyes.

I say nothing back to you, afraid of what might come out.

"But I don't want Rob to know where I am. I don't want him wondering where I go all of these nights . . . ," you say and purposefully leave your sentence open. *So, yes, there will be more.*

"Okay, are you ready for this?" *Am I ever? Does it matter?*

"Yes." I should note that this is all done in a voice softer than a whisper. If I didn't have the misfortune of knowing you so well, maybe I wouldn't be able to despise the words that you are speaking to me.

"Okay, first I am going to show you how to put the screen back on the window. You have to do this right after I leave, in case your parents hear something and they come to check on you." My heart rate triples at your foreshadowing. You show me the hooks on the window that will hold the screen. "Here, let's use the top sheet."

You whisk it off my bed like the magician pulling the tablecloth from the undisturbed set table. You are seamless, making no noise whatsoever. My window has a crank that opens it. I have always thought that it looks like the neck and head of a giraffe, peering into my room. You grab him by the neck and twist my giraffe slowly until the cold air of the night brings shivers down my spine.

"You are such a strong girl, I know that you can do this. I think that those arms of yours are getting stronger by the day." *I do not remember you ever touching my arms. I do not see you every day. Do you see me?*

I manage to smile back at you, guessing that this is how Eve would want me to react.

You hand me the sheet, looking confident in yourself and too confident in me.

"Goodbye, my angel." *Aren't angels dead people? Dead people who are good? Why do you call me that?* I have allowed myself to return to my body and I know one thing is for sure: I don't feel good.

"Bye," I shove the word out of my mouth, and although it comes, it is almost all air. I watch as you stand in the frame of my window facing me. What if the down-the-street neighbor is a compulsive food addict and he sees you as he goes for the Chips Ahoy?

"Hold it tight!" You hiss at me and I am reminded that you are the snake that was under my bed. I lean back from you, causing the sheet to pull tight.

One time, when my family went on vacation to Lake Tahoe, before you cut me in half, I went rock climbing. Well, not real rock climbing—the kind that you do on a fake wall with a harness and all. My brother was my partner. I imagine that fun day, repelling down the manmade wall to my happy family below. Now you, repelling from my bedroom window, feet dug into the white stucco of my home . . . it doesn't feel fair.

I am mad. With every inch you descend, my anger puffs just below the surface of my skin. Eve would tell me to keep it cool. But I can't control myself. Wanting to have never met you and have never been put through all of this. Wanting to score the first goal in my game tomorrow and go to sleep so that I can get a perfect score on my science test.

The fury freezes me. With four feet of the sheet left, I hold it tight. The signal, you had said, that I was near the end of the sheet. Well, I am at the end of my rope. Even if I wanted to soften my grip, I cannot. Like my toy gorilla, my eyebrows pull to the center of my face and my hands become tight fists.

Through this Thursday night you look up. But you cannot see me through the night. From your angle, you do not know who I am. You do not know that I have been growing indestructible. You do not know that you have chosen to mess with the wrong person.

I have four feet of sheet, but I refuse to give you any more.

I feel strong. I feel capable. I give a short yank in response to my power. I can easily hold you here. But my tug makes you think, this is as far as things will go. And, suddenly, things get lighter.

I am surprised that I don't fall back toward my bed. Instead I stand upright and feel myself tower stories above you. I look down in response to the loud and short burst of cry I heard on impact.

Did my parents hear? I quickly replace the screen. Replace the top sheet. Replace myself in bed. Replace the phone inside the book under my pillow.

The insides of my house remain surprisingly still. I hear the smallest noise as you ever so slowly close the wrought iron gate to the side of my house.

I try to get settled in my bed, but my mom just washed the sheets, and they don't feel clean anymore. I try to get settled on my pillow, but it doesn't feel soft as it is supposed to. I slide my left hand under my pillow to adjust the book that hides the cell phone, when suddenly I am jolted by a vibration.

I lift my pillow case and remove the small Nokia from the book. No one else I know has a cell phone. *Why are you calling me? You never call me afterwards.*

"Hi?" I start. I know you are calling because something has gone wrong.

You are remarkably calm, almost monotone in your speech. "I broke my leg."

"Oh. Are you okay?" I know the answer. *You are not okay, you are crazy.*

"Yes, I am driving to the hospital. I am going to say I stepped off the curb."

You are not crying? You climbed the steepness of my hill with a crack in your bone? I notice the hum of your Subaru as you drive yourself to the hospital, armed with your prefabricated lie.

I hang up the phone and allow myself to wonder about you. *Are you human? Do you feel pain?* As I try to make my bed comfortable again, I scoot my body to the far side of the bed that you never touched. I fluff the other pillow, one that I have never used, and wish for your leg to cause acute agony. I pull my legs up into a fetal position and loop my hands around the tops of my feet. I hope, in some way, your ankle hurts as much as my ankles do.

CHAPTER TWENTY-SEVEN

Circle of Love

On October 17, 1989, the Loma Prieta earthquake rocked the San Francisco Bay area. It struck at 5:04 P.M. during the warmup of the Bay Bridge World Series where my Oakland A's were taking on the San Francisco Giants. A slip along the San Andreas fault line resulted in a 6.9 quake, which caused widespread death and damage.

I was seven, and having an afternoon snack of Campbell's ABC soup at the kitchen counter with my mom. I felt it before she did. Looking at my soup, I watched a current in the center of the bowl come out of nowhere. I had yelled to my mom, "What's going on?" She grabbed my hand and pulled me under the built-in desk in our kitchen.

As the roof started to bend and the house filled with angry noise, she said to me, "Holy shit, this isn't going to cut it!" My mom all but dragged me outside, and for the long remainder of the fifteen-second quake we watched the house sway and finally come to rest with only minimal damage. My feet felt numb. My young ears had heard my mom swear for the first time in my life. I will never forget the shaking I felt that day.

Or the shaking I feel now.

When I talk about this, when I share the other side of my life with people, I shake. I don't just mean that I feel shaky. I mean that my whole body shakes. And, depending on whom I am telling and how much I have to tell, the Richter scale has a unique reading. Today, exactly like the day in October, I am at a 6.9.

I knew that this moment was on its way. The anticipation builds tension within my plates. It is hard to have someone think they know me. Then I share the other me, and now they see the abused me, the split me's or the real healing me depending on who they are. And I have no control over that.

People from around here always complain about the San Francisco fog. Sure, summer is only just heading out and the idea of a sunny weekend on the beach is blanketed by the rolling fog. But I like the fog. The white clouds offer protection and intimacy from the vast sky and sun. It makes me feel surrounded and safe.

Teri and I have taken the team to this beach in Marin for the past three years. It is less than an hour from campus and we spend the weekend here in old military barracks, building our army for the season ahead.

People hear that we are going on a "team retreat" and they think it will be fun. "Team bonding?" they ask. I guess, in a way, we do bond. But it isn't always fun. The retreat is an environment for the machine to be opened up, the internal pieces to be closely examined, and the machine to be fine-tuned and, if necessary, repaired.

My life coach, the first person I ever told about Julie, is here. I met Kathie because of Teri. A few years back Teri had me start working with Kathie on a weekly basis because Teri knew that something wasn't right with me before I knew. It took more than three years of working with Kathie an hour a week to even begin to find my wound. That's over a hundred and fifty-six hours of digging. It was a long journey to get here, and Kathie and Teri have both walked with me through unknown and undiscovered territory.

Teri brings Kathie to run our retreat. It's the one time in the entire season where Teri steps down from the platform of head coach and allows someone she respects and trusts to take the reins. Kathie has been a Division I head coach before, and since her retirement she has become a life coach as well as a trained facilitator to work with groups and enhance dynamics. She is Teri's best friend. She is one of my angels.

We are sitting in a circle, close enough so that if I reach out, I can touch Teri to my left and Kathie to my right. *What if I reach out and grab them?* I think holding on to them might help me from floating to the ceiling.

Our twenty-four athletes also sit close, and I find it hard to look at them. Some of them know a little, some of them know a little more, and some of them know nothing. I look at the face of a freshman sitting in the circle to my right and I scan her eyes for who she thinks I am. I am the fun-loving and happy assistant coach who helps to balance the intensity of Teri. I am the one who, during the recruiting process, went with her to get frozen yogurt and spoke deeply with her about her desires and dreams for college swimming. I am the one who threw her out in our game of dodgeball yesterday. I hope that she can handle this.

The trial is supposed to start in exactly two months. One minute it feels as though the sixty days will take forever. The next minute it feels as if time is ticking too fast. *What will it all be like? What will it feel like?* Geoff says that I will be on the stand for up to a week. *How many questions will they ask me? How can I be sturdy enough to answer?* Everyone says it will be worse than the preliminary hearing. *How could anything be worse than being asked if it felt good?*

I know I have to tell my team and I balance the two primary reasons in my right and left hands so that they do not reach out and grab Kathie or Teri. On the one hand, they need to know because this is going to take me away from them. It will take me away on the days that I am sitting on the stand. It will take me away on the days I can't stop thinking about what the defense attorney will ask me or did ask me. It will take me away for some time, but will eventually bring me back a stronger coach for them.

On the other hand, I need them to know for me. I need them to know so that my army keeps growing.

"Kristen, are you ready?" Kathie asks me and as she sees my shaking hands—the most obvious point of reference—she sees the impossibility of her own question.

The girls have just finished an exercise Kathie calls "beneath the iceberg." They were broken into small groups and shared statements that begin with "If you really knew me you would know that . . ." Kathie explains the exercise and talks about the ninety percent of the iceberg that is below the surface, relating it to the part of ourselves that we want people to see and the part of ourselves that is hidden below the waterline.

Every time we embark on an activity like this with our girls, I am surprised by something I learn about them. We take an oath of confidentiality before the weekend and I am honored that they are willing to open up. Some of them have faced tremendous hardship in their young lives—have lost a father to cancer, have seen their dad hit their mom, are battling with depression of their own. It is important for me to share that I am not so different.

The final piece of the iceberg exercise will be me telling them about, well, *me*. As I look at the faces around the circle, I think back to the day each of these girls told me that they had decided to come to Cal. I allow that feeling of happiness to come into my heart and pour fuel into my soul for the trip ahead. I feel courage in their courage and strength in their strength. And, still, I am scared.

"You each just had a chance to share something beneath the surface with your small groups. I hope that you feel stronger and more connected than you did before." Kathie has an undeniable presence about her. She is 6'2", but her presence comes from somewhere deeper.

The girls look around the circle at each other. Some of them look drained, some look physically lighter, and some look like they have just been through something that they didn't know they signed up for. They certainly did not sign up to hear what they are about to hear next.

The circle reminds me of last year. The introduction reminds me of last year. We were here, on our retreat, but in a different room and a different building. Like today, Kathie and Teri sat to my right and to my left, a little closer than through the other activities of the weekend. I look back on "my telling" a year ago and I was almost a different person. That day I told the entire team for the very first time. That day I only managed to get the bones of the story out. The magnitude of my shaking felt more like an 8.6. *Does that mean I am getting stronger?*

Suddenly last year's team understood the vacant look in my eyes, and understood why I was absent for the many days that I could not go to practice. Or get out of bed. Suddenly my army had grown.

Now nine new freshman to share my pain with and open my heart to. *Can I go through this again?*

My eyelids feel heavy in exhaustion and my pupils dart in anxiety. I shake in anticipation but feel a sense of calm readiness. It has grown dark outside and the protection of the fog is untraceable. I hate that I always look for headlights in the dark.

Teri senses my shaking. I have tried my best to hide it, but as Kathie continues on and I know she is running out of words before I start mine, Teri knows I am struggling. She leans her entire upper body forward, grabs her chair right underneath the seat, and slides it just close enough to me that I can feel her being. I am not sure if I grab her hand or she grabs mine. I am pretty sure we reach for each other at the exact same moment.

One day, when I had just started processing the trauma, Teri and I were at Starbucks. She was eating a protein plate with a hard-boiled egg, cheese, and fruit. I was begging oatmeal to go down my throat.

"It's interesting how things have a way of working themselves out . . . like the fact that you are a coach now." Teri spoke these words to me and I could sense her looking out of the corner of her eye to catch my reaction. Call me stupid, but I had never put two and two together. Is it irony? Grace? Healing? Whatever it is, I had never thought about the fact that I am what Julie was.

My hand brings me back to the present as it settles in the warmth of Teri's palm. Kathie continues, "Kristen has something that was frozen deep in her iceberg, for a very long time, and now she would like to share that with you."

Would I really 'like' to share? I would have liked for it not to have happened in the first place. I would have liked to rewind my life and seen through the mask Julie wore. I would have liked to sit here and tell these girls how life is fun and exciting and easy.

I look at the faces looking back at me. They are young. The youngest, five years older than when Julie snapped me in half and eight years older than when Julie first began washing my brain. I look into the eyes and wonder what my girls have seen. Have any of my athletes faced what I have faced? The pain of all of the years and all of the times echoes through my veins. Certainly, my story is extreme. But what if they have touched this pain, if only for one second? Like a hand on a burning stove, seeing evil means feeling pain.

Kathie settles in the chair next to me and mimics Teri as she pulls closer. She rests her hand on my upper back. I feel the backside of my rib cage expand with welcomed air.

The words, the letters, feel like molasses in my mouth. My brain is jumbled with all of the things that I want to tell them about and my heart hurts in anticipation. "Some of you know this, and others of you don't. I have been going through some-thing really hard." I look down at the carpet, which desperately needs to be replaced or at the very least cleaned. Looking down and avoiding eyes is a comfort condition of my victim self. The carpet doesn't make a face that says: "I don't want to hear this. I don't believe you. Why are you telling us this? How did you allow this to happen? This is disgusting."

"For the past year and a half . . ." As an opening statement to my story, I have to keep adding time. Each time I move from a number of months to a number of more months, I am surprised that the following story doesn't grow easier to tell. "I have been facing bouts of serious depression and flashbacks from times of my childhood and adolescence."

I use both terms because, when this all began, I was not an "adolescent." I was a child with a child's mind. "I have been diagnosed with acute PTSD, anxiety and situational depression."

I want them to understand where I was in my life, who I am now, and where I am headed. I need to give them background, context of the child who was tricked into a grotesque trap.

"On the outside, my upbringing looked perfect." It really did. I wish that this short sentence could give them a snapshot into the rolling hills of Moraga and my parents' unlocked front door.

"Things went wrong in Junior High School, when my science teacher touched me." My mind is drawn to the black chalkboard at the back of the meeting room. I imagine erasing it clean. "What he did, exactly, is blocked from my memory." I wish I could just hold up the empty chalkboard and say, "when I try to remember what Mr. Witters did, it feels like this." Would they understand then, or just think I am even more crazy?

"I went and told the person I trusted the most, my PE teacher." The cadence of my speaking feels erratic, moving from rapid to delayed, and I hope I am speaking loud enough for them to hear me. I cry and I shake through all of this, but still I continue. "She was young and married and I looked up to her in every way possible. I was her TA, her student, and she coached me in three sports." I build the house so that they can see the fire.

"Then two things happened that were just too much for me to take." I am purposely going into far more detail than I did last year. This is my chance to ask for understanding, and asking for help requires telling.

It feels as if I am at preschool and I have just shoved two Legos in my mouth. I can't breathe and I can't ask for help. This is the worst part and I know I'm going to have to clear my air pathway on my own.

The first Lego is green. "My PE teacher, she said she would take care of everything. I became completely dependent on her. I became isolated and she began abusing me." It comes out quickly and scrapes the roof of my mouth along the way.

The next is blue and feels smaller yet heavier. "My science teacher found out that students had reported his behavior. I thought my PE teacher had turned him in on my account. They put him on paid administrative leave. He disappeared and ten days later committed suicide. He left behind his wife and two young boys. I blamed myself."

I feel my shoulders sink into the frame of my body as I feel the weight of my fourteen-year-old world. Getting the Legos out of my mouth feels good, but remembering is always hard.

"It was too much for me. I split in half." I allow myself to look at my audience for a brief beat of time, to make sure I have not scared them too badly.

My eyes capture the image of the same freshman I pegged yesterday, sitting just to my right. It is an image I might remember for the rest of my life. Head tilted, she is staring at me. Her lips parted slightly, her eyebrows raised in astonishment. A small tear lines her lower lashes. I want to yell out to her. I want to say, "I wish I didn't have to say this to you! I wish this were not true about me. Do you still want me to be your coach? I am sorry you have to hear this!" But, instead, I look back at the safe and stained carpet.

"I lived a double life. A perfect high school life where I got straight A's and a life for her." I wish with my entire being that I could change this last pronoun. That I could say "him." Maybe things would be possible if it were a man. I know it is healthy to tell the truth and I force myself to use the dreaded word again. "I became her sex slave."

I imagine my freshman to the right watching a show about child sex slaves in Thailand on Dateline NBC. The reference makes her understand just how bad it was.

I go through the structure of the rest of my story; how it all ended, my time at UCLA, and the time in my life when the memory of this was frozen deep away.

I walk them through the past year and a half, the discovery of my other self. "I told Scott in May of last year. It was the week after our travel meet to Irvine." I allow the pain of those days to sit in my bones. And as I feel heavier in my chair, I can see my two lives come together for the first time. I see myself coaching and healing, teaching and remembering, succeeding and struggling. And as I scan over the past year, I realize that it was a singular me who went through both the highs and lows. I did not have to split in half. My role as their coach gives context to my story.

"Many of you probably remember that meet . . . those of you who were there. It was when I first told you I was having a hard time. We did not talk about what it was or why. Just telling you made me feel better. Some of you told me you would pray for me." I remember myself sitting in the breakfast room of the La Quinta, crying hard, and not caring if someone walked by as I told my team that I was struggling and I needed their patience. The team has changed a lot since that day; freshmen have filled the locker spots of graduated seniors. But, still, the bond and sense of belongingness that comes from being part of this team remains.

I remember that weekend. I remember the sound of the train. I remember the image of Teri telling the team the next morning. I remember what kept me in bed that night.

"I came home from that meet and told Scott. He told me I had two choices. The first I can't repeat because what he wanted to do is a felony." I leave a pause for them to imagine the idea of Scott planning a murder. "The second option was to go to the police and see how the criminal justice system treated her."

I remember that day, the leather sofa feeling strong and sturdy beneath me as Scott gave me his options for moving forward. I didn't know why I trusted him, only that I did.

"On July first of 2010, the same day that I made recruiting calls to many of you freshmen for the first time, I went to the police." I remember that day, making phone calls in the morning, sharing my excitement about our wonderful Cal program and knowing that my appointment with Detective Parker awaited me at 4 P.M. I think that my job got me through that day, too.

"I told the police everything. They did an investigation. They made me do taped phone calls. Later in July, when we were at the LA Invite, Teri sat in my room when I did recorded calls and got Julie to admit to everything." I know the entirety of the circle, with the exception of Kathie and Teri, are astonished at this. The image of me, at a swim meet, coaching athletes and recruiting prospects, running an investigation at night. And with Teri at my side.

I can feel the aftershock within the circle.

It is important to me that my athletes know Teri's role in this and who she has been for me. Teri is the visionary of the program and thus often the cursor for keeping it in forward motion. But to me she has been a floatation device. It is important for the circle to see her ability not only to lead but also to support.

"During Summer Nationals"—I continue to draw a timeline that relates to their swimming so that they can see me from their perspective—"a judge issued a warrant and they arrested her."

"In March, less than forty-eight hours after this team won an NCAA Championship, I had to face her in court and take the stand at the preliminary hearing." I look up at them now, making eye contact with a sophomore who had shocked the swimming world and won an NCAA title at that meet when she was only a freshman. Her eyes grow wider and her head tips trying to understand the extreme high and low I had to face within a week's time.

"Teri was there. It was two days of detailed accounts of what happened and horrendous questions by the defense." I remember sitting on the stand, picking off the blue sparkly nail polish one of the juniors had painted onto my fingers on the last day of the meet. "I need you all to know all of this, because what we did at that meet made me strong enough to take that stand . . . and take my stand."

I look up. The sophomore—the defending NCAA champion—has taken the hand of the teammate to her right. And then she turns to the left, reaches out to her other neighbor, and they join hands.

For a moment I remember last year. Then, just a freshman, this young girl had been willing to share her nauseating account of her parents' immigration from Cambodia. "They were being hunted like pigs, and they had to leave everything in their lives," she said in a low and serious tone that stood in opposition with the fast tears that left her eyes. For a moment we make eye contact and I see her eyes grow concerned for me, her coach.

The carpet calls my name. Seeing people care for me or cry for me feels hard and good at the same time. Hard, because I never wanted anyone else to feel an ounce of this pain—not during, not after, not now. Good, because it feels as though the evil is defrosting out of my soul and out into the open.

"She has been in and out of custody for the past year and this is scheduled to go to trial on October 31st." I march on.

I stop in the realization that I have no clue what the next few months of my life will look like. I speak my internal thoughts that come racing out, somewhat out of order. "There might be a plea bargain; this might be in the news. I might be on the stand for a week. She faces anywhere from a year in jail to life in prison. It is a very complicated case."

I drift off in speech and drift off in thought. I look down at my hands, still holding Kathie's and Teri's. The grip has loosened slightly, and the tremors have lessened but not disappeared. *Am I done? How long did that take and did I do okay? Are these kids okay after hearing that?*

I am busy analyzing all of what I just said when Kathie interrupts my evaluation, "Is there anything else that you would like to tell them about your healing?"

"I'm in therapy twice a week. I have the best therapist in the world. He is an angel."

Kathie leans in closer and covers the outside of her mouth with one hand so that the girls can't see what she is saying. I read her lips ask in exaggeration, "Do you want to tell them about your book?"

I don't know why, but every time I talk about my book to people I feel a tiny bit embarrassed. *Who do I think I am that I can write a book? I am not an author. Are they secretly laughing inside?* The feeling of embarrassment tends to rank very low on the Richter scale.

"So I am writing a book. I have a writing coach. He is amazing. I love it and I think it is pretty good." I actually think it is very good, but I shouldn't say that, should I?

Kathie's voice is loud and by the way she is rubbing my back. I know that she is proud of me for what I have just shared and what I have survived.

"Is there anything else that you want to say?" She leaves the center of the circle open for my closing remarks.

"Thank you. For being on my side. For getting me through this when you didn't even know you were. When you swam fast or asked for advice or decided to come to Cal, you helped me." I imagine my athletes lined up like little ducklings behind me. I know they will never go to court. I don't want them to. I want to protect them, the way Julie should have protected me. And I know that they will be waiting for me when I get back to the pond.

"Anything else?" Kathie wants to make sure she has given me the room I need.

I can barely get it out. My tears are different this time, like the relief of a sudden and heavy rain on the Sahara. "I need this."

The room is quiet. I allow myself to look at my team—my team of athletes and my team of people. They are connected now, not only as they hold hands for me, but as they hold a piece of my pain. I look at their chests—swimmers are known for having big upper bodies—and I notice that they are drawn in together. I think of the team, just before the start of the meet, leaning in for a team cheer.

"Do any of you have questions for Kristen?" Kathie wants them to know that they can talk to me.

Typically backstrokers and freestylers are long and lanky. A 6'3" relatively shy sophomore raises her long and bony arm as no exception to the rule.

"Yes?" Kathie asks.

She is smiling almost. She looks more confident in her question than she usually looks on the blocks. "Are you going to publish your book?"

I look at her and realizes she wants to know me. She wants to read the words I did not have time to speak here tonight. The words I wasn't allowed to speak then. I feel happiness radiate from my center and with a sense of courage I lift my head in response, "I hope so."

CHAPTER TWENTY-EIGHT

Phone Found

I am in the car. You are here, talking to me. I have difficulty finding the meaning of your words. I am trying to take in where we are, figure out how I got here, and decipher who I am.

The steering wheel remains straight and we are driving down a straight road. This road I know to be Larch Avenue, and it is located between my house and JM. Looking through the windshield, I see a sunny end-of-winter day, indicating this must be March: that middle-season month which wavers between cold and warm. I think that we are headed more east than north, but it is certainly a combination of the two.

My eyes photograph my environment for safety's sake. To my right there is a short cul-de-sac of almost new homes. They sit proudly on Windeler Court, and the young landscape makes the short street look neat by default. To my left is Wandel Drive, a significantly older neighborhood built along with the majority of Moraga, probably in the late 1970s. Wandel and Windeler face each other directly and could share a street name, but apparently they are so different that they prefer not to. The house to my immediate left, the first of the tired houses, is a bit of an eyesore. The Hispanic house with its yellow stucco and adobe tile roof sits uncomfortably with Japanese juniper and lava rock in the front yard. I wonder if the nonneighbors on Windeler laugh as they look across the street.

The steering wheel is black. Not beige like your Accord, not grey like your Suburu. It is black and much rounder. It feels both new and uncomfortable as I realize that it is under my hands. I press into it, hoping to draw my attention from my surroundings back to the inside of this moment. My hands curl, starting at the line opposite the top joint in the finger, and find stability in the grooves on the underside of the steering wheel. Having never seen these before, I am surprised the indentations are there. Having never driven before, I am surprised that I stay on the road.

Now knowing where I am, I can begin to peel my ears open to listen to you. I am driving Kristen's car, her bright red Jetta that she and the Maggies jet around town in. But I have never driven before. Usually when I am around, you do the driving. So this is a new experience for me. Being out in this bright sunlight is also a new experience for me.

As I sit in the driver's seat to the left, I bring my eyes into focus and see you to my right. You are sitting where I usually do, in the foot space of the passenger side of the car. I am surprised that you can make your body so small. But, then again, you would fit your body anywhere if it meant that you got what you wanted out of it.

Somehow I know that this time is different. Somehow I know that you want something different. The air in the car is stiff and you are stiff. And you are not touching me. I circle my mind in accessing this scene.

Was there a plan to see you today? It is the middle of the day in the middle of a week. My mom expected me home fifteen minutes ago.

Did you tell Kristen a plan and did she forget to tell me? Kristen and I have grown apart; we have had to. But she wouldn't forget to tell me something that had to do with you. That is why she created me.

How did you get in the car? I hamster wheel through my history and cannot remember. *Did you jump in the car after Kristen's soccer practice at Campo? Did you wait for me to drive by on Moraga Road, and did you flag me down into the Jack in the Box parking lot? Did you leave a note on my car to pick you up somewhere?*

Kristen was most likely having an average day for her above average self. Suddenly you appeared, and then so did I. Just as I grow frustrated at not being able to see how you ended up next to me, you turn my emotions into fear.

"Your mom found the phone," you say to me, thinking that I am Kristen. You are calm as your words flat-line on tone and volume.

Behind the steering wheel I freeze. My hands stay at 10 and 2 and my foot maintains pressure with the gas pedal. I envision a five-year-old running into the street to chase a ball and know certainly that I would not be able to stop for him. And why should I? My life is over anyway.

My mind maps the distance to my home; as the crow flies, it is less than half a mile. *Is my mom in there? How do you know that she knows? Is she already dead?* I think of her body limp on the living room floor, her head bludgeoned and bloodied by your hand.

Or will you wait for my dad to join the party? Perhaps you planted the bomb long ago and you will make me drive this very car into the darkness of the night. You will take me away forever, so that I cannot hear the explosion of my parent's life.

I do something that I am not entirely proud of nor that I can entirely control. I let out a wail. My jaw unhinges and, somewhere between a scream and a shriek, I yell.

I might yell because it feels as though it is over for me. I might yell because of what you might do or what you have already done. I might yell because the physical pain caused feels like a heart attack. But rather than having a partial blockage in the left ventricle, my heart squeezes due to the tremendous force of two worlds colliding within the walls of my body.

As the pain of the inside comes barreling to the outside, I realize one thing. I have made Kristen's family my own: my house, my mom, my family, my life, too. I have come to love them as much as, or quite possibly more than, she does.

The scream is loud and is contributed to by every cell of my body. I wonder if the minivan speeding in the opposite direction will slow in response to what might be read as a siren.

With the release of my primitive and irrational noise, you touch me. With your hand on my leg you say, "Oh, Kristen, it's okay, sweetie." You move your body closer to the center of the car as you reach for me.

I do not want to be comforted by you and do not use the word Kristen. I shake with your touch and become silent immediately.

"Shush, my dear, there is a way out of this," you say as I notice that the tips of your teeth are pointed inward, toward the hollowness of your throat. You seem confident and contrived in your plan. I think that you might be smiling.

My fear forces my eyes to remain unblinking ahead. I listen. But I also do more than listen. You can't see this, but I turn on a miniature and invisible tape recorder so that I will not miss a single sound.

"I already talked to your mom." You look at me and I know that you can sense my fear of how this may end. "She's absolutely crazy," you say and I look at your wild and darting eyes. "She waited for me to get off of work and then she followed me. She followed me all the way from JM almost to Campolindo. She was tailgating me and waving her arms like a whack job in the car behind me. She started laying on the horn, so finally I pulled over." You pause here and I digest what you are saying without reply.

My mom knows that the phone has to do with you. She doesn't think that it could have to do with Kristen and her boyfriend Adam. She went right for the monster. This is bad.

"I pulled into the TJ Maxx parking lot, where there were a lot of people. I was scared of what she might try to do to me," you say, although I know that you are not scared of anything. "She went nuts. She threw the phone at me and screamed, 'what the hell is this?'" you say, trying desperately to make your voice sound crazier than it already is in mimicry of my mom. "She broke the phone to pieces." You shake your head in disbelief.

I think of my lean mom, throwing her tantrum on the hardness of the concrete lot. I can almost feel the fire that she threw at you.

"I told her that she didn't understand the situation fully," you say, and your mouth twists into a grin. *Yes, if she knew the situation fully, she would kill you.* "I told her that you have been having a really hard time with the Mr. Witters thing—with what he did to you, what he did to those other girls, how he disappeared, how he devastated his innocent wife and kids." You look for my reaction, but by now there isn't one.

Instead, my mind is with my mom as her feet and her fury burn into the concrete. You give me the words to imagine her role: "Then she said, 'I thought that nothing happened to Kristen'." Your eyes penetrate me as I record you.

"I told her that something happened in the spring of your eighth grade year. I told your mom that you made me promise not to tell anyone. Still, your mom was angry at me and said, 'well you should have told us. We are her parents. We could have handled it with her.'" You pause for a moment and watch me.

Could my parents really have handled it? My eyebrows lift with a piece of hope, and it is too bad that you notice this.

"But that's a lie. She would have blamed you. She would have looked at you differently. Not like me." You move your hand up my leg and smile in full at me. "So I did what I had to," you say, moving back to the conversation with my mom. You stop moving your hand and for that I am grateful. "I told her that you were suicidal. I told her that you would kill yourself if I told her about Witters. I told her that I bought the cell phone for you to use only when you really needed to talk about what had happened to you."

"Did she believe you?" My words come out along with the carbon dioxide that has been amassing inside. It is rushed and panicked, but I need to know the answer.

"I am not sure," you say, and my heart squeezes. "She kept saying that she felt as though she were going to have a stroke. I mean she was really worked up," you say, and let yourself laugh in the face of my mom's unravelling. "She called your dad on her new cell phone; she barely knows how to work that thing. She had me talk to him and I told him the same thing I told your mom."

I imagine my dad getting the phone call and your voice giving evidence that Witters had abused me. *Where is my dad now?* I imagine my dad reporting to the Moraga police and searching for Witters's grave. *Would his body be inside? Would my dad feel better if they dug him up, put him in handcuffs, and then buried him again?*

"Did he believe you?" I ask the same question with a single pronoun replaced. As I await your words, I believe I know the answer.

"Hook, line, and sinker," you say, glowing in gloat. Although unfamiliar with the saying, I know that it means yes. My heart calms and sinks at the same time.

"Then your dad and mom fought on the phone. They hate each other. Their marriage won't make it. They don't love each other the way you and I do," you say, and you reach for my hand. I let my right hand leave the steering wheel to appease you and hold your bony and frozen hand.

"It is going to be fine. Tell the story I told you. Leave an old pair of running shoes in your locker tomorrow. I will buy a new phone tonight, charge it, and we will be back on track by the end of the week." Now your voice moves in a march as you dictate commands to me.

I can't say that I am surprised or sad. I can't say that I am relieved or disappointed. All I know is that I am still alive. Everyone, besides possibly Mr. Witters, is still alive. I am still alive and I am still scared.

"Do you have it all?" you ask me, and still I wonder how you got to me with a plan before my mom. I push pause and then rewind on my recorder. "Here, just let me out here, and I will jog to my car. It's back over by TJ Maxx." Nearly five miles away, I look down and notice that you don't seem phased by running the distance without proper running shoes on. Your ankle must be feeling better. Your pain was temporary. I wish that I could drive a knife deep into your lumbar spine so that you could never walk again.

"Okay," I say, and I notice how rarely I speak.

"You can do this," you say as though you believe in me. *If you only knew who I actually am.*

"I know," I say, and I do.

You get out of the car at an empty street corner. I do not stop to wonder if a Moraga family has seen or recognized you in the daylight. Instead, I focus solely on the single task at hand.

I make my way through the only right turns that lead me home. I pass JM on the way, and as I see the kids loading into the cars to my left, I understand the possibility of life.

Now I am steering past my old preschool at the bottom of the hill, and I drive faster than Kristen normally would. I need to get this over. Kristen has a History paper due tomorrow.

I park in the usual spot, the extra triangle of cement in the righthand corner of the driveway. Here, in the same place that I was born, I put the car in park. I allow myself to pause and remember that June night, after the June show. In the stillness of your car and in the aftermath of your kiss, Kristen plucked pieces of her DNA and glued them together to form me.

As I enter the house, I know by now that the external eye cannot detect the extreme difference in my appearance. I walk into the kitchen to take care of business.

The counter is white and the tiles are made distinct by the near black grout lines that separate them. Each tile, the same size and the same shape, is never allowed to touch another. My mom is standing next to the raised kitchen counter. Her body is tight and her arms and cheeks are drawn in.

"Can you explain this to me, Kristen?" my mom says and points with her nose to the evidence sitting on the counter. The black book is open, and it's exposure makes me feel like my insides are hanging on the outside of my body.

Keeping the phone a secret was my job. And the book was the perfect cover. When closed, the black binding and the gold print look like a necessity for any Spanish-learning high school student. When closed, the book looks perfectly normal from the outside. Kristen looks perfectly normal from the outside. But now everything is opened.

The book is empty and so am I. I have failed. I wish that I were allowed to cry. I look over to the book sitting where it was never meant to be.

My pupils struggle to focus. The florescent light of the kitchen combines with the daylight from the west-facing window to illuminate the display. I can see the jagged edge of each page and I think of you carving it to contain an awful secret. I think of the wounds you have gashed on my life and the internal split and bleeding that has come at your will. As I stand staring at the truth of the book in the kitchen, it feels as though my mom can see the truth of me as well.

I reach inside and push play on my recorder. "It's a book that I kept a cell phone in. Natali bought it for me because I was having a hard time with Mr. Witters," I say and try to draw some emotion into my voice. "She is really helping me, Mom," I say and take a break for a response. I look down at the linoleum floor below.

"Well, I don't like it. I don't like that you are talking to her in the middle of the night. I don't like that you are talking to her instead of us." My mom stops short and I can see in her eyes the warning that Julie put there: "don't push too hard, your daughter will kill herself."

"I know you don't. I am sorry. It's just that this . . ." I stop myself because my emotions are growing here and on the verge of becoming real. "It has been hard," I say.

"I know it has, Krick. And we—your dad and I both—love you a lot. You know that, right? That we love you?" She looks deeply into my eyes as she asks this. I hope that what she really means is that they both love both—that she and my dad love Kristen and Eve.

I nod my head yes and hold onto the hope for a moment that she loves me the same. I walk toward her, with the empty book to my left. She stands with her arms open, and though I worry that upon contact she will know that it is not Kristen, I long for her embrace.

In the center of the kitchen, in the center of the home, I allow myself to have a slice of what I have given Kristen. I feel her arms around me and with her touch I can feel what real love is supposed to feel like. I can feel what Kristen lives for.

So I head up the stairs to change, imagining the ordinary evening ahead for Kristen. Maybe she will study with Maggie Red, or maybe Maggie Black will come over for dinner. Maybe she will think of me once or twice before the day's end. Maybe she will not. And as I think of her studying Ponce de Leon or chewing baked rigatoni, I feel proud that she is safe. I think of the new phone, slipped inside of a running shoe, and I know I will do better next time.

CHAPTER TWENTY-NINE

Civil War

O kay, I'm just going to say it. Sometimes it feels impossible. All of it.

Impossible that it happened, impossible that it is still happening. Impossible that she was partially right. Her voice sneaks back into my ear, "they will never believe you." I was convinced she was right, then. I am being convinced that she is right, now.

Today was a routine court hearing. Geoff called me last week and let me know that the defense had made a motion to make Julie's cash bond a property bond. For exactly one year she has been out of custody, roaming the streets with the possibility of being anywhere, the possibility of telling anyone any kind of story she has made up. But after a year a criminal's bail expires and the down payment is absorbed by the bail bond company. For this reason, Julie's family is desperate to keep her carriage from turning into a pumpkin and her having to go back to jail.

I thought that it was as simple as a judge saying "okay" and Julie getting what she wanted. Apparently, the family has enough property to cover the $1.2 million in bail, as long as a judge agrees to allow property rather than cash. I thought that the hearing was a pointless fight. I thought my presence was a pointless pain.

Tomorrow is the first day of school at Cal, and what I wanted was to be with Teri to start the new season. Our new freshmen come in for their initial meeting with Teri, me, and their designated "big sisters" on the swim team. I need this sense of purpose in my life right now. If there is one thing that Teri does better than any other coach, it is to create a support system for our athletes. This is an initial step in the creation of that system, and it was incredibly important for me to be at Cal and not at court.

But then there was the text from Scott five minutes before the first athlete meeting today.

It feels as if my feet are made out of helium and it makes me feel as though I want to take the push pin off of my cubical wall and drive it right through my fingertips. There are parts to this all coming out that feel liberating, parts that feel devastating, and parts that hurt so bad I can't feel anything at all. As I read the text from Scott, I start to float toward the ceiling tiles. I imagine how good the blood would feel as it filled my fingernails.

"I'm so glad that you aren't here." When I get a text from Scott, my phone reads "my boy."

"Why?" I type the three letters so quickly that the action appears as a single motion.

No answer for twenty seconds. That is twenty seconds too long.

"Why, babe? You are scaring me," I demand.

"Thirty people here for her. Tsubota . . ." As I read Scott's text, I remember Mr. Tsubota. He was my teacher, too. He taught a class at JM called Team Sports. Basically, it was a glorified PE class that the jocks always took, and of course I jumped all over that. I liked Mr. T, as we called him, and I was always scared that he would know what Julie was doing to me through all those years, because his office shared a wall with her office. I think Julie was scared, too, because she eventually made me come into the shower area in the back of her office when she would rape me.

When I first began to remember it all, I imagined the look on Mr. T's face when he found out that Julie had done this to me. As a look of "Ah-ha" spread across his face, I pictured him finally understanding the reason that Julie was always spending sunny lunch hours in her office with young teen students. I wondered if he might even call me, or find me on my fake Facebook page, and apologize for all of this happening to me.

I think of Scott sitting in the courtroom looking at Mr. T. Scott was Mr. T's TA in junior high school. How is this for Scott? Why is this other teacher supporting this other evil? I am endlessly angry that Scott's adolescent mentor, another role model, is dragged into all of this. I am sorry for Scott and my heart sinks into my feet. As I worry about Scott, weight fills my shoes and it feels wonderful.

I continue on with the text from Scott.

". . . Mrs. Christiansen." My sixth grade Core teacher. I remember this iguana-faced, heavyset woman. With thick glasses and a booming voice, she was widely agreed to be the best Core teacher for sixth grade. Our junior high school worried that going from a single class in fifth grade to a full seven course load was too much for sixth grade students. "Core," the solution to their problem, was a combination of History, English, and Life Skills that took up three periods of every sixth grader's life.

I remember my Core class, and Mrs. Christiansen's assignment of the "Big Ten"—a compilation of each student's "biggest" life markers in the first eleven years. A school project, not only turned in for a grade, but also kept in the junk drawer for years turning to decades. How many of those "keepsake" projects are parents supposed to hang on to?

I remember my mom and I spending hours on my Big Ten book, the red spine we made out of duct tape, the colored pencils sprawled across our massive dining room table that we used rarely for dining and more for nightly homework. Each memory with its own page, its own picture, and its own explanation of the meaning it held in the chronology of my little life. *Is it still sitting at the bottom of my parents' junk drawer?*

As I stare at the text from Scott, I wish I had Mrs. Christiansen in *my* army. Her crossing enemy lines and fighting for the South feels like a continuation of my slavery. I look at the Mason-Dixon line and understand why most victims never pick up arms. I see that Julie was right: the South is much stronger than I ever imagined.

My Big Ten book, made for Mrs. Christiansen's sixth grade Core class. The last piece of evidence before the murder of my innocence. The last photograph before the death of my youth.

Mrs. Christiansen, do you remember my Big Ten book? Do you remember my braces, my flat chest, my neck gear? Do you remember the innocence in my eyes? But there you sit, so there you must not remember.

The more names I read, the more daggers drive into my chest.

". . . Mrs. Rubino."

With small glasses and a small face, there she sat as the middle school secretary. A guardian of the campus, the gatekeeper of the comings and goings. I remember hearing, from whom I am not sure, that Mrs. Rubino had concerns about "how much time

Mrs. Correa is spending with the young girls. Especially Kristen." It was a concern that haunted me and stayed tucked somewhere in my brain. I let it out only when I went to the police and gave them the name "Suzanne Rubino" as a possible witness for the prosecution. Sadly, she will not sit on our side. Perhaps she has been fooled as I was.

I am relatively certain that this is the longest text message Scott has ever sent: ". . . Pattie Forrester."

Mrs. Forrester was the other female PE teacher at JM. She was the softball coach for the two Maggies in high school. She was a close part of our community and the first lesbian I ever knew. "Do you guys know about Patti?" Julie used to say with a grin and lingering on the word "about." Julie would continue on to tell us that Patti was gay, that she was in love with another woman, and would make fun of Patti and her sexuality. "She bats for the wrong team," Julie would say, and I would conjure up a confused image of Patti at bat when the rest of us were in the outfield.

As a twelve year old in Julie's class, I was taught to look at Patti differently because she was gay. When I finally realized just what Julie was doing to me, and what all that really was, I was terrified of being portrayed as Patti had been. Julie's voice sneaks back in: "They won't understand, they will think you are gay." Now I imagine Patti taking Julie's side. Now, I look at Patti differently because, so sadly and truly, she is batting for the wrong team.

I continue on with the text from Scott and I come back down from the ceiling tile. Upon my descent I occupy my body, and I begin to feel again. I feel the disappointment in the other people in my life at that susceptible stage. I feel the sadness that Scott has to face this same disappointment. I feel the fear that these people have joined Julie's army and that her army is stronger than mine. I feel the grief of Julie being right; they believe her.

I want to sit with Teri in these meetings, but I am having a hard time focusing. I feel like a puzzle, and although I had been mostly put back together, Julie just dumped a bucket of water on me. The pieces of me shrivel away from each other and the paper curls in sadness.

I fight hard to stay present in the meeting and I do everything I can to dry myself out. As we make our way through the first meeting, I see a freshman sitting across from the Head Olympic Coach, and as the minutes pass, I watch the freshman's nerves find a bit of ease. My eighteen-year-old athlete finally allows the corners of her lips to smile in Teri's presence.

Teri's office is warm and the lack of a cooling system is something that she complains about routinely. I would never admit this to Teri, but I like how her office feels, warm and comfortable. Safe. I can't help but think of Julie, her cold office and her cold soul. I am proud of the safety net we are building for our athletes. It is a net that I thought I had. Our net hangs under the trapeze of college swimming, life away from home for the first time, and growing up. My net was for fishing: to find, capture, and kill.

As we take a small break before the next meeting, I desperately try to hide the hook drawing blood from the side of my cheek. Just as Teri looks at me and sees that "this is just too much" look, she says, "I got this next meeting. Go take care of yourself. You don't have to pretend that you are okay." Teri knows I am struggling after telling her the recent update of Scott's text message and the grand march to support evil.

I walk out to the front of Haas Pavilion, where fans line up for basketball games in the winter months prior to March Madness. Hundreds of new students are hurrying through campus to find their classes before the games begin tomorrow. There is a piece of me that feels entirely alone.

The trial is in two months. *Who else will be there to support Julie? What will the media coverage be like? What if they take her side, too? How am I going to get ready for this?*

For quite some time I sit on the stairs across from the pool. I call some of the usuals: Scott, my mom, the Maggies, and Chelsea. They each give me kind words and they each throw me a rope of hope to hang on to. Although my seat bones hurt from being here too long, I finish my calls and decide to stay a while. I see my hope and I see my angels, but I still feel alone.

No one was there. No one knows how it was then. No one knows how it is now.

No one is here.

But me.

Yes, there is part of me that was forced onto an island. I lived and continue to live here alone, without family or friends or Julie. It hurts when people deny that the island exists. I hate it when people think that I asked to be a castaway. It feels scary and safe to have people be able to see a landmass surrounded by water. I am getting better at asking people to come visit. I know the island well. I see the world differently because of my unique viewpoint. My visitors help and, when I show them around, they can imagine what it is like to live here. But no one else does. When the sun comes to rest on the horizon behind the ocean, I am the only one who can see through the dark. I am the only one who has to stay through the cold winters, the hurricanes, and the flash floods. I am the only one who can fully absorb the sun of the summers or be made to fly by the tradewinds from the west.

It's just me.

I am alone.

But I feel okay.

I stand up and look out at the ocean that surrounds me. I look at my island and remember the God I found in Teri's guest bedroom.

I feel stronger than before. Stronger because Julie's army is stronger and I have no other choice. Stronger because my puzzle has, yet again, been put back together. Stronger because I have found something bigger than myself and something bigger within myself. Stronger because I have no other choice.

CHAPTER THIRTY

Puppeteer

"She called you? What did she say?" Your voice is rushed and has raised an octave in fear and utter panic.

"What?" I say to you, wanting to yell, but only using my lips to make the shape of the single word.

"Shhh," you hiss at me out of the side of your mouth. Your eyes are staring straight ahead into the darkness of the night. The greenish glow of the numbers on your cell phone illuminates the side of your evil head.

We are smashed in the back seat of your car. The phone rang about twenty seconds ago, piercing the silence of the night and quite possibly my life. You took your hand from me and said, "It's Rob. Be quiet."

Aren't I always quiet? Sometimes I wish you knew the difference between me and Kristen. I know when to stay quiet. I know exactly when to speak to you.

You had answered the phone and you were short with him: "Hi. What do you need?"

Is this how a normal newlywed couple talks on the phone to each other?

As Rob had talked, I leaned toward you an undetectable inch in an effort to hear what he was saying on the other end. I have much better hearing than Kristen does. It is almost as though you and I are both on the phone call and listening to his words, which give way to your current state of rage.

"Well, what did you say to her? Did you tell her I was out with the soccer team?" Your voice booms through the cloth seats of your Subaru station wagon. The car that you bought "for me," as you had said, "so that you could have more room to play." *You make me sick.*

I spend more time wondering about Rob than Kristen does. *Does this phone call mean that Rob thinks you are actually out with your soccer team? Or is he an insider going along with the lie?* His voice is only a muffle on the other end and, with your darting eyes, I believe you might kill me if I lean any closer.

Suddenly you turn to me, and mouth the words that I fear from the time I leave my house to the time I return home. "Your mom knows that you are gone."

I think of my mom and of Kristen. I feel as if I am driving 95 miles per hour on the highway, I blink briefly, and all of a sudden there is a car coming directly at me. I stare at the driver and I see Kristen. Her life is about to end. My life is about to end. My head swirls around as I realize I have failed to protect her. This is my job. I must have been the one driving on the wrong side of the road.

You quickly finish the conversation with Rob. My insides feel stretched as I anticipate the collision. I allow myself to speak, hoping there is something I can do to save the day. "What did Rob say?"

"You heard what he said," you bark at me.

My eyes burn as I realize I don't have an answer for this. I feel as though I don't even weigh an entire pound as I begin to float to the ceiling of your car.

We are at the top of the hill and I imagine my dad's large fist knocking on the rear window of your station wagon. Our parents could be anywhere.

I wonder if they would recognize me?

"Call Adam." Your voice is calm again. You look at me and hand me the phone. It is after midnight. *What will Kristen's boyfriend say when I call him at 12:37 A.M.? Will he know that it isn't her?* His mom or dad will most certainly answer the phone.

Adam is a good guy, one of Kristen's best friends in the world. But as a couple there isn't a whole lot left between Kristen and Adam. I think Kristen has taken away the spark on purpose, because there certainly used to be a fire. When they first started dating at the beginning of sophomore year, she was attracted to him.

But now with me dealing almost exclusively with you, she avoids being with Adam. I think she worries that even the slightest touch could remind her of you or remind her of me.

"Call Adam," you say again. Adam was your idea. You wanted Kristen to have a boyfriend, and the scruffy haired water polo player and swimmer fit perfectly. "It will keep people from asking questions," you had said and, for once, Kristen agreed with you. Partially because it protected the façade. Partially because Kristen actually liked Adam.

Kristen is good at a lot of things, and she was good at making Adam like her. She thought that he was cute, you had the requirement of a boyfriend, and Kristen didn't really know that she would end up caring about what score he got on his Chemistry exam.

Then Kristen started to fall in love just a tiny bit. Adam would write notes, and her heart would beat hard when she would read them. As someone who was invented to keep the silence, I worried a little that Kristen's feelings for Adam could risk everything. I agonized when Kristen would get distracted and look for him in the hallways at school, or when she would lose herself in thought over where Adam would take her on their next date. Maybe I should have had more faith in Kristen. Look at the mess I have gotten us in.

But when dinner and a movie are over, on the drive home in the red Jetta, Kristen knows that you will always be waiting at the dropoff spot. You don't let her have a boyfriend, or dates, or a normal slice of life. You sit waiting for her. And she has become scared of Adam's touch, just as she is scared of you. So, when the pair comes to the end of a date, Kristen quickly puts the brake on any feelings, on any physical progress, and on what might have been. Now Adam is only a statue.

Why am I thinking about all of this? I need to deal with the current emergency. "What?" I ask you in a voice that I myself can barely hear. *What was it that you just said to me?*

"Call Adam and tell him that you need to talk to him." *How are you so easily able to form complete sentences?* "Tell him to meet you at the office building at Moraga Way and School Street." You are climbing into the driver's seat, bending yourself into a nonhuman shape, as you give me directions. Your aggressive action contrasts with my still and young body. I am paralyzed on the edge of the back seat, unable to move and unable to control anything in my life or Kristen's life. My heart races, my mind races, but the only external change is the widening of my eyes as I watch you spring into action.

You settle behind the wheel, turn the car on quickly, and leave the headlights off. You slip down the hill toward the dropoff location. "Here, call him and tell him that you need to talk to him and that it is an emergency."

I have no choice. I can't protect Kristen any longer. She is going to have to do this. She is going to have to face Adam, face her family, and face her future. You are so busy driving that you don't notice a stunt double in the back seat.

I bend over slightly as the two cars collide faster than full speed. The pain is sharp and loud, but without you knowing to turn around, Kristen has replaced Eve.

My panic changes. I think of my mom, of my friends, of my dad, and of my life. I think of what people at school would say if the secret came pouring out.

I dial the numbers quickly, knowing them by heart and desperate for a way out of this mess. I remember how excited I used to get when I would call Adam, nervous now for a different reason.

"Hello?" His mom sounds mad, although I know she loves me and will forgive me for this intrusion.

"Hi . . . um . . . sorry it is so late. It's Kristen. Is Adam there?" I hurry my voice out of my mouth and I realize that I sound different than Eve just did in the car with you.

"Yeah, it is past midnight, Kristen. Are you okay? Where are you? Adam is asleep." She sounds worried for me and I imagine her in a long white nightshirt—a takeaway gift from an A's game—and a pair of flannel pants.

"Yeah, I'm okay," I lie and avoid her second question. "Can you wake him up? I need to talk to him about something."

"I guess so . . . Hang on." I look at you and I mouth the words, "She is getting him." I realize that I haven't had to look at your face in a long time. Eve has been doing the work. You smile a deep smile in knowing the first stage of your plan is working.

"Hey . . ." His voice sounds deep and tired, and I notice how much it has changed since I first started dating him.

"Hey, I need to talk to you. Can you come meet me? I need to talk to you," I say again, because I have no idea what else to say. You look at me and mouth "emergency." I nod and do as I am told. "It is an emergency," I say, and tug on the heartstrings of a well-meaning and innocent sixteen-year-old boy.

"Of course . . . where are you?" Adam takes his time with the first two words, showing me how much he cares. Sometimes I wish he wasn't such a good guy.

I give him the coordinates and hang up the phone. I am shaking, and I look at you for the next ingredient in the creation of getting out of this. I allow the current situation to seep into my brain.

How did my mom find out that I wasn't in my bed where I belong? Did she scream? I imagine the lights being turned on in a hurry all around the house. The emptiness my mom is feeling in her gut must be the same as the one that sits in mine now. It must feel the same as when she found the phone.

Does she think I am gone forever? Does she know I am with you? Did she call your house first?

"When he gets here, you tell him what happened with Mr. Witters. Tell him that he touched you and you don't want to talk about the details of it. Tell him what you told your mom when she found the phone," you say as though you have said it a million times.

I don't want to talk about the details of it. A sense of vacancy fills my head.

"Tell him that the only person you can talk to is your junior high school PE teacher. That . . . I was the only one here for you through all of this." You purposefully repeat the "'I." *Is that what you really think?* "Tell him that your mom is jealous of our relationship and that you just don't want to talk to your mom about Mr. Witters. Tell him that you were feeling really sad, needed to talk to me, and that you snuck out. Tell him your mom will be mad if she knows that I was with you, and so you want to pretend that you were out with him." Your voice might as well be accompanied by a low and slow beating drum.

You had this all planned out, didn't you?

Just as I think that this might all be over, that for better or worse people will find out, you find a way to slither out from trouble.

"Okay." I have the instructions drilled into my head and ready for use. You settle the car into the dark parking lot only a block from both Maggie Red's and Maggie Black's houses. I was always a little jealous that they live only a few houses from each other. The office parking lot is empty, just as it is on the weekend when we often bring our roller blades here for free skating.

You pick up your phone for another call, this time I am guessing back to Rob. Like my usual guesses with you, I am wrong. I watch as you dial the numbers to my house. *What are you doing? Who do you think you are?* I am scared.

The other line only rings once. Again, I can only hear your side of things. "Jeanne, it's Julie. Rob called me and told me Kristen is gone." Your voice sounds entirely different than it usually does, slower and less deliberate.

Time passes. I know my mom is talking. I can't hear what she is saying because my hearing is not that good.

"Yeah, I have been drinking a little. I am out with my team. But I wanted to make sure everything was okay. Do you want me to come help you find Kristen?" Oh, that's it. You are pretending to be drunk. This is where it would help to have Eve.

I don't know what my mom says, but you smile into the phone as though you are much smarter than she is.

You continue in your conversation. "No, I haven't talked to her in a really long time." You let your mouth linger on the word "time," and again you pause as my mom talks to you. "I haven't talked to her since you told me not to and broke my cell phone." You smile at me.

"Whoa, Jeanne, I'm just trying to help. I have no idea where she is." You look right at me and even I am almost convinced of your words.

Does my mom believe you? I hope my mom feels some relief in believing I am not with you. My poor mom.

You end the conversation and begin a new one with me. "I'm going to leave you here so that Adam doesn't see me." *But wasn't I supposed to tell him that I was confiding in you? It isn't Adam that you are scared of, is it?*

I look out into the vacant lot, not feeling a sense of fear in being here alone. It is the middle of spring and it is not so cold out. Plus, it is better than breathing the same air as you.

"Bye," I say feeling emotional and emotionless at the same time. I am terrified that my parents will figure this all out. They have never found out that I have left the house. *Why did they call you? Is this all going to end tonight? Will my parents ever be able to look at me the same way again?*

I feel incapable of emotions as I look at you and your hollow eyes that give way to your hollow heart. Here I see myself only as a puppet. You hold me like a sock concealing your veiny hands. In the car, in the apartment, to Adam, to my parents, you control what I say, what I do, and who I am. You make me Eve and then you make me Kristen. Somewhere along the way my insides got scooped out to make room for your control. My stomach turns as I think back to what you were just doing to my body, and I realize the literal truth to this figurative analogy.

"Bye, my sweetheart. You can do this, I know you can." Your eyes dart back toward the possibility of what lingers in the darkness. You all but run over my foot as you pull away in a hurry that does not match with the way you claim to care about me.

The night is still. Nothing happens in Moraga, especially after midnight. *Why am I the exception?*

I am not sure how much time has passed, because my focus remains on the task at hand: saving you so that I can continue living my other good life.

Adam's headlights are the first I see since yours disappear. I can tell by the large square shape barreling through the night that Adam is driving the greenish-blue family Suburban. I imagine him searching for a set of keys in the darkness of his quiet house.

As I prepare to climb in, something happens in my brain. Yet again, another shift. I think of the lie you have fed me to feed him. I picture the details of your words playing out before me. Me and you, sitting together and talking about Mr. Witters and what he did to me. My mom hating you, an innocent and good-intentioned mentor. I see it, feel it, and then I believe it. Now I don't have to lie.

"Are you okay?" Adam has large and beautiful hazel eyes and they grow wide as they look at me, his girlfriend, sitting in an empty parking lot in the middle of the night.

"Yes, I am okay." As I roll through the tall tale, I use my vision. I allow myself the emotion that I would have about what happened with Mr. Witters, the need I have for a confidant like you, and the frustration at my mom for not understanding. I lose myself in the lie and, as usual, he buys every word.

"Kristen," he says and moves himself closer to me. Good thing the center console separates us. "I am so sorry," he says and I cling to the depth and realness of his words. The faint smell of chlorine fills the car and I look at Adam's hair, bleached by the pool and the sun. I wish I were allowed to love him.

"I'll be okay. I'm really glad that you know." At least he knows a piece. Maybe this will give him a fake reason as to why I don't like the final part of our dates.

"Yeah, I am glad that I know, too. I am glad that you have your PE teacher, too." The irony of Adam's words hangs near my heart. *What if I told him? Could he save me? Would he want to?*

"So, can you take me home? We'll just tell my parents that we were talking about all of this." Not an entire lie. It's just that it was twenty minutes of talking, not two hours.

"Of course." He looks at me as he turns his head over his shoulder to back out of the parking space. We head toward my house, up the steep road, to the four-way intersection where you had parked the car such a short time ago. As Adam turns right, and we move closer to my house, my chest tightens as I foresee the bright lights in the night of my parents' search.

Am I having a heart attack? What if I just die right now? Not such a bad option.

My vision comes back, the one that I had right before climbing in this car to sit with Adam. I believe your lie and so I get ready to tell my parents the "truth."

"Where were you?!" My mom has run to the curb and is frantic as she looks at Adam's face. My dad follows close behind her. I press play on the story, like the Kricket doll with a recording that comes out of automated lips. Adam sits there and plays along perfectly.

The crease in my dad's brow disappears and my mom's eyes soften. I speak to my parents and I believe my own words. "This has been really hard, Mom. With Mr. Witters killing himself and everything." I wonder if she will ever know what "everything" means.

I march up the stairs, putting weight in my steps to prove a point and partially glad I don't have to worry about a creaky floorboard this time. I close the door to my bedroom, stare at my bed, and wonder. *How did my parents know I was gone? How did they not find out I was with you?*

I pause in light of the night's events. I stand in the darkness of my room feeling silenced by your lies. Through the fear of the night, nothing will change for me. For the first time within the night, I allow myself to feel. *Without chains, without handcuffs, I am your prisoner.*

CHAPTER THIRTY-ONE

Mirror Mirror

As I sit on a random suburban street somewhere in Tennesse, I am surprised at how capable I feel. After all, traveling has not always been this easy for me. As I wait for the digital clock on the rental car dash to hit 5:30, the time for my dinner appointment, I am proud that I have arrived here.

Airports have long been hard. It is only now that I can see why. Before I opened the curtain of my youth, I did not know why they were terrifying, just that they were.

First, there was the worry of whom I would see from my dark and scary past that I wasn't ready to bring a light to. Then there was the idea of being alone, which made me feel hollow inside. People have always just assumed I was born an extrovert, and there is some truth to that. I like people, and being around people has always filled me up. But much of my life has been about hiding from the possibility of being alone; about hiding from myself.

I sit here, alone and still living. I have heard people talk about God; that with Him, they are never alone. For me, my faith is different. I am still alone. But in my faith I feel a sense of safety in being alone.

One of the very favorite parts of my job is recruiting. It's ironic because, if you ask any other college coach about his or her least favorite part of the job, you will almost certainly get back "recruiting" as a single-word, no-thought-given, answer.

I am passionate about finding the next athletes, the next students, the next souls for our program. What we have at Cal is sacred. And finding the next people to join us is a sort of pilgrim-age for me.

As I check my teeth and fix my bangs in the rear view mirror, I prep myself to have dinner with one of the top young swimmers in the country. Jessica will be taking an "official visit" to Cal in a few weeks to determine if our program is the right next step for her. My journey to see her is about becoming a bridge from her life in Tennessee to her life in Berkeley.

As an athlete, I like the feeling I get in my stomach, the tingle I get in my fingertips, before a competition. As I head into the house, my body responds just as though I am about to start a race. I imagine my dear friends with desk jobs. As I tell my lungs to get a deep breath of air before the games begin, I am lucky that I have a job that can make me feel butterflies.

I walk toward the house, grateful I am not walking toward the courtroom that I will be in a few weeks.

It is always awkward at the beginning. After all, I am new to them and they are new to me. But the trick to outrunning the awkwardness is to genuinely and sincerely invest my emotions and interest in a recruit's newly remodeled basement, the draw-ing on the refrigerator, or her pet turtle. So, suddenly, she will open to me and I open to her.

"If you were to come to Cal, it is important that I see this." I make a motion with my hands to signify her family, her kitchen, her dogs—to signify her world. "So, if you get a little homesick in the fall, as most freshmen do, I will know what you are homesick for." I smile at her and I am proud that I am such a strong re-cruiter. Unlike a used car salesman, I see myself as an effective ambassador of my program because I believe so passionately in the holistic importance of what we do with our athletes.

Jessica, the superstar of a swimmer I am visiting, looks out across her family and she smiles. I see in her eyes the deep pride she has in the many opportunities she has created for herself. I see the pride she has in sharing her humble and kind family with an almost-stranger such as me. I look at Jessica and see a seventeen year old with the world at her fingertips.

As we eat dinner, Jessica tells me about her experience with the US National Junior Team. She speaks of her travels to Berlin, Peru, and Canada. I hear about her many trips around the United States and the world, without her parents and with her team-mates. Her face lights up when she talks about the spoils of being a top athlete, the free gear, the slices of local fame. Jessica has top universities knocking down her door with full scholarship offers, and at seventeen she is going to say no to all of them but one.

At seventeen I was finally saying no to the one.

What would I have been able to do in high school sports if I were not keeping Julie satisfied all those years? Would I have been like Jessica? With some extra sleep maybe I could have swum a little faster? Maybe I could have represented the US on the Youth National Team? Maybe I would have gotten a USA cap with my last name printed on it?

Jessica's mom has printed out all of Jessica's academic achievements for me so that I have them on record. It is important that we find athletes who are a good fit for our program and students who are a good fit for our university.

As I review Jessica's coursework and course marks, I compliment her on her solid grades. "Wow, these are really impressive, Jessica. Especially with all that you are balancing." It is true, the grades are impressive, mostly As and a few Bs. But I can't help but see the two C+'s in Calculus and think of my own report card. I can't help but think about all that I was balancing.

It's not that Julie told me I had to get good grades. I just knew, in order for no one to know, that I had to be one hundred percent perfect. And that meant getting as close to one hundred percent in every class, on every test, on every essay, that I could. My secret, my pain, became my fuel to perform.

But I struggled to trick everyone in Spanish. There must be something to trying to learn a new language when running low on sleep that just doesn't work so well. I remember Mrs. Taylor pulling me aside and questioning me about my underachievement on my recent quiz: "Salsa, tienes un momento."

"Si." Just responding in Spanish was shaky for me. I liked my assigned Spanish name Salsa, but I hated everything else about that class. I hated Mrs. Taylor, not because she was mean, but just the opposite.

As Senora Taylor went on to voice her concern about my recent grade, I looked at her and bit the inside of my lip hoping she didn't know. When she asked me why I was always so tired during her first period, I felt the cold tile of the school floor fall away from my feet. *What if she saw Julie in the hallway putting stuff in my locker? What if Mrs. Taylor had talked to my mom at back-to-school night, and my worried hen had asked this teacher to watch out for me?* As I used the excuse of a morning swim practice that I did not have, I saw the softness return to Senora Taylor's kind eyes. I promised myself to pay more attention in Spanish class.

The white paper of Jessica's transcripts glare up at me and remind me that I wasn't allowed any mistakes.

"I get awesome grades," Sally pipes in. Across the table Jessica's younger sister adds her mark on the conversation. Sally just started the sixth grade four days ago. Since the start of dinner, Sally has been adding her bits of opinion whereever she can. I can feel her hurried desire to grow up, to sit at the adult table, and to talk about important life topics. As I turn my eyes to this exuberant new middle schooler, I see just how young she really is.

Just like me at that age, Sally hasn't quite caught up to those around her. "I am the smallest on my soccer team," another fact she slipped in earlier in the evening. "But I'm really fast," she can't help adding, and certainly doesn't want me to think of her as a second-class citizen because of her stature. Ah, she even plays soccer like my young self. She is the youngest family member and looks at Jessica like she walks on water.

Sally doesn't wear makeup, she doesn't need a bra, and her teeth are still getting straightened by her retainers. She relies on her mom to wake her up for school, to make her lunch, and to protect her. I wonder if Sally is allowed to go trick-or-treating without a parent on Halloween. I have noticed that her young smile never leaves her face, and although she is desperate to grow into the accomplished and older shoes of her big sister Jessica, she is still very much a kid.

As I look across at Sally, I find a tiny piece of my peace in understanding how I was manipulated. There I sat, eager to grow up. And there Julie sat, ready to destroy.

Sally's eyebrows stay glued higher on her forehead than they should be with everything I say about Cal and college swimming. As I pull my focus back to Jessica and the task at hand, I forgive the eleven-year-old, high eyebrowed girl, who was betrayed. If this all had happened to Sally, I would find just the idea of blaming her a travesty all its own.

A part of me feels lucky to be sitting at this table, with Sally and Jessica and this force of a family. It allows me a snapshot of my past—when this began and when it ended. It allows me a glimpse into my future of dealing with athletes whom I get to coach and teach the way I should have been.

Part of my role in recruiting is to get to know as much about each prospective athlete as I can. A sort of investigator, I ask Jessica, "So tell me what you like the most about your club team."

After I ask this question, I jog through the possible answers that a recruit can give me.

If Jessica tries to change the subject quickly, I wonder why. *Is there something about this coach that she doesn't want me to know?* What if her eyes grow distant and her voice becomes so weak that she suddenly looks like a tiny grey mouse sitting at the dinner table?

What if Jessica begins talking about how her coach is like a second father? *Aren't coaches supposed to be just that—a coach and not another father? What if her dad shifts his body weight in his chair, crossing his arms, and a sense of concern radiates out of him? Is her coach making her dependent on him for some later purpose? Did he give her a pair of Oakley sunglasses?*

If Jessica spends time talking about how much fun her coach is, and how they text all the time, my mind wonders if her coach took her to a movie last weekend and if they got a Slurpee on the way.

It is not as though I am paranoid or feel insane when I ask this question and anticipate the answers. It is just who I am and what I see as a result.

Last year before Oprah went off the air, I heard that one in four girls have been abused by the time they turn eighteen. I quickly count that I have been to see eight recruits this summer. Is it possible that two of them have felt this pain?

Allison or Krista? No.

Leslie? I doubt it.

Katrina, Samantha, Suzan, Marcie all seem to have their lives all together. But isn't that how I seemed?

Nora? Maybe.

I hope not. I hope that Oprah was wrong.

Part of my unraveling was the newsbreak of the USA Swimming sexual abuse scandal. *Who are these coaches?* A while back I looked up just how dangerous these predators are. I had to clamp my jaw from dropping off the skeleton of my head as I read a study from the National Institute of Mental Health: "The typical child sex offender molests an average of 117 children, most of whom do not report the offense" (NIMH 1988).

As the question finishes coming out of my mouth and I await Jessica's response, I imagine her coach. I respect and know him well.

Like music to my ears, Jessica says, "He's a really great coach. Sure, there are relay decisions that he makes that I don't totally agree with. But he means well." Jessica looks at me, hoping that her speculation on her coach's faults have not caused alarm in me. I wish she knew that the exact opposite is true. Jessica's ability to see her coach as a human, nothing more and nothing less, rests my worried mind.

I cross Jessica off the chalkboard in my brain and I wonder if the odds just increased for the other girls.

As we finish dessert and I say goodbye to the family, I leave them with departing words of comfort: "I just want you to know that if we are lucky enough to have Jessica join us at Cal, Teri and I will do everything we can to ensure her growth. We will support her with her academic pursuits, with her athletic endeavors, and with a team environment that is open and honest and positive. We will do everything we can so that Jessica leaves Cal a stronger, more confident, and more capable young lady." A look of ease blankets both her mom's and her dad's faces. In the three hours spent with them, this is all they really needed to hear.

All I needed to hear.

All my parents heard from Julie.

"I am helping her get through something really hard. She will only talk to me about it." Julie's lies to my parents sweep across the early evening landscape, always assuring them that she would protect me and look after me in the wake of Mr. Witters's death.

I walk across the front porch to my rental car, I look out at the darkening clouds, and see the flashes of a late summer lightning storm in the distance. As the streaks of light illuminate the sky, I am grateful that I have a job that continues to strike healing and understanding on to the darkness of my past.

CHAPTER THIRTY-TWO

Take Your Marks

It's kind of like walking around daily life with cotton balls shoveled deep in the ear canals—and as though, instead of walking through the typical and slightly boring air, a warm and safe cloud caused floatation, like an astronaut. It has its own language and its own rhythm. It's like being in the womb as a full-grown human. As with osmosis, troubles and wants pass through the membrane of the skin. It is the most simple form of being. I believe I was born to be surrounded by water.

I know I am getting faster. I mean, not to be arrogant or anything, but I can feel my body adjusting to the water again. It's only two weeks before the biggest high school meet of the year and I am at my first morning workout since coming back from having mono.

People always say that 'spring is in the air.' Today they would be right. The air just above the interface of the water has a chill in it, but wears the distinct smell of a warm day ahead. I let the carbon dioxide leave my lungs in a huff as I realize how relieved I am to be back at workout.

Today's practice isn't hard by any stretch of the imagination. The swimming world calls it a taper, meaning that before a big meet the workouts aren't as hard as they are throughout the year. Thus the workouts "taper" down as we get ready for the competition.

I have missed the majority of my taper, being stuck at home with mononucleosis. Usually I like staying home from school when I am sick. No one knows that every once in a while I fake being sick just so that I can stay home and sleep—and spend time with my mom. But this was no facade. Maybe my mono was karma for all those times I lied about being sick?

And could the timing be any worse? I have worked so hard this year in swimming, determined to become a better swimmer than a soccer player. The pieces of mail that drift into my mailbox on collegiate letterhead are all signed by the soccer coaches, not swim coaches at universities. I don't know what it is about soccer these days, but I feel as though I have chains wrapped all around me when I try to play. I am sure it is a difference that no one else can see—a change that only exists in my mind. I still score goals, but I just don't really want to be out on that field.

Soccer makes me think of you.

"That looks pretty good, Kristen," Dave says as I come into the wall after a short sprint of my best stroke, butterfly. I love telling people that I am a butterflyer because the surefire response is something to the effect of "oh, that's the one I could never do." It makes me feel tough and gives me a sense of ownership of my broadening shoulders.

"Yeah," I say, looking up at Dave. I remove my goggles using my index finger and my thumb. I place the suction cups on my forehead so that I can look at my coach unobstructed. Dave stands smiling over me and a wide grin spreads over his face. "I think I am getting back into things," I say to him.

"Actually, I think that you look better than you did before you got sick." Dave's voice radiates positive energy. He smiles at me and he has one of those smiles where you can see both the top and bottom teeth—the kind of smile that reaches his eyes and the beginnings of crow's feet that border the outside edges.

Dave is about thirty, I would guess. I don't know his exact age because we have never talked about it. All of the girls agree that he is cute, but I stop myself from thinking that way before I even start. I know that trouble waits on the side of that road.

But he is also a great coach. He holds kindness in one hand and respect in the other. Being a junior in high school now means that Dave has been my coach for varsity high school swimming for three years. Sometimes after workout we go running together to get in a bit extra cardio exercise. I love running with Dave. First off, it certainly beats running alone and, secondly, I know that our jogs are helping me towards my goal.

Also, if I am running down the street with him, I know you won't pull over and try to whisk me off.

"Maybe this mono thing isn't the worst thing after all?" Dave says before it is time for me to push off the wall for my warmdown.

I hope Dave is right. I made a deal with him that if I make the Junior National cut in the 100 fly that I have to start swimming year round. Right now I only swim for the high school season and summer league. But if Dave wins the bet and I make it, I have agreed to start swimming with the club team and swim all year round. This would mean a little less soccer as swimming would move into the spotlight of my life.

I have to drop two full seconds. In the scheme of life that seems like nothing, but in the scheme of swimming two seconds seem like everything. I had been right on track for this, but then a 103-degree fever veered me wildly off-course.

My mind swirls as I move through the water knowing that this cut is essential. *College coaches don't even recruit swimmers who can't even make Junior Nationals, do they?*

As I slide my head to the right to take a breath, I look at the pace clock turning its arm on the corner of the pool deck. I think of the laps, the work that I have done this year. I let all of the strokes and streamlines come into the forefront of my memory. I think of finishing a practice with my heart pounding so vigorously that my ears burned with noise; of holding my breath underwater to the point where my lungs felt as if they were bleeding on the inside; of searching, day after day, for that feeling of deep and intense pain that made my body feel . . . feel so real.

I know I can make the cut. I have to.

I pull myself out of the water with ease, feeling my stomach growl with anger—anger after today's workout and anger after mono. I look down and feel my suit a little baggier than it used to be.

While the boys get started on reeling in the lane lines, Dave lets Allison and me into our private changing room.

"Here you go . . . You two are such divas," Dave says, smiling and shaking his head back and forth as he opens the lifeguard shack for us to change in.

Our high school pool is in the process of being replaced, so that this season we are training at a tiny neighborhood pool, just a block from high school. With no locker room, and only a bare-bones bathroom, getting ready for school is no easy feat. After a week of sharing the mirror with ten other girls applying makeup for the day, Allison and I began to beg Dave for another room in which to change.

Allison is two years younger than I am. I guess that you could say she is like my little sister. We started swimming together during summer league about five years ago and became friends immediately. She follows in my footsteps, purposely imitating me. She loves wearing my old clothes, she is taking the same classes this year as I did when I was a freshman, and she was a TA for PE in eighth grade.

"We're not divas!" Allison says back at Dave with her sassy voice. She puts her hand on her hip and tilts her head as a diva might. She swings her wet brown hair over her shoulder as she playfully puckers her lips at Dave's remark. She looks a little like a mouse, but a cute mouse. Allison might be the most hyper person that I have ever met. Maybe that's why I like hanging out with her: when I am tired, she brings enough energy for both of us.

"We are *kind of* divas," I say to Allison and I smile. I think of all of the other girls shoved into the tiled floor bathroom. I feel the tight bound carpet underneath my feet and feel guilty only momentarily. It's warmer here than in the bathroom, and at least I can get myself looking halfway normal as I head off to school.

"Hurry, Krick!" Allison says to me with great excitement as I pull on my dark blue Gap jeans. My legs are still a little damp from the pool, as I don't take the time to dry them completely. "Hurry, so you can drive us to Burger King for Cini-Minis!"

I look over at the toothpick of a body standing next to me, pulling a sweater over her straight arrow of a body. *No wonder she's a good swimmer.*

"Okay, I'll hurry," I reply, because the sound of hot cinnamon rolls sounds too good to deny this morning.

"Hey, Krick. I almost forgot to ask you, how'd it go in bio yesterday?" Allison stops tying her shoes and focuses her concentration on my forthcoming answer.

"It went absolutely awesome!" I say back to her, knowing that she is talking about the drysolpolia fly project that we got back in AP Bio yesterday. "Maggie and I got the highest grade in the class! The only one hundred percent given to anyone in Mrs. Scott's two AP Bio classes!" I say back to Allison, not worried that I may sound as if I am bragging. I let the pride of yesterday's feat pull my lips tight into a smile.

I look back out at the pool through the small window of our special changing room. The water is calm now. *If I can just get that cut, everything will be better.* After all, everything with school is perfect. Now with the highest overall grade in AP Bio, I sit in striking position for valedictorian of the school. I'm worried about AP Calculus because, quite frankly, I don't get it. And I am not so sure that I can fake it. But even if I am not the valedictorian, my 4.2 GPA looks pretty good.

As I stand staring out the window, I see Dave round the edge of the pool to take down the backstroke flags. I bend at the waist quickly, and grab my V-neck t-shirt to slide over my bra. My face reddens as I imagine Dave seeing my body. "Crap, Allison, Dave's outside," I say with a teenage laugh.

"Who cares? He sees us in practically nothing every day at workout!" Allison says back and I look at her, realizing her body has nothing to hide from Dave. I smile and stop myself from thinking of the other side of my life. "Oh, yeah," Allison continues, "I forgot to tell you . . . when you were out with mono, Dave told me to loop this sheet over this bar to cover the window." Allison throws an old navy blue sheet up to block my current view of the pool. My heart smiles a little with the good intentions of my swim coach.

I finish getting ready in a hurry, and Allison and I head to the car. We pass the crowded and noise-filled bathroom that houses our teammates. I see my red Jetta smiling back at me from the parking lot.

I am not the only one who has my own car. Almost everyone in our entire high school does. There are three unspoken options when it comes to turning sixteen in Moraga. The first, and most normal, is a used car—maybe one that has recently come off of warranty, but one that is almost always nicer than those parked in the teachers' lot. What is the price difference between a two-year-old Jeep or a three year-old Mustang and a new car anyway? Maybe the cost is that Moraga parents can tell themselves that their kid is not spoiled because it is a used car. The other two options exist on opposite ends of the spectrum: one being a new car, which just screams that money is not a problem or even a consideration for a family; the other being no car, which means that a family shouldn't really be living in Moraga, but they somehow make it work in order to live in the school district, which is widely considered to be the best school district in the state.

As I turn the key and press my left foot on the clutch, I look at the clock on the dash of my car. It reads 7:28, and I realize that we got out of practice early on account of our taper. My rushed movements slow and I am grateful to have almost an hour, since class starts at 8:24 today. "Yay!" I say to Allison. "We can stay at Burger King and eat our Cini-Minis there!" I say as I wonder what time the adjacent Long's Drugs store opens. I forgot my mascara today and I want to look nice for Adam.

Adam and I broke up for a little while because he was frustrated with our relationship. I'm glad we are back together, and I hope he doesn't get frustrated again. We both went to homecoming with other people this year, and it made me feel as though I had a huge spotlight shining on my face. All of the girls in my grade were going around talking about how hot Adam is and how stupid I was for breaking up with him. It was very glaring that the boys did not have the same reaction to my status as a single sixteen year old. I knew Adam still liked me, so I made him start dating me again. Everything is back in order.

I look over at Allison buckling her seat belt. I can tell by the smile that she is trying to hide the fact that she thinks it is cool she will arrive to school with me today; that instead of getting dropped off in the front lot with the other freshmen, she will pull into the student lot at the rear of the school; that instead of waving goodbye to an overprotective parent with an outstretched curious neck, she will march into school with a mildly popular upperclassman.

As I pull the stick shift toward me into second gear, we pass the high school. The dying landscape that surrounds the building stands in sharp contrast to the acclaim of the classrooms. The gym, though on the opposite side of the campus, sticks its head up and I think of the many high school dances held within its walls. I look to the right and see the progress the loud construction workers are making on our new pool. It's supposed to be ready right in time for my senior season. I look at Campolindo High School and believe that I will miss it when I am gone. Whoever told me that high school is better than junior high school was undoubtedly right.

As we approach the main road, I ease off the gas as I approach the red light waiting for me. But that is not all that is waiting.

An earthquake. A lightning bolt. A flash flood. A crisis, but one that only I know and one that only I can see. There, parked on the side of the road, your maroon Subaru Outback. The thoughts of the morning—the dreams of swimming fast, of mascara, of looking perfect—fly out of the moonroof above my head.

I know I will see you before I see you. I know this is your car without considering that Moraga is crawling with many cars of the same make, model, and color as yours. But I know that this one belongs to you.

And then, halfway between the street and the building that houses my locker, I see you. Your back is toward me, but I know your legs, I know those mesh shorts, and I know only you would wear shorts with a North Face jacket. With the windows of the car closed, I know the precise sound that your jacket makes as you glide toward my locker.

I gave you the combination. I had to. I think of the purple lock on my locker that is different from any lock in the hallway. "Get a different color. And don't get a combination lock. Get the kind where the numbers line up. That way, I can get in and out faster and no one will see me." These are the directions you had given me on the phone. Now, today, I look at the clock and realize that you are entering the hallway less than an hour before school.

Is Mrs. Bartlett, my History teacher, in her classroom already? Will she see you? What will you say? As the worried question marks stack up in my head, I realize that you already have an answer. I realize you have a plan for everything.

I look at you, and I see the small brown paper bag tucked under your right armpit. As if I have the superpower of x-ray vision, I can see what is stacked inside.

First, my favorite kind of candy: a bag of sour watermelons that might as well have a note attached to it that reads "I give you candy so that I can pretend I am not raping you."

Second, a bagel with chive cream cheese, just like the one you would bring me in eighth grade. If this were to have a note, it would say "See, things are just like they always were. Except for now I follow your every move."

And last, but by no means least, a new battery for the cell phone, which I now keep in a pair of running shoes that hangs off of my backpack. They dangle as if to tell the world I am an athlete ready to take off running at a moment's notice. I wonder if people would laugh or cry if they could see the secret hidden inside.

My eyeballs shake as I look at you walking into the hallway of my life. I had all but forgotten about you this morning. All but forgotten what you are going to do to me next time you "have to have me." All but forgotten you were sick with mono only a month ago.

I force my eyes away from you. I pull them to the left and point out of the driver's side window before I even know what I am pointing at. "Hey, look," I say to Allison, pulling her attention with me. "Look at the hideous car. Would you still be my friend if I drove that?" I ask and force my trembling mouth into a smile.

"Gross. That is gross. No way would I still be your friend!" she says as she looks across the intersection at the stopped PT Cruiser. Allison laughs so that I know she is joking and I try to laugh alongside her. I make a halfhearted stop for the righthand turn, but then quickly press my foot on the gas, unable to stay this close to you any longer.

Would Allison still be my friend if she knew about you?

On the main road now, we head past the front of the high school. We inch further away from you and I can pretend that I never saw you there. I can pretend that you were never there in the first place. I can pretend that you were never born. I lean forward and look quickly in the rear view mirror that hangs from the windshield. I do not check for you. I do not look for a police officer who has caught me rolling through a stoplight. Instead, I look at my eyes. I look at my blank lashes and the plain face looking back at me. I step harder with my right foot, determined to get both my Burger King breakfast and my mascara to continue the masquerade.

PART FOUR

"And Here I Stand"

CHAPTER THIRTY-THREE

Curtain Call

If life were a play, this would be another dress rehearsal. The place, the people, the props all look the same. For the past three weeks the defense attorney (the little leprechaun of a woman Julie hired in the wake of her first attorney) has been engaging in the plea negotiations. Another sunny fall day in northern California. Another trek to the courthouse. Another sleepless night before. Another chance to see if an agreement between good and evil can be reached.

From what we have heard, Julie fired Thorman immediately after the preliminary hearing. After the judge handed down her ruling, Julie made her own ruling that it was the fault of her counsel. Once again, Julie refuses to accept guilt or blame. Her new attorney, Elizabeth Grossman, reminds me of a little leprechaun.

Here we stand again, just past the metal detectors. Per usual, my mom and dad are already here and, as I look at them, I wonder how long they have been waiting for me. To my right, I see Maggie Blakc with her tissues, and to my left, I see Scott with his box of files from his morning case. I look through the small window that leads into Department 36, the stage for much of these proceedings, and wonder who may be inside. "There is no one here for her, Krick," my mom says to me as if she can hear my thoughts.

Let me be honest; I have mixed feelings. Over the past three months I have been in training for a trial. I have done the heavy lifting in my therapy. I have visualized sitting on the stand. Over the past year and a half I have built a base of patience—having court dates get moved, pushed back, and canceled. And, in watching Julie's army grow, I have grown strong.

How will her army feel if they hear those phone tapes in an open court? What would they think if the Facebook messages are read? Would they stay on the same side of the courtroom after they hear my testimony? What look will appear on their faces when the book, the one with a cut-out hole in the precise shape of a late 1990s cell phone, is brought out from evidence? I know that a trial is my chance at having the full truth come out.

Then, like a spiral that comes to my brain without warning, I remember the questions asked by the defense. I remember my many hours of testimony and worry that I don't really remember what I said. I know I told the truth, but once I was done with an answer, I had to crumple it up and throw it away, so that I could unfold the answer to the next question. I imagine the leprechaun dragging me through the dirt, tied with rope and chained to the back of her Prius.

I think of my team at Cal. A sense of peace fills my insides as I allow myself to imagine the legal proceedings blowing over like fallen leaves. Right now a life-size question mark is standing between me and the road ahead, one that is heavy and hard to carry. Really, I have no idea if and when my battle will go to trial. Last week the only agreement that was made in plea negotiations was to move the start date from October 31 to November 7. I allow myself to imagine my question mark being lifted by a crane and the path ahead being clear of Julie and sitting on the stand. I would be able to travel to all of the competitions this fall. I would be able to be a better assistant to Teri as she walks closer and closer to being the Head Olympic Coach this summer. I would be able to be me again. Or would I?

As I look at Scott and my dad talking about what may or may not happen today, I am reminded of the same conversation that they had this time a week ago. I look to Scott's face, as he sees these scenarios every day. He has a soft dimple in his cheek and relaxed lines around his eyes; he thinks that nothing new will happen today, that this is just another checkpoint before we are moved to the marathon of a trial. I look from my mom, then to Maggie, and finally to my dad, and I sense that they feel the same. Two years ago, I never could have imagined the scene before my eyes. They all almost look comfortable here, waiting for just another day in the courtroom. But as I watch this day unfold, a strong sense stirs in my soul and says this is not just another day.

Behind me the door opens too quickly for comfort. My head swivels, prepared to defend myself from the sharpshooter Julie has hired to kill me. I see Joyce and Geoff, my prosecution team, entering the side entrance for attorneys only. "Kristen . . ." Geoff's voice is deep and low and comforting. He takes his time with my name, tilts his head, and I imagine him lightly holding my hand as we walk down what would be the darker, rockier path of a trial. "How are you doing today?"

As I shake my head to indicate that I, in spite of all of this, am living and breathing and walking, I see Joyce appear from behind Geoff. At literally half his size, it is hard to think that the Border Terrier of Joyce is the boss of the entire attorney general's office. I imagine her chasing Geoff through the office hallways and nipping at his heels. Geoff, the Bernese Mountain Dog of a man, listens intently to the directions Joyce barks at him as they prepare for the next trial.

"Hi, Kristen." Her words move faster as do her eyes. She shoots a glance into the window of the courtroom to our right, peering quickly with her striking blue eyes. *Is she looking for defense counsel?* The wiry gray hair on her head matches her electric personality. She has done a full survey of the situation in a matter of one full breath and suddenly she is back to her immediate company: "Hello, family." Her voice is slightly shrill, and while it doesn't comfort me as does Geoff's voice, it comforts me as I imagine her in front of any judge. This woman is a fighter.

Behind them a new face follows. "Hi, Kristen, I'm Investigator Doti." I have spoken to her many times on the phone and her petite figure surprises me. As I shake her hand, my own feels clunky, and I am surprised at how slight Imelda Doti is. I had pictured a bigger, more sturdy woman at the other end of the phone as she hammered me with questions. Her dark skin, dark hair, and dark eyes look up to me. I see her searching me for signs that I have endured the pages of abuse she has read about in the police reports. Her hand moves quickly to that of my mother and father, introducing herself and reminding them that she is going to interview them at a coffee shop after the court proceeding today. Her tight mouth, her aggressive energy, and her Latin American heritage remind me of an overly excited Chihuahua, and she is panting with anticipation.

The brief conversation touches the surface of the weather outside as I prepare myself for my entrance. Geoff and Joyce pass through the swinging wood door first, and then my procession follows the same order it always does. Scott puffs his chest and enters first, leaving his right hand stretched out behind his back for me to grab. I hang on, being toted into the courtroom and into an open seat. Maggie walks at my heels, close enough that if I stop, she would run into me, but yet not close enough. My parents follow a respectable distance behind as if to say they are here to fight with me and for me, but not lead me into battle.

We head to the back row, at the back of the room, just in front of the window where I watched Julie walk as a free person for the first time. We leave a bank of seats open, the seats where Julie's supporters have sat so many times before. Like ghosts without hearts, they have vanished.

Judge Maier, the beautiful blond judge who handles the master court calendar, is not on her bench yet. Maier has been the judge we have appeared before regularly since the preliminary hearing. She must be in the back, in the "Judge's Chambers," a term that previously held meaning for me only for the end of *Law and Order* episodes. Now it is where my justice will be debated.

Out of the back a blond-haired woman comes quickly. She is not Judge Maier, but almost. Ironically, she looks much like Maier. She is blond and well put together. "She's ready for you," the judicial assistant says before disappearing back into the cave of debate. The leprechaun and my dog pack scurry to follow her.

Alone in the courtroom. Almost alone. I have my army strategically placed around me. To my right is a small contingent of attorneys sitting in the roped off area that is reserved for lawyers only. There are five of them, two of whom I recognize from Scott's holiday party a year ago. They are "higher ups" in the district attorney's office, individuals who may or may not know about my case. Their eyes are looking in my direction, just past me, and focusing in on Scott. I search their faces in an attempt to read their thoughts: "Why is he sitting there?" or is it "Is it appropriate for him to hold the shaking hand of a witness?" Part of my heart hopes that they know and instead are thinking, "Wow, look at Scott. Look at his wife and what they have been through together. They are strong." But their light smiles and daily conversation between each other tell me that they do not understand the gravity of the situation.

"Kristen," Imelda has slid her body between me and Maggie and I jump at her quick word.

"Yes," I reply, but my eyes are glazed over and my response feels like a prerecorded tape playing from the speaker of my mouth.

"I wanted to ask you a few questions." She holds my eighth grade yearbook in her hand, the most recent piece of evidence that my mom has found. Are her questions proof that we are paving the path toward trial? "Can you show me where you are in this book?"

I hear her questions, but the words float into my head and, instead of being processed and resulting in an answer, they simply swirl about. I picture the process: picking up the book, opening the book to the index, finding the page number of my various appearances, flipping the pages and reading the page numbers, looking at my face from before. Suddenly her request becomes impossible. My mouth, my brain, and my hands that would turn the pages feel as though they are filled with drying concrete. Imelda does not notice my internal struggle; instead, she stops on a random page, thrusts the book in front of my face, and says, "Is this Correa?" I haven't been given time to answer the first question. Now, another. My heart races and I feel my neck stretching like a giraffe's, my head filling with helium, and me beginning to be pulled from my body.

I do not answer. Imelda's eyes dart back and forth, looking at both of mine. I wish with every ounce of my DNA that Maggie were sitting next to me, that Imelda would stop barking at me and just let me get through the "right now" of life, that she would somehow understand that it is not me as soon as I enter the courthouse.

I take the energy I can muster and I crease my body in half, leaning toward Maggie. I give her a look with my eyebrows drawn together. She knows what I need her to do, but somehow I find the words to ask, "Mags, can you answer these questions?"

Maggie is aggressive, and if she could have, she would have put a muzzle on the dog. Instead, she does the next best thing and plays fetch with Imelda, going through the pages of the yearbook, pointing out the key players and the important notes scribbled in black and white—a snapshot of the moment in history just before my life broke into two.

The hairs rise on the back of my neck as I sense something to the right of me move. It is not the pod of lawyers, who are still there and have stopped staring—an indication that they have figured out exactly who I am and exactly why Scott is there. The movement comes from behind the glass partition, behind the sign that reads, "Communicating with inmates in custody is a federal offense punishable by law."

She is in all green. And her face is almost green. Her clothes hang on her body and she looks smaller today. She moves like a mouse behind the glass, peering out into the galley of the courtroom, stealing glances of the hungry army that is there to shred her to pieces. I wonder if she is thankful for the safety of her glass cage.

I am gripping Scott's right hand as Maggie and Imelda talk quietly and quickly on my left. I wonder if I ever hurt Scott's hand, clamping down with my anxiety and hurt and pain? I look down, realizing that the fuzz on top of his paw is wet, realizing also that as soon as I saw my demon, I began crying. Scott holds my hand steady, making no effort to wipe or dry the fallen tears. He just lets them fall.

My eyes are pulled back to the glass, and I catch a glimpse of Julie looking directly at me. Is that really her? She looks different. I am shaken. Her head is low and I can't see the whites all around her pupils as I could at the preliminary hearing or when she was on top of me hurting me. Her eyes look sunken, her cheeks hollow, and her brow has softened. But mostly her mouth looks different. Usually her mouth is pulled up at the corners, and her heinous laugh lifts her lip above her upper teeth so that the gum is exposed for the onlooker. The laugh that drives a dagger into my soul, the laugh I used to laugh along with, the laugh she used at me when I feared getting caught, and the laugh in my direction as she sat with Barbara and Amy, the two former students who have joined Julie in support.

This new look, I have seen this Julie before. But where? Not always, but often on the drive home. In the glow of the streetlights Julie would tell me that it was all my fault. And the look on her face—this look—told me that she was wrong. As a fourteen or fifteen year old I had mistaken this look for remorse. But my soft heart grew harder and wiser, and by the third year of captivity I realized it was not remorse. It was, and is, the downward spiral of an addict. After the hunt, the purchase, and the high comes the fall. This is her fall. Is this her defeat?

The back door of the chambers opens quickly and I jolt in my seat, wondering briefly if others notice my external symptoms of PTSD. Again, the assistant look-alike comes out of the back. She grabs a large black covered book on the judge's desk.

Scott leans his mouth to my ear, "She is getting the calendar. They are picking new dates. It's on for trial. They are just going to push it back." Scott speaks so softly that no one else can hear him and I am thankful for our secret language.

My brain tries to make sense of the words Scott has whispered. I struggle to imagine them looking at the calendar and arguing through the logistics of the trial. My mind is quickly tempted back to the face. What have we taken from her? Brazenness? Arrogance? She is stuck back there, without her army. Perhaps that is the reason for her metamorphosis. Perhaps the Julie I know will be back just in time for trial.

My body jolts again, and I look up expecting to see the judge's assistant. But when my eyes meet Joyce's eyes, my heart stops beating as she walks swiftly at me. She passes through the half gate that keeps the audience from the stage of the court and takes the row in front of me, until she is directly square in front of me.

It is not a yell in volume, but it is a yell in intention. My eyes meet hers, and I believe my ears are ready to hear. Her cheeks are tight and I am surprised to see her eyes riddled with emotion that she is working to contain. "She is going to plea."

Somewhere, in the pit of my center, between my stomach, my chest bone and my heart, I feel something. I feel peace. I could reach inside my body and put my finger in the very middle of who I am and touch my soul.

And as quickly as the sensation came, the peace blows out of my body and I am numb.

The buzz around me stands in sharp contrast to my immobility. Joyce, after telling me, continues on to my family to repeat the words they have surely heard. "She is going to plead guilty today." I turn my inside tape recorder to 'on,' because I cannot feel this now, I must transcribe the words to feel later. "She is going to plead guilty to three counts of a lewd act with a minor fourteen or fifteen and one count of forcible sexual penetration. It will be a max term of eight years. She has also waived her appellate rights."

From somewhere within my army comes a question for Joyce, I believe it might be my dad. "What about the sex registration?"

"She will be a registered sex offender for life." A puff of pride fills Joyce's chest as she pulls the waist of her pants up closer to her belly button. I make an addition to my list of memories to remember.

I can sense that my dad is crying. Maybe my mom, too. Imelda moves and Maggie Black reclaims her rightful position at my left flank. She is crying, an unusual sign for my toughest friend. I want to feel what they are feeling, but my insides are insulated with bubble wrap. I let Scott hold me, and as Joyce returns to finish up in the Judge's Chambers, Scott proceeds to fill us in.

"So what now?" I am pretty sure that it is my dad with yet anther question.

Scott explains the next move in the peace treaty. "She'll come out here and they will read the counts and set a sentencing date."

Today? They will read the counts today? And as if my mom can read my thoughts she asks, "Today? That will all happen today?"

"Yes," Scott replies. He turns to me and, at our table for two, he says in my ear, "It's over. We won. We did it." His voice echoes through my ears and begins to melt the ice that has frozen my feelings. My eyes begin to drip with tears as reality thaws.

I look up and see Julie's attorney entering the glass cage. I imagine her with a bucket of fish to feed a shark. But instead she is armed with a pile of paperwork. Ah, time for the South to sign the Emancipation Proclamation.

I am reminded of a different type of signing that what will happen in the next three weeks. It is one my favorite times of year to be a college coach. November 7: National Letter of Intent signing day in which our high school senior recruits sign their NLI in a contractual agreement that they will attend Cal. Signing ceremonies, in which athletes from all sports sign their prospective NLIs for their prospective schools, will take place. The celebration of jocks: balloons, cakes, collegiate apparel, high school assemblies, families, photos, principals, handshakes . . . and teachers. The happiest moment in these young athletes' careers, set in time by one thing: their signatures.

Julie's stringy hair falls in front of her face as she signs her name. She doesn't seem to have the energy or the care to slide her hair behind her ear. I remember that. The feeling of giving up or wanting to give up. But now, with my hair pulled and pinned neatly into a bun at the back of my head, I am proud that I did not give in, that I walked through. And, at last, victory lies on the side of God. My tears come now in full and with a partial sense of happiness.

After all, how happy can I be that a part of my life was stolen in the first place?

I am expecting Julie to join her attorney at the defense table, but she does not. Judge Maier takes her place upon her judge's throne and looks down at me instantly. Joyce and Geoff sit tall ahead and to my left, on the side of good. The bailiff is in place and that stage is set. The judge begins to discuss the terms with limited interjections from both the prosecution and the defense. The legal language swirls in my head and I translate by listening and looking at my interpreter, Scott.

"In the matter of The People v. Julie Correa, how does the defendant plead to count one, lewd act with a child fourteen or fifteen?" Judge Maier's voice, much like the look she shoots at Julie, is convincing and almost angry. I am proud to have a judge like her taking up arms for me.

There follows a pause in the courtroom that makes my heart spin. The leprechaun leans over to the monster and Julie leans down to listen. My eyes are locked and I do not blink for fear that I may miss what I have been waiting half of a lifetime for.

"No contest," Julie whispers. A voice that I can barely hear and have never heard before. Scott tightens his grip on my hand and, with a quick pump of our combined fist, we celebrate.

The term "no contest" echoes in my head. I am sure it will give my mom reason to be frustrated and I know that most of my army would have liked a "guilty" plea in retreat. But as the words leave Julie's mouth, they find my ultimate satisfaction. The devil drops her pitchfork, puts her hands in the air, and hides her tail between her legs. As if she is saying, "I'm not going to fight anymore. You are right. You are good. I am wrong. My army is gone and yours is strong. I give up. It's simply . . . no contest."

The judge moves through the other lewd act charges, and Julie's voice remains barely audible. And then the victory of my most contested battle: the force charge. The tipping point of the case, the chains that kept me in bondage, the fear that gave me PTSD: the force element is what caused my personality to get chopped in half. It is the truth of what happened to me.

"How does the defendant plead to count 4, forcible sexual penetration of child fourteen or fifteen by means of force, fear, or duress?"

This time there is no pause and no private attorney conference. In a voice that I have heard before, the Julie that I know and knew too well, the monster, is back, "No contest." It is a yell. Her last stand. As if to yell, "fine!" I am reminded of the tantrum of a two year old. The final pout as if to say, you won but I am still right.

She is still sick.

Judge Maier finishes the logistics. Just as I think we are done, she looks at me; "Mrs. Cunnane. Thank you for being here again today. And thank you for the letter submitted to the court. I look forward to hearing your thoughts through your victim impact statement on December 13th." Her eyes pierce through the space that separates us and we may as well be the only two in the court. She sees me, and I see her. My mouth remains shut, and my eyes say a silent thank you.

I walked into the courtroom not knowing what I wanted to happen. I walk out now, and I know what to expect next. I am able to feel my feet again.

My people encircle me. They talk about what has happened and look at me, searching for my reaction. Still partially frozen, I give them what I am able: "I am happy." But my voice comes out flat and I know they wish for more from me. I am not there yet.

We decide to grab lunch, and we walk to the usual post-court restaurant. Back to The Copper Skillet of the preliminary hearing, I realize we have become regulars at this greasy spoon through the many court dates. Scott walks in and shakes hands with a variety of local sheriffs and officers who have, at some point along the line, testified at Scott's court cases or given him police reports. It's proper that the good guys surround us.

We settle into the booth in the corner. I slide over the vinyl seats. The springs protrude and remind me of sitting in the same spot in March as I awaited the verdict of the preliminary hearing.

I have always liked sitting in the corner. I have always preferred to be close to the table. I like small spaces. They make me feel safe. As I burrow into the most awkward seat at the table, I feel an undeniable sense in my tummy. I look at my family, at my army, settling into their positions. I feel Scott, as always, sitting a little closer than the average husband would. My shoulders settle into my body, I take a breath, and revisit my belly. I am not hungry or sick. It is not the sense of peace from earlier. Instead, for the first time in my life, I believe that I was meant to bring a baby into this world.

CHAPTER THIRTY-FOUR

Dragon Slayer

It is dark. So dark that most people wouldn't be able to see. But I can. I am used to this.

We are in your apartment. I am also used to being here, although that doesn't mean that I like it here. Or that I like the dark for that matter.

"Have you heard from the Davis soccer coach yet?" you say as though we are having a normal conversation. There is nothing normal about any of this. You are trying to act like the mentor you should have been: "I am sure that they will be contacting you. Maybe you should write them a letter."

I hate it when you talk to me as if you think I am Kristen. Kristen is the one who plays soccer, but you don't know that I am not her. You also don't know that she likes swimming more than soccer now. After all, how would you know such a thing?

"No, I haven't heard from him." I say, and go along with the game that I am Kristen. Kristen has not heard from Davis, not that she would be interested in going to UC Davis anyway.

I should note that this is not a conversation that occurs in a coffee shop or on the telephone. It is some time after midnight and we are, as I said, in your apartment. The corduroy-like fabric of the aging couch itches under my bare skin. You have your cold, bony arms draped around me, and you hold me as though you care about me. I know that you do not care, because if you did care I would not be here. I would be in my bed. I would be asleep. And most certainly you would not have just done what you did to me.

This is the order of events as always. It's not as though we get to your apartment or I get in your car and we chat. You always hurt me first, and then you talk to me as if I am your friend or your partner or your child or all of the above. I play along with all of it because what other choice do I have?

Before I can get to the possible options in my head, my mind reels quickly through the image of Mr. Witters driving off a cliff in Big Sur. The scene changes every time I press the play button, and I replay it all the time. I have never been to Big Sur before, but I have seen pictures. I actually have never been outside of the county, although Kristen has.

Big Sur is located just over an hour south, and the dramatic cliffs of the northern California seascape look angry in my imagination. Kristen never thinks about this. She never gives her mind space to consider what happened to Mr. Witters and acknowledge that she may have been the reason. But I think about it all the time because it makes me scared. And being scared fuels me. I don't eat. I just think. And this fuels my effort to keep Kristen and myself safe.

There he is. Mr. Witters in his blue pickup truck. Just receiving news that a high school girl came forward. *Which one?* Gripping the wheel, pressing the gas, propelling into the air, suspending in time before meeting his death below. *Did he think of his two little ones on the way down? Did he scream? Or was he even in the car? Is he really dead?*

The pending fear brings me back to you. "I got a letter from Emory and a letter from Princeton," I say. Kristen was excited when she got these letters, especially the one from Princeton with its prestigious Ivy League letterhead. She thinks that her perfection in school and in sports may help her get there. But I never let her dreams run very far.

"You can't go that far away," you say, as though you can read my mind. You clench your arms around me and I envision you moving your arms up four inches to my neck. I feel as though I can't breath as I imagine you choking me.

I only let my mind wander momentarily as I think of Georgia and New Jersey. Still, I know that neither Kristen nor I will ever have a future without you in it. I imagine the apartment that you will have when Kristen goes to college. I think of you walking ten feet behind her as she heads off to Psychology lecture. Still, it is better than you killing her. At least Kristen will still need me.

"I know. I won't go that far," I say, and you relax your grip enough that my diaphragm also relaxes, drops, and lets the much-needed air in. "Marc wants me to talk to the swimming coaches at UCLA." I say this before I can even fully consider the words that have left my mouth. I know that swimming in college is Kristen's true dream. I also know that going to UCLA is what she thinks about when I let her get away with it. My job is to protect Kristen. Maybe I am trying to protect her dream.

"What about Davis?" you say in a whisper that tells me much more than your spoken words. You think that Kristen should go to UC Davis because you did. "Davis is less than an hour away. I can get to you when I need you . . . and things won't change." You take a short pause before saying, "I thought that you were going to be just like me." Now your voice changes to a whine, as though the mere consideration of a different school is a betrayal. "We are soulmates."

"Davis is still definitely in the picture. I just want to keep my options open just in case I don't get in," I say, knowing full well that UCLA has much more difficult admission standards than Davis does.

I don't say this, but I think Kristen would rather die than go to Davis. She wants nothing to do with you and rarely ever sees you. She sends me instead. And she doesn't want to be a PE teacher anymore. She would rather be anything than a PE teacher. I know that she hates putting on her soccer cleats, because she is scared of remembering you.

With her 4.2 GPA, she is too good for Davis and too good for you.

"Okay, well, I think that Davis is the best option," you say in a stern and steady voice. I do not turn to look at you, because I know that you are staring at me without blinking. I hate it when you do that.

I remain silent and still in the darkness of the room. There is a lot of time that goes by where you and I say nothing to each other. And that silence has been growing. Before me, when Kristen had to deal with you all by herself, you talked a lot. You justified things, you explained things, you cried, and you pleaded. But now you mostly just do what you do.

All of this makes me wonder. Kristen is just starting her senior year in high school. It has been three full years since she was your favorite eighth grader. *Do you have a new favorite? Is there someone else that you have been using your words on?*

This is selfish. And I would never say it to you. And Kristen doesn't know that I hope for this. But every time I have to sit on the floorboard of your car or hide in the damp bushes at the top of my hill, I fantasize about there being someone else. I pass the minutes by imagining Nora Hope coming home from college, showing up at the Moraga Police Department, and saying, "Julie Correa raped me." I picture the mother of an eighth grader, one of your TAs, walking into your office in search of her daughter and finding an unwanted and undeniable scene. *What would happen then?* You would be taken away. Not me. My heart flutters at the thought of this freedom.

I know that it is wrong: to wish this on someone else. But I am now entirely alone. And it has to be that way. Kristen has to take care of Kristen's life and I have to take care of you. So I imagine, I hope, that there is someone else out there, feeling what I am feeling. And hating what I hate. I think that we would be really good friends.

"Yeah. Davis is the best option," I say to break the silence and make sure my high hopes don't get the best of me. "What are we going to do if I don't get in?" I ask.

Part of my job is to be one step ahead of Kristen. I need to know what Julie's plans will be should something go wrong with my Davis application. I need to know if life will end instantaneously, if she will kidnap Kristen there on the spot, or if she will move with Kristen and hover about. And, if that is the case, I need to figure out how to keep Kristen's parents safe and without suspicion of the shadow. I have a lot to maintain.

I await your response and hope that you don't know the strategic reasoning that lies behind my question.

"I don't know what we will do . . ." As you say this, I am sure that you actually know exactly what you will do. You have a plan for this because you have a plan for everything. "I guess it would be okay," you say to me, and I hate that I can feel the temperature of your breath on the backside of my ear lobe.

Silence follows and I realize I have gotten nowhere. "What would we do?" I try again. My success pivots on my planning.

"I don't really know. I have always assumed that you would go to Davis. That is what you told me." You voice is factual and cold. I wonder if you realize that things have changed since you went to college. You are now almost thirty-two years old. People talk about how things have changed in the past decade in terms of applying to college, especially the University of California public schools. Supposedly, they are among the best universities and are still affordable. I am certain Kristen could get in anywhere, but still I wonder if you are aware things are different now.

"I'm really scared I am not going to get in." I knock on the door again and pull my body toward my center. I am a veteran when it comes to dealing with you and my guess is that you will respond to this act. You can't help yourself when you think you are helping me. It's all part of your sickness.

"Oh, sweetie. Don't be scared," you say as you get closer to me. You begin rocking me back and forth ever so slightly as if I am your child. "We can work it out. Maybe I'll just have to come visit you."

My body freezes and I am stiff. I do not respond to the rocking and you know all too soon that something is wrong. Or right, depending on the person asked.

The words ring in my ear canals, "I'll come visit you." I can't help it. I do what I am always halting Kristen from doing. I let my mind run. I see Kristen, at UCLA, with a life—a real life and real friends. And she is walking to class and there is no one to follow her. I think of you 400 miles away, getting on an airplane every so often to come "visit."

The apartment is so dark that we might as well be in a run-down building in Mexico somewhere. I have been so scared that I might as well have been your captive. I know that my handcuffs are invisible to the naked eye, and no one can see my chains other than me. But they are real. Or at least they have been until this very moment.

"Visit," I allowed myself to repeat out loud in wonder. *Visit? Visit!* Visit is not the term used by a crazed and obsessed maniac you had me believing you are. Visit does not fit with your daily statements of "I can't breathe unless I have you," or "You know I will never really let you out of my sight."

My body is a statue and you can feel it. I do not care and I am not scared. "What?" I say and I let my voice sound like an adult. Although I do not move, I feel as though I am growing an inch with each passing instant.

"Or I can move there," you say quickly, and you try to sound stern. But it is too late. In the darkness of the room I have already seen the door ahead of me opened ever so slightly. The brilliant beam of light has caused my pupils to shrink and has made my brain see exactly who you are.

The door is slightly ajar as I allow light to shine on the past four years. Like a prisoner of war, I see my chance. I see my way out of here and Kristen's life without you. The ropes and the cuffs are only props on the stage of a horrible nightmare. But now I am beginning to wake up.

My bones sink into the couch as I see reality. *You are not going to follow me. You are not even going to give up your life. You do not love me and you do not have to have me.* I let myself smile, not only in my heart, but also on my face. You cannot see me as I still have my back seated toward you, but still I think that you know that everything is going to change.

"What is it?" you cry at me, forcing craziness into your voice. "I'll move, I'll move. Don't be mad, sweetie, I'll move." I pretend to listen to you and pretend that I am listening to your words. "What's wrong? Are you mad at me? What's the matter?" Your questions run together without giving me room for response. *Ha! You mistake my change in demeanor. This may be the happiest moment in my life!*

I can feel your worry as you sit behind me. Your paranoia may be partially warranted here. Not because you can't live without me, but because of what I might do in knowing this, that everything you have said has all been a lie.

"Okay," I say in a quick voice. "I'm okay," I say, knowing that it's going to be true.

As the night lingers, and you hurt me once again, I cannot remove the smile that lies inside of me. I let you do whatever you do, but I am planning. I have practiced my patience for years and I will need it once again. But I see things for what they are now. You are a monster, a dragon who breathes fire. But dragons only live in fairy tales.

CHAPTER THIRTY-FIVE

Complete My Sentence

I hold in my arms a number of things that will help me through the next few hours. The first and most important is Scott's hand. The other things include a conglomeration of artifacts from the abuse, along with the ten-page statement that it is meant to reveal my current state.

My Victim Impact Statement: I had to stop myself from laughing when I opened the letter from the Victim's Assistance Program. It was over a month ago, and it was meant to give me information about the day that defendant Julie Gay Correa would be sentenced for the four felony counts to which she had recently pled no contest, which by all standards is the same as a guilty plea. Included in the number of papers was information about the rights that victims have to speak about the crimes committed against them on sentencing day. "What is a Victim Impact Statement?" the title of the page asked. And below was the simple statement that brought some amusement: "A chance for the victim of the crime to summarize how he/she has been affected." *How am I supposed to sit down and write a summary of the unraveling of my life?*

Now as I pass through the metal detectors today, statement written and rewritten, read and reread, I know I must be ready. It is 1:30 P.M. on December 13, 2011, and I am ready to fight my final battle towards getting my life back.

Department 36 has just reopened from lunch, and I enter without hesitation because, for me, it is important to find a seat near the back where I feel bulletproof. I need a spot where I can sit, look squarely at the door, and not have to wonder who snuck what in their purse behind me. I notice immediately the barrier in the middle of the room, as the yellow caution tape of a crime scene smiles back at me. This line offers separation between my side and hers, and I know that Scott has made this arrangement with the acting bailiff in the courtroom. I am surprised that the room is already full.

The back row is already filled up with my people: friends who have proven their fortitude during this storm, family that has become more immediate with the need. It is, without any doubt, the largest my army has ever been. I keep my eyes focused on my half of the room, catching quickly the eyes of my Aunt Judy and two closest cousins, who have flocked here from Utah.

My feet cooperate in walking me to the empty row, second from the back. I know, without anyone saying a word, that this row has been saved for me and my first line of defense: Scott, Maggie Red, and Maggie Black. My entry is not as graceful as I would like, as I wear a pair of black high heels that are hardly part of my daily coaching wardrobe. They make me walk a little like a horse, and the fact that my knees feel like putty adds argument to the question whether I have hooves or feet.

I settle into the wooden pew, and Scott lets go of my hand just long enough to take off his suit jacket. He slips it over my legs, which are covered in black tights and are sticking out of a new grey sweater dress. His gesture reminds me of the time we went to an Oakland A's baseball game and he used his jacket to protect my cold legs from the Bay Area fog. But this time, my legs shake for another reason.

Maggie Black holds my ammunition of paper and Maggie Red holds my right hand. I feel surrounded and safe as I see Chuck and his wife walk in to take my side. Suddenly I feel strong enough to lift my eyes and look at my competition.

Her side has dwindled and changed. No more JM teachers. No more former JM teachers. I glance at Scott, and I can tell he is searching the other side of the room for the same thing. Perhaps his call to the superintendent of the school district worked after all.

Also missing from Julie's fleet are her brothers and in-laws, who were all there for her initial arraignment. Perhaps they could read into the truth of a "no contest" plea.

My mind has a hard time clinging onto those who are not there, and immediately focuses instead on those sitting in support. Her mother looks limp, with grey hair and glasses, appearing as if she may have gotten even smaller since the preliminary hearing. Her eyes seem vacant, and I wonder if the absence is courtesy of a Valium prescription, or perhaps her brain knowing the truth and her mind not willing to handle it.

Her father is back in the room, and I haven't seen him since the earliest of court days. In another setting and on another day, I imagine that this man may be kind. He has lines around the corners of his lips and the unmistakable lines of crow's feet at the corner of his pale blue eyes. My heart momentarily aches as I see too kind a face to have to bear witness to this. *If his face matches his insides, what then went so horribly wrong? Was Julie just born this way?*

Rob is here, looking straight ahead. He peers through the same pair of glasses he wore over a decade ago. His thin lips are drawn tight, and I wonder why the hardship of the year has not taken any sort of physical toll on him. Like a statue, he is unchanged and unscathed.

There are no kids in the courtroom. I can swallow and I can breathe. Two months ago, Geoff had called and said that Julie may bring her kids to give a statement about "what a good mommy she is." A new movie reel was set on play in my mind. Two dark-haired boys with dark circles under their eyes, stammering over redrafted statements to the court, pleading to the judge for their mom's freedom, begging the question 'Was coming forward the right thing?" I feel calm as that possible scene is ejected.

Her sister Kara is there, but that is a given. It's ironic that Julie always said she didn't care much for her sister. Kara sits there, ashen grey skin, and moves her neck and head just the way Julie does. *Is it genetics or the commonalities of evil?* I would be lying if I said I wasn't scared of her. Yesterday, on my walk with Scott, I thought that she was in the white SUV that passed us. I was sure she was going to shoot me in the chest before I had a chance to share my insides in court. Of course, it wasn't her. *Or was it?*

And Julie's other favorite students, Amy and Barbara, are back. Their moms have joined them. The four of them sit closely in a pod, held together in seeing that my army has grown with increasing representatives from the Moraga community. A slice of me hopes that their lives will change with their choice to sit on the far side of the caution tape.

It hurts every time. It doesn't get easier or harder; it remains exactly the same. I see Barbara's head rise, and her eyes are drawn to the right. From a sturdy-looking door, a bailiff leads Julie into the room. She is in all green again, and I wish my mind would not drift back to the time I knew her as Natali, the coolest teacher at the school. But I can't help it. I see her and, just for a split second, I think of the role she *could* have played in my life, the role she *should* have played in my life, and the role that she *did* play in my life. Had it stopped with soccer tips and the safe haven office lunches, the fabric of who I am may be different. I look at her and know that Natali never existed. As with each time my eyes meet her being, I double over in pain seeing that she is real.

Julie is led to a table on the righthand side of the room. Her forces are lined up behind her, and she turns to them. With a smile that reminds me of religious cult leader Warren Jeffs, Julie thanks her side for following.

It is quiet, outside of the light tapping of my heels at the end of my shaking legs. I have drawn this scene in my head a million times, each with a different script and each with a different result. And now I am here.

Judge Maier enters, and I believe we make eye contact across the room immediately. I slide my body an inch closer to Scott's as the judge settles in her chair, so that I can maintain a direct visual line with her. Her blond hair falls on the shoulders of her black robe just as it did during the previous proceedings.

She has never looked more beautiful.

"In the matter of The People versus Julie Correa. May I have appearances, please?" Judge Maier breaks the silence of the courtroom and solicits responses to begin the proceedings.

Give her the max sentence of eight years! I want to yell to the judge, but remain quiet and listen.

"Elizabeth Grossman representing Ms. Correa. Ms. Correa is present in court in custody." Elizabeth stands, her outfit, her hair, her makeup looking more as if she were going to a craft fair than to court. Next to her, Julie also stands and looks straight ahead, attempting to avoid the media cameras angled at her from the opposite side of the room.

"Good afternoon, your Honor. Geoff Lauter for the People from the Attorney General's office."

Geoff's voice booms and he looks the part of the good guy.

Judge Maier reviews the evidence that she has examined before coming to sentencing today: letters from both sides, evidence from the case, probation reports, professional evaluations of Julie and the entire transcript of the preliminary hearing. Judge Maier then asks Geoff if he is ready to present his speakers.

Geoff said yesterday that the defense would likely lead, so I'm not prepared for this order of events. He stands up for our side and says, "Normally my experience is the defense goes first, and then the prosecution goes second." With his gentle approach, Geoff makes his opinion known, while at the same time shows respect for the judge's decision.

Quickly Maier agrees, and a podium is placed on the defense's side of the room.

Grossman has a casual feel about her as she begins her parade: "The first witness we're going to call is Dayle Carlson."

His shoulders are drawn in, his hair is grey, and his glasses are round. Carlson reviews his own accolades, which include being a probation officer for a number of years. With every word that comes rumbling out of his lips, I worry that he will say something that will take the wind out of our argument. My mind becomes a Rolodex, shuffling through the possibilities of what he will say. Maybe he will cite another similar case that was worth much less time and provide case law for Judge Maier to make a lighter judgment. I have to slow my mind, hang on to Scott, and simply listen.

Carlson describes the work that he has done reviewing the case, and he begins to paint a picture of a perfect mom raising her family. He tilts his head and looks toward Julie: "I actually saw the family together in Utah, saw these boys interacting with their peers and with other adults and was duly impressed by that." My spine shortens as I imagine these two boys. Carlson continues, "Julie Correa was living there, and it was a life devoted to her two young sons. She was a stay-at-home mom. She was involved in all of their activities." I shudder at the thought of Julie as a mom.

Carlson continues on to argue that Julie should have a lighter sentence, claiming that there is ample evidence that she has changed her life and regrets her actions. He reminds the court that there are no other victims as he refers to this "singular relationship."

The term "relationship" hangs in my ears. I imagine Julie and I strolling down the street toward the movie theater for the afternoon feature. My jaw clenches as I remember the taste of the alcohol Julie gave me so that I could fulfill her needs. I wish I could stand up, catch the word "relationship" coming from his mouth, and use my claws to tear it to shreds. My scream stays inside my body.

"And for those reasons, your Honor, I urge the court to impose a five-year period of imprisonment." It is obvious that he is finished as he returns to his seat in the first row of the defense.

My eyes are drawn to Geoff, who speaks with anger rattling the back of his throat. "Your Honor, I have a couple questions."

"Certainly." Maier takes no time for her consideration.

"What exactly do you mean by 'relationship'?" It is as if Geoff can read my mind.

"Well, relationship is—I mean by that a lot—a lot of things," Carlson stammers. "We all have relationships. You and I have a relationship now. It was in the context of the interaction between the two, between the teenager and a teacher, that relationship."

"Did you mean also between a sexual abuser and a victim when you said "relationship"?" Geoff's words hang in the still courtroom air.

Grossman looks relieved that Geoff is done, but the brief pause quickly comes to an end as Geoff continues, "You've been a defense consultant since which year?"

"1984," says Carlson in a murmured reply.

Geoff's voice is loud in opposition, "So, you haven't been a probation officer since 1984?"

"Yes," Carlson admits to his nearly thirty-year hiatus.

"How much money were you paid to prepare the report you submitted to the Court today?" Geoff pries. He asks a question I have never considered, but now I am excited to hear the answer.

"Five thousand dollars," Carlson states in a near whisper.

Scott shakes my hand as if he is rooting for Geoff. "That's all I have, your Honor." I can't see Geoff's face, but I can hear a small smile in his words.

Grossman has a line of character witnesses for Julie. My mind races with what they might say: *Sure, Julie said she had sex with a fourteen-year-old girl, but she's not so bad! Julie has changed! Julie got railroaded into taking a plea!*

I allow air to fill my lungs as I look at my former classmates. Before Grossman invites them to the podium, I know that they will speak. Amy and Barbara each have a stapled stack of paper in their hands that they have been preoccupied reviewing since I first spotted them.

Barbara stands first and I am reminded that we had ballet class together when I was five and she was four. *Does she remember our dancing days?* She still looks the same as she did then: beautiful brown hair and light freckles. She is half Asian, and her almond eyes give her a distinct and tropical look. In high school she was the girlfriend of Scott's best friend. In a different life, she would be sitting on my side, and we would go to coffee after this was all over.

Barbara begins: "I have known Julie Correa for going on 16 years now. I was a former student of hers as well. I believe I was the year underneath the victim. After I left middle school, we remained in touch throughout high school and indeed college . . . in fact, I had Julie and Rob attend my recent wedding."

Barbara pauses and takes a deep breath. Her face is riddled with emotion, and I am well-aware of why. She continues, "While I was at J.M. I was also a victim of sexual abuse by another teacher. I confided in Julie. She was the only one I confided in. And she did help me through a very difficult period in my life." Her tears soak the papers below.

I know it is wrong because Barbara is on the wrong side, but I cry along with her. I look at Barbara and see a beaten puppy that has ended up at the SPCA, only to be picked up by the guy who runs the local dog-fighting ring.

I can feel that Maggie Red next to me is concerned. Her hazel eyes are not looking at Barbara, but at the judge. She is wondering, which in turn makes me wonder. *Will Maier be swayed by Barbara's compelling testimony?*

Her tears are enough to draw sympathy, but not enough to interrupt her cadence. I hope I will have the same ability. She leans her head to the side and speaks about her fondness for Julie: "She was the only one I ever talked to openly. I was never made to feel like I had to do anything or say anything. She never took advantage of the situation. She never made threats. She never made inappropriate comments. She was nothing but supportive and, like I said, helped me to overcome it myself. She was pretty much the only adult I felt that I could trust."

That was on purpose, Barbara! That's what she did to me!

Now I wish Barbara would stop, but she continues: "I know that she's well-respected by her peers and her colleagues, and I know that she is truly sorry for what's happened. We've had many discussions since then. I know that she's a dedicated and loving mother." My mouth opens wide, and a silent scream leaves my mouth with the horror of how devastating the truth is.

She digs deeper. "I don't feel like there was anyone else . . . I know that no one else has come forward, and I feel like if there were anyone else, I would have been pretty much ideal. And despite her plea, I remain friends. She is a trusted friend of mine, and whatever she did in the past doesn't change how she helped me, and I will be forever grateful to her.

As Barbara finishes, I am bent over in pain. Scott is rubbing my back and Maggie (I am not sure which one) is holding my right hand.

Barbara passes through the galley and hands the torch next to her mom. Mrs. Louie, just like Barbara, has not changed much. I am sure that close up she has more wrinkles and lines, but from far away she looks the same as she did when she pulled into the parking lot to pick Barbara up from dance class.

She is the Caucasian half of Barbara, and I am almost certain that her strawberry blond bob is a wig. She is comfortably overweight, as many Moraga moms are, having completed the life tasks of bearing children and nestling into the security of the golden brown hills in this little corner of California. On cue, she begins to talk about the four daughters she has raised.

It feels as though the courtroom is filled with figurines, as Mrs. Louie recounts the phone call she received from JM: "I would never have received that phone call, I would never had known that my daughter tried to commit suicide, I would never had known that I needed to get her more help than she already was getting, I would never had known all these things had it not been for Julie Correa. Julie Correa listening to her students and recognizing a serious problem and reporting it immediately. I will always feel that had it not been for Julie, I would be the mother of three daughters and visiting the grave of the fourth one. I will be forever grateful to her. That's all." Her voice is shrill in an effort to prove her words. I know that Mrs. Louie isn't evil; she truly believes that Julie saved her youngest daughter's life. As Mrs. Louie finishes her kind and grateful words about Julie, I find a tiny window in my heart that breathes forgiveness.

Amy stands from the second row, sporting shoulder-length blond hair and towering around the six-foot marker. As Amy approaches the podium, it is clear that she is pregnant. From outside sources, I know that it is with twins. I hope Judge Maier doesn't find sympathy in her swollen belly.

Amy lists her own life accomplishments, which feel as though they have little to do with me, or Julie, or the four felony counts to which Julie has pled guilty. "After college, I moved to Australia to play professional basketball for three years after attending the University of Portland on a full-ride basketball scholarship. Julie was also a supporter of my personal growth and athletic career. She has been a very important person in my life."

"Mrs. Correa was one of the one [*sic*] teachers who really cared for her students and wanted to make a difference in our lives. Some might say she gets too close with her students, but I truly believe there were no ill intentions there. She made herself available to all of us, which kept a lot of us out of trouble." I can see it now, Julie befriending Amy and growing close to her. *What would have Julie done if the day where I got strong enough to walk away would have come sooner?* Julie needed a backup plan. Amy should be thanking me . . . her grooming ended with grooming.

"Being into sports and athletics, obviously I gravitated toward my PE teachers and played sports and hung out in the PE office, just like students who are into music spend their lunch times in the music room. It was great to have such a young and supportive teacher to help you through troubled times as a student or to even help you work on your volleyball serve." I think of Julie helping me with my volleyball serve and then afterward, slamming my body into her cold office floor. My toes curl in response to Amy's happy memories.

As Amy finishes, Grossman shuffles the papers in from of her. "Can we ask Heather Anderson to please come forward?"

With long brown hair and a black-and-white top that I am sure she purchased just for this occasion, Heather begins to read her long letter to the court. She looks relatively well put together, but she has lines under her eyes that makeup cannot hide. Her body looks tired, maybe from having four kids, maybe from drinking too much diet soda, or maybe from a combination of both.

As she speaks, her words have little to do with the fact that Julie raped me hundreds of times. Heather wears this ridiculous look on her face, as though the court should feel privileged to listen to her. She has her eyes opened too wide and she presses her small lips together at the end of each sentence, as if she may have just stolen the show. At one point, she laughs and says, ". . . we can just say I do a lot of charity work. And I'm also a member of the Relief Society, which provides aid to those in need across the globe."

In a chipper voice, Heather explains, "Julie's been my friend and neighbor in Saratoga Springs for just over five years . . . Our children are actually really good friends, and they spend a lot of time together. Boys are at my house quite a bit, and mine love spending time at hers." My mind spins thinking of Julie supervising a play date.

"I don't think what she did was the right thing to have done, but it's still, even being here today, really hard for me to accept the reality of it. It's just not the Julie that I know. It's just not the person that—everyone at home wants their kids to hang out with her kids because of how good they are and what a great family they are. She's a devoted mother of two incredibly respectful and intelligent children. She is extremely close to her family and her children, and her family are a reflection of her quiet, caring personality."

"Julie is a very selfless mother. Whenever I see Julie, she is with her children at a park, at a game, at a practice, riding bikes, at the pool, golfing, or playing soccer in her back yard. In all the years I have known Julie, I can count the number of times I've seen her without her two boys on one hand." *Then why did Julie want me to come to Utah?*

"Julie puts a lot of time and thought into motherhood. We have long discussions about what our kids should be exposed to. I can recall one conversation where we discussed which video games and which television programs were acceptable and which ones weren't." I remember Detective Parker telling me that her kids were in front of the TV when he came to question her.

"When you're just around their family, you see how tight they are and how much they love each other and how much those boys love their mother.

Stop! I want to yell, but I hold myself back. I curl into my ball as I think of this incredible mom Heather is describing. *I wish I didn't have to do this.*

Heather continues with her nose in the air, "And living in a predominantly L.D.S. community, Julie has been extremely respectful of others' beliefs and traditions." Suddenly I can sit up straight again because I see the scene vividly unfolding before my eyes. Julie, in her protected Mormon cul-de-sac, has befriended Heather.

Heather, BE CAREFUL! Again, I hold myself back from yelling. I imagine Julie, sipping caffeine-free hot chocolate with Heather. Julie asks questions about Joseph Smith and Brigham Young, nods her head when necessary, and inconspicuously watches as Heather's twelve-year-old daughter fills up her water cup at the kitchen sink.

I look at Heather, and her stupidity is not something that I mock. Julie tricked me once, too. She tricked my mom, my dad, my brother, and my friends. That's the whole point of who she is. It's not as though a serial killer goes around and acts like a jerk or makes flippant statements such as "I wonder whom I should knock off next?" Julie knows how to slither her way into people's lives when they have something that she wants.

As Heather finishes, my attention is turned to Rob. Sometimes it is just as hard to look at Rob as it is to look at Julie. I remember the surprise when I saw Rob for the first time. I expected an All-American boy to go with my All-American PE teacher. It was in eighth grade, and Julie brought him with her to watch one of my club soccer games. Rob is dark and different-looking. I remain confused about his nationality. As he stands, computer paper in hand and ready to give his statement to the court about his wife, I feel uncertainty and fear fills my thoughts.

Did he listen to the taped phone calls? Did he know then? Why did he lie about her phone number? Did he watch as she raped me? Is he the same as her? Is it possible that he is worse?

His skin looks as though it may be made primarily from wax. As the words rapidly begin to slip out of his mouth, they occupy only a single note on the scale.

"Mr. Correa, because you're reading, you're going fast. Could you slow it down for the court reporter, please?" Maier's voice is not kind but factual as she makes an attempt to bring Rob back from the beginnings of a filibuster.

He takes a breath and his eyes move back down to the safety of his typed words. I wonder who typed them. With his monotone speech, he sets the foundational stage of how he and Julie met in college, what they each majored in, his occupational history, and the life events that led them to Utah. He rolls through the poor educational system in Concord, a new job opportunity, and a subsequent move to Utah. But the hair on the back of my neck stands in wonder: *Why is Julie not teaching anymore? Why does Rob feel the need to explain his move? What are they hiding?*

I look at Rob and I feel too much emotion for a single being. I bend over in my ball so that I can yell in my head and not out loud in the court. He talks glowingly about his wife: "I have never seen this behavior from Julie firsthand, and never heard anyone speak of these behaviors or actions until last year. However, I will not distance myself from Julie. I do hold Julie in high regard as she is a person of many great and positive attributes. She gave herself as a teacher and mentor to all her students. She had demonstrated outstanding and positive coaching ability. Her mothering touch to her two boys is sweet, nurturing and beautiful. She provides strength and guidance for me to take care of these two boys."

Why don't you talk about the night that you covered for Julie? Or about whom you thought that Julie was talking to on the phone almost every night from 1996 to 2000? Did you ever see a long piece of blond hair in the drain of your shower that you knew didn't match your new bride's head? Julie admitted it. Please, tell me that you're sorry.

While I have had my private conversation, Rob has continued on an emotionless rant about his wife: "For my community, those in our neighborhood want Julie to return. She is an active at-home parent who's regularly involved with activities of our boys, but also the neighborhood children. She has set up soccer games, baseball and basketball games, and other activities that involve all neighborhood children of all ages."

"Her background as a PE teacher, her instinct is to be all-inclusive. She regularly monitors and protects all these kids and provides a safe and fun environment." *Did you say SAFE?!* I start to feel split in the middle again. *Am I taking away a wonderful mom and a centrifugal part of a community? Or, is she once again on the prowl?*

"My last desire is to speak for my two boys" as Rob begins to talk about his sons, I close my eyes and cling onto a prayer that I am doing the right thing. "They need their mother. She has provided well for them and cares for them deeply . . . they are still in development. They very much need guidance, mentoring and nurturing, all of the elements that Julie provides. These two young boys truly love their mother. They miss her deeply and would love to have her home. I will do the best I can in her absence. However, I cannot replace Julie in their lives. I beg for leniency for Julie because of these two boys. At their age, they need a mother figure in their lives." I try to ignore it, but I crave the noise of a rumbling train.

The cheap school clock ticks on the wall just over my right shoulder. Suddenly I see the plan of Julie's side to take time off the clock. It is almost 4 P.M.

My heart rate jumps. *How, in less than an hour, can my family, my friends, my husband, and I all speak about the impact that this crime has had on my life?* Yesterday, on the phone, a very kind woman from the Victim's Assistance Program called to check in with me and remind me to take my time when speaking to the court. I listened to her, but as the tension now builds in my body, I wonder if I am going to have to switch plans to the two-minute offense.

Stopped dead in my tracks of panic, I am swiftly brought back to the pain of the present moment, as Julie stands to address the court. She tips her entire body forward, to slide the chair away from her disappearing waist, and stands. I am scared that she will walk to the podium, as I am scared anytime that she moves her body. Instead, she remains standing next to her now upright attorney.

Grossman holds her hands together, cupped just a few inches below her belly button. Perhaps she is praying that this will go smoothly. She doesn't fully turn her body to Julie, but peers at Julie out of the corner of her eye. Her head is softly tilted down, as if to listen intently to Julie, this kind and sorrowful mother. It is as if the screenplay included emotional instructions for body language: "make your client appear human, solicit sympathy, and offer a caring ear to the rapist on your right."

I grip Maggie's hand and Scott holds me tighter, as though we are on a roller coaster climbing the hill for the final fall. Julie has a letter that she does not hold, but rather rests it on the table. Her eyes look downward and her hands rest on top of her typed words. Her body position mimics the day that she wrote down my PE mile time as I crossed the finish line.

As she begins, her voice is high-pitched and familiar. I have heard this tone before, at the Claremont Hotel, when I got angry on the pretextual calls, and the nights of exceptional hurt when she would cry on the drive home from her apartment.

"After over a year of silence, I am grateful for the chance to express myself today in this setting. I am hopeful that what I have to say in the next few moments will give you, Kristen, what you need to move forward, away from what is causing you such anguish. I can only do this by speaking from my heart and giving you what I believe is my truth about our past connection."

My body returns to the safety of my ball as I hear her words. An unspoken disgust from the people on my side draws their eyes to me to see if I am still breathing. My ears wait for an objection from my side, demanding that Julie never speak to me or use my name again. But she continues, from her heartless heart.

"First, I want you to know, if I knew then what I know now, I wouldn't have allowed things to happen the way they did. Although I have been through an absolute nightmare the past year and face a difficult future, this is not the reason that I would change the past if I could. The reason is that it was never my intention to hurt you. I cared deeply for you and always wanted to do what was best for you regardless of my own needs."

My ankles hurt.

"I know in some ways this seems contradictory. If I cared about you, why would I do something that could potentially harm you? Why did I allow the relationship to happen? I have thought long and hard about this and can offer you this explanation: at some point I began to view you as a peer instead of the teenager that you really were. I believed that you were mature enough to make your own decisions. This was an error in my thinking. Maybe I did it to make it all okay in my mind. Maybe I did it because that is what I wanted to believe. Why it happened is probably, in a lot of ways, inconsequential to you now. What matters is that it was wrong—and I am very sorry."

But you said that you weren't sorry! That you would do it all over again! That it wasn't wrong! You said all of that fifteen months ago, frozen in time by the taped calls. I open my mouth so that I can yell in my head. I gag a little, and if there was anything in my stomach, I would throw up all over my cousin's beautiful brown hair in front of me.

"For as long as the relationship lasted, it never sat right with me. I don't know if you remember this, but we had many discussions about it. I want you to know that, although it was dreadfully wrong and I should have put a stop to it, I didn't feel as though it was an option at the time because I didn't want to hurt you emotionally."

My body shakes. My hands turn to fists. *You have almost ruined me emotionally.* I gag again.

"I know that this thought seems ridiculous now, given the pain that you are in, but you need to know that I tried to do my best with the circumstance in which I found myself. I convinced myself that if you got good grades, succeeded in sports, had boyfriends, and went to dances and school functions, what we had wasn't affecting you in a negative way. This was a grievous error in my thinking. And again—I am very sorry."

Julie may sound sorry. I look at Maier to see if the whiny voice is convincing to a judge. I cannot tell what an outsider thinks. But I am, unfortunately, an insider. Julie is only sorry that she got caught.

"After things ended between us, I never stopped worrying about how it might have all affected you. I didn't want to be responsible for causing you any harm. I did not contact you and never intended to do so. When you made the pretext calls over a year ago, I am sure you wouldn't deny that I was very suspicious of your intentions. After the first call, I knew that for my own good, I probably shouldn't continue to talk to you. However, because you told me that you needed help, I made a decision that if potentially helping you put me at risk, then so be it. I felt I had a responsibility for your well-being. To turn away and put my best interest above yours would have been unconscionable. I risked everything because I wanted to help you, not to hurt you."

My forehead touches my knees as Julie speaks to me. I have my hands cupped over my ears, yet I can still hear every word.

"I have read your testimony and letters to the court and can't help but being more than a little bewildered as to why you seem to fear me now. In my recollection of things I cannot think of a single thing that I ever did to make you believe that I would ever purposely hurt you."

It must be nice that you don't remember grabbing my wrists or popping out of a bush to talk to me. You are unable to recollect the threats and the stalking and the cell phone and the hiding? I punch Maggie's leg as my anger grows, and I don't stop to think I may have left the beginning of a bruise on her thigh.

"When things were over between us, I never contacted you because I did not want to disturb your life. When we talked on the phone, you asked if I ever considered calling you and I told you, 'No, I was going to leave that up to you.' I am proud to say that, in my forty-three years, I have tried to conduct myself with kindness as my guide. Nothing that has happened in that past fifteen months has changed that. I believe that anger and hate poison the soul and are exhausting emotions. I do not have any interest in harboring such feelings toward you. Please know that I have no interest in revenge or in contacting you in any way. I am most interested in closing those pages on this chapter in my life and returning to my family and friends, the people who truly know me and love me."

My brain has a hard time imagining what these people look like. *Are their arms stretched open? Do they bring flowers and make signs that say, "It's okay that you raped someone! WEL-COME HOME!"*

"I also want to use this opportunity to apologize to my former colleagues and the teaching community in general. I believe that teaching is truly one of the most noble professions. I became a teacher because I wanted to help people and make a difference in their lives. I wanted to be the kind of teacher that my students felt comfortable enough with that they could approach me with their problems. It was a difficult dance sometimes to allow access to myself at that level and maintain the position of authority. Even though I was able to affect many students in a positive way by being that kind of teacher, I see now how it can also go horribly wrong. The complexities of human behavior and emotions are sometimes hard to understand, and just when you think you are in total control, things can go careening out of control. I see now that my lack of clear and definite boundaries was a danger to not only myself, but to those around me."

I can't help but think of the center divider in a car, the console that includes the parking brake and most typically two cup-holders. I am in my driveway and thanking Julie for taking me to watch Meghan's dance show. She leans her whole body past the boundary, onto the passenger side of the car. She hugs me and kisses me half on the cheek. Without moving at all, my life is forever changed.

Julie continues her act: "I am sickened by the fact that, in-stead of boosting the reputation of the teaching profession, I have sullied it. I wish there was a way that our justice system could allow me to use my story to help other teachers see what I did not see. Maybe on my own, I will find a way to impart that knowledge to other teachers as a way to make amends for what I have done to hurt the profession. Only then would I feel as though I have contributed more than I have stolen from a profession that I loved and still do to this day."

Impart your knowledge? I wish you were dead.

"Finally, I would like to address the Court, and more specifically your Honor. I wanted to assure the Court that, no matter what my sentence, I intend to serve it in the most upstanding and dutiful manner. Due to my privileged upbringing and education, I believe I have much to offer in the prison setting. In paying penance, I will seek to give more to the system than I receive. I hope that I can assist in a constructive manner and that my life in prison will be full of purpose.

Julie pauses, and I know what is coming next. My head hurts as I listen to the words I have dreaded since coming forward: "Finally, your Honor, I feel that I would be remiss as a mother if I did not ask you to consider my children as you sentence me today."

I bend tighter into a ball, and this time I allow my mouth to move as I let the words quietly leave my lips: "Please make it stop. Please make it stop . . ." I am rocking a little, and if you didn't know me, you might think I belonged in a psych ward.

"Even though they were not alive at the time, I shudder to think that, in a way, they are also victims of my indiscretions. I know that it is not possible, but I would serve double time if I could serve it after their childhood and spare them from being without me at this time of their lives. I will not be at peace until I return home to them and make amends for my absence. Please consider them when considering my sentence today. Thank you."

I wonder where they are, what they are doing. I wonder if they would have been better off if I was not here; if I was a statistic on a train track. Slowly I turn, half to look at the clock and half to look outside. It is a crisp winter day and the sun feels far away. The excited approach of Christmas brings hustle to the air. I imagine my mom and I, stopping at the makeup counter in Nordstrom's, picking out gifts to go under the tree. I imagine a smile on my face and innocence in my heart as I sample the eye shadow. *Where would my life be, who I would be, if Julie had not put me here?*

CHAPTER THIRTY-SIX

Growing Wings

It's probably one of the worst workouts that I have ever had. But I can't help it; I can't seem to concentrate and this feels impossible to explain.

I hear the loud rumbling of the flow-masters on his Chevy Trail Blazer headed down the street to pick me up. Workout is finally almost over. *Is this a date?*

I haven't told my friends how I feel about him. *How could I?* I don't think that they would understand. *How could they understand when I don't?*

It's not as though he's perfect. He's not tall and striking like Adam. He does okay in school, but I don't think he worries about it the way I do. But he might be perfect for me.

The underwater lights surprise me as they click on right as I am headed into a flip turn. They illuminate tiny fragments in the water and remind me that I don't particularly like swimming at night. It kind of feels wrong, having to swim when the sun's not out. At least the water in the pool is warmer than the air outside. And I am not one to break a promise. I got my Junior National time last high school season, so here I am doing year round swimming. Swimming has almost fully taken the spotlight.

It is the fall, the days are growing shorter, and the nights are growing colder. But my insides feel warmer.

I have known Scott Cunnane for as long as I can remember. His older brother played on a baseball team with Marc when I was seven. Scott teases me about that now, how he remembers me and my bright blond hair running wildly behind the backstop. He teases me about just about everything.

Sometimes I try to remember if he ever asked me to dance at the JM school dances. Sometimes I try to remember if we had math together in seventh grade. Sometimes I wish it didn't take me this long to notice him. Sometimes I wish it didn't take this long for him to notice me.

In the same grade at the same schools, I guess that we have been friends by association. He came to my fourteenth birthday party, but I don't think that we ever had a real conversation. Until now.

And now, as my mind strays to him, I can feel my training partner Brian pulling ahead of me. Brian and I both swim butterfly, so we are always racing each other. Today I am losing. Something must be wrong with me because I don't care. My body feels as though it is made of tootsie rolls, and I feel like molasses in the water. I let Brian pull away with indifference, and I don't think about what my coach will say or what others will think. Instead, I think of Scott.

He was the powder puff coach for our senior girls' football team a few weeks ago. He made me the quarterback and drew up every play with me as the pivotal piece. I was afraid it was just because of my athletic ability. *But then why would he chase me with a handful of mud after the game? Why would he hug me first after we won the championship game under the lights?* I guess that's where things started.

Or maybe things started in Leadership Class. This is my first year in Leadership. Every other year I have taken Choir, but lately when I sing, it makes me feel as though I am going to choke to death.

Last week for Leadership we went to a ropes course to work on group dynamics, whatever that means. "You're my partner," Scott had said when we were instructed to pair off. He tugged at the drawstring that dangled from my pink windbreaker and pulled me alongside of him. With a twinkle in his eye, he looked over at me. "You'll be good at this."

I hope that Brian cannot see me smiling underwater through his goggles. I think back to the ropes course. I had secretly agreed with Scott, confidently thinking that I would be good at any physical challenge. But as I climbed the first tree, the ground felt as though it was pulling away from me, and my head began to spin.

I tried to gain my composure as I would before a penalty kick or a race, but nothing worked. My lungs tightened as I looked down and realized that I did not want to fall. And a near panic attack set in as I realized I did not want to die.

I never knew I was scared of heights and I thought that Scott would be frustrated as we fell behind progressing pairs. But there he stood, holding my rope and softly encouraging me from below. "Come on, Tree Trunk, you can do it." He calls me Tree Trunk because he thinks my favorite pair of boots look as if they are made out of a tree log.

Scott didn't help me get any better at navigating the tree, but he made me feel better. With the inclusion of the cohesion game "Mojo," the day wasn't a total bust. Each pair, with backs pressed up to one another, turned around at the sound of the whistle and made one of four faces at each other. The goal was to see which pairs knew each other well enough to make the same face on the same turn. We redeemed ourselves, as we were the only pair to make it a perfect four for four.

Now I can only see the tips of Brian's toes and the bubbles that trail off of them. *Oh, well.* I take a pause as my head comes forward in my stroke for a breath and I steal a glance at the parking lot searching for Scott's car.

We are still training in the same rinky-dink pool that we used last year. The high school pool is supposed to be ready any day now. "I was the first person to ever swim in that pool," Scott said to me yesterday, with his unmistakable mischievous grin leaving his sentence incomplete. I looked at him a little shocked and a little intrigued.

"It's not done yet," I said back to him, knowing that an incredulous look was spreading across my face.

"It felt done to me. I jumped in after volleyball last night," he said and smiled.

I gave him a smack, "Scott!" I said to him as he absorbed my fake blow and caught my hand between the two of his. "You could get in trouble," I warned. I often wonder how Scott does and says what he wants, yet still slides under the radar of authority.

"What's going to happen to me?" he said with air in his words. Maybe his casual and carefree confidence can rub off on me.

With practice coming to an end, I do not worry that I will have wet hair when Scott picks me up. I hurry through the process of putting clothes on a wet body so that I can get into his warm car faster.

"Hey wet head," he says as I climb into his black two-door SUV. He pats me on the head and then wipes his hand on the cloth seat behind me. He makes a disgusted face, as if I have lice or something, but his broad smile says he doesn't care.

He drives me on the windy road from Moraga to Lafayette, and I do not let myself think about the many other times I have been passenger on this hill. We arrive at Togo's and I plop out of the car.

"What are you doing?" I exclaim as I turn over my shoulder and see Scott climbing over the center divide of his car.

"My door doesn't open anymore," he says with a shoulder shrug as he swings his body out of my side of the car.

"Really? How long has it been like that?" I ask him, getting a little laugh out of him as he brushes the lint and dog hair off his black and yellow North Face fleece jacket. His friend Nick told me that this is the first time he has ever taken a girl out on a date officially.

"It's fine. It doesn't bother me." And somehow I know that he is telling the truth. Most Moraga kids wouldn't stand for such an inconvenience. But it doesn't bother Scott. "Like I told you . . . Don't sweat the small stuff, Mojo." He has been calling me Mojo since the Leadership retreat and last week, when I got a C+ on my AP Chemistry quiz, he put his hand on my back and reminded me of this, his favorite saying.

"Yup, you're right. Don't sweat the small stuff," I say with a smile. *But what about the big stuff?*

Scott opens the door for me, and I am glad that we are getting sandwiches rather than having some fancy meal. He walks boldly up to the counter and orders: "I'll have a large Italian on wheat and a turkey and cheese only on white." Scott turns his back to the freckle faced teen behind the counter who has begun making our sandwiches. "That's what you want, right?" he asks, sounding very proud of himself. "I remember from last year in English class."

Scott sat behind me in English, and I would often sneak bites of my sandwich to settle my growling stomach before the pending lunch period. I always have a hard time making it all the way to lunch without eating. I am also always tired, and my snacks help keep me awake. Tired from morning workout and from whatever else.

I can't believe he remembers.

"You always used to kick my chair last year. Why did you do that?" I ask him as I remember trying to concentrate in my English class.

"Oh, so that's why you transferred out of that class?" Scott says, teasing me just enough to make me smile, but not so much that it makes me cry.

"No, I transferred because Mr. Jacobs is a bad teacher. And he was going to give me a B for no reason." And it is true. He had it in for me, and I wasn't about to let my perfect GPA go for a teacher who was rumored to be smoking weed during brunch period. I wasn't learning anything, anyway. So I transferred mid-quarter to the hardest English teacher in the school, Mrs. Beason. "It ended up being a good move for me," I explain myself to Scott. I throw my drying hair over my shoulders so that my Campo sweatshirt doesn't get too soaked. "I learned a lot; I got an A. Plus, Beason is my all-time favorite teacher," I say, not pausing to remember who used to be my all-time favorite teacher.

"But it wasn't a good move because then I never saw you anymore," Scott says and stops chewing for a moment to let me know he is serious. The air is still between us. I know there is a football game tonight and I know I have a soccer tournament tomorrow. I know that Togo's will eventually close and that my mom will want me home for the night. But, still, I wish I could somehow sit on this restaurant chair forever.

"Because I liked you," Scott says, almost out of the blue. I look at him as though he can read a question mark in my mind. "You wanted to know why I kicked your chair . . . because I liked you." His voice grows a little softer as he looks down to his jean pocket, pulls something white out, and sets it on the table. It's a Blow Pop. "Watermelon flavor, right?" he asks to verify my favorite.

I look at him and try to pinpoint a day that he would have noticed my mouth turning green. He is not the first to feed me a watermelon flavored candy, but this is my first taste of love.

We drive to the football game, and although there is silence, there is not an awkward moment between us. Past Campolindo and onto the campus of Miramonte High School. We are in enemy territory tonight, but I have never felt so safe.

A sea swarming with high school students, staff, and parents. Half of the community is here, but I am only aware of a single person. Scott walks in step with me as we find our friend pool in the stands. I look at Maggie Black and feel a little lost, imagining trying to explain this feeling to her.

I am a jock, so I care about football games. That's not entirely true—I care about every game Campo plays. But as we square off with our crosstown rivals under the Friday night lights of a romanticized high school football game, I can't seem to concentrate.

Instead, my nose fills with Scott's scent. Pert Plus never smelled like this before. And my heart speeds as Scott wraps us together in a blanket he brought from his trunk. My mind races, wondering if he packed it just for this purpose. He holds me and gets closer with each ticking minute on the game clock.

I feel protected in the small space of a cocoon. I feel my insides shift, and I feel my self changing.

The game ends, and I only know so by the physical movement on the wooden bleachers. They bounce in celebration of our unlikely victory. *Could this night get any better?*

"Hey, Krick. Hi, Scott." It's Maggie Red. She smiles at me with her perfectly pink lips. But her smile is the same one she gave me the first time she ever saw me holding hands with Adam. I wish I could tell her that this is different. "There's a keg at Burton Valley," she says and awaits my response. "You guys wanna come?"

This won't be hard for me to get out of. My friends are used to me turning them down. But this time there will be a different reason.

Just as I begin to search for it, Scott answers on my behalf. "I think I should get Kristen home. She has a soccer tournament in Lodi tomorrow." He was listening to that, too.

I stand, surprised that Scott doesn't want to join in the fun. I know that he drinks on the weekends, but it doesn't bother me. It doesn't bother me at all.

I break from Scott to give Red a quick hug. She holds it a little longer than normal, and I wonder if she knows.

The Blazer is loud and it shakes as we make the way toward my house. "So, what are you doing tomorrow night?" Scott asks me as we turn the corner at the top and I avoid eye contact with the bushes to the side.

"A bunch of us are getting together to watch a movie. Do you wanna come?" I look at him out of the corner of my eye.

"If you are going to be there, then yes." He squeezes my hand that rests on the center console. I am happy that he leaves his there.

We pull into my driveway, and for the first time all night I am nervous. I suddenly feel unsure of myself. The car jiggles to a standstill, and I feel awkward and anxious all at once.

"Oh, let me give you your fleece back," I say as I lean forward and begin to unzip the warmth. Scott let me borrow it on the walk to the car because he knew I was cold.

I look at him and, before he says anything, I know that my feelings are shared. "No, you can keep it. I mean . . . you can give it back to me tomorrow. It's cold out there."

I open the car door and immediately wish that I hadn't. I don't close it, though, in hopes that he will go through the obstacle course of getting out of the passenger door and walk me to my door. I am grateful to see him cover the distance twice as fast as last time.

We walk up my driveway and onto the mossy bricks that lead to my solid oak entry door. There are still lights on in my house, though it is almost 10 P.M. Scott carries both my hefty swim bag and my overflowing school bag, which reminds me that I haven't been home all day.

Suddenly my heart sinks to my toes as I see movement in the adjacent window. It's my mom waiting for me. Go figure.

Scott sees her, too, and I can feel a puff of air leave his chest with disappointment. We both know that there will be no goodnight kiss tonight. It would be too risky.

"Okay, well . . . thanks. Call me when you get home from your soccer game tomorrow," he says as he hands me my baggage. He smiles so that I can see my single most favorite physical attribute, his deep and defiant dimples. Although I wish he wouldn't, Scott allows me to leave him on the steps to my front door.

"Yeah. Thanks . . . I'll call you when I get home tomorrow." I try to ease the excitement off my voice. I wonder how I will pass the minutes until then.

I press my thumb down on the latch of the front door knob and feel the cold sting of the iron below. My bags press heavily into my shoulders, but my feet feel light as I step inside the entryway.

I make casual conversation with my mom about the details of tomorrow. She tells me what time we are leaving, but I hardly hear her.

I am exhausted as I set both bags down near the foot of the stairs. I am light as I begin the trek toward my bedroom. I know I have never felt this way before. The carpeted steps feel different under my feet. I can feel how much Scott likes me. I can feel how much I like him. And no one picked him for me. I think, if truth be told, he picked me for him.

I am so distracted that I float up the stairs with no worry or care of what I have left at the bottom. There, on the tile entryway, hiding in plain sight, is my school backpack with an old pair of New Balance running shoes tied innocently to the arm strap. Each day at school, I walk up and down the hallway with these shoes dangling. They swing back and forth and annoy me every step of the way. They are heavier than they should be. And only you know why. Because in the bottom of the left shoe, under the flap of the removable insole, lies the secret cell phone.

The distance grows between me and the bottom of the stairs, between me and the phone, and between me and you. I am tired and I am tired of thinking about you. I do not worry if you will worry. Actually, very faintly, I hope you do.

I brush my teeth and I take my time in the mirror, as a teenager should and as I never have. I look at myself and see what Scott sees. The bright yellow and black fleece bounces boldly back at me. I pull the zipper an inch higher and hide my chin in the comfort of the fabric. I look at myself, Scott collared around my neck, and all I can think about is him.

After spending some time picking at my face in the bathroom mirror while replaying the events of the night in my head, I walk to my room. I elect to keep the fleece on although I am not cold. I lay down in my bed with nothing hidden under my pillow. And for the first time in a long time I am allowed to dream.

CHAPTER THIRTY-SEVEN

Sitting Tall

By now, Julie has sat down. Just beside her, Grossman continues to stand, and is giving her drawn out conclusion. She draws upon the parade of character witnesses who have just testified for the monster. I am sitting as upright as I can, but my heart is still racing in response to the grotesque letter Julie read to me minutes ago in open court. The clock ticks and, suddenly, I am sure that we will run out of time.

I try to quiet my worrying mind and I close my eyes. My tranquility is bombarded by Grossman's defense: "But I do object, and I object over and over again, and throughout these proceedings to a characterization of what occurred as a child molest or a grooming or that Ms. Correa is a pedophile who was lurking about the schools. That is simply not the case." I think of the bagel, the sunglasses, the hat, and the lunches.

"And the cold, hard, difficult, painful reality is that a relationship sprang up between human beings that should never, ever have occurred, but that does not mean, to make sense of it, that we have to turn Ms. Correa into a pedophile . . . and . . . attempts to squeeze her into that box are not gonna heal Kristen . . ." *What is going to heal me, Elizabeth Grossman? These words of yours?*

As Grossman speaks her gross words, I wonder if I would still be able to love Scott if he represented monsters like Julie. She keeps going: "In fact, what we've tried to do is very comprehensively educate the Court and the People about who Ms. Correa actually is. And the truth is, is this was . . . a human being who is a decent, thoughtful being who committed a grievous error . . . but that doesn't turn her into a monster." Grossman steals the word "monster" right out of my brain.

Hate and anger bubble under my skin as I look at Grossman. She is incredibly unfortunate-looking. Her short and stubby stature gives way to a pointed nose and grey curly hair. She wears glasses for her beady eyes and for her likely sloppy notes. When trying to make a point, she slides them down to make eye contact with the judge. When it is a point she feels with especially deep conviction, Grossman removes them completely to make unfiltered eye contact with Maier. Often, she uses the arm of the wire-rimmed glasses as a magical wand of point-proving.

Grossman's voice is an attempt at soft and sweet, which stands in opposition to her body language. She continues, ". . . in Ms. Correa's entire life she has had sex with two individuals, her husband and Kristen."

I double over. I punch Maggie's leg again. I open my mouth for my silent shriek. I think of Julie forcing my hand down her mesh shorts. I think of the smell of Scott's hair gel. My toes curl within my shoes and my hands become fists: they cannot be the same thing.

I can tell Grossman is reaching a crescendo in her performance, as she takes a brief pause to position her glasses toward Julie and to add dramatic effect. "An inappropriate . . . relationship . . . took place between two human beings . . . No one is disputing that, least of all Ms. Correa, but it doesn't mean that you need to sentence her like she's a dangerous pedophile or now call her a child molester. There is nothing to suggest that that is true." *WHAT ABOUT ME?*

"Ms. Correa did not rape Kristen. In out-of-court statements Kristen has claimed she was raped. This is simply not true." I allow my lips to move again, *Please make it stop!* But nothing comes out of my mouth for fear of being removed from the court. And, again, I am silent with fear.

Grossman finishes with a handful of lines about how a sentence of five years would honor me and honor what a wonderful person Julie is. As she closes her arguments, my eyes are drawn to Geoff, who has shifted his weight and turned his eyes to the clock, now within forty minutes of five. He barely waits for his opposition to finish. His confident male voice is a relief to my ears: "My we approach briefly, your Honor?"

As they walk toward the bench, I realize the tactic behind the long drawn out testimony. *Have they used up all the time this case is allowed?*

They stand, their backs to us and their faces to Maier, and I wonder if I have ever felt so differently about two people in the same room. Geoff, the epitome of justice, and Grossman, the epitome of evil. Then, as I look at Scott to my left and Julie ahead of me to my right, I see an even sharper contrast of good and bad.

Grossman brings her right hand to her hip, shifts her weight, and tilts her head as a stance of objection. I can't hear any of the words, none of us can, but I like watching Geoff battle against Grossman. It is clear she is unhappy and her game plan is not panning out. The two retreat from the judge's bench and take opposite loops back to their respective tables. Maier slides closer to her audience, and I imagine her chair having wheels on the bottom of the legs.

Maier's eyes are kind, but the weight of the day can be seen now, just below her lower lids. "In speaking with Mr. Lauter, it appears that there are a number of individuals who would like to give statements, and it is clear that we won't be able to complete this before five today."

Panic rattles my head. *When will I go? Now? What about everyone else? If not today, then when? How much longer will I have to wait?* Without recognizing it, I string together a number of questions of a person who is ready.

Maier turns her face toward her like-looking assistant, who in turn knows to hand Maier her calendar. "Ladies and gentlemen, we are going to start with some statements on behalf of the People and the victim. However, it's clear that we're not going to finish today, so just informing you we will start again at 8:30 tomorrow morning."

I expect Geoff to give an introductory statement as Grossman did, but he jumps directly into the battle, presenting my mom to the court. "Why don't we start off right now with Mrs. Lewis, Jeanne Lewis, who is Kristen's mom?"

My mom has been sitting one row in front of me, across the aisle, to the left. Her head has swiveled periodically from the judge, to the current speaker, to Julie, and most frequently to me. She sits tall, and I have always admired her upright posture. She stands on cue, making her way away from my dad and Aunt Judy. As she passes Judy, I am startled by the similarities between these two sisters born only ten and a half months apart. Though Judy remains active in the Mormon church, she and my mom remain best friends. I look at my Aunt Judy, grateful that she has been there for my mom when I have only been able to be there for myself.

The podium has been moved to our side of the room, and seeing it away from Julie's reach makes me feel safe. My mom shakes a little, and I shake a little more for her. Her white turtleneck reminds me of the one that Marc's friend sprayed ketchup on at Jack in the Box when we were little. Just as she wore her hair then, the ends are curled under and her bangs run straight just above her eyebrows. I have always been jealous of her dark complexion, wondering how Marc received that DNA sequence and I did not. She has light lines on her face, and I wonder how many Julie has drawn. As a complete picture, she is pretty as she approaches 65.

She has a stack of papers in her hands, and as she looks down, I wonder about her words. In an action opposite from Julie, she puts her papers down and looks at the judge directly. From across the room, I can feel her strength as she begins to speak from her heart. "I just wanted to say a few things in reference to the many people here that have commented about what a wonderful mother she is, what a wonderful home she has. I too had that. I was a stay-at-home mom who really cared about my child, who would have done anything to keep my child safe." *This is not your fault, Mama! Keep going!*

"I asked her to stay away from my child, not because I thought it was sexual, but I could see that there was an intensity there that was very scary for me . . ." My mom tries to make the audience in the courtroom see how this all happened.

"Anyway, let's get back to the happy home with the two happy kids, which is what I had. And I'm mad. Yeah, I am mad. This predator came into my home . . . it wasn't so happy anymore, and to this day it isn't so happy anymore. My daughter cannot come to our home. I decorated our Christmas tree this year knowing she could not come and celebrate the holidays with us. This is something we live with, Julie, every day. Every single day." I cannot be sure, but I believe my mom is strong enough to look Julie square in the eye.

My mom's words seem as though they are climbing a ladder, "As far as her psychological evaluation, it came up in court in the previous months, and it was really offensive to me for them to get up there and say Julie is okay. Okay? There's a little girl back there with blond hair who was a little kid at the time who is NOT okay! That is the problem with child molestation!"

She turns her whole body to face mine and our eyes meet, unobstructed, across the court. She speaks to me with the room as bystanders: "Kristen, are you *okay*? Are you *fine* like Julie?"

Her questions hang in the air and I float just above my head so that I can see what the court sees as they discretely turn to look at me. My face is wet, my blue eyes reddened and puffed with pain, my body shaking and intertwined with the support of my external structures.

Her cadence isn't controlled or even, but it is perfect. Anger and devastation radiate off of her skin. I have never been more proud to be her daughter. "She did unimaginable things to us. I'm sure you read the reports. She came into our home when we weren't home. She hid in my daughter's closet, and she molested our daughter as we slept on the opposite wall. Who does this? Did you do that, Julie?"

My mom redirects her attention to Maier: "She took Kristen in the middle of the night. Now, keep in mind Kristen is way too young to drive a car by then. Somebody took her to Julie's apartment. It was Julie. And she molested her in that apartment."

As my mom talks to Maier, she walks that line between being in control of her temper and out-of-her mind enraged. In her fury, she continues: "She knew what she was doing wrong. She drove 10 miles out of her way to get home. She drove via Orinda, so people in Moraga, the people who think she's so wonderful, would not see her."

Fueled by the argument made by the defense that Julie was a exceptional role model for her students, my mom continues: "She is known for having crossed the line for many other girls in our community. Kristen may be the only one that did come forward in this case, but when the story broke, people in our community were not surprised about this. There were a lot of girls' names that were guessed as the victims because the victim's name in the paper said Jane Doe, and I'm just saying that this is not a huge surprise to our community.

My mom pauses and repositions her slender frame to face Amy and Barbara: "And in addition to that, Barbara, I have sympathy for your molestation issues, and in light of your near suicidal attempt, you must see how this issue feels to Kristen because the issue is very similar." I steal a glance at Barbara, who begins to weep. My mom continues, "And as a matter of fact, one morning when Kristen was 14, Ms. Correa rang our doorbell at 7:00 in the morning, and she wanted Kristen to implicate Mr. Witters as having molested her. It's just indescribable to me that she wanted Kristen to come forward against Mr. Witters when, at that very same time, she was molesting Kristen. *That* . . . is Julie Correa."

My mom leans her body over and collects her unread statement. As she turns, my mom stands tall. Through her glasses, my mom keeps her eyes locked on her seat as she returns, as if not to be tempted into a physical attack on Julie. Once secure in her seat, she turns to me and nods her head quickly, as if to say, "Here we go." Oxygen enters my lungs as I find heritage in my mom's posture.

Before I know it, my mom has been replaced at the podium by Marc. He wears a brown sweater and his dark brown hair short on his head. My friends obsessed over Marc when he was an upperclassman in high school. Somehow, his baby fat was stretched into a sculpture that reflected his hours of swimming and water polo. And still, as he stands here today, he is handsome. As he begins, I can hear his years of law school and law practice entwine with his years of being my big brother.

Marc begins, "There were a number of people that came up today and talked about how the things that Julie has done are out of character, but the things that Julie has done are not like cheating on taxes or something that would be surprising when you found out that something somebody had done. You're not even talking about a seemingly devoted wife who you find out has had an affair. That's something that would surprise you about somebody's character."

"We're talking about a teacher who raped her student, and that's it. There's no—there's no other gloss to put on it. And she didn't do it once, and she didn't do it twice, she did it over and over again for a period of years. Of course that's out of character because it's *inhuman*. It's *inhuman* to imagine that somebody could actually do that, to use their power and influence to nearly ruin my sister's life."

Marc pauses and looks over his shoulder at me. "And anyone weaker than Kristen I think would have been ruined by this, and for that I wanted to tell you, Kristen, I—this is the most courageous

thing anybody I know has ever done. And you coming forward is
not because of vengefulness . . . You did it because you knew it
was right, and you did it because you knew you had to. And for
that, I respect you more than anyone in the world."

With a slight smile on my face I listen to Marc as he continues:
"One of the things that Julie got up here and said was that she
always wanted to do what's best for Kristen, and I'd like your
Honor to . . . question what it was that Julie did that was best
for Kristen, *ever.* Was it using her power as a teacher to—as she
says, the most 'noble profession'—to lure Kristen into her—into
her trap? Was it plying Kristen with alcohol to get her to submit to
sex? Was *that* the best thing she could have done? Was it coming
into our home and violating the sanctuary of our family? Was *that*
the best thing she could have done?"

Marc shifts his weight but maintains control, "Or was it raping her over and over again? Was *that* the best thing that she
could have done? I, for one, am hard-pressed to understand what
exactly she did that was best for Kristen."

Marc shifts his hat from being my brother to being an attorney: "And I don't know what defense counsel means when she
says that Ms. Correa is not a pedophile. She's the very definition
of a pedophile. Kristen was 14 when this started to happen, and it
happened over and over again. The pedophile implies something
that happens over and over again."

"Defense counsel says that she's not a child molester, but she
is. Just because you say something doesn't make it true. Kristen
was a *child* when it happened and she was *molested*; therefore,
she's a *child molester.*"

"The final thing that I'll say about what defense counsel said
is that Kristen wasn't raped. Well, maybe defense counsel needs
to brush off her copy of Black's Law Dictionary because rape is
sex with a person that can't consent or hasn't consented, and
Kristen didn't consent to it. She was a minor. She was forced to
submit to this sex, and that's the bottom line. She was raped over
and over again.

I want to clap for Marc but the courtroom stands quiet. *Julie,
you messed with the wrong person . . . the wrong family.*"

Marc's walk to the final row of seats is aggressive. As he sits,
I am surprised to see his wife stand in response. Like Marc, my
sister-in-law Emily wrote a letter to the probation officer. Of all
the letters, this one may have found a permanent place in my

memory. Emily compared my trauma to that of her own fourteen-year-old self. As she recounted her father's cancer-ridden body being carried "in a body bag down the stairs," and the subsequent daily life of seeing that image every day, I suddenly realized that in so many ways all pain is the same.

Emily and I don't look alike. Her long dark hair waves down her back, and I watch as she turns her own pain into power. She is mid-speech and looks confident for someone who had not planned on addressing the court: "But, to me, it's really insulting when you think about the fact that Kristen is going to have to deal with this *every single day* for the rest of her life . . . And it disturbs me to talk about this abuse like it had a beginning and it had an end. It's not going to end for Kristen . . ."

I have never seen this angry and brave side of Emily before. Perhaps there is some beauty in all of this pain: "Having said that, I just also want to say, as a mother, listening to the people speaking on Julie's behalf bring up her two sons so often is really disturbing, and I just want to say I wish . . . her sons the very best . . . But when Julie chose to start a family, she knowingly brought them into a world where this precise scenario where we find ourselves today was likely and indeed inevitable because Kristen is too strong to remain silent about the repeated sexual abuse and rape that happened." I am reminded of the time just before the darkness of remembering Julie. Getting my dream job at Cal, marrying Scott, buying my house, winning the 2009 NCAA Championship, building my army, and suddenly I see my life painted by Emily's light. *All these years, all this time, I was growing strong enough to face you.* My vertebrae separate with air, and again I grow.

"And I just wanted to end by saying," Emily looks at Julie, "it's because of people like you that being a parent can be so terrifying. Kids are afraid of monsters in their closets, but what about the ones that are right in front of us?"

The time has ticked within striking distance of 5:00 P.M. Maier wraps things up and we gather ourselves to leave. I sit still for a moment as I watch the faces around me begin to make adjustments in plans for a surprise second day on the battlefield.

We make our way outside and Teri walks in step with me. She grabs my arm just above my wrist and stares into my eyes, just as she would one of her athletes before a big race: "We'll see you tomorrow." We have a small break in our training right now due to final exams for the fall semester at Cal. As Teri approaches being the Head Olympic Coach for the USA, I have watched as her plate has grown increasingly full. And as the first woman to serve in this role, I have seen new hope and expectation put on her shoulders. I open my mouth in objection, knowing she needs a break.

Before I am able to voice my concern that Teri has too much on her plate, Teri takes back her authority as head coach: "Kristen, stop. Please. I will be here." And I know I need her. I need everyone.

Arrangements for tomorrow morning are being made around me when a small dark-haired girl I saw scribbling notes in the courtroom slides in next to me with her notepad. "Can I wait until after tomorrow?" I ask as a preemptive strike to her wanting a quote from me.

"Yes, of course, but I just need to know if you want your name on the article for tomorrow morning." My assumption that she is a reporter is confirmed.

I am standing alone, away from my strategizing army. I imagine my first babysitter reading my story over her morning coffee and dropping her jaw in horror. I can almost hear Julie's words perfectly: "No one can ever know. They will never understand what we have." I imagine the black ink on the grey newspaper shaped into the letters of my name. I stand tall, look her squarely in the eye, and say with a single bullet, "Yes."

Just a few short hours later, my face glows in the computer screen as the article appears online. My story is being told.

MARTINEZ — A Contra Costa County judge will sentence a former Lamorinda middle school teacher to prison Wednesday after the victim, now an educator herself, speaks about being molested by the teacher in the 1990s.

The victim, Kristen Cunnane, who said she didn't want her identity protected by the Jane Doe moniker, was surrounded by friends and family members Tuesday when Julie Gay Correa's sentencing hearing began with Correa's supporters extolling the former Joaquin Moraga Middle School teacher and sports coach at length as an amazing educator turned stay-at-home mother of two young boys.

Yellow police tape divided seating in the courtroom to provide a barrier between supporters for Correa and Cunnane.

One such supporter, another of Correa's former students, said Correa provided her with key support when she was molested by another teacher at Joaquin Moraga Middle School during that same era.

"She was pretty much the only adult I could trust," the woman said.

Correa, a 43-year-old Utah resident, pleaded no contest in October to four felonies for sex crimes from 1996 to 1999, beginning when the victim was 14 and Correa was 26. Cunnane, an associate head coach for UC Berkeley's women's swimming program, first reported the abuse to police last year.

"It was never, never my intention to hurt you," Correa said to Cunnane in court Tuesday. "I care deeply for you and always want to do the best for you.

"At some point, I began to view you as a peer instead of the teenager you were," Correa said.

Her attorney, Elizabeth Grossman, told the court that Correa has been mischaracterized by the prosecution as a pedophile. She described Correa's contact with Cunnane as "a relationship between two human beings that shouldn't have occurred."

Cunnane's family took offense at her remarks.

"We are talking about a teacher who raped her student. And that's it. There's no gloss to put on it," said Cunnane's brother, Marc Lewis. "She's the very definition of a pedophile. Kristen was 14 when it happened, and it happened over and over again."

Cunnane's mother, Jeanne Lewis, said she had asked Correa back then to stay away from her child because there was an intensity about Correa that scared her. She didn't know at the time her daughter was being molested.

"I see people here who really respect Julie. I do not," Jeanne Lewis said. "She did unimaginable things to us. She came in our home, she hid in our daughter's closet, and she molested our daughter as we slept on the other side of the wall."

The sentencing hearing continues at 8:30 A.M. Wednesday in Judge Clare Maier's Martinez courtroom. ∎

I look at my name. I look at my article. I look at my day. I look at my life. Fear has turned to fuel as I imagine tomorrow. I will be there. Ready to take my final stand.

CHAPTER THIRTY-EIGHT

Run with Me

M y legs hurt. My lungs burn. But it doesn't matter.
Sometimes in northern California, we get these crystal
clear warm winter days. If I took a picture, my Aunt Judy in Utah
might start to think that the rumors about California weather are
true. The sun is convincing and gives reason to believe that the
North is not so different from the South. And today is certainly
one of those days.

But I know the truth. It's the beginning of December and the
beginning of the cold. I can smell the damp, almost moldy mud
next to the running trail. The recent rain makes the leaves hang
heavy. The soles of my feet hurt from pounding on the cold pavement. The tips of my fingers tingle, and I hope that Scott doesn't
notice my Rudolph-looking nose.

We run in stride, although I am sure that this is slower than
his ideal pace. I am a good runner, but he is better. "Okay, it's
time to get serious," Scott had said to me this afternoon with the
end of the last class of the day. "Let's *actually* go running today."
The corner of his mouth pulled into a smile as he slid closer to
me and we leaned against the side of his black Chevy Blazer. As
cars too nice for a high school parking lot raced by us, I didn't
care who saw us together. Actually, if truth be told, I wasn't even
aware that a single other person existed on the planet.

"If you say so . . . ," I said back to Scott. It is Thursday, and
we have been planning on going running every day this week. But
we keep getting . . . distracted.

Scott's right, we need to get serious because winter sports are right around the corner. My fourth year on the varsity soccer team starts in less than a week, and his varsity basketball tryouts are next weekend. He's a point guard, so his fitness is everything. I should let him stay on task.

On Monday we went up to the running trail near his house to take a run. "I want to show you my bedroom," he had said to me innocently enough. Gullible, but excited, I had followed him to the back of the house.

Things have been progressing since our first date. The night after my soccer tournament, he kissed me. Actually, he kissed me more than once. And since then there's been more. I don't know if it is going too fast by other people's standards. But I don't care about other people. Something happens to me when I am with him. My skin cells become magnets and I feel a deep thirst inside. I need him.

We never had the typical teenage conversation that made us "officially" a couple. We didn't need to. We both knew and know that, once this started, it might never end.

"Both of my parents work," Scott had said on Monday as we got to his room. With his usual grin, he laced his fingers with mine and pulled me to his loosely made bed. I had wondered if he had planned this and pulled his comforter tight before he left the house that morning.

We don't have sex. We haven't even really gotten that close. I don't think I am ready, and I think Scott might know that. But at least I'm not scared of thinking about it, which wasn't the case when I was with Adam. Scott makes me feel safe. He's not that big, but he makes me feel surrounded.

Instead, we kiss until our lips are sore. If truth be told, we do get a little workout in. And even with a tired jaw, I would opt to go an hour more. Scott can kiss as if he has practiced a million times before. I like that he has not.

Tuesday and Wednesday ended up in similar ways. So today we are doing what we have been telling everyone else that we have been doing all week: training for our winter tryouts together, although I won't really need to try out for soccer. We decided to come running on the trail behind both Maggies' houses. It's a ten-minute drive from Campo, closer to JM, but Scott said it would be better so that we wouldn't be tempted by the bed in his bedroom.

"When are we going to start our star-gazing project?" Scott asks in a smooth sentence, and I notice he is not breathing quite as hard as I am.

"I don't know. Maybe this weekend," I say in reference to our Geology assignment. Two weeks ago I dropped Honors Physics and joined Scott's third period Geology class. We sit next to each other, and now my hardest class has been replaced by the easiest of the sciences, playfully coined "Rocks for Jocks."

"I can't believe your parents let you switch out of Honors Phys," Scott says with a smile, knowing that he singlehandily convinced me that the move was a good idea.

"Oh, no . . . it's not like that." I pull my brow down and look at him as we bounce in sync. "My parents never tell me what classes to take. I don't think that they really care, just so long as I do my best." I allow myself to wonder why, then, have I always been in the hardest classes with the notation of Honors or AP before the subject line? I think of a giant red balloon, full of self-created pressure, that has been tied to my wrist for all of high school. It floated up and down every high school hallway, attached to me with a ribbon of perfection. And it is only now that I realize in the recent weeks, it has begun to float away.

"So it's just you that's a perfectionist. You're my goody-two shoes." I notice Scott's possessive adjective and smile. I smile simultaneously at the fact that the only other person who ever teased me this much was my grandpa. I have missed him every day since eighth grade. Maybe he's back.

I reach out with my right arm and give Scott's left a playful but firm slap. I have not told Scott this, but my initial favorite attribute (his dimples) has been replaced by a new and very convincing winner. Despite the chill in the air, Scott wears a short sleeve t-shirt that has been worn far too many times and now is only paper thin. My hand lands squarely on his left bicep, and I am glad his shirt does not impede the sensation of his thick and solid arm. I squeeze my hand shut and hang on for a brief moment. He has the best arms.

He squeezes back, both to let me know that he likes my touch and also to make his arm tense and feel even stronger. We look at each other and talk without speaking as we continue our run.

The path follows a creek, the same creek that borders JM and the same creek that middle-schoolers often sneak off to for weed sampling. My heart feels a little stiff as we near our old middle school.

"Did you get a new lock for your new locker yet?" Scott asks in the start of a new conversation.

"No, not yet. No one will steal my stuff. What is there to steal anyway?" I force myself to joke as I think of my new locker. People never want the bottom lockers, but I honestly don't mind it. Again, this was Scott's idea; he was the one who noticed the empty locker below his. He knew I was carrying all of my books in my oversized green North Face backpack. I moved in under Scott immediately, not conscious that this was the second time someone had picked out a new "locker" for me.

"I don't know. You keep all of your stuff in there and I am worried someone is going to see that you don't lock it and steal all of your color-coded Calculus notes." Scott smiles and his grin reaches the corner of his eyes. He always pokes fun at the fact that even my notes are pretty.

"I'm not worried about that," I say, because I am not worried about anything. At least I don't have to go to my locker anymore and worry about what will be in there.

Three days after I kissed Scott for the first time, there was a frantic note in my locker. No new cell phone battery, no bagel, and no candy. Just a note that read in your sick script, "Why haven't you called? Do your parents know? Am I in trouble? Write back and I will pick your note up tomorrow." I had crumpled up the note, walked to the bathroom, and thrown it away in a metal depository meant for tampons. After all, who would dig around in there?

From that day on, I refused to go to my locker just as I had been refusing to call you. That night after my sandwich date with Scott, when I left the phone downstairs, felt like the first night of the rest of my life. I have not called you once since and I only think of the darkness haphazardly. It feels remarkable.

My stride becomes bouncy, although we are headed up hill. The swoosh of my Nike running shorts becomes more noticeable and I am breaking away from Scott. Suddenly I feel strong and swift.

He thinks we are racing, and I guess we are. He thinks it is fun, and in some ways it is. But as I make my way up the long incline, I clench my jaw and think of you.

To the left of us is the creek, but we are pulling away from it as we run toward the top of the hill. To the right of us is an imposing cliff that looks like a gargantuan half-eaten hamburger from Burger King. The sun is lowering on the horizon and a spectacular sunset is likely less than an hour away.

My body feels empty, but I have fuel. I think of last Wednesday, when you were waiting in the 7-Eleven parking lot. You know that I stop there for coffee before school on the days without morning swim practice. I didn't see your car in the corner until it was too late. I rushed inside to the coffee bar.

"What is going on? You have to tell me," you said as you filled a cup that I knew you would promptly throw away. Your voice was low and snake-like.

"Get out of here. I can't talk to you," I had said, looking over my shoulder as though someone might be watching me.

You slammed a lid on the top of your coffee. You paid and scurried to your car for the protection you thought you needed. I stood and stirred my French vanilla creamer into my coffee. I felt a sense of force from your new fear.

Scott and I are now only halfway up the hill and I think of last night and the night before, standing in my room and looking at your headlights circling my cul-de-sac below. I think of my swim practices and the sound of your engine humming as you tried to watch through the fence. I think of the fact that I know I can never be home alone again. I think of the running shoes and the unused phone, which is now buried deep in the mess of my teenage closet.

I swing my eyes to the left. With our ascent of the hill I can see the entirety of JM below. There, sitting in the safe arms of the Moraga hills, fuels my final push. I pull away from Scott, trying desperately to forget what I am thinking of, and beat him to the crest, my predetermined finish line.

"Whoa, I wasn't expecting that," he says as we stand at the top of the hill. We chug the air, and though it would be much more comfortable to put his hand on his knees, he wraps his arms around my shoulders and pulls me in.

I am hot from the climb and my wet bangs brush his scruffy chin. I might smell and he might notice that I am sweating, but I make no effort to pull away. Instead, we stand there, our lungs fighting for both air and the small space between us. Our hearts work hard at the same time.

I do not feel scared.

Without reason or even conversation, we decide to head back. We turn to jog down the hill to recover from our battle. Or so I thought.

I can see you and I know that it is you immediately. You are coming toward us. You are just to the left, running on a trail off to the side of the pavement that dodges and weaves between bushes and trees. Still, I know that our paths will intersect.

The space between us is rapidly closing because we are both traveling. I wish I could stop, or even turn around. *How would I possibly explain a sudden change of direction to Scott? And what if he didn't follow me?* Then I would be alone with you.

You are less than twenty-five yards away. I use the most common distance of a racing pool to gauge my safety. As you approach me and I approach you, I wonder how you knew where to find me.

Did you call Maggie Black? Did I tell her that this was where we were running? Did you call my house and pretend to be someone else and did my mom tip you off? Did you see us on the street and then follow us? Or have you been following us since we walked off of our high school campus? Were you hiding in the brush during Scott's and my first foot race? Did you see us hug at the finish line and do you now know that I am finished dealing with you?

Ten yards, and you do what I expect you to do. "Oh, hi, Kristen!" you exclaim. You make your voice sound surprised and jubilant, and you make a terrific attempt to make your face reflect these same fake emotions.

Like so many times before, I follow your lead. "Oh, hey, Natali!" I force an exclamation at the end of my sentence, and I hope that Scott doesn't notice that my hands have started to shake. I realize that I have not called you this in many years. I have not used this name since the night of the dance recital, when everything changed. What once was the sound of my most admired mentor feels like charcoal smoldering in my mouth.

Scott puts his hand up to wave, and he pulls his lips into a smile I have never seen him make before. "Hey," he says to you, and I remember that he would have known you from JM. Although he would have never had you as a teacher, the school is small enough that you would have known him, too. I can tell by the drumming of Scott's footsteps he doesn't think we will be stopping. But I know different.

You have now come off the dirt trail and you stand solidly in the center of the path. While it would be physically possible for us to pass you here, it would be rude and awkward enough that Scott would know that something is wrong. I am sure that you are banking on this.

I see in your eyes an invisible glare. You have picked my boyfriends before, but you know nothing of this new scene. "Hi, Scott, right?" The tiny blond hairs on the back of my neck cut short by the constant rub of my swim cap stand on edge as you say my new favorite word. The three of us slow to a standstill at the roadblock of your body.

"Yeah. Hi," Scott says, and I wish that I could reach back out and hang onto his arm again.

"Can I talk to you for a second?" you say to me as you try to sound as casual as you can. But your intensity burns in the late afternoon sun and, before I answer, you grab me just above the elbow and pull me away from Scott.

What is Scott thinking? How good is his hearing? Will he know immediately and, if he does, will he run away?

My arm feels as though I have gangrene where you touch me and I know that I could never live through being your captive again. You take me off of the trail, about fifteen feet from Scott. I turn slightly, careful not to lose sight of him.

"What is going on?" You are only an inch from my face. You take your cold and bony hands and wrap them around my head, just behind my ears. I can smell you, and my tonsils gag in defense.

I am frozen, but my main fear lies in Scott leaving. I say nothing.

"Tell me right now, Kristen." Your mouth spits the K and the R in my name and I hear that you do not love me at all. Actually, you hate me. "Is it . . . this? Is it . . . him?" Your eyes leave mine momentarily and I see you look at Scott. You are ready to pounce and, if I told you the truth, you may shred his face into bits.

This image makes me brave and so I lie. "I think that they know. They know something. Stay away. For your sake, stay away," I say, mimicking your intensity. I lie to you as you have lied to me. You loosen your grip, and through the window of your eyes I can see you looping the reel in your mind of what may come next. The police lights almost reflect in your pin-pricked pupils.

You slide your hands away from my head and they fall silently alongside your frail body. You look grey and with sunken eyes, I wonder if you have either eaten or slept in the weeks that I have refused to call. I have always hated how your forehead and your brow protrude from the rest of your face. But today it is even worse. You look like the Cro-Magnon that we learned about in AP

Bio. Your body is starved and your face reflects that it is willing to give up nutrients for the vital operations of your body.

I, on the other hand, have never looked better. I take a little longer getting ready these days, and I have never gotten this much sleep in my life. I never cut brushing my teeth short and I even tried flossing. I look back to Scott, the person making me healthy.

"Okay!" I say loud enough for my new running partner to hear. "Good to see you and get that all sorted out." I turn my back on you and, as I run toward Scott, I am surprised that you do not take a blow to my skull. You stand in your spot, shocked and scared.

"What was that about?" Scott asks once we have stepped out of earshot. We are running again, and the distance feels like freedom.

"Oh, she thinks I am mad at her about not coming to any of my club soccer games," I say to Scott, but I don't count this as a lie.

"You used to be really close to her, didn't you?" Scott asks, and I can hear a minute slice of worry in his voice.

"Yeah, I used to be. But she is kind of . . . weird. Like kind of intense," I say, trying to explain the recent transaction.

"That was kind of weird. What happened just back there . . . That was kind of weird." Scott's pace has slowed and he looks at me, below the surface of my skin.

"I know . . . sorry. I think that she wants to be friends or something. Don't worry. I doubt that I will ever see her again," I say, and I hope that my statement is true.

We finish our run, and with each stride I leave what just happened behind. I push you, and all that you have done to me, to the back part of my brain. I leave it there, locked securely in a safety deposit box. It stays contained and unable to contaminate the happiness of today.

CHAPTER THIRTY-NINE

My Final Push

It's not what I would have picked, but it will work. It's probably more of a spring or summer dress, but with black stockings and the same black shoes as yesterday, I guess it will do for the middle of December. As I enter the courtroom in my pinstriped blue dress, I realize that I have made it.

I feel relief to see the caution tape, which is still here, but sags a little from the weight of yesterday. Geoff is already sitting at his table and crunched over his notes in preparation. The podium stands just behind him, to his left. Grossman is huddled with a few of her special agents. Though the court is not full yet, I take the same seat as yesterday. As the door of the court opens and closes, I notice that people from both sides do the same, finding security in their spots.

The corners of my mouth curl slightly as I witness my army as they march in. It seems as though for each supporter of Julie, there are two or three for the North. As my friends and family members enter, they find my eyes to make contact. Some come over to squeeze my hand, some give me a quick pat on the shoulder, and others respect my space, but all give glances of support. All in their own way and without words tell me I am ready.

Geoff also turns to look for me and, upon locating me in the growing crowd, comes back to check in. "So I think we will start with Maggie . . . Ford, is it?"

"Well, actually, my dad wants to speak and so does the other Maggie," I say to Geoff, and hope there aren't too many people.

Geoff looks back at me and my words, somewhat surprised that things have changed overnight.

"Okay . . ." Geoff's brow lowers in slight confusion over who is who. "So we have your dad, both Maggies, Scott, and you. I'm sorry, I don't know the Maggies' last names."

I am about to respond, but as typical in a situation like this, Maggie Black does it for me. "I'm Maggie Rinow, formerly Barnard. And this is Maggie Presutti, formerly Maggie Ford." Her words come out too quickly and I am suddenly aware that others have anticipation about speaking today. Geoff remains confused.

As Geoff tries to scribble Maggie's rapid words on his paper, the placidness of Maggie Black's words shuffle in before he has had time to bring pen to the paper. "Geoff, honestly, don't worry about it," she waves her hand in front of her face in dismissing the minor detail of last names. "We can just say our name for the record to the judge once we get up there."

Geoff does not need any convincing. "Sounds great," he says, and quickly returns to his post. I settle into the safety of my immediate surroundings.

Suddenly the pain slices again as I see Julie's face. But this time the pain dissolves quickly. My eyes are drawn to her cuffed hands and cuffed feet joined by a belt around her waist. A rattling chain links the bondage of her hands and feet. *Is this how she entered last time or every time? How could I have never noticed before?* The sound of that chain clanks as Julie approaches Grossman and effectively adds to my feeling of safety.

Julie is accompanied by a young and handsome bailiff, who catches my eye frequently whenever I have sat here in Department 36. His short brown hair reminds me of an actor in *Saving Private Ryan.* I imagine in a private moment, he would offer to enlist for my side. He removes Julie's shackles before she sits down, but somehow I know that he doesn't want to.

With minutes until 8:30, Judge Maier comes from the back. I find difficultly in imagining her going home last night, having dinner with her family, and wearing different clothes than yesterday as she appears identical in her black robe of judgement. I find surprise in her words starting so quickly; "We are back on the record in the matter of The People v. Julie Correa. May I have appearances?" As the attorneys stand and speak the beginning words they did yesterday, I am aware that Barbara is not on the other side of the tape today.

"So I'd like to call Mr. Lewis, he would like to give a victim impact statement." Geoff stands in respect as my dad makes his way to the podium.

I wonder if Julie is surprised at how much my dad has changed since she knew my life. He is older, yes. But the day I left to swim at UCLA, he began swimming masters every morning. And while my career went from a walk on, to a full ride, to a retired Division I athlete, my dad has remained a loyal daily swimmer for more than a decade now. The work ethic that my dad taught me as a child has left him fit and healthy. I look at him, my eyes barely blinking, and find myself glad that he is standing up for me.

For an accountant known by my friends as being shy, his voice is sharp, loud, and effective as he gets right to business. "Ms. Correa groomed Kristen and groomed our entire family. We thought she was a great and wonderful role model for Kristen. We have never been more wrong. Kristen was 11 years old when she met Ms. Correa, who was at that time 28. She made herself part of our family and then molested our daughter. It is as simple as that."

I steal a glance at my mom. She turns to Aunt Judy, and just by the private smile they share, I know my mom has helped my dad write his words.

With a slight rumbling in the back of his throat, I imagine the growl of a male lion protecting his cub. He continues: ". . . Ms. Correa got away with these crimes because she was a trusted teacher, a family friend, a newlywed, and most of all because she was a woman." As my dad speaks, I realize I have heard these exact words said by my mom in private. Now, with full proof that these words are as much my mom's as my dad's, I smile inside. I think of my mom and dad working late last night in partnership as parents. The scene stands in contrast to Julie's common words: "Your parents won't be able to handle this. You know their marriage won't last through this." Perhaps my dad is more of a man than Julie ever gave him credit for.

"Your Honor, Barbara Louie is not the only student whom Julie reported as being suicidal. After we found the cell phone and the book, my wife was beyond upset, having a gut feeling that this came from Julie. We approached Julie and she told us that Kristen had been abused by Mr. Witters and was suicidal. The phone she said was meant to help Kristen through hard times.

Julie told us that we should be thankful for her for helping out our daughter: just as Mrs. Louie was for her helping Barbara."

My dad shifts his weight to the opposite foot and I take a moment to look over at the other side. I wish Barbara were here to hear my father's words. I imagine her listening, and suddenly standing up to cry out, "That's what happened to me. There was Witters and then Julie was there to pick up the pieces. She did the same thing to me!" I imagine Judge Maier slamming her gavel down as everyone in the court, other than me, murmurs in shock.

My attention is brought back to my dad as his voice grows louder.

"Julie, were you in our house telling us that morning that our daughter had been abused and then did you sneak back into our house that night? Or did you take Kristen from our home that night and make her ride with a blanket over her head to your apartment?"

"You may have confused Kristen's memory with what Mr. Witters did or did not do to her. You certainly confused us. But Kristen is not confused here in what she remembers about you. You planned this, you integrated yourself into my family, and you slithered your way into Kristen's young trust."

His words are riddled with a "how dare you" attitude as he digs his heels into the courtroom floor. His long-sleeved sweater is a staple of most men over fifty, with the neckline of a polo shirt and the bottom tucked neatly into his khakis. He looks angry.

I know my dad was scared when I decided to go to the police. I know that he worried when I decided to use my name. What would people think of me? Of his parenting? What would people at Cal think? At his office? And as I see him finish his address to the court, I believe he finally understands.

As he returns to the Irish twins of my mom and aunt, my dad's blue eyes meet mine. I am transported to the day I told my parents that I was going to the police. I could feel his unease and concern. But now I am reminded of standing with him, outside of our favorite taqueria. In an awkward action he put an arm around me and said, "If this is what you need to do, we'll do it. We'll go get that bitch." He sees me today, understanding a part of both my pain and my plan. As he walks back to his seat, I can tell that he wishes he could give me a fist pump just as he would after a 200 butterfly. His eyes tell me he is glad he had faith.

"Your Honor, there's two friends of Kristen's both name Maggie." Geoff rolls seamlessly into the next chapter. He turns to the audience as he stands, smoothing his tie down the front of his body. "One is Maggie Barnard."

In my hours of interviews with Detective Parker, I was surprised that Maggie Barnard's name came so frequently out of my mouth. "I will need to talk to this . . . Maggie Barnard, or I guess it's Maggie Rinow now?" I had laughed a little under my breath, thinking *you can just call her Maggie Black.* Parker had given me a courtesy couple of hours so that I could call Maggie before he did. I was on the way to see Chuck and, as I passed over the Alameda Bridge, I called Maggie.

It's not that we weren't friends anymore, it's just that we were different friends. We are the kind of old friends who are in each other's weddings as bridesmaids, that see each other on holidays, call for birthdays, and always care about the other's happiness. But we weren't stones in each other's life where the timing of a phone call or the towering dishes in the sink didn't matter.

I guess it's a bit like discovering gold in the Klondike Territory of Alaska.

Through the cold I have found a nugget of sisterhood that will last until I lay on my deathbed.

Without trying very hard, Maggie is beautiful. In her sweater and dress pants, Maggie has never been shy as she bulldozes into her statement: "Julie Correa is a chameleon. She has made her supporters believe she is a good and conscientious person. I was a student of Julie's in the same time period as Kristen, and I know a different side of Mrs. Correa. I know the 'fun' side that allowed us to go off campus with her, the 'cool' side that only allowed select students to eat lunch with her, and the 'silly' side that called us by nicknames and ignored teacher rules and allowed us to call her nicknames."

I remember Maggie looking up to Julie, reading her actions and mimicking her mannerisms, the same way I did. Maggie quickly continues: "I also know the 'elitist' side of Julie, as I watched her handpick Kristen, over me, to be the favorite of our grade. I know the 'giving' side of Julie, who gave Kristen Oakley sunglasses, hats, and other presents. I know the 'selective' side of Julie, who only brought Kristen—not anyone else in the lunch group—a bagel for lunch. I know the 'mean' Julie, who would pick on students of lesser athletic ability or the handicapped,

most specifically, Carolyn Gow, a student in our grade who was
mentally handicapped with, if I remember this correctly, Prader
Willi Syndrome. Carolyn lacked the hormone that controls hun-
ger and was therefore very overweight. Julie called her 'Caroline
Turpentine.' Carolyn often got upset and asked Mrs. Correa to
stop. Correa told Carolyn that it was just a new nickname and all
of the other cool girls had one. Carolyn did not have the capacity
to understand boundaries, and Julie thrived on that. I remember
once Carolyn asking Julie if Rob chases her around the house
to get her and get on top of her. Julie threw her head back in
laughter and said, 'what then, Carolyn, what would Rob do then?'
Julie would continue to egg Carolyn on. It left me embarrassed
and mortified not knowing either how to protect my handicapped
classmate or my own dignity in standing up to a teacher."

I hear Maggie's words with a sense of regret. I remember Carolyn for a moment and wish I had been able to make life better for
her.

Maggie's flatline voice stands in contrast with the goofy side
to her that first made me her friend. But her presence now has
power. I allow her words to pull me up, from the very top of my
head. I sit straight in listening. Maggie takes no pauses: "Now
I don't know how to protect my best friend. In July of 2010, I
saw another side to Julie—a monster. Kristen called me and told
me what Julie did—not once but over and over. I have sat with
Kristen through all of these court proceedings and have watched
with Kristen in difficulty as Julie changes the mask she wears to
court. At the preliminary hearing she laughed, when she brought
her supporters she glared at us, and yesterday she gave an empty
apology and cried.

"You saw the act. The script read with the emotion of remorse.
But it is not how she feels. She did not pick up the phone last
year and say 'Kristen, I'm so glad you are okay and I am so sorry
for what I did.' Instead, she was suspicious and not wanting to
speak because she did not want to be sitting here today."

Maggie points her defined nose and her high cheekbones toward the defense. I feel her fury as she finishes: "She is a chameleon. She fooled me as an eleven to fourteen year old. She fooled
many people in this courtroom. Please do not let her fool you."
She takes the only pause of her speech to look Maier squarely in
the eye.

As Maggie rounds the corner of the gate that separates the audience from the stage, she walks with accomplishment in each stride of her step. As her shoes hit the ground, I realize that Maggie has been to every court marker. Today, in the final hour, she was given a voice.

To my right, Maggie Red rises. I am not sure what Maggie Red's approach will be, as she is the softer of the two, but the look in her eyes and sound of her stilettos on the floor convey a conviction I have not seen before.

"Your Honor, my name is Maggie Presutti, formally Maggie Ford." *You mean Maggie Red*, I smile to myself. She makes the most of her 5'2" inches, as she stands tall as she looks directly at Maier.

I remember the day before third grade started, I was walking with my mom into Safeway and I stated, as only an eight year old would, "Mom, I have decided I am going to be best friends with Maggie Ford. She is really nice and really fun and I want her to be my best friend." I guess we never looked back.

"In April of 2010 I got a phone call from my best friend Kristen, though I could hardly understand her through her sobs. She said she had something she had to tell me about her past . . . As Kristen divulged the details of the abuse, I was shocked and devastated to learn what my friend had lived through."

I am teleported back to the call. *Had I not made that call to Maggie, the friend who made me tell Scott, would I be here today?*

"We have spent a lot of time in this courtroom talking about the horrendous abuse that Kristen endured at the hands of Julie Correa, but I would like to give you a snapshot of how this continues to impact Kristen today. Kristen has been diagnosed with PTSD—a condition that many of us are most familiar with in terms of war veterans. In many ways, Kristen, too, has lived through a war. She is plagued by vivid flashbacks so intense that she becomes paralyzed in fear. These flashbacks prevent Kristen from being able to go to her family's home in Moraga. While my memories of the Lewis's house include hide-and-seek in the backyard and slumber parties in the family room, Julie Correa has shattered those happy memories for Kristen and replaced them with flashes of her hiding in Kristen's closet or under her bed."

"In addition, Kristen suffers from depression. I have spent countless hours on the phone with her while she tells me between sobs that she is having trouble just getting through the day. Kristen often has anxiety so great that she can't eat, can't sleep, and can hardly function."

I appreciatively remember Maggie ending our conversations with "what did you eat today?"

"Kristen confided in me that she was not sure that she wanted to have children out of fear that something so terrible, like what happened to her, could someday happen to them. Over a decade later, in the wake of Julie's abuse, Kristen is still struggling to just hang on."

I sense movement in the courtroom, people shifting weight with Maggie's words. Maggie was the only one who knew that I have been hesitant about having children. Now my parents and my friends see my darkness in a different light. I become aware of the bones in my palm as Scott squeezes my hand, letting me know it is okay to be scared.

"Julie has used the explanation that she thought she was in a 'loving romantic relationship' with Kristen, which she believed to be consensual. Hearing that makes my blood boil. What 'loving relationship' includes secret cell phones in carved out books, breaking into a family's home and hiding in closets, or jumping out of a two-story window to avoid being discovered and breaking your leg? Certainly no relationship that I've been in. But most importantly—and I cannot emphasize this enough—what 'loving romantic relationship' includes an adult and a child and a fourteen-year-age difference? This all began when Kristen was fourteen and Julie was literally *twice* her age. Julie attempting to explain her actions by saying that she was in love with Kristen is delusional and downright offensive. Let's call it what it actually is: Julie is a pedophile."

Maggie is angry now and her voice may be louder than even her most contagious laugh. She seems to spit her words in a way that I did not know she was able to.

"Yesterday, many people spoke on Julie's behalf and said that she is a wonderful person and these accusations are out of character for the 'Julie Correa that they know'. It was excruciating trying to digest what these people were saying. Julie has admitted her guilt. Furthermore, we are not talking about a minor indiscretion or a lapse in judgment. We are talking about raping a child hundreds of times over a period of four years. Had this been a lapse in judgment, Julie could have stopped after the first time. Julie could have stopped after the 150th time. She did not. She continued over and over again. Perhaps everyone's perception of "Julie Correa the upstanding citizen and wonderful mother" is just an illusion."

"Many people ended their speeches yesterday by talking about Julie's sons, and I'd like to do the same. While they spoke about those boys, I attempted to calm Kristen as she visibly shook. The Correa boys have been something that Kristen has cried to me about many times. I understand that Julie does not want to be separated from her sons. I have two children of my own, and being separated from them is my worst nightmare. With that, I have this to say: having children does not at all change the crimes that were committed. Having children does not lessen the gravity of Julie's actions. Having children does not absolve Julie of those skeletons in her closet. Those two innocent boys did not ask for this—they are two additional victims in the aftermath of her horrendous crimes. Julie, I'd like you to put yourself in the position of Jeanne and Rob Lewis. Imagine that one of your sons gets to be fourteen years old and a teacher that has 'fallen in love' with him begins breaking into your house and hiding in his closet and doing unspeakable things to him. As a mother, I hope you now understand that not only have you horribly abused Kristen, but you have completely violated the entire Lewis family."

"Your Honor, I appreciate you giving me and other supporters of Kristen the chance to have a voice. As an advocate for my friend, I ask that you show Julie Correa no leniency. Kristen has a long road ahead of her to put together the pieces of her almost broken life. Julie's crimes are monstrous and inexcusable and she deserves due punishment. Thank you."

Maggie picks up her papers, aligning them as she taps them on the podium. I know that she is proud to have fought. Red whips her body around and looks right at me. Her eyes seem to say, "I'm protecting you now, my dear friend." I pull my lips tight across my face, in between a smile and a frown as I attempt to say "thank you." Red returns to me and picks up my hand.

"We are going to need to take a brief break," Maier speaks quickly so that Geoff doesn't play his next chess move. Her eyes glance below her to her left. "This is just a lot of transcribing for my court reporter. Are you okay?" Maier asks the quickly writing woman in a kind voice, which soothes my anxiety. I turn along with Maier and see the court reporter, who looks a little green. I realize, somewhere deep inside my chest, that I am not the only survivor in this room.

Scott pats my back as he gets up. I know him well enough to know that he needs this short break to move his body before it is his turn. I wonder if he has a nervous stomach like mine. Before he leaves, he evaluates my immediate surroundings to determine if my structure is sturdy enough without him. With a half-smile he turns the back of his pinned stripe suit to me as he leaves.

As promised, Teri is there again. As if on cue, Teri sees Scott's open seat and slides across the walkway into it, without ever standing completely upright. If I didn't know any better, I would think that she and Scott planned it this way. Teri holds my left hand in between the two of her much colder palms. She wears her rimless glasses and I am grateful that I have an unobstructed view of what she is saying to me: "Kristen, you can do this. You have a lot of people who are proud of you." Her voice is shaking and her mouth drawn into a deep frown. With her eyes completely full of tears, and her face dry, she continues: "I am really proud of you. I am really proud, Kristen, and you can do this and you are almost done." We look at each other and I see so much of who I want to be—and so much of who Julie could have been. A single drop leaves my eye as I know that Teri's words are both true and hard to come by.

Chuck has brought his good wife, Joan, again today. In my year and a half of working with him, I have drawn great inspiration from her and her repetitive battle with cancer. Chuck has often shared her road, her setbacks, and her current remission. She is a classy lady, with an outfit precisely picked the night before. She leans her fragile body forward and exits the court to use the bathroom. Without explaining myself and feeling invigorated by Teri, I leave the safety of my Maggies. I slide in next to Chuck and sit closer than I have ever sat to him during a session. I feel safe in the cubby of his arm shadow. In making no attempt to move away from me, he tilts his balding grey head closer to me and says, "You all right, kiddo?"

Not that it really matters if I am okay or not, I do a scan of my body and realize I can feel every square inch of myself. My feet are anchored into the ground and the beat of my heart in time with the cause of my war cry. "Yeah, I am ready."

"You are doing the right thing here today. You're an okay gal." As he gives me a quick hug, the wooden door swings open and Joan and Scott return. I, too, return to my spot.

"How are you doing, Kristy?" Scott has taken my hand again, and I notice the shaking of his leg next to mine.

"I'm numb." It is true. Although I can feel my whole body, my emotions are buried somewhere much deeper inside.

"It's okay. You have to be to get through something like this." His words hand validity to my journey.

"Yeah, you're right. I'm numb, but I am ready. I guess I'll just have to feel it all later." I look at him out of the corner of my eye.

"I'll help you remember." He can't quite look at me and I sense there is something more he wants to say, but he needs to hold it all together. I see Maier reenter the courtroom and I feel the time between me and my husband disappearing. I hold his hand tight just as I would in the middle of an especially hard night. I pull hope from him.

"We are back on the record." The pieces of the stage fall back into place without any countdown or yelling of the word "action." Maier turns to Geoff, "Mr. Lauter, you may continue."

"Your honor, I would like to call Scott Cunnane, Kristen's husband."

Like a ghost, Scott is gone from my side. He struts to the front of the courtroom and looks tall for his average height. Is it that he feels comfortable in this courtroom? He has appeared here a number of times in his young career as a prosecutor. But his swagger comes not from comfort. Poised with purpose, he attacks the enemy.

"Your Honor." He stands at an angle and I am glad that I can see his face. "I am the husband of the victim." Scott holds either side of the podium in restraint. I imagine Scott transforming into a werewolf, jumping over the wood podium, and tossing the tables before him in the air. He finally gets to Julie and pulls her stone cold vampire body to shreds.

"Now, although you are here to sentence Julie today, this is not a happy day for anyone. This is not a victory. This is an ordeal, and it will continue to be an ordeal everyday.

"To some degree, your Honor, everybody in here will live with the scars from what Julie did to Kristen. The day in 2010 when Kristen told me about the sexual abuse she had endured at Julie's hands . . . that was the hardest day of my life. And from that abuse we're left with pain, sadness, and a new perspective on life.

I can feel the anger in his words, but I can also feel something much bigger and much heavier. The corners of his lips are pulled downward with the weight of sorrow. His emotion occupies every air molecule in the room.

On our wedding day, as I walked down the aisle and Marc conducted the ceremony, Scott cried the entire time. He said his vows with confidence and clarity, but his tears never stopped. The same is true today.

"I want you to know, Judge, this case has left me personally with a lot of sadness and a lot of anger. And it's easier for me to express the anger, so I'd like to start with that." I think of Geoff calling us to let us know that the defense was going to paint Scott as the angry husband. The corners of my lips lift in a small smile, in opposition to Scott's, proud that he has a plan.

"Judge, I hate Julie Correa. I hate everything that she did to Kristen. I hate the way that she acted throughout this process, how she came in here and laughed in Kristen's face and mocked Kristen. I will never forget at the preliminary hearing when Kristen bared her soul and answered every question that you won't answer on the stand." Scott directs the emphatic "you" at Julie.

"You won't take the stand, but she did. And she answered every question about the abuse. And her attorney asked, 'Well, isn't it true, Kristen, that that felt good?' And you laughed in her face as she cried on the stand and couldn't answer."

His voice is increasing in speed now and louder than any speaker to date.

"I hate that Julie is using children to get a lighter sentence here, knowing and admitting that she raped a child.

"I hate the fact that people stood up yesterday and said, she should get a lighter sentence because Kristen is the only child that she abused. As if to say Kristen doesn't matter. Look, she didn't abuse anybody else, it is just Kristen. Tell that to Kristen. She's the only one and that her sentence should be lighter for that. You said that." Scott accuses Julie as his face grows a color of red I've never seen him wear before.

"Judge, I hate the nights that we can't eat dinner together because she's crying. I hate waking up in the middle of the night because she's shaking . . . that gives me so much hate. I hate that my wife has PTSD because of what you did. And I hate, above all, that we are here at sentencing and you, Ms. Grossman, stand up and you, Julie, stand up and you blame Kristen. You've already admitted your guilt. You were there when she entered her plea and you still blame Kristen. That's what I hate."

Scott pauses with purpose and shuffles his feet so that they point directly at the enemy.

"You admitted your guilt, and you still say things like . . . you thought she was a peer. You were twenty-eight. She was fourteen. I'm twenty-nine. I don't think of a little eighth grade fourteen year old as my peer. That's ridiculous."

"You *let* it happen . . . is what you told the Court yesterday. You're sorry that you *let* it happen. You don't *let* oral copulation happen. Sexual penetration, that's not something that just happens, Julie. You don't use those words for that.

"How did you end up inside Kristen?" My heart stops in surprise that Scott's words have turned so vulgar. "That's not something that you *let* happen, so stop using that language. An indiscretion is what you said it was. Your attorney said an egregious error. Orally copulating a fourteen year old under duress is not what we call an error; that's called sexual abuse."

"And I can go on and on, Judge, with the hate; and that's not why I'm here."

Scott pauses again and glances back at me.

"I'm here to stand up for my wife. What she's done here is heroic, and I couldn't be more proud of her and that's why I'm here, that's why we're all here. We're here to support Kristen."

"This day, your sentence, is about Kristen. It's what she's gone through, what she's going through today, what she's going to go through, and what she's going through for the rest of her life."

"Julie spent years grooming Kristen. She coached her. She taught her. She mentored her. And then she raped her."

"And, Judge, this is the sad part: the abuse left Kristen isolated. Who could she tell about the abuse? Who would understand her? Still to this day people blame her. This is why people don't come forward. She was left by herself with the pain, the confusion, the shame, and the guilt. All by herself."

"And that's why I'm here today because I want Kristen to know, and everybody else in here, that she is not going to carry the pain by herself anymore. Because she went through this, we are going to share the pain with her. I want you to know that, Julie."

"Through this process, I got to see firsthand just how Julie manipulated Kristen. I was there. I got to listen to the first phone calls. I heard everything that you said to her, how easy it was for you to step back into that role, Julie."

I like how Scott spits her name.

"You remember one of the first calls when you and Kristen were talking about us being high school sweethearts—because, Judge, we met in high school—and you laughed. You mocked. You mocked us. And you continue to mock us. I saw on Facebook all those Facebook messages. You remember, when you changed your picture, you wanted Kristen to see what you look like today in case you could start up—start abusing her again. Do you remember that when you changed your picture? You do."

"I heard you on those calls. You let Kristen take the blame. I think you said, 'I wasn't strong enough.' It's been fourteen years, so you must still believe that. You must still believe that it was the child's fault, just as you said yesterday."

"Before you get sent off to prison, I want to be very clear with you: Kristen didn't do anything wrong. She didn't do anything wrong. She was the kid. She was an innocent kid, a kid that I grew up with, that was my friend, that you raped. I went to school with Kristen. She didn't do anything wrong. All that Kristen did was show up for her first day at JM, and you were there. You were there waiting in that office with those windows that overlooked the girls' locker room, big bank windows just as you see here looking over all the girls in the locker room. And you were there to be her friend, her mentor, her coach, and then rape her."

"And it's not an accident. It's not an accident that a person like you puts yourself in that position, puts yourself in the position of a coach, of a teacher, of a mentor."

"You're sick. Is that funny?" The entire audience turns to see if Julie's laughing. Though I guess that she may not be, I know Scott has a plan to expose Julie's typical courtroom behavior. "You're sick. That makes you laugh."

"But it wasn't just the access. It wasn't just your access as a teacher. You had to do so much more to get to the point of raping that girl. You had to put in so many hours of planning, of plotting, of stalking, of sneaking. And that's why you're going to prison today. That's why you're going for eight years. You earned every day of it. Every day that you spent manipulating Kristen, manipulating her family, sneaking into her house and raping her, you earned every single day."

"So, Judge, when you consider imposing anything less than eight years, please, think of Kristen, please think of myself, and please think of the rest of Kristen's support here today as we try and heal ourselves and we help Kristen heal."

"Julie took a piece of Kristen's soul. She blackened part of her heart, and together we now carry pain that we shouldn't have to."

"In closing, I want to share with you the most painful moment of my life. I told you that that day that she told me about the abuse was the hardest day."

Scott's shaking now, just as I typically shake. But, finally, I am still and listen to the devastation of my crying husband.

"And, Judge, it's not because she told me about the abuse. It's because afterwards she asked me a question that no husband should ever have to answer. It breaks my heart."

Scott tries to inhale, but the sobs stop him.

"Judge. She asked me if I could still love her. And for that . . . eight years is appropriate."

The still courtroom moves, and I see heads bend around me to wipe tears in tissues and rub eyes with shirtsleeves. Maggie squeezes my hand and I stare straight ahead, hoping Scott's words can penetrate my skin and dwell in my heart forever.

I may own the only clear pair of eyes in the court, but I cannot cry because it may impede my ability to see the beauty of my life.

Scott closes his remarks, grabs his notes, and passes Geoff. As he walks toward me down the aisle, I see a change in his face. His eyes are tired from crying, his cheeks have a soft dimple back in them, and his big eyebrows are a bit higher than before. He glances fleetingly at his dad and his brothers but, as at our wedding, maintains focus on his bride.

I wish I had time with him. He sits down and pulls me close, making a quick moment for the two of us before we are separated again. Time evaporates. Geoff looks at me before he says my name: "Your Honor, Kristen Lewis Cunnane would like to address the court."

Maier says nothing. She nods and I wonder if this is what she can manage. Scott pats me, just between the shoulder blades, and Maggie Red lets go of my hand after a pulse of love. I push my weight through the heels of my black shoes and stand upright. I am taller than when Julie knew me. Taller than when she raped me. I have grown. I feel taller since yesterday.

I begin my march up to the podium and I stare intently at my destination. I do not look at the people who love me, but instead feel their love inside of me. The sound of my shoes is so loud it almost hurts my ears, and too soon I am behind the wood structure. I see Geoff, standing in respect. And I know he will stand with me.

When I was twelve, I didn't sleep the entire week before my big swim meet. I would lay in bed, close my eyes, and envision my 50 butterfly over and over again. The heat of the summer day, my competitors around me, the roar of what I thought a big crowd, the scorch of the summer sun, the dive, the turn, the finish. And, of course, the win.

I have practiced this, too. I have practiced with Chuck and without him. My imagination is what allowed me to live through Julie in the first place. I might as well use it again.

I am dizzy and the court is spinning. I force my diaphragm to drop and let air fill my lungs. The globe stops spinning and time waits on me.

I grip the stand, and in my mind I let the lights dim in the courtroom. A soft spotlight is cued to illuminate me first, then Maier, and then the space between us. Quietly behind me, my Grandpa Lloyd stands straight as an arrow. The audience cannot see him through the darkness of the stage, but I know he has made the trip from heaven for me. Having died early in my eighth grade year, this man had a contagious love of life. Today he is here to remind me where I came from and to remind me who I was before Julie.

My hands are tight on the sides of the wood edifice. I look down at my nail polish, black as night. Two years ago my nails would have been pink. Two years ago I would not have been here. I see my black, short nails, and I think of Eve. I am glad she is a part of me.

The pages of my impact statement stack before me. I imagine picking them up, one by one, and handing them to my judge. I will not talk to Julie; she has not earned my response to her audacious statement.

One more breath. They will wait.

"Honorable Judge Maier." I stop, look at her, and before I begin I believe she knows everything I am going to say to her. Her head is tilted slightly to the right, and her eyes say, "Speak, child, I will believe you."

My words feel a little sluggish as they leave my mouth, but I am grateful that my vocal cords are firing.

"To try to describe the impact that these crimes have had on my life is like trying to dig through my DNA, unravel it piece by piece, and somehow lay it out on the table and make sense of it for you. If I could, I would make a small incision in my chest, open my heart, and hand you a piece of the hurt I feel every day."

I make a small fist with my right hand and put it up to my chest.

"This statement, much like my survival through and after the abuse, pulls the air from my lungs and causes my knees to go weak. To walk in my shoes, and feel the impact of Julie Correa, you must first understand who I am."

My back pulls my body perfectly straight with pride in the life I have. I look at the words before me and I am excited to pass them to my judge.

"I stand before you today with much to be proud of. Since turning eighteen and finding physical freedom from Julie Correa, I have created much success in my life. In my time at UCLA, I was an academic and athletic All-American, graduating with honors. I was an Olympic Trials semi-finalist and team captain for the swim team as well as an NCAA Post-Graduate Scholar. I received my Masters in Education from Cal with a 4.0 GPA. I am married to a prosecutor for the Contra Costa District Attorney's Office, my soulmate, my best friend, and the bravest and softest man I know, Scott Cunnane. We own our own home, have two dogs, and in most respects have a tremendous life together."

I think of Scott, of the words he has just spoken. I think of the life that I look forward to getting back to.

"Professionally, I have my dream job. I am the Associate Head Coach for the Cal Women's Swim Team. In my six years at Cal, we have finished in the top five in the country every year, and we have won the program's first two NCAA Championships. I coach numerous All-Americans and several Olympians."

I can feel Teri sitting behind me. I think of the text I got from the team captain yesterday that read, "I have been thinking about you nonstop today."

"In my time coaching at Cal I have come to see the importance of my job and the impact I possess as both a teacher and a coach for my athletes. For my profession I sit down in family rooms throughout the country and promise parents that I will mentor and protect their maturing seventeen year olds through the next phase of life. I make a promise to care about their swimming second and their well-being first. As I have watched these athletes walk into our program and into my life, I have come to understand the importance of having a role model. I take my job with grave seriousness and would stop at nothing to protect these young women. They trust me and I understand the significance of this trust. Who I am now, the person you are looking at today, is not the person I was then."

Without invitation, a flood of images race into my brain. A movie reel plays on fast-forward of my life before Julie broke it. As I speak to Maier, I see my words press play.

"When I was eleven years old, I started sixth grade at Joaquin Moraga Intermediate School. In the heat of a late August day, during roll call on the blacktop, I saw Julie Correa for the first time. Her reputation preceded her as she was the favorite teacher of the seventh and eighth grade athletic girls at JM. As I stood in line waiting for my name to be called, I saw the person who would be my teacher over the next three years, who would be my volleyball coach, softball coach, and basketball coach. I saw the person whom I was supposed to look up to and aspire to be. I saw the person who would do what she could to ruin my life.

"I stood there that day, without a bra on, with braces on my teeth, no makeup on my face, and never having kissed a boy. I stood there, wanting to get to know my new PE teacher, innocent of knowing how she would manipulate my admiration for her."

It feels as though my heart may be bleeding inside my chest as I see the young Kristen standing in line. I grab her hand and say, "Come on, we will make this as right as we can." And now I know why I have to keep speaking.

"Over the next three years I came to respect and look up to Julie more than any other figure in my childhood life. I wanted to be just like her—go to UC Davis, become a PE teacher, coach sports in school, and get married as she had recently done. She was revered by the other JM students, staff, and community. She was revered by me."

The wood door behind me slams. I almost jump, but convince myself to stay on the ground. Maier said she had other cases to-day. Is it a man reporting for his DUI, or someone hired by Julie? "Don't turn around," I tell myself, and the Eve part of me digs my nails into the podium. I keep reading my words to the judge and allow the light between us to grow brighter.

"A snapshot of the role that Julie played on the stage of my middle school life is preserved in the pages of my eighth grade yearbook. In her own writing and in her own words . . ."

I open the blue cover of my eighth grade yearbook to a center page that I have marked. I smooth my hand over the open page and look down at Julie's slanted script somewhere between print and cursive. I remember thinking then that her handwriting looked so different from mine . . . so much older than my fourteen-year-old bubbles. I begin to read her writing, the secret nicknames, the inside jokes, and the casual banter written by Julie herself for my judge to hear.

"*'Kristen. I will never forget the year of Krrr. Sheesh—there are so many memories! Lunchtime bonding, 20-minute runs, cement wall bonding, perfect attendance pact, your 'what are you saying basketball looks', Slurpee runs, bake potato tosses, Washington D.C., Bagel King, Perhaps, phone bonding, and just so I don't forget anything, any time Kristen was around. Thanks for making this an enjoyable year. I will never forget it. You have a bright future ahead of you. Shoot for the stars—they are within you reach. My thoughts and best wishes will always be yours. Natali, Natooli, Toolie, Tool, Tootie, Toot, Julie.'*"

I close the book and look at Maier, who has just let out a full exhale of air. She does not turn her head, but looks quickly at the defense table out of the corner of both eyes. As her lids lower slightly, I sense a sliver of anger in her as she hears the real written words of Julie's trap. I close the blue pages of the book and return to my typing.

"I remember the days just before eighth grade graduation, bringing my yearbook home, and reading this along with a personal card Julie had given me with an end-of-the-year gift—an Eddie Bauer watch. A sense of happiness stirred in my soul, thinking I had something special in Julie. I thought I had someone whom I could turn to through the hard things in life. I thought that I had someone who cared deeply about my happiness, health, and growth. I thought that Julie would be a permanent fixture of positive influence and support as I grew up."

For just a heartbeat, I allow myself to think of Barbara's speech and her telling the court how Julie attended her wedding. I remember the pause I took at the altar with Scott, to look at the crowd of my life and soak in their love. *What if Julie's face had been among those on my wedding day?*

I look back down my path of light as I share with Maier what I thought Julie's words meant and what I know them to mean now. I feel powerful as I dust off the deceit of the devil. I look at Maier, with a sword of truth in my hand and charge forward.

"As I read Julie's words now, I see them for what they were and what they have always been. 'Grooming,' a term used often in sexual abuse scenarios, is preserved here in black and white. Over the course of three years, from the time I was eleven until I was fourteen, Julie systematically got closer to me, integrated herself into my friend group, and acted more as peer than as teacher. Like a predator hunting prey, Julie used the trust and influence inherent to her position as an admired teacher and coach to insert herself into every aspect of my life. 'Lunch Time Bonding,' as Julie called it, in which only select friends and I would spend time in Julie's office, was a chance for Julie to weave herself into inside jokes and the daily happenings of thirteen and fourteen year olds. 'Slurpee runs,' that I was never supposed to tell my mom about, were a chance for Julie to take me off the closed school campus and in turn test my loyalty to her and my ability to keep a secret for her. And when saddened by the death of both of my grandfathers in my eighth grade year, I remember confiding my sadness in Julie while doing the '20-minute runs' with her, rather than my classmates, during Tuesday PE periods. This was Julie's way of ensuring I would turn to her, not my family or friends, in a time of need. As a young and naive fourteen year old, I did not know that my reliance on Julie was dangerous. I did not know that she would use my trust and shred my world to pieces."

I pause here, letting the sadness of who Julie is and what she did to me fill the courtroom like a cloud of smog. I feel like floating away, but my Grandpa Lloyd's tall stance behind me reminds me that it is time to stand and fight. As I climb to the summit of my speech, I know that oxygen is becoming scarce for my audience, who waits behind me in the dark.

"Through my teen years, my life appeared extraordinary. I received impeccable grades and played a key role on numerous sports teams. But as I succeeded in tangible terms, my life was split into extreme polarities: that of an accomplished Moraga teen and that of a terrified sex slave."

A strange picture appears in my head as I speak. I see a photograph taken of me and my soccer pal Meghan sitting back to back with a soccer ball. With a high ponytail on my head, I look to the outside world as a proud freshman who has made the varsity soccer team. But something behind my eyes, a darkness that only I can see, reminds me of what happened the night before.

I lower my eyebrows and refocus the light between Maier and myself as I continue.

"From the fall of 1996 until the fall of 2000 I lived in perpetual terror. Julie tracked my every move, watching my swim meets from the top of hills with binoculars, timing her drive to work to pass me as I drove to Campolindo, putting things in my high school locker on a regular basis—the list is too long to include everything here. The stalking became so severe that it became safer for me to assume that Julie was around each turning corner."

"Perhaps the most telling physical proof of Julie's tracking is held in the evidence locker for this case: the Spanish-English Dictionary in which Julie handcut a hole and hid a secret cell phone that she bought for me. She demanded that I keep this book with me at all possible times and she used this cell phone to monitor my whereabouts. Julie insisted that I call every night and give her updates on my parents' suspicion as well as plan the next scenario in which I was to meet her. For me, this phone and the book with the empty spot in the middle were the equivalent to my handcuffs, my ropes, my bondage."

I look down at the podium and imagine that my black book is there. I imagine touching the cover first and then opening it to touch the empty hole in the middle. I remember what it looked like sitting innocently next to my History book and assigned English books in my locker. I remember turning it on its side to fit neatly at the bottom of my green North Face backpack.

I wish I had the book to hold up to Maier and say, "See, this is what Julie did to me. This is the hole she cut in my center." I wish I could put the book above my head, high enough for the whole room to view, and shout, "You don't believe me, Amy, here is my proof! Look, Barbara . . . at my wounds!"

I take a full breath to calm the swelling anger in my belly. I look at Maier and then back down to my paper and continue.

"Julie has pled guilty to four felony counts, but the amount of times she raped me is countless. Perhaps it is closer to four hundred."

My voice slows as I allow Julie's words to come rushing at me. My heart rate increases as I share Julie with the court.

"'I just have to have you' was Julie's most typical statement when wanting to arrange a meeting. Sometimes Julie's words ran rampant through my head: 'I can't live without you . . . No one will understand this . . . There is something special about you that makes me do this to you . . . You drive me crazy . . . Your parents will never understand. If they catch us, I will take care of them . . . Your friends won't like you if they think you are a lesbian . . . Hide here, on the roof if they show up, and then, when they leave, I will take you away . . . If anyone finds out, I will be in big trouble . . . This is not wrong, but other people will think it is wrong . . . I will have to disappear like Mr. Witters . . . If I can't have you, no one can . . . This is your fault. I wanted to wait until you were older, but you made me.'"

Like a symphony, the beat of my heart increases as do my words. I can feel the emotion of the audience behind me as they scoot closer to the edges of their chairs. My heart is racing, and as the door slams loud behind me, my body jolts again. I am shaking now, and I look down at my black nails, which cling to the podium. *Stay with this, Kristen. Don't turn around. You can do this. Eve is a part of you now, and you have to do this together.*

"Julie's words scared me then and scare me now. They left me paralyzed in fear. They kept me doing, saying, and acting exactly as she wanted. Yes, they kept me calling her when I was supposed to or driving to meet her when she told me to. I had no other choice. I did not want to lose my family. I did not want to lose my life. I did not want her to kill herself."

The shaking that was once fear is now anger. I think of Grossman and her words yesterday. I wish I could turn around and throw a dagger into her heart—a dagger that would make her wake up with the same memories that I wake up with. My words have diesel fuel now.

"Julie sucked the innocence from me just as she stole my ability to cry for help. Her words kept me quiet as did her actions. People in this room, even Julie herself, question the legitimacy of my fear. But Julie's aggressive and irrational methods made me believe I was trapped. It was Julie, not me, contrary to what the defense mentioned yesterday, who jumped out of my second story bedroom window. She even broke her leg in the process. Julie also hid under my bed or hid in my closet while she waited for my parents to go to sleep. Julie jumped over seven six-foot fences to get to my home and get to me because she did not want my neighbors to see her coming down my street. When I questioned Julie, she grabbed me by the wrists and said, 'Don't you think I know what I am doing?' Julie also followed me on running trails and to 7-Eleven stores for stops for coffee before school. She would make me hide my face under a blanket as she drove me to her apartment in Lafayette. Julie, when pulled over and questioned by a Moraga police officer in the middle of the night, lied boldly, telling the officer that I was a family friend, that I got sick in the night, and that she was just taking me home. The officer, much like many people in the room, believed Julie's words. I was left there that night, certain that no one could believe the nightmare in which I lived."

My monologue here feels a bit as if I am rambling. *Maybe I should slow down for everyone. But why should I?* It never slows down for me. The wondering where she is, or the remembering what she would say, charges like a freight train. It doesn't come in a neatly paced package.

"The toll taken on my life through the time period of abuse is enormous. Julie drove a wedge between me and my family as I tried to operate in a way that would keep them safe from her. I had difficulty maintaining existing relationships and establishing new friendships through high school. I was always tired, sleeping little even on the nights I was allowed to sleep in my own bed. And when I did sleep in my own bed, I had to keep the secret cell phone, either hidden in the book or in the shoe, underneath my pillow. I was constantly sick, running off of the stress of trying to protect my life and the fear of wondering what would happen should I fail. My life was split in half by Julie, and from having to exist in two worlds; I have faced severe psychological hardship."

Take a deep breath, Kristen. Read these next words, feel the cut, and share pain for the world to see. It is your key and you can do it. I balance my weight between my two feet and take another inhale.

"And the abuse itself, the mouth-souring details that neither people who love me nor the people who support Julie want to hear, but that must be told." My cadence is extremely slow.

"The physical pain I literally suffered by the hands of Julie is rape. The burn of the carpet on my back as Julie pressed her body on to mine was torture. The smell of the antibacterial soap Julie forced me to wash my genitals with before returning home can still bring me back to that cold shower and those cold nights. The gagging felt in the back of my throat and sense of suffocation, as real as the nights Julie forced herself on top of me, are enough to make me want to bite my own tongue off inside my mouth."

My face draws into a grimace and I wonder if I have exposed myself too much. My body hurts, the inside of my legs feels sore, my back burns, my nose turns, my throat can't swallow, and I can almost taste the blood from my tongue filling my mouth. The manifestation of the physical symptoms makes my body shake, but as I look at Maier's face, I am certain that she feels my words. I crawl through my memory to share a specific day with her.

"I remember once, in the middle of Julie 'having me', telling her I needed to go to the bathroom as she was causing me extreme internal pain, the thick brown carpet in her apartment feeling like quicksand. For a moment, I imagined running down the stairs and down the street to a pay phone at the nearby BART station to call my parents. But what then? I had no clothes on. And what would my parents do? And what would Julie do to my parents? And what would Julie do to me? And what would Julie do to herself? With the inevitable end of life coming if people found out, instead of running, I returned to Julie. As I often did with the abuse, I allowed my brain to separate from my body, a coping mechanism called disassociation. This particular time, my brain left the scene of the crime and crawled into a picture. As Julie used my body, I pretended to lie inside a painting that hung on the wall; this picture of a sleeping lab often offered me escape from rape."

I allow myself to be filled with the image of my pup. I feel at peace for a moment, thinking of being curled up with him. Just as I felt safe then, I feel safe now. I continue my march.

"Julie has admitted her guilt. But her plea does not encompass the pain that she caused, and continues to cause me and my family and friends. Perhaps the extent of this pain can be felt in looking at my current life over the past two years."

I enter my mind and fast-forward from the time of abuse to the time of remembering. I often have an internal debate over which period of my life was darker. Without the abuse, there would be no remembering. But remembering means seeing Julie's master plan, from start to finish, through the eyes of an adult. Which is worse: the hours of Katrina, or the subsequent wreckage and downfall Louisiana faced for years after the hurricane? I begin to tackle the question.

"The abuse I suffered from the defendant was so extreme that my brain was incapable of storing the memories. For a decade, the trauma was buried inside of me like a black ball. For ten years, I was blind in seeing what Julie did to me. I was a stranger to my own past. Abuse Induced Amnesia, a medical term given to victims like myself, allowed me to continue living void of recognizing what I had been through.

"In the spring of 2010, owing to a variety of life circumstances, the black ball that Julie had put inside of me began to resurface. In the form of extreme depression and intense flashbacks, I relived what Julie had done to me as a child. The shame, self-blame, and fear that Julie had instilled in me filled my entire being. I was in emotional pain as well as physical pain and thought that no one could ever understand the darkness and disgust I had seen in my life."

The door opens behind me again, and my head is tempted to turn around. I beg my eyes to focus on the words beneath me and the loneliness behind me. I think of Scott's speech about sharing my pain. I imagine shoveling pieces of my past into little mounds amongst a vast field. My family, my friends, and my judge stand on their own mound. I hoist my shovel into the air and then drive into the ground as I begin to share my dirt.

"In May of 2010, I was at a swim meet in Irvine, California. I had not told my family, friends, or even my husband what Julie had done to me. I assumed that no one could ever look me in the eye, nor love me again knowing what I had been through. The flashbacks were coming like flooding rain, and when I closed my eyes, I would be jolted by a new memory: Julie making me hide in a bush and wait for her in the cold, or Julie being under my bed and grabbing my ankles when I thought that she would be in my closet. The suffering was crushing."

I take a moment for a long blink, and as I squeeze my eyelids together, I hope that my mom can handle what I am about to say.

"Our team hotel was adjacent to a train track. As the devastation felt as though it were pulling me apart into a million tiny pieces, I was tempted out of bed and in front of the next coming train. It felt as if it might be the only way out for me: finally the release of the loneliness, sadness, and darkness Julie put into my soul. Through that night the pain rivaled that felt throughout the worst of the abuse. I dug my fingers into the mattress, holding onto a deep faith that there might be a way through rather than out."

My fingers ache as I remember that night. My body aches as I imagine my bones being pushed together by a train. With clarity I know my fight today seems less a match than my fight that night.

"I knew then as I know now that me speaking the truth about my past has a grave effect on me, my support system, Julie, her family, and everyone in this room. But coming forward—saying something and asking for help—is what I had to do in order to heal. I have found tremendous support from family, friends, and strangers, and they have allowed me and encouraged me to tell my story. Speaking the truth was my choice in continuing to live."

I think of the stranger who hugged me in the bathroom at one of the court hearings after seeing my face wet with tears. I think of the people behind me, those who have spoken in court and those who have listened all along.

"In that choice, I began intensive therapy with a psychologist specializing in trauma. I have been diagnosed with depression as well as post-traumatic stress disorder. I have a long list of medical diagnoses and residual effects, including not being able to visit my parents' home. This home became my prison, where week after week Julie raped me, where night after night I had to call Julie, and where day after day I had to live a split life. This home is where I should be going to celebrate Christmas in a few days, but I can barely stand to think about. My effort to heal from what Julie did to me often feels like a full-time job."

My body feels heavy as I think of my burden. My words feel as though they are made out of mud, but I continue trudging along.

"At the onslaught of remembering, I would feel overwhelmed by just looking at food. Brushing my hair felt pointless. I would spend hours scared to fall asleep, fearful of vivid nightmares about Julie. When I did doze off, I was often jolted awake, sometimes by screaming, sometimes by tears, and sometimes by shaking, all of which existed outside of my own control. I trained my eyes to avoid contact with the knives in my kitchen, worried I might not be able to contain the pain inside my skin. Each day brings new pain as it does new healing. This is just a process for me."

My arms feel frail, but my feet sink solidly into the ground. I think of yesterday, and the buckling pain brought by the idea that Julie is a mother with two living, breathing children. Used repeatedly as an excuse by the defense, Maier must feel the toll I have felt over Will and Marco.

"I remember specifically, in the summer of 2010, feeling as though I was trapped. I knew I had to speak in order to heal and in order to live. I also knew that Julie had children. She had contacted me when I was a freshman at UCLA to tell me that she was pregnant and also so that we could 'get clear on what our relationship really was—something that no one else would understand or believe.' My brain allowed Julie's justification of the abuse to continue to store my memories in a tiny black box. I have since learned that my little black box has a name and physical location in my brain; the amygdala and the hypothalamus. But the idea that Julie had her own children was also stored there. And upon remembering my abuse and reporting it, I found myself trapped in knowing that I needed to speak but that Julie's children deserved a mother. So where did that leave me? I talked to my psychologist about my feelings of being trapped, and he told me something that stuck with me; 'Kristen, it is not the fact that a mother is a molester or a father is a serial killer that causes damage to children. It is the secret. You must tell the truth. You owe it to yourself and to those children. They will find a way out of the cycle.'"

I allow myself to think of them now. I pause and say a short prayer for them before I continue. *May they know truth and happiness. May they be okay.* Like a caged bird, I let the responsibility of what will happen to them leave my shoulders and fly somewhere above my pay scale.

"The criminal justice system has provided both a road to recovery as well as another trauma that I have had to work through. After reporting the abuse to police, I was told that I would need to conduct pretextual calls in order to gain evidence for a stronger case. After taking my statements and reviewing the physical evidence of the book, the picture of the cell phone, the poem Julie wrote me, and a number of other items, Detective Birch Parker told me that, without the calls, the case would likely be dropped. I was terrified that, after I had gained the courage to come forward, nothing would be done. I was mortified at the idea of speaking to Julie, and oftentimes the words that I knew I needed to say just would not come out of my mouth."

I punctuate this statement with a pause. My mouth pulls to a tight close as I remember gripping that phone with her awful voice coming out the other end. No one ever told me life could be so hard.

"I was coached through these calls by Detective Birch Parker and was told to use the same language and terms Julie used while abusing me. For example, instead of saying 'oral copulation' Parker told me to call it what she did then, and say, 'Remember when you kissed me down there?' I spoke in the helpless and lost voice that Julie demanded I use through the years of abuse; I was taught to talk to her in a certain way."

I allow the light between the judge and me to expand and cover the defense table. I do not look over at her, but my guess is that Grossman drops her head slightly, as her argument from yesterday is deflated. I like how this feels and I envision shoving Grossman's face in the mud.

"Detective Parker even encouraged me to take the entirety of the blame on the phone calls as a means of getting her to admit that the illegal acts occurred. Julie was extremely suspicious in talking with me, and while taking the blame caused me severe internal strife, it quickly made Julie feel safer and bolder in her admission of the past. Suddenly Julie wanted me to come to Utah, and her intensity over the phone terrified me. She claimed that even with her current life, her husband and her kids, there was room for me and that life was long. I am sure that to an outsider, these calls are confusing . . ."

I look at Maier, and with my eyes I try to get her to understand. *I was coached in those calls. Our only goal was to get her to admit that those things happened. Please don't let the defense use those callas against me!*

"But the little girl that you heard on the phone is who Julie made me be for her. She bought me white pajamas from the kids' department, she made me sing and dance for her, and she made me act even younger than I actually was. Julie always told me that people would never believe me."

I pick up my yearbook and slide it behind the smaller green journal I have also brought as ammunition. It has no lock, but a small leather flap that folds over and fastens it closed. I remember the process of having new memories, and feeling as though I had discovered an unwanted treasure. My hand would scribble quickly through the lines of the journal so that my memory did not have to sit inside my body alone. I do not open the book, but instead press my hand on the cover to feel its truth.

"While doing the pretextual calls, I held this green book with my notes and my memories of what she did to me. I used these Post-it notes to mark pages and to get Julie to admit to a wide range of the crazy things she did to me. I was taught to think no one would ever believe me."

"After the calls Julie proceeded to change her Facebook photo to not include her kids. In her Facebook message on July 14 she says, 'I changed my picture for you—it is more recent and without others.' She began contacting me obsessively via Facebook messages, which created an intense fear and paranoia in me that Julie would return to California, find me, and murder me. Through these phone calls and messages, I saw Julie's obsessiveness resurface and once again saw her sinister ways of trapping a person she identified as vulnerable."

I allow myself to think briefly of Julie's statement yesterday and her stated desire to help me over Facebook. I also allow myself to imagine Scott and what he does for a living, standing up here and arguing truth in the fight against deceit. A wave of control enters my body as I lobby for my truth.

"I have also faced great pain in seeing the faces of fellow students or respected teachers who have reported to various court hearings in support of Julie. The original defense counsel on the case shredded at my soul as he questioned me through the preliminary hearing. He argued, just as Julie did back then and does now, that this was my idea, my fault, that it felt good, and that I wanted it. And, again yesterday, the many speculations made about the legitimacy of my pain or realities of my memory. Here Judge Maier . . ."

I take a breath to make eye contact with Maier so that I can imagine handing her my upcoming words.

". . . I offer you explanation of why I am the only one to come forward. The double-sided shame and pain felt as a heterosexual woman who was abused by a trusted and respected coach compiled with the horror of today, of yesterday, of the last fifteen months. And, still, when I made the choice to live and fight for my life, I made the choice to stand here and tell you the unspeakable truth of what Julie did to me, no matter the pain I feel."

I am suddenly aware of the soles of my shoes. I can feel the cold tile of the floor beneath me. I feel planted and sprouted and grown as I continue.

"Because of Julie Correa, I have PTSD. What does this mean? Through the time before Julie's arrest, and while she was out on bail through parts of the past fifteen months, I operated under the same assumptions I did through the years of abuse. Walking into the garage in the early morning before swim practice meant wondering if she would be in the back seat of my car with a rope to choke me, crouched in the corner of the garage with a gun to shoot me, or having rigged my car with a bomb so that I would blow up on the way to work. These fears may seem far-fetched to an outsider, but as a child who was raised on the inside of Julie's operations, I was taught to believe that Julie would stop at nothing."

"Yesterday Julie questioned why I would fear her. Each day, after each night, on every phone call, with every surprise appearance, Julie gave me reason to fear her." I think back to my fourteen-year-old self collecting these coupons of terror. I take a deep breath to settle some of the shaking caused by over a decade of aftershock.

"I am tremendously proud of the road I have traveled that has led me to stand here today. I am devastated that this happened to such a young, innocent, vulnerable, and good eleven-year-old girl in the first place. There is not an hour that goes by within each day where I do not wish that this had not happened to me. Other people can say what they wish, but hear from my own mouth and in my own words, I never wanted Julie to touch me or kiss me or rape me. I never wanted a relationship with my teacher twice my age or a romance with a married woman. I never wanted any of this."

The sentences feel like black syrup coming out of my mouth and I wish I could take a bucket and dump it on Julie's army. Black goop, draining all over their clothes, seeping into their eyes and down into their mouths. *Maybe then they could taste what she has done to me?*

I look back at my paper with anger and my voice grows into a growl.

"While doing the pretextual calls with Julie, Detective Parker had instructed me to ask Julie if there was anyone else. She paused before her reply and an eerie silence stood between Julie and me on the phone. Julie, in a tone that concerned me, said: 'I don't *think* that there could ever be anyone else.' It has taken me great pain, consistent therapy, and more tears than anyone should ever cry to discover one thing: there is nothing inherent about me that made Julie do what she did. I did not ask for this and this was not my fault. Julie is a predator; one of the most dangerous and malicious kinds that exist on earth."

"Many people saw Julie as a great teacher, a caring coach, and a good person. Many people still see her this way. They simply cannot believe that she did this to me. These people have dug another wound in my heart."

I feel myself slowing here. Not because I am afraid to speak, but because I can feel a metamorphosis with each letter that leaves my lips. My shoulder blades widen. My brow grows heavy and thick. A small stripe of fur lines my spine. And my tongue brushes over my teeth as they sharpen to fangs. A wild cat lowers her body in the forest.

"But I have been there, behind the curtains in the middle of many hopeless nights, and seen Julie's face and the look in her eyes and the drive in her soul. What they cannot believe, I cannot remove from my memory."

My head swivels to the right and I allow myself to look. Now strong and solid, I can handle seeing the other side of the room. I allow the reality of my memories to give me fuel as I turn my glance into a glare. I see faces looking blankly back at me. As I look at them, I strip them of their control and I march on.

"From what I have seen with my own eyes, Julie is not only capable of doing this again. She is incapable of not doing this again."

I grab my focus and place it back on the paper. I let the light between Maier and me regain strength.

"'I don't *think* that it could ever happen again.' I disagree with Julie. Through the recent months and weeks, it has become more evident that child sexual abusers walk among us, in places and positions of trust. They are coaches, priests, teachers, Boy Scout leaders. They are men and, sometimes, they are women. And as these abusers are uncovered, and the victims stack up, it is clear that sexual predators do not strike in isolated incidents and against single victims. When given the chance—when we have a gut feeling or see something in a shower or notice a lingering touch—we must blow the whistle for society to hear."

I can feel Teri sitting behind me. I can remember worrying about what she would think if I came forward, if I used my name, if this awfulness was somehow tied to Cal. Suddenly I feel as if this is the biggest accomplishment I have made as a coach and the biggest gift I could give my athletes.

"As a coach, it was my duty to lift my head and come forward. As a judge, it is your opportunity to protect future victims, protect the law, and protect the truth."

"I have told you this once, but I remind you once again, that I have a good life, a life that is worth living, a life that is full of meaning and, now, full of healing. Yet, still, what Julie did to me was so devastating that she almost took everything good that I have away. More than ten years after the fact, the cut she made was so deep that it nearly killed me."

My lips draw into a deep frown and the continual tears accelerate. I imagine Scott, rather than crying in the courtroom audience, sitting by my grave and wondering why.

Again, my anger grows. But this time my fury festers not at the army but at Julie alone. I cannot allow her to do this again.

"What if the next person does not have what I have? Does not have parents and a brother and a family that will come with her to court? Does not have friends that will hold her hand through the darkest of despair? Does not have a job that heals her every day? What if she doesn't have a husband who sits with her through sleepless nights and quiets her shaking body?"

I feel as if I am down on my knees and that I am begging, that I am holding desperately to the ends of Maier's black robe, looking up to her, blue eye to blue eye. I am pleading to her. I think of the words spoken on my behalf before me and I imagine that it is not just me kneeling, but my entire army.

"I have many people in this room to thank for my survival. I have needed them. After all, I have lived through a lot in my life. This did not happen to an 'at risk youth'. It happened to someone with too much to lose. This did not happen to Jane Doe. It happened to me, Kristen Lewis Cunnane."

I look at Maier and she cannot help herself any longer. She turns her head to the side and the corners of her lips draw to a smile that could define compassion. If she could, she would tell me that she is proud of me.

I imagine her now, lifting the boulder off of my back that has led me to kneel before her. She takes my hand and I stand upright, speaking fully in my twenty-nine-year-old adult and capable voice.

"Our society must look at what Julie did to me as we would look at a man jumping out of the bushes on my way home from court today, holding me down, and raping me. Far too terrified to say no, much too young to say yes, what Julie did was rape me: over and over again, in her office, in her car, in her apartment, on the carpet of my closet, on the sheets of my childhood bed. Yes, she comes in a different package, but make no mistake about who she is. To me, she doesn't deserve to breathe the air that you and I do. Julie is not sorry for what she did. She even says so on the phone calls. She is only sorry that she got caught. Julie took something from me that she can never give back and, for that, she should lose her freedom."

"I ask you that you weigh my pain and loss in considering the maximum possible sentence for Julie Correa. Once my coach, teacher, and mentor, now the admitted molester and rapist that she is."

"Thank you for allowing me to be a part of this process and for allowing my wound and word to be heard."

Just as the people before me did, I take a moment to collect my papers and the rest of my proof. I look at Maier and I wonder if I look as tired as she does. I turn my body and face my people. Instead of looking at them individually, I see them as a whole— the panoramic picture of the people who gave me my life back and taught me how to walk again.

My knees feel as though they are made of Play-Doh, but I make it back to Scott. He puts his arm behind my body around my shoulder. He pulls me close to his center and lowers his mouth to my ear: "You were amazing."

With Scott holding me, I feel my shoulder blades sink deeply into my frame. I feel heavy in my seat. The spinning of my insides stops, and I feel completely still. *Is this the solstice that mountain climbers feel at their summit?*

"We will take a break before we come back for any finishing comments." As Maier and her staff retreat to chambers, I am surprised that my stomach does not turn in anticipation of what will come.

"I did everything I could," I say almost silently to Scott. My whole body feels the truth of my statement, not just in speaking to the judge, but in living through the process of bringing Julie to justice and in living through the darkness of the abuse.

I did everything I could. Now I will see if it was enough.

CHAPTER FORTY

Fly

The air smells still and cold. The darkness of night surrounds me as I begin my march. My feet move, not because they want to, but because they know that they have to. The orange streetlights paint the cement below, and I make no effort to hide from their illumination.

I am headed up my hill. It is February 19, 2000, a day after my eighteenth birthday. As I pass the familiar homes of my neighbors, I do not care if they see me tonight. In fact, maybe a tiny part of me hopes that they will. Perhaps they can be witnesses.

I had hoped that you might just go away. But in my heart I think I always knew that would never happen. I have refused to talk to you since late October. Since then you have followed me everywhere. Even so, life is better than I ever dreamed it could be. And now is the time to banish you completely, to remove the final chains.

My legs feel sturdy and strong. They connect me to the slope of the ground below. I stand upright and breathe in the free night air. I think of nights before, and remember traveling this same path. Like a scurrying mouse constantly looking for cover, I darted up the hill to you, the biggest trap of them all. And now I do not hide. Instead, I think of all of the things that I have to live for.

Scott gave me concert tickets and a silver bracelet for my birthday. I love his presents, but I love the fact that he picks them out himself even more. I didn't know that it was possible to love so many things about a single person.

Last night, on my actual birthday, my parents let me have my first ever boy-girl sleepover. I didn't really even have to beg for it. I just asked and they said it was okay. After all, it's better than the parties when no parents are home. At least they wouldn't allow alcohol.

My house was packed last night. And my friends, both boys and girls, stayed over. It was a much different scene for my eighteenth birthday than you had programmed in my head. Instead of you taking me away to a far off land, I was at home, surrounded by people my age, embraced by the person who matters much more than you ever will.

"Come on, let's go up to your room," Scott had said with a sliver of mischief in his eye and a dimple pulling deeply into his left cheek. Last night around midnight, when people had started to go to bed, Scott saw his opportunity. "No one will notice," he promised.

"What if my parents hear us?" I had said to Scott, thinking of my sleeping mom and dad upstairs. But as I questioned Scott with my words, I never questioned him with my heart.

"We can be really quiet," he said with a smile, and he didn't stop to wonder why I never smiled back.

I followed Scott last night, just as I have been following him for the past four months. He led me by the hand, up the stairs, and I felt relieved as his foot creaked on the second stair from the bottom.

We slid into my room, which has been growing increasingly neat. Scott promptly opened his hooded sweatshirt and pulled out my birthday presents. He didn't need to tell me that he had wrapped them himself. We sat at the end of my bed, which I have repositioned in the recent months. Before I opened the bright blue wrapping paper, I read the card. On the front was an old-time photo of a blue-eyed boy kissing a blond-haired girl on the cheek. On the inside, the words that made me melt into him, the same words that I read just before leaving tonight: "I love you."

And so, before I knew that I was getting a bracelet or concert tickets, we made love. It wasn't the first time, although it always feels like it is. He didn't rush me or push me into it. It just happened because it was supposed to happen.

Every time I am with Scott, I feel as if he washes me a little cleaner. When he teases me, I feel you leaving my soul. When he touches me, I forget that you ever did. And the closer we get, the deeper the scrub.

I am not sure if my parents know that Scott spent the night in my room last night or not. I think that they might be suspicious because they caught him walking down the stairs this morning. But I don't really care. I want them to like him, but it's not like he will go to prison for staying the night in my room.

As I pass the dip of the last driveway before the top of the hill, I know that you will be here. Before I see your car, I know that you will be at the top of the hill waiting for me. Probably a hundred times or more, you have said: "If something goes wrong, I'll meet you at the top of the hill on your eighteenth birthday." My birthday was yesterday, but I know that you will be here. Again.

I look to the left and I am proved right immediately. The tail-lights of your Subaru station wagon are asleep, and I wonder if the engine has had time to cool off yet. I cross the center of the sleepy four-way intersection with poise. I look intently at the bushes and the fence and get power from the usual hiding spot.

I can see the back of your head. The scraggly hair that you never tie back has a low profile in the driver's seat. You are crouched low, so that in the unlikely event that a car drives past you, you can quickly disappear. *I hate you.*

I press my back molars together and take a brief moment to fill my nostrils and lungs with a full breath. I stand tall at the passenger side door and let the air out as I open the handle to the unknown.

The smell hits me and nearly knocks me over. For a single heartbeat, I think of slamming the door and running straight down the hill, up my stairs, and blurting the whole truth to my mom. But I can picture the look on her face, the utter devastation, and I have no choice but to do this myself.

I can barely look over at you, but I know I have to. My eyes fall on the skeleton of who you used to be. You looked bad on the running trail, but tonight you look far worse, almost dead.

"Oh . . ." It's more of a breath than a word. I feel your exhale on the left side of my neck. "Oh, thank God you're here," you say and let out your toxicity. I wonder if you have held your breath for almost four months. I also wonder what God you now believe in.

I shake my head "yes" and make no noise because I am scared that I will scream so loud that the Moraga Police Department might hear me five miles across town.

"I waited here all night last night." *I know you did.* "I thought that you would meet me the night of your birthday. I thought that was the plan." You run your sentences together in the most frantic way possible. "I have been going absolutely crazy. I have been going insane. I don't know what to think. I don't know what to do with myself."

You are driving now and I realize that you are accelerating down the steep hill away from my house. You grip the wheel and, in the hue of the dashboard lights, I can see every vein in your hand.

I have heard that you are going crazy, but not from you. The other day, as I was driving with my mom, she turned to me and said, "Do you ever hear anything from Natali anymore? Like, do you ever see her at sporting events at Campo to watch former students?" I could feel her watching me out of the corner of her eye.

Although my stomach had turned with the sound of your name, it felt good to not have to lie to my mom. "No, I haven't talked to her in a long time. I think that you were right about her. She is a little weird," I said, returning the corner-of-the-eye stare.

My mom had continued on: "Well, apparently she is really struggling. She has lost a ton of weight and everyone I talk to asks me if I know what is going on. Like, she might have cancer, or something really bad is going on."

Or something really good. "Well, that's a shame," I replied, reverting back to my lying ways.

We are turning out of my neighborhood and onto the main street. You take the turn much too fast, which causes my unbuckled body to lean toward you. "Come here, sweetie," you say and use the momentum of the car to reach out to me.

My spine becomes erect in defiance of the centripetal force. "I can't get near you. I am really sick," I say as I look at the blurred trees out of the window. As you drive the car, I know this is not the time to take control of the situation. "I am just going to sleep until we get there."

Without talking about it, we both know where we are going. You have always said that you would book a room at The Claremont for when I turn eighteen. "It is the only place nice enough to celebrate," you always said in regards to the single five-star hotel in our area. Now as you drive to The Claremont, I have my eyes open only a millimeter. I know this is not how you fantasized it to be.

You grip the wheel tighter and tighter, and with each clamp of your hand, I am surprised that you are physically able to apply any more pressure. Just slightly, you begin to rock back and forth. And as you do, you say in the tiniest voice, "What am I going to do?" Your voice is a near whisper and it sounds as if you are crying. But from the peephole of my eyes, I know that your face is dry.

Do you know that this is almost over? I think that you do. You are smart enough to see the writing on the wall. If you are certain, it would be much better to kill me now and kill the possibility of being caught. I watch you carefully in case you reach under your seat and grab the gun I have convinced myself you keep there. Your hands remain on the wheel.

You drive because you have to. You have to take me to the room and you have to hope that I am still your slave. You are too sick for any other option. You must be absolutely sure that this is absolutely over.

Besides your rumbling, the car is quiet. I lean near the door with my hand ready to pounce for the door handle at a moment's notice. The car speeds, my mind prepares, and within ten short minutes we have arrived.

I have seen The Claremont before. It sits at the start of the Berkeley hills and overlooks Cal and the San Francisco Bay area. Its perfectly white exterior is elitist even from an airplane overhead. We pass the entrance, which boasts an odd juxtaposition of redwoods and palm trees. My heart clenches when you do not pull in, and I move my hand an inch closer to the door handle. I open my eyes fully now and you think that I have awoken, when really I am just getting ready.

Your wheels point to the right and we follow a road that perimeters the hotel. You accelerate up the street and turn right again into a back parking lot. "I found this entrance yesterday." You sound proud of yourself, as you always do when you have discovered a new and twisted way of hiding me. You pull past the white arm of the gate that has opened to let you in. My eyes lock on the video camera that monitors the comers and goers of the hotel. I hope someone is in the security booth tonight.

Once the car is parked, I do not wait for you to check the surroundings. I promptly get out of the car. You come to my side of the car and are surprised to find me already standing outside of the car door. Your worry heightens.

You turn your back to me and, again, I think of running. The sound of your jacket, the hover of your body, forces my hands into fists and I am determined to stay here and fight you.

You lead me through an inconspicuous white door on the side of the imposing building. I look longingly at the guest entrance to the left. "There's a service elevator here that we can take." Your whisper makes me sick. "No one will see you. No one will know you are here," you say, as if we are special agents on the same mission. I do what you say, while I hope that just a single guest needs to make a midnight run to the convenience store.

Walking past half-filled laundry bins that the maids push up and down the hallway, we make our way to the service elevator. Before my eyes is a worn and overworked space that stands in contrast to what I envisioned this hotel to be. I guess that in the morning hours the air is warm with the smell of freshly washed sheets and busy with the hurry of getting rooms ready for the next guest. Getting ready for me.

The elevator pulls us up to the sixth floor. I try to memorize everything about everything, although I don't really even know the point of this. The service elevator opens to a hallway of printed brown and gold carpet—much too busy for my taste.

We are here. I know because you stop squarely in front of the white door and reach into the front pocket of your rain jacket. You turn and look at me, in hopes of a reading that will tell what will come next. But I stare stonefaced ahead and wait to enter.

The room is beautiful, although I wish we were in a ware-house. Two overstuffed, oversized, and likely overpriced chairs occupy the opposing corners. The furniture is cherry wood, which I know to be expensive. My mom inherited cherry wood furniture from her wealthy great aunt and still has it in her bedroom. I quickly bring my mind off of my mom. The walls are a dark gold with lighter gold stripes, and I take the time to look at them and wonder if they are painted or if they are wallpaper.

I linger at the door and let you enter further than I. You sit on the bed, and a fan belt in me starts to turn. I think of Washington, DC. I think of UNO in your room. I look at you now, much thinner than you were four years ago. There is no fat to soften your soul. And without the extra weight, your evil has nowhere to hide. I see the king bed, I see you, and I know that your sick mind has, and always has had, a plan.

I look past you momentarily to gain further strength. Past you and your bed is a large white-framed window dressed with velvet curtains that puddle heavily on the ground. I am both surprised and grateful that you have not pulled them closed. I am also glad to see who I see sitting there.

Eve, perched with her little body on the little sill, looks smaller than she usually looks. I realize I have not seen her or let myself look at her for a long time. She wraps herself in the drape for warmth and I smile knowing that you cannot see her. Our matching eyes meet, and she shakes her head. Just one time. A single nod to let me know that she believes in me. That I am ready and that she is ready, too.

I am suddenly deeply aware of space and distance. My primitive brain accesses my surroundings without forethought. You are between me and the window on the bed. I am closer to the door than you, which is latched with the chain of the extra security lock. Across from the bed there is a desk. On it is a small CD player that spins with music you think I like, but actually makes my ears bleed. The volume is on low; you left it playing while you came to get me. I wonder if you had it on last night. I know that you were here last night.

Almost touching the CD player is a gift bag, which I know contains my birthday present. I know I will never open it. There are dark and unlit candles on the desk, and I wonder fleetingly if there are matches hidden somewhere that I could use to light your hair on fire.

"Come here, sweetie," you say and your voice is hollow, as if it has traveled down a long hallway to get to me.

"I told you . . . I am sick. I have a really high fever," I say, and I look at Eve whose eyes approve of the continuing tactics.

"Just come here, honey." Your voice has turned to a beg. You pat the bed next to you.

"If you cared about me, you wouldn't want me to do things when I am sick," I say with a sense of defiance in my voice. I think of the "things" and dig my heels into the carpet beneath my still feet.

"I just want to hold you . . ." Your voice trails off, and I watch you start to cry. And this is not a fake cry, it is a cry that comes from deep in your center and results in wet and heavy tears. You pull your legs to the center of your body so that you are only a ball toward the bottom of the bed.

I do not go to you. The cells of my body will not allow it.

Instead, I back into the chair closest to the door and once again fake sleep. I have tried this before, pretending to be sick. And you have always done a version of what you are doing now—unraveling as though something catastrophic has happened to you. You have always won this battle: I have always eventually caved to you and whatever you have wanted to do to me. But now I won't give you an inch. My cells have grown strong and I will not let you touch me.

I calm my body into the fabric of the chair, but my mind is sharp as I watch you. Your nasty hair streams in front of your face and falls out of the circle of your body. You pull your arms out of your fetal position and bring them to your temples. Just as you grabbed my head on the trail, you grab your own head. Although my eyes are just barely open, I can see your hands clamp on your hair and begin to pull it away from your head. My eyes want to grow wide as I witness this new behavior. You are a maniac.

You know that I am awake. You must. You rip at your hair in hopes that it will rip at my heart. But you can no longer reach my heart: Scott owns it. And you are incapable of reaching me.

As I sit and you decompose, the seconds tick to minutes and the minutes roll into more than a full hour. My lips touch loosely, and I know in this time you are realizing the truth. I am patient and I watch carefully as your emotions drain your energy.

"Okay," I say, and I allow my voice to sound like the adult that I have newly become. "Take me home." I stand and I feel as I am towering. I look to Eve, and she looks more like a fairy than a human now. She stands straight but can still fit within the frame of her window. I cannot see them, but somehow I think that she might have a soft and silky pair of wings.

"No," you say and hang on to the "o" much too long. Your lip turns into a pout and you glare at me. Your eyes seem as though they have sunk to the back of your head.

"Take me home. Now." I allow myself to look through you. I see you only as a pile of skin and bones. I move closer to the door.

"No . . . Don't do this. No, I won't let you go." You come out of your ball completely and put your feet on the ground in dispute.

I know I can make it to the door if I need to. I look at Eve, and we both believe I will win tonight. Eve looks at me and tells me exactly what to say: "Take me home right now. Take me home or I will walk down to the front desk and tell them . . . everything. I will tell them what you have been doing."

As if I have a rope that reaches inside your chest cavity, I rip your heart out. The rope burns your esophagus as I make this threat. Here on the hotel floor: a smoldering piece of lava as proof of who you are and what this has been.

Your tears stop. Your rocking stops. You stop.

You stand up and look at me and you know. The window is open only a sliver, just enough for your hope to fly out. And along with your hope, out slips my angel named Eve. I look over my shoulder as I have turned to the door in hopes of seeing her one final time. But she is already gone.

We leave the hotel the same way we came. I twirl my ponytail in an effort to leave a strand or two of hair behind, just in case you do not do as you are told.

The car is silent, and turn after turn we make the way toward my hill and toward my house. I am not sure if you notice, but I try to touch the car in as many places as I can, leaving evidence of my identity. Still, my right hand never drifts too far from the handle, and I am very conscious that should I need to, I would confidently throw myself to the asphalt.

Finally, we get to my hill. I look at the parking complex where you have hidden so many times, waiting for my parents' car so that you can safely sneak into my home. The engine pulls us to the top of the hill, to the intersection. You circle around, and we are back to the place where this all started.

The car slows and comes to a park. I know what I must do to rid you from my life. "I won't tell anyone," I say and I am certain that I will not. Although it feels as though my arm weighs a thousand pounds, I lift it and put my hand softly on your shoulder. My entire body is tense, but I relax my palm, trying to convince you of my words.

You do not respond. You do not say anything at all. You stare into the emptiness of the night and of your future. But you relax a little with my touch. Your shoulders drop an inch, and I know that you won't be following me any longer.

"I guess this is goodbye," I say and take my hand off of you purposefully so as to avoid the end that usually happens.

"I guess this is goodbye . . . forever." You match my words and confirm my sense that I will not see you again.

I pull the car handle open for the last time. "Never say forever," I say back to you. You look at me and your lips pull into a hopeless smile. And as I close the car door, I know that someday we will meet again.

I stride from your car, across the four-way intersection. As I move farther from your car, I am relieved that with each step there is not a bullet in the back of my brain. I walk down the hill with even more brazen confidence than I walked up it. Hurrying from light to light, looking to be out of the dark.

Up the moss-ridden brick steps and toward my home, I choose not to sneak around the back and enter my house the usual way. Instead, I walk to the front door and step right in.

It is dark and I am not loud, but I am not quiet, either. I move much more quickly than usual as I approach the steps. As I begin to climb them, I feel a sliver of sadness in my soul. *Am I sad about you? Am I sad to have seen what you really are?* I know the answer to both questions and the answers are both no.

I think of my dear friend with the dark hair and the street smarts. I think of her standing in the heat of your fire. I think of all of the things about her that I love, her fortitude and her faith, and I know I will miss them. I hope that she did not fall out of that window to a lonely and pointless death below. I hope she flew away and I hope that she is finally safe.

But by the time I reach the final stair to turn to my room, I allow Eve to fly out of my memory as she did The Claremont window. And as she leaves my memory, you do, too. My house looks clean and feels warm and protected, just as it always should have. I pass a family photo on my left and in the darkness I know exactly what it looks like. Just as I smile in the still shot, I smile in my heart. I think that nothing bad has ever happened to me in my entire life. I am certain that you never existed. I am sure that I have never been abused. And I know what my future holds.

CHAPTER FORTY-ONE

The End . . . and the Beginning

"Pee-pee! Come meet your friend poo-poo!"

Tears fill my eyes immediately as I begin to laugh and cry at the same time. The kind of laugh that isn't a courtesy, but an uncontrollable and unpredictable reflex, similar to a cough or a sneeze.

The kind of laugh only solicited by a two and a half year old sitting on the potty.

My laugh is matched by hers and, as she looks at me, she begins giggling uncontrollably with squinted eyes and tiny teeth. It is Thanksgiving Day, and while twenty members of our family are enjoying the best turkey on earth, I sit on the hard honeycombed pattern tile of our bathroom floor and wait for the next joke to come out of my Annie's silly mouth.

"You are my funny girl. I love being your mommy," I say with my forehead tilted toward hers.

"I love being your Annie," she says in her toddler voice and matches my move, pressing her forehead into mine. She looks up into my eyes with her beautiful blues. Her blond hair, stringy from a full day of horseplay without a wink of a nap, falls from behind her ears.

I scoop her up, wipe her up, and as she clings to my neck, I feel full with more than mashed potatoes.

Clutching Annie in her silver sparkly princess dress, I leave the bathroom to find Scott, wanting to share the hilarity of our daughter with him. I find him sitting at the Thanksgiving table, baby spoon in hand facing a high chair and making an O with his mouth.

As he makes the spoon into an airplane, I am saturated with how much I love Scott. How much I love him for who he has been for me and who he is now as a father. How much I love him for how he opens his own mouth when trying to convince our six-month-old Billy to take a bite of food.

My eyes are lifted to see our home, our beautiful and big and amazing house, that we moved into just over a year ago. It has been nearly four years since Julie Correa was sentenced, and my life is starkly different. For a brief moment I am transported back to judgment day.

"I took home the prosecution's packet first and spent quite a bit of time on it that I don't have time for during my day," Judge Maier had said that day, looking sad. "Then I did the same with the defense's packet of materials. The weekend was very hard for me." I didn't think it would be hard for her; I thought that her decision should be easy.

"And I first tried to make a decision and living with it, and then I decided not to and just let the facts sit with me."

My tummy had rumbled in nerves.

"I saw incredible speaking here in the past two days. What I heard, I have to say, Ms. Grossman presented an amazing packet of materials. She's a very good defense attorney. She is a professional. Both attorneys were passionate and very eloquent. The speakers were so moving and persuasive. I don't think there was a person in this courtroom that wasn't moved. I know all of the staff had to, when we left bench, had to deal with our own emotions connected with the intensity of this case."

"So the struggle that I had—and I'll describe it—is that I'm being given basically two different versions of the facts. The one from Ms. Correa is almost Romeo and Juliet, or should I say Juliet and Juliet, two star-crossed lovers, destined for one another." I had gagged at the Juliet Juliet comment.

"And the side I hear from the victim is that Ms. Correa is a Svengali. She's presenting herself to the outside world as a wonderful teacher who goes above and beyond the call of duty by being around students at all hours, and yet she is secretly plotting incessantly to ensnare an innocent girl into a relationship that is a pseudonym for years of molestation."

"The other salient factor that has been emphasized by the defense is the defendant's children's loss of their mother. Clearly, Will and Marco have suffered in this past year and will suffer immeasurably from the time without their mother in their daily lives."

I had clung to Scott that day as Maier conceded that these two boys were factors in her decision.

"Ms. Correa's supporters, her parents, her colleagues, paint a persuasive picture of a talented, intelligent woman who excelled in athletics and was very committed to her students."

"The victim's family and friends, Kristen's family and friends, paint a much different picture, that of a girl whose life was ripped to thunder by the predation of a morally depraved human being."

"To solve this riddle and to tease apart these sides to see which side was presenting the fiction was initially difficult for me. I finally decided to look at this incident and how it developed from the perspective of a middle school student."

"I have a sister who is a teacher. And we have both discussed the awesome and fearsome power that we both wield in our respective positions. We have both discussed the need to constantly remind ourselves that our words can have an impact much greater than we realize. My sister speaks to me of how she guards herself from speaking to a child in anger. She calls it barking at them. She knows that a child's day could be ruined. My sister speaks to me, also, of how the children have crushes on her, both boys and girls. And when she says that, she is not speaking at all in the way that we, as adults, would look at a crush. She is talking about loving, adoring, seeking to emulate, seeking to have that person love them and find them special. That's what that child wants, and that's what that child would give anything to have that special, important adult do for them."

Julie was that person for me! I had wanted to yell out loud that day four years ago.

"So many girls . . . remember middle school as the worst years of their life. Middle school girls are struggling with their identity. They are struggling with conformity. They want to fit in more than anything in the world, and they are taking their first steps to independence. They are seeking to differentiate from their parents' values. They start to care more about their peers' opinion of themselves rather than their parents'."

"Ms. Julie Correa sought to make herself one of their peers. She not only breached many boundaries with the victim, but there were many warning signs beforehand."

Scott had stretched his back up straight in attention and I knew that he liked where Maier was headed.

"The duty of a teacher is to respect the boundaries of the teacher/student relationship. Teachers are almost like rock stars to their students. Students have crushes. Students may even behave in inappropriate ways. But it is the teacher's responsibility to understand the child's perspective and to protect the child at all costs from any inappropriate connection."

Maier drew in a deep breath and looked at me: "And I want to emphasize, again, that the child did not put that out there. It's the teacher that construed it as an inappropriate connection. I want to make clear to—to Kristen that nothing she did caused what happened here. Ms. Correa breached that promise; even if you believe her statement that the victim wanted the relationship, it was the teacher's job to prevent it from occurring. And the truth is Ms. Correa is the one who wanted the relationship."

"Ms. Correa is the one who created an inappropriate environment for not only the victim, but for many girls in middle school. Ms. Correa, essentially, still blames the victim."

Suddenly there was an anger about Maier not present before.

"Several speakers noted this, but I saw the quotes from Ms. Correa's statement as quite striking and, actually, helpful in seeing the legal fiction that she created. The quotes I wrote down were, 'What I believe is my truth about our past connection.' This is not connection. This is a molestation. This is the beginning of her letter. She still characterizes molestation as her 'past connection'. The reason—and I'm quoting—is that 'it was never my intention to hurt you. I cared deeply for you and always wanted to do what was best for you, regardless of my own needs'."

Maier had put her notes down and had looked at the courtroom in front of her: "Have you ever heard a more hypocritical statement?"

She brought her notes back in front of her petite and pretty nose: "Why did I allow the relationship to happen? I believed that you are mature enough to make your own decisions." Maier slammed her paper down and looked at Julie: "That's a fictional construct. There is no teacher on this planet that has the right to make that statement to any student, ever."

Scott squeezed my hand and leaned his head toward mine.

"The defendant must have been aware that she started to have inappropriate feelings for this victim, perhaps, for years;

and yet, Ms. Correa failed to seek help. She did not say, 'Ah, this is uncomfortable. I do not like what's going on here. I've met an eleven-year-old, and I feel some feelings. I'm watching her turn twelve and starting to touch her, to ask her to be closer to me. I'm looking at her at thirteen and I think of her as somebody I want to have sex with; then there is something wrong with me. I better go get help.' No, she didn't. She had years to make this decision to not take this to the direction that she did. And yet she did not stop it."

"Circumstances and aggravation under Rule 4.421(a), the crime did involve a high degree of callousness. The victim was particularly vulnerable. The manner in which the crime was carried out indicates planning, sophistication, and the defendant clearly took advantage of a position of trust to commit the offense."

"The circumstances in mitigation, Rule 4.423, the defendant has no prior record. And I say this hesitantly, the defendant has apparently not re-offended since this occurred."

"The additional circumstance which was extremely hard for me and painful to reconcile is that two young boys will suffer the loss of their mother at a time when they, too, will be receptive to outside forces. Ironically, the oldest of the defendant's two sons is almost eleven, the age of the victim when she first met the defendant."

"The defendant will have no opportunity to monitor her sons' relationships with teachers, with coaches, with Boy Scout leaders to see if she notes an overly friendly friend."

My eyes were drawn that day to the back of Julie's head. It was never my intent to take a mother away from her sons.

"Ironically, this defendant has denied for herself by her actions, not by this Court's sentence, the opportunity to be a guide to her sons in this time in their lives when teachers and peers become powerful influences."

Maier had slowed the cadence of her speech, emphasizing her next words: "I want to note that Ms. Correa was originally charged with crimes that, if convicted and sentenced consecutively, she could have spent over 100 years in state prison."

How different my life would look if I never had to worry about a free Julie Correa.

"My sentence is as follows: I am designating Count Four, a violation of Penal Code section 289(a), to be the base term. I am imposing the middle term of six years, and I'm running that consecutively with one-third the midterm of Counts One, Two, and Five, violations of Penal Code section 288(c)(1), for a total of eight years in state prison."

Not sure who grabbed me first, but my body was wrapped in the arms of the army around me.

My eyes are drawn back to the current scene of my full Thanksgiving table. Four years since she was sentenced, four years until she gets released. *How are we already at halfway?*

I try to absorb the happiness of Thanksgiving. I listen to the joyful banter of our growing family and try to dismiss Julie Correa from my mind.

As I spot the marbled grey granite countertops of the kitchen, I am loosely aware that my home looks different than it should, than those of my friends. As I survey the scene, I know why I have this home.

Once the sentencing was over, I agreed to have my whole story told in the local Contra Costa newspaper. As they prepared to write the story, they requested documents from the Moraga School District, the content of which was devastating.

"Kristen, you will not believe what we found," Matthias Gafni, the reporter handling the story, had said after I had slid my iPhone to answer.

I had stood that day, still as a statue on the hardwood floor. Time stopped, and if I didn't know better, I would have sworn that my heart stopped beating, too.

"They knew. Kristen, they knew what was going on." Matthias delivered his words with as much softness and kindness as possible.

"What do you mean?" I had managed to ask, almost breathless.

"Walters knew that Witters was abusing girls. There is a letter from a high schooler in 1994 warning Walters of Witters's behavior."

As I stood in wonderment, I remembered Mr. Walters, our oversized bear of a principal. I thought he was a good guy and always remembered how to spell "principal" because he was our "pal."

"Kristen, there is evidence of so many warning signs. The school allowed for this culture. The school allowed this to happen to you. It's unbelievable." Mathias pressed on. I was lightly aware that this kind soul had become my friend through our hours of interviews.

We would come to find out that there was ample evidence that the Moraga School District had turned a blind eye to various abusive situations and inappropriate conduct by teachers.

As a child, I was betrayed by my teachers. As an adult, I saw that my betrayal could have been stopped.

What could have been sadness boiled in my veins as anger.

In the following weeks, Scott and I walked the dogs and spoke almost exclusively about our options for holding the administration, the people who were supposed to protect me, accountable. We made a decision, and that decision started with Marc.

"Marc," I had said in a more serious tone than I typically used for my brother. "We need to do something about this," only vaguely caring what others would eventually think of me.

"Let's make those bastards pay for all this pain. None of this should have happened in the first place." Marc replied an octave too loudly.

Having my own brother's newly founded firm represent me in my civil case was not a choice; it was the only option. With love and care, he and his law partner led me through every hill and valley.

"Kristen, I need to talk to you about the school district's response to our claim," Paul had said on the phone a few months after my original call to Marc. Paul had taken the lead on my case so that my brother could mostly be my brother and Paul could mostly be my attorney. As I listened and wondered at Paul's words, my world stopped once again.

"What?" I managed a single word. I stood still on the shag carpet of Aunt Judy's house in Utah. Briefly, I forgot about the rampant morning sickness my pregnancy with Annie had brought me.

"They are blaming you. They are saying that our suit is frivolous because you were a contributing partner in the relationship. Basically, they are saying it is your fault the abuse occurred," Paul said with a soft and quiet voice in his British accent.

But didn't we just prove that it wasn't my fault in the criminal case? I thought that it was impossible for it to be a fourteen-year-old's fault.

Paul had continued on that day to soften the blow and give me a play by play of the next legal hearing, but I couldn't hear him. I could only see my tears fall on my swollen belly and listen to my thoughts. *Will this battle ever really end?*

With more ups and downs than I could have ever predicted, the civil battle did end, though the war of pain will never truly be over.

"They have agreed to settle at $2.85 million," Paul had announced over the phone. I was standing in my office at Cal when my phone rang. When I saw that it was Paul calling, I knew what he was going to say. It had been months of trying to settle with the insurance companies for the Moraga School District. Their first offer was $100,000.

"Really?" I could not believe it was over. I stood up and looked out across the pool from my towering office. It was dusk and the sun was setting. With only a few lap swimmers, the pool looked peaceful.

"Yes. And if you are okay with it, we will go ahead and accept. Talk to Scott. Think about it. And let me know tomorrow," Paul had said, and I could feel his pride.

"We did it, Krick!" Marc's voice came in as he clicked on to speakerphone, more than a year after our first business call.

"I'll talk to Scott," I had said. "But this sounds fair." I knew then, as I know now, that no dollar amount could make me wonder whether the pain was worthwhile.

After all, I am always aware that the pain almost won. "I don't know exactly how to feel about this," I had managed to say.

"Feel proud, Kristen." Marc uses my name in full.

"Remember," Paul chimes in, "this won't affect the students. This will be paid by the insurance companies."

I had taken a little bit deeper of a breath in relief.

And so, within days of giving birth to Annie, Scott and I sat on our front porch as a courier on a motorcycle walked up with our portion, a check for $1.78 million.

We sat on the money for a while. Our life stayed exactly the same other than a few extra bank accounts with lots of zeros and not having to think twice about what we ordered from Amazon.

It's nice to not have to worry about money as we used to. It's hard to have people say things like, "You don't need to work because you don't need the money." It's frustrating when people treat us differently.

The money we have is a signal of our small victory. You can't put a school district in prison. But I would be lying if I didn't say that I am a tad sensitive about the money. I would give it back with interest if my ankles never hurt again, if I didn't have extra worry about my kids' babysitters, or if I was able to go to my childhood house—which I still can barely think about.

There were other victims in the civil lawsuit against the school district. These victims, all of whom were abused by Witters, elected to remain anonymous under the Jane Doe Moniker. I felt far away from these women and yearned for a sense of solidarity with them. But my name was public and their names were not. Months after I settled, the school district awarded two of the victims a settlement more than twice as large as mine.

Just over a year ago, we found it. We were looking through the real estate listings on Scott's phone, just as we had hundreds of times before. On our final night of vacation at a cabin in the Sierra foothills, Scott and I cuddled on a couch while Annie slept in her crib directly above us.

"Let's check it out," I had said to Scott and looked out of the corner of my eye at him, hopeful that he would be willing. Scott had never liked going to open houses like I do.

"Yeah, we have to. It looks amazing."

And it was. Filthy and tired from a week's vacation with one-year-old Annie, we stopped at the open house on our way home. Complete with a pool, old oaks, a tire swing, and more square footage than we will ever need, sat our estate. A place to put our money, a place to see the fruits of our labor, it was a home to find our peace.

"We are going to need to have lots of babies to fill up this house," Scott said, pulling me close in the family room during the open house. I had looked at him to see his usual dimples and a twinkle in his eye.

We bought it two days later.

I pause in my memory to survey the scene around me: The closest members of my army, my family, laughing and building memories together in my home. The babies Scott and I have already added to this space, giggling like monkeys and sporting Scott's dimples. I take a deep breath and blink back tears.

"No. Way." Scott had looked at me in amazement. We had moved in only two weeks earlier, but almost every box had been unpacked on account of my obsessiveness.

"Can you believe it?!" I had squealed. The house seemed silent during Annie's nap.

Scott wrapped his arms—the same arms that I fell in love with in high school—around me and we stood looking at the two lines of the home pregnancy test.

"I looked it up and I have the same due date I had with Annie: May 6th. They will be exactly two years apart."

"So how far along are you? Do you feel okay?" Scott asked quickly, being fully aware of my acute morning sickness with Annie that lasted more than the morning and most of the pregnancy.

"I think six weeks and I feel great," I said with pep in my voice.

That would all end soon, though, as I became very ill with my pregnancy. Nausea and vomiting gave way to weight loss and fatigue. Plus, keeping up with my Annie proved to be a hard battle. But I had battled far worse.

And so the month passed, my belly finally grew once again, and in March, I marched with the Cal team to the NCAA Championships in Greensboro, North Carolina.

As I stood at Teri's side once again to accept our 2015 NCAA Championship trophy, tears fell fast and hard from my eyes. I would try to take a deep breath, but my crying would not slow.

Even then, I didn't know exactly why I was crying. Was I happy or sad? Amazed or relieved? Perhaps it was because we hadn't won an NCAA Championship since 2012. Perhaps it was because we had some of the best swimmers in the world and we figured out a way to have them perform at their best and make each other better. Perhaps I was just exhausted, eight months pregnant and swollen everywhere after three days of standing on a pool deck at a swim meet. Perhaps, deep down and against my strongest personal desires, I knew it was my last.

The job that saved my life, that healed me, that showed me there was a different way, became the wrong job for me. Either that, or I became the wrong person for the job. Or maybe it was both. Either way, with two tiny people to look after, traveling across the country for meets, recruiting, waking up early for morning workouts, and staying late for team dinners got increasingly difficult.

I tell people that it was the hardest decision I have ever made, leaving Cal. And it was. I am always met by a sideways tilt of the head and an unspoken question of "don't you remember how hard everything else was?"

And if there were volume to the conversation I would say, "Yes. I remember. But none of that—reporting to police, making phone calls, the civil suit—was a choice. That was surviving."

So weeks after having Billy, I had a scheduled phone call with Teri.

"Hi, Kristen, I am going to let you start," Teri had said on the other end of the phone.

Without wanting them to, tears returned to my eyes and, in skipping the small talk, I said, "I don't think I am the right person for you anymore. I don't think that the job is right for me anymore."

"Okay, take a deep breath. I know," Teri had said in a calm and slow tone. We continued on for more than an hour and finished in agreement that it was the right choice.

Leaving Cal felt wrong in so many ways. I imagine it is what it feels like to break up with someone when you are no longer in love but still love deeply. It hurt. It physically hurt. Like ripping off a worn and tattered Band-Aid.

But just as the exposed wound may bleed at first, it eventually scabs and scars and heals. I think that there will always be a mark.

Sitting back at the Thanksgiving table, I know I have so much to live for as Scott says, "Let's all go around and say what we are thankful for." Certain that in most families, this would have been done before the feast, I am glad that we are not most families.

Annie wiggles off my lap to go visit her Grandma and tell her the latest joke she made up in the bathroom. The instant she leaves, Billy reaches across his high chair and leans for his mom. My arms are not empty more than a moment.

As I bounce Billy on my lap and listen to the gratitude lists of others, I wonder how it would ever be possible to summarize what I am thankful for. I begin to make a list in my head.

As the tallies grow, I battle. Chuck called this part of me Chicken Little. I often have a hard time enjoying the happiness and magic of today as I am worried "when the next shoe is going to drop," as Chuck puts it.

My kids are amazing, but what if something bad happens to one of them? What if Julie gets out of prison and comes for me? And comes for them? My life is great right now . . . I want to press pause!

I tell myself that all of the pain I have faced has been worth it and all the pain I may face in the future will be, too. And as Annie comes barreling into my lap, and both my arms are full, I know that my heart is, too.

It is my turn to talk, and with a single word and swoop of my hand I say: *"This."*

Mountains to Climb

As I unbuckled my chatty two year old from his car seat and grabbed the hand of my bouncy four year old to cross the street for preschool, my phone buzzed in my pocket. When I made it to the safety of the sidewalk, I let go of my kids' hands as I wondered who would be calling me at 8:58 A.M. I looked at my iPhone screen expecting to see "Maggie" or "Mom." Instead, I saw an unknown number. A voicemail was transcribed from this number that read:

> "Good Morning, this message is for Kristen Cunnane. This is the Central California Women's Facility calling in regards to Julie Correa. She will be paroling on March 24th. 2018. This is just a courtesy call. You also will receive a written notice to the address you have listed."

As I continued to walk down the corridor toward the preschool classroom that cold January day, I smiled and chatted with a few of my favorite preschool parents. I appeared to them as I always do, a mostly put-together mom trying to make it to school on time. Though as I mingled, my heart was clenched and my brain had drifted thirty feet in the air as I realized the impending change in my life.

Julie was being released from prison.

For months and years I had been trying to keep a mental log of how long Julie had been in prison and how long she had left to serve. It felt as though a ticking time bomb was buried some-where deep in my chest and I was allowed to enjoy life only until it exploded.

I had always tried my best to account for the unknowns; the time she had already served and a possible reduction of her sentence due to "good behavior." I knew we were getting close, but now instead of a rough estimate, we had a date: March 24.

Through the years that Julie was in prison, I had the luxury of being able to reason with myself: *It is the middle of the night—that sound in the backyard cannot be her. I do not need to check the back seat of my car because she CANNOT be in there—she is in prison. My kids are safe—I know where she is.* Suddenly I knew that safety was going to be stripped from me in just over two months.

Just as it was through the abuse, through the work with police and the phone calls, through the court hearings and my dealings with the school district, I disassociated. On that cold preschool morning, a layer of my brain separated from my body so that I could care for my children. I had to be in a safe place so that I could process this next major hurdle.

I got back in my car. I closed my eyes and took a few deep breaths. I clutched the steering wheel as tightly as I could. With an exhale I was able to let the reality of the voicemail sink in.

Then I made a plan.

As with all of my other plans, I started with Scott.

"She's getting out March 24," I blurted into the phone as I sat in the preschool parking lot.

"Wow . . . Okay. You will be okay, Kristy," Scott said. And after a quick pause he added, "We will be okay."

Scott came home that night with some information about Julie's parole and some ideas about how we could keep ourselves safe. My head began to swirl with thoughts of home security, a neighborhood watch, restraining orders, and talking with Julie's parole officer. Suddenly I was back in the trenches of it all once again.

The amount of therapy, writing, talking, interviewing, and working that I have done to recover from Julie's abuse and devastation feels like the tallest mountain I will ever climb in my lifetime. I am proud that I made it to the summit and glad to have the mountain behind me. But part of being a survivor means realizing that there will always be mountains on the horizon. Some may be small, like having a rude woman in the gym say, "How in the world did your parents not know?!" Some will come unexpectedly, like a nightmare or a flashback. And some are large. Julie's release from prison was much larger than I wanted it to be.

I found myself not looking forward to my birthday in February because that meant time was passing. I felt incapable of filling out the two-month calendar in our mudroom. I calculated everything in my life to the "before" and the "after" of the release.

My anxiety grew.

"So what *can* we do to help make this easier?" my new friend Missy asked me at a mom's dinner out to Mexican food. I had gotten close with a bunch of the moms from Annie's preschool class, and as we snacked on chips, I looked around at my growing army.

"I think I just need to make a list," I had said.

The very next morning Missy and I met at Starbucks after preschool dropoff and began hatching our plan. What could I do within reason to keep me and my family safe?

I wanted to let the world know she was getting out. The more eyes that are open and aware, the safer I should be. Missy and I wrote down the steps I could take, both in my house and in the community, to make me feel as secure as possible. We wrote down the various law enforcement officials, such as the parole officer, whom I needed to communicate with. The list was long and full of time-consuming tasks. But at the bottom of the list was the most important item of all. Listed simply as another item on my to-do list: "Trust that God will protect me."

I completed every task on that list. By the time I got to my final agenda item just days before her release, I found a sense of peace. I had done everything in my power, not only to protect myself but to heal. When the list was completed, I simply made the decision to go forward with my life.

On March 24 Scott and I loaded our family up and took the kids on a spring ski trip. It was one of those trips where everything went perfectly. Fresh snow from the weekend before combined with the sunshine we had all missed through the winter. Who wouldn't feel happy to watch their blond-haired babies squeal down the bunny slope for the very first time?

As we drove down from the mountains from our perfect trip, I knew I was coming home to a new reality. I knew Julie was no longer confined to the boundaries of a prison and that she was a free woman. *Or was she?*

The parole officer had assured me that Julie would have to wear an ankle monitor for a number of years after her release. Julie would also have to register as a sex offender for the rest of her life. People now knew the truth about her. Her life was different because I had held her accountable. I had done all that I could.

As the kids rocked to sleep in their car seats as we made our descent, I looked out of the corner of my eye and saw Scott smiling. I knew that he was happy about our trip, but I also knew that our vacation was not the reason for his smile. As he reached over to me and put his hand on my tummy, I was reminded of the positive pregnancy test I had read with him just before we left.

And so, as we rode down the mountain of our vacation and of the difficulty of Julie's release, I knew we were headed into a new chapter of our lives. Yes, there may be moments of fear and darkness. But with Scott's hand on my soon to be growing belly, and the soft snore of my kids behind me, I knew that the light would continue to flood in.

About the Author

B orn in Moraga, California, Kristen Lewis (Cunnane) was a star student and multi-sport athlete during her middle school and high school years. She went on to become an Academic All-American and captain of the UCLA women's swim team, ultimately earning a spot at the Olympic Trial semifinals in 2004. While receiving a masters in education at Cal-Berkeley, she volunteered as an assistant for the Cal women's swim team. The following year Kristen was hired to be an assistant coach, and eventually became an associate head coach under renowned Olympic head coach Teri McKeever. Given chief responsibility for recruiting, Kristen played a key role in the success Cal had in winning four NCAA championships between 2009 and 2015. In 2015 Kristen retired from Cal to spend more time with her family. Kristen now coaches and consults privately for athletes looking to compete in college and is determined to share her story and educate others about sexual abuse. Kristen is enjoying raising three young children with her high school sweetheart, Scott Cunnane.

Made in the USA
Columbia, SC
19 February 2020

88151192R00248